CHRIS SCOTT'S first motorcycle adventure got him halfway to Wales aboard a moped. A long affair with bikes followed while working as a despatch rider in London on anything from IT250s to a 900SS (with one especially productive week on a nitrous-oxide-assisted XS650). Most winters were spent attempting to explore the Sahara on trail bikes; adventures and misfortunes described in *Desert Travels* (1997).

Since then he's made films of his rides in the Yukon (*Call of the Wild*, 2001), *Desert Riders* in the central Sahara (featured on National Geographic Channel) and *Gorge Riders* in north-western Australia (2005). But most frequently he returns by whatever means to the Sahara where he occasionally runs tours. His other books include *Sahara Overland* (also for Trailblazer) and the sandy parts of *Rough Guide Australia*.

Adventure Motorcycling Handbook
Fifth edition 2005; reprinted with additional material and amendments 2006

Publisher
Trailblazer Publications
The Old Manse, Tower Rd, Hindhead, Surrey, GU26 6SU, UK
Fax (+44) 01428-607571
info@trailblazer-guides.com
www.trailblazer-guides.com

British Library Cataloguing in Publication Data
A catalogue record for this book is available from the British Library

ISBN 978-1-873756-80-5
(ISBN-10: 1-873756-80-1)

Editor: Anna Jacomb-Hood
Series Editor: Patricia Major
Typesetting and layout: Chris Scott
Cartography: Nick Hill
Cartoons: Simon Roberts (www.sr-illustration.com)
Index: Patrick D Hummingbird

Global travel by motorcycle is unpredictable and can be dangerous.
Every effort has been made by the author, contributors and the publisher to ensure that
the information contained herein is as accurate as possible. However, they are unable
to accept responsibility for any inconvenience, loss or injury sustained by anyone
as a result of the advice and information given in this guide.

Printed on chlorine-free paper by
D2Print (☎ +65-6295 5598), Singapore

ADVENTURE MOTORCYCLING HANDBOOK

CHRIS SCOTT

with contributions by
**ARNO BACKES, ANDY BELL, CHRIS BRIGHT, DAVID BROWN
BOB GOGGS, GREGORY FRAZIER, GRANT JOHNSON
SIMON McCARTHY, NICKI McCORMICK, SHAUN MUNRO
LOIS PRYCE, DR PAUL ROWE, SAMEER SHISODIA
GEORGIE SIMMONDS, TED SIMON, ALEC SIMPSON,
MACIEK SWINARSKI, AUSTIN VINCE & RICHARD VIRR**

and additional material by
**JEREMY BULLARD, SAM CORRERO, TOM GRENON
GEOFF KINGSMILL, PHIL McMILLAN, LEWIS MILLER
CYNTHIA MILTON, ANDY PAG, PAUL RANDALL
RONNIE SKÂRNER & RICHARD WOLTERS**

Illustrations by
SIMON ROBERTS

and additional graphics by
ALAN BRADSHAW

TRAILBLAZER PUBLICATIONS

Acknowledgements

Contributions from riders all around the world help make the *AMH* what it is, a collection of guidelines for adventurous travel by motorcycle, principally in Asia, Africa and Latin America. So a big thank you to the thirty-odd contributors listed on the title page as well as credited photographers who supplied material for free or for negligible fees. Some of their biogs appear on pp.271-2.

A request

Every effort has been made by the author and the publisher to ensure that the information contained in this book is as up to date and accurate as possible. Nevertheless things will change; even before the ink is dry. If you notice any changes or omissions that you think should be included in the next edition of this book, please write to the author at Trailblazer (address on p.2).

Updated information and a whole lot more at:
www.adventure-motorcycling.com

Cover photo: Ladakh with a Bullet © Chris Bright

CONTENTS

INTRODUCTION

Adventure motorcycling

What exactly is adventure motorcycling? As far as this book is concerned it involves a challenging unsupported journey into the wilderness or a significantly strange country. For most of us living in cities in developed countries, a visit to a wilderness involves leaving the security of the paved highways of Europe, Australasia, southern Africa and North America, and heading onto the dirt, while an exotic destination adds all sorts of challenges that are patiently waiting for you out there in Central and South America, Africa or Asia.

Mainstream touring on or off the highway is a fun way of getting to nice places or enjoying the thrill of a sharp-handling bike. But the *Adventure Motorcycling Handbook* sees motorcycles not as toys, but tools with which to escape from the mundane and predictable, and to explore the wild or exotic regions of our planet.

Since the last edition of this book the popular appeal of taking on an adventurous motorcycle journey has grown significantly. Though challenges will always be there if you want them, it's no longer seen as an eccentric pursuit for a few hardcore individuals. Equipment need no longer be custom made and it is now possible to rent motorcycles right across the globe, enabling you to explore a given area without having to quit the job and sell up.

In Latin America, Asia and Africa, or in mountains and deserts closer to home, reaching out into the back country requires planning and confidence in your abilities, be they riding half a ton of bike through mud, or dealing with a shipping agent in a foreign port. In some situations the unfamiliarity adds an edge to your travels that you won't necessarily appreciate at the time. You'll be pitted against your wits, stamina and resourcefulness, but part of the education of hard travel is that give yourself a chance and you'll find you have greater reserves of these qualities than you ever expected.

Sure you'll be glad to cruise restfully along the blacktop and stay in hotels once in a while. But ask any of the many contributors to this book and in most cases they'll vividly recall the places where the riding was most demanding, where every day was hard-won and threw up an unexpected challenge, a breathtaking view or a memorable human encounter.

This book spells out the practicalities of paperwork, the cost of a Big Trip, as well as which machine is best and how to equip it. It's followed by an outline of routes around the world and ends with a selection of two-wheeled adventures from all corners of the globe to give a taste of what to expect.

There'll be times when you curse the very notion of ever leaving home. But make no mistake, it will be a lifetime's achievement that will remain with you forever.

HISTORY OF THE *ADVENTURE MOTORCYCLING HANDBOOK*

In the summer of '91 I was dishwashing in a Mexican restaurant, recovering from a broken leg and another costly Saharan fiasco. The job was not too intellectually taxing so I decided to get into writing, having enjoyed writing about my travels for bike magazines in the 1980s.

I decided to compose a short report on what I'd learned the hard way in a decade of motorcycling in the Sahara. Many riders, myself included, had trouble-strewn first trips on account of a complete lack of hard information on all aspects of adventure motorcycling.

I bought myself an Amstrad, worked out how to turn it on and, after a lot of wasted paper, dropped off a 30-page report entitled *Desert Biking: A Guide to Independent Motorcycling in the Sahara* at the Royal Geographical Society in London. For all I know the original is still tucked away in their archives today.

Rather pleased with the end result, I figured the report might have some faint commercial value and proposed this idea to the

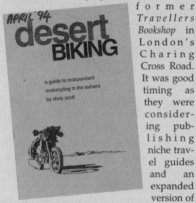

former *Travellers Bookshop* in London's Charing Cross Road. It was good timing as they were considering publishing niche travel guides and an expanded version of *DB* fitted the bill. I spent a couple of months padding out the RGS report into the 100-page first edition of *Desert Biking* which was eventually published in late 1993. It did

not exactly hit the bookshops: batches were Xeroxed in a copy shop in Notting Hill as demand trickled in, then stapled and sent out.

Chris Scott

Following the moderate success of this handmade version, a revised and suitably expanded paperback edition (right) was published in September 1995. The updated format included the addition of 'travellers' tales' in the back.

Seeing promise in this format, Compass Star Publications picked up the idea and took it a big step further with the publication of the snappily retitled *The Adventure Motorbiking Handbook* (AMH) in November 1997. It featured the practicalities and yarns of *Desert Biking* and also, with the help of a web of contributors who now help make the book what it is, attempted to cover the globe.

Chris Scott

At the same time I created the AM Website which now features hundreds of riders' trip reports and my occasional tours.

Which, fifteen years down the line, brings us to this fifth, Trailblazer, edition of the *AMH*. Enjoy the trip.

PART 1: PRACTICALITIES

Planning and preparation

Prepare. That is the first word of the first chapter of this book. The motorcycle adventure you are considering is going to be expensive, physically and mentally demanding, and maybe even dangerous.

Thorough preparation gives you confidence in a venture that will always include elements of risk. Short of joining an organised tour or renting a machine, by tying up every loose end you can think of before you go, you can set off knowing that whatever happens your chosen bike, documentation and knowledge of whatever lies ahead are as good as can be expected.

Certainly spontaneity is wonderful thing, but make no mistake, even if you're just heading off on a two-weeker to Morocco, up to Cape York, or down to the Baja, there'll be enough unexpected dramas to deal without adding to them with inadequate preparation.

How do you want it?

Ask yourself how much of a commitment you want to make to your motorcycle adventure. Do you have an urge to see some exotic part of the planet, but still like the idea of coming back to your job and house, or are you ready to take an entirely new direction in your life for several months or even years?

Time was when unless you had heaps of money you could not just nip overseas, do some exploring and come home. These days the possibility of **hiring bikes** across much of the globe, as well as joining **organised tours** (even round the world!) can make the commitment merely financial. But even with these easier options most of the considerations outlined on the following pages must be addressed. It's just that with a rental you miss out on a whole load of freight and carnet tedium, and on an organised tour riding your own bike, you pay to have much of that done for you. This book focuses on the biggest adventure of all: **doing it yourself**, but even if you pay up to join a tour from Alaksa to Patagonia, you may still choose to buy and prepare your own machine.

So, you've seen the light and you're going for it. When? As a rule a first time, independent, trans-continental journey such as crossing Africa, the Americas or Asia needs at least **one year** of preparation. If you're heading right around the world (RTW) you might want to **double** that time; if you're just taking an exploratory nibble into the above three continents, **six months** should do. Preparing to explore a wilderness region of your own country may only require **a few weeks**. All of these times can be comfortably halved if you're joining an organised tour or renting a machine locally. And they all assume that you're undertaking your preparations while continuing with the full-time employment which will help fund the trip.

You may not think so now but within a few pages you'll be getting an idea of the mushroom effect of Big Trip Planning. The more you learn the more there is to consider. For some the idea of riding round the world may seem like too much and they'll have to either postpone the venture or downsize it to something more manageable such as options discussed in the box on p.12.

Time and money

Ask yourself realistically if you have the will and opportunity to put the money together in the time you've given yourself – let alone the will to be on the road for months. To cross Africa budget on **£4000/US$7200** (at early 2005 exchange rates), plus the cost of your bike. Asia is much cheaper; you could probably ride from Europe to India and back for around £3000/$5400. To cross the length of the Americas costs at least as much as Africa (especially if you have to fly your bike over from Europe), and a genuine RTW trip is going to set you back around **£10,000/$18,000**, mostly in fuel and freighting your bike from one continent to the next. Many have achieved the above for less, some a lot more, but these estimates account for at least some of the unplanned expenses which most trips encounter.

Doing it yourself, your big trip is like a major civil engineering project; traditionally it will be **late and go over budget**. It's rare that a first time DIY-er leaves on their original departure date, so don't set this in stone and don't give yourself impossible goals. Although some biking trips add up to nothing more than doing something hard in a short space of time, be aware that this puts you under extra stress in an already stressful situation.

Be wary of **over-ambitious goals** or, if you're like me, factor in over ambitious goals and be happy to scrape home having done less than you planned. As I wrote in *Desert Biking*'s introduction years ago 'Expect your itinerary – conceived on the living room floor with [a map] a couple of cans and all the chairs pushed back – to go to pieces once you're out there.' Once you find yourself riding out of an African port into the chaos of the city, or off the end of a sealed highway into a remote area of dirt tracks, reality bites. Sitting directly on the sharp end of your adventure, you want to be sure you've got all your ducks in a row. And you're with someone you can trust...

Travelling companions

Most people will instinctively know whether they want to ride alone, with their partner sitting snugly behind them, their mate in the mirror, or in a group as part of an organised tour. Nevertheless, below are some considerations to mull over when considering travelling companions.

Alone

The perils and rewards of **doing it alone** are clear cut. On the debit side there's no one to help you in times of difficulty and no familiar face to share your experiences with. No one can help pick up the bike or guard it while you nip into a store in a dodgy neighbourhood. All this will make your trip hard and inevitably introspective. This may be because you don't know anyone who's crazy enough to set off on a trip such as yours, or you're independent-minded and like the idea of doing it alone.

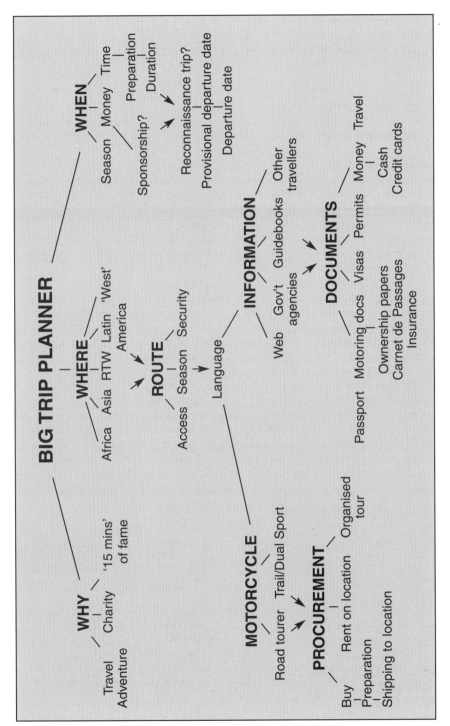

BIG TRIP PLANNER

WHY
- Travel
- Adventure
- Charity
- '15 mins' of fame

WHEN
- Season
- Money
- Time
- Sponsorship?
- Preparation
- Duration
- Reconnaissance trip?
- Provisional departure date
- Departure date

WHERE
- Africa
- Asia
- RTW
- Latin America
- 'West'

ROUTE
- Access
- Season
- Security
- Language

INFORMATION
- Web
- Gov't agencies
- Guidebooks
- Other travellers

DOCUMENTS
- Passport
- Motoring docs
- Visas
- Permits
- Money
  - Cash
  - Credit cards
- Travel
- Ownership papers
- Carnet de Passages
- Insurance

MOTORCYCLE
- Road tourer
- Trail/Dual Sport

PROCUREMENT
- Buy
- Rent on location
- Organised tour
- Preparation
- Shipping to location

RENTALS AND ORGANISED TOURS

The opportunities for joining a tour or renting bikes all over the world are greater now than ever before. Don't be put off by the idea of joining a tour to a remote location or renting a bike abroad and doing your own thing. Both these options allow you to dip your toe into the adventure motorcycling experience with only a financial commitment.

For many it's a worthwhile endeavour. Without taking on a Big Trip from a standing start they can discover that this foreign travel malarkey is not so hard after all. I would say 20% of the people that have come on my Sahara tours (in 4WDs and on bikes) have gone on to have their own adventures, including packing it all in and going round the world.

You can even see it as a **reconnaissance trip** (something that is recommended, on p.45, as a practical shakedown anyway). Only on this occasion you'll be testing yourself rather than your machine.

Some trips were never meant to happen but disappointment is so much easier to handle on a shorter trip with less invested in it.

When you have the momentum that months of preparation and expectation have created, your pride is too great and you decide to just go through with it, however bad or uncertain you feel. If it's just a few weeks' overseas rental, or a tour that has not turned out as expected, the disappointment need not seem so galling and you might be able to get it right next time.

It all sounds miserable until you consider the rewards of solitary travel. Riding solo your social exposure can be more acute; unless you're a real hardcore loner you're forced to commune with strangers who'll often make up the richest (and sometimes the most frustrating!) aspect of your trip; you have to look *out* at the world instead of being protected by the bubble of companionship. And unless you're going somewhere really outlandish, you're bound to **meet up with other riders** and in most cases be very glad to ride with them.

Tough overland stages like the Sahara, Far Eastern Russia and Patagonia, or intimidating regions in Africa, Central Asia and Central America are where overlanders often bind together, irrespective of their origins or mode of travel. Alone you can choose to join in the safety of a convoy, and when you feel like going your own way, you can split with no strings attached. This **freedom** to be your own boss is probably the biggest attraction of riding solo. A romantic location to rest up for a while, or who knows, maybe even a promising romance, can be explored with no pressure that your companion wants to get on; it is this disparity in pace that often causes tensions in groups.

Overall, you'll get more of a **raw experience** alone but at times may have the option of companionship – an ideal scenario for most. Be under no illusions that at times it will be utter misery and frustration, but this is all part of the nature of adventure and typically your fortunes will swing the other way before long.

Two's company

The advantage of travelling with a friend is that, psychologically and literally, the huge load of your undertaking is halved. Two people also tend to be **braver**; checking out a crowded market café or following a remote short-cut become shared adventures instead of missed opportunities if you're alone – even if behind it all is a mild competitiveness of 'sure, I'm n-not scared...'. There's no doubt about it, you can have a lot more fun if there are two of you and you get on.

One drawback to travelling in company is that you tend to remain rather exclusive to social interaction. There's no need to be outgoing because there's always someone to talk to, whine at or help you out. You can miss out on a lot that travel has to offer by reclining in the security of your **companionship**, because there's no need to meet others.

Another problem which won't surprise anybody is **getting on** with each other. Alone you can indulge your moods which will swing from one extreme to another as days go by. In company you have to put on a brave or polite face when you might not feel like it; your partner thinks they're the problem, becomes resentful and the whole day becomes edgy as you wish the road would open up and swallow your buddy.

Having a united goal doesn't seem to help, once the rot sets in your whole trip can be shrouded in tension and misery. If it gets bad, there is only one solution: **split up**. It may well be that they want to take the high road and you the low road, but whatever it is, it's far better to accommodate differing personal wishes, even if they mean temporarily terminating your fellowship.

It's well known that these conflicts occur in the stress of expeditions which is effectively what you're undertaking; try and anticipate how you might deal with these sorts of problems and don't feel that separation down the road turns the trip into a failure. **Discuss** the possibility of this eventuality during the planning stage and prepare yourself and your bike for **autonomy**.

With a group of two or more, one thing that may be obvious but ought to be mentioned is **choose the same bike**. This has countless advantages in fault diagnosis, quantity of spares and shared know-how.

Two-up on one bike? Well as long as the machine is big and powerful enough like Kevin and Julie Sanders' 1150 it can of course **reduce costs**. It can

---

ADVENTURE MOTORCYCLING MINDSET

As a plan takes shape trust your instincts and resist the pressure to be seen as brave individual or reluctant member of a team. Do what feels right for you. You must be psychologically fit before you ride off to face the countless trials that adventure motorcycling throws in your face daily. Without what I like to call an 'optimistically fatalistic' attitude your trip may develop into a catalogue of miseries.

My first trip on a half-baked XT500 started just like this and it was amazing I got as far as I did before the desert turned on me halfway across the Sahara (see *Desert Travels*). Turning back then was the right thing to do and a decision which probably prolonged my life. Returning after just five weeks but a lot older, it was not an enjoyable trip in any way, merely a depressing baptism of fire. Many motorcyclists are attracted to the idea and romance of an overland journey without truly facing up to the gruelling practicalities of the commitment required. Your own trip is likely to be one of the major events of your life, give it your best chance: don't bite off more than you can chew – a tour or rental may be much more fun. And if, along with the time and money, that inspiration or confidence never arrives then postpone the trip or don't go.

also mean one person can navigate or film while leaving the riding to the rider, all of which can make life easier and more fun.

The long-range **comfort** of the pillion really does need to be considered carefully. Do not set off on an unfamiliar machine and hope that just because it has an extra set of footrests it will be all right. It helps of course if both parties can confidently handle the bike, though usually this is not the case. And of course the weight of a passenger will for most riders rule out difficult off-road sections.

Big groups

Outside of tours, big groups are much less common than solo or twinned riders, if for no other reason than forming a group of like-minded individuals is a tricky proposition. Numbers fluctuate during the planning stage and even on the road the chances of a bunch of riders staying together for the whole trip are very slim. As in any group, the dynamics evolve as the trip moves on, although inevitably a leader will dominate from the start, alternately respected or despised by the others. Expect never to want to talk to certain members of your merry gang by the time you return!

With a large group there is usually a shared or even officially-established **goal** which itself can cause pressures. It may help with sponsorship, and the mutual support is enviable but, as you'll find on the road, most people are more comfortable alone or with one or two companions.

Road-based **tour groups** need not be as bad as they sound as it is not normal to ride in convoy, day after day. It's more common for all riders to set off at their own pace and meet up in the evening. On off-road tours or those in remote regions, you will have to **stick together**, for better or worse.

GETTING INFORMATION

However many of you are going, now your plan is underway there's work to be done. The countless things you need to know are all out there, but finding them is a lottery. Luckily, one of the best sources for your specific two-wheel undertaking is right in front of your nose but the *AMH*, or any other guide book, can only be as up to date as when it was written.

Embassies and tourist offices

An obvious place to start, but not very useful except in the most general terms concerning documentation, vehicle importation regulations and possibly a free map or brochure. Some embassies and tourist boards have a habit of glossing over domestic upheaval or hard facts, and neither place will be likely to advise you about the condition of remote routes or what facilities you might find there. Sitting out cushy overseas postings, inevitably detached from what's really going on, consular officials are more interested in promoting mainstream tourism or trade rather than hare-brained motorcycle stunts.

Government overseas departments

On a par with the usefulness of an embassy is your country's foreign ministry. In the UK it's the **Foreign & Commonwealth Office Travel Advice Unit**; in the US it's the **Department of Foreign Affairs** (both with usefully updated websites; linked at www.sahara-overland.com/news). Whatever they might claim, these civil service departments are primarily concerned with avoiding international incidents involving their nationals, if not urgently discouraging casual visits to countries with whom political relations may be strained. Take everything they say with a liberal helping of salt and accept the inevitable taint of politics and convenience which colours their advice.

National motoring organisations

Again not a lot of help for the aspiring adventure biker but sometimes useful on documentation and essential when it comes to coughing up for a *Carnet de Passage* (see pp.21-3). In the UK this, along with an International Driving Permit, is all the RAC and AA can do for you. To be fair adventure motorcycling is such a minority form of motoring, you can't expect them to take it seriously. Both are businesses which make most of their money providing roadside recovery and insurance.

News media

Following news reports in the media (newspapers, TV, radio, or on the web) is the best way of keeping up with the news in the region you're intending to visit. In the UK you still can't beat *The Times* for its detailed foreign coverage, but you've only got to live abroad to find out just how sketchy and polarised your home country's media can be, focusing on the more sensational conflicts in former colonies. Inevitably Australian media is strong on Asian affairs, North American is good on the south of that continent, and Europe good on Africa and west Asia. The **web** of course is available to everyone and you'll be able to use a variety of sources, though when certain news breaks, you'll find them all reporting the same thing, fed by a news agency.

Travel magazines and travel guides

Travel magazines are geared towards producing glossy photo features to attract related advertising and if you regularly subscribe to such a magazine you'll know what to expect. From the adventure biker's point of view, travel magazines' (and their online counterparts) best feature can be the latest visa or political information in the news pages, as well as readers' letters and other information. You'll find the travel supplements of weekend papers tend to circulate the same stories over and over, although these occasionally include 'trendy' motorcycling once in a while.

At least as good as the news pages and readers' letters of travel magazines are the free newsletters produced by travel guide publishers like **Lonely Planet** or **Rough Guides**. Both contain travel information from readers and you can get on their mailing list for nothing. The established *Planet Talk* is currently the best, with latest hot spots and readers' tips as well as a customary advertorial from authors of forthcoming editions, although really you can find as much news in many places on the web, not least the Lonely Planet *Thorn Tree* website.

Useful motorcycle publications

When they cover travelling at all, rather than pegging the latest megabike, most mainstream bike magazines tend to feature lame stories alongside scantily-researched 'how-to' text boxes, because although it may be gaining popularity, outside Germany adventure travel is still a minority pursuit in motorcycling. In the UK, only the monthly *Motorcycle Sport & Leisure* runs occasional intrepid touring features.

If you live downunder, watch out for *SideTrack* and *Trail Bike Adventure* magazines, both inspiring publications focusing on the huge opportunities for adventure sport riding in Australia. In the US, *Rider*, *Cycle World* and *Motorcyclist* all carry travel features.

The Internet

Newsflash! Far and away the most effective and wide-ranging source of information is on the Internet.

My **Adventure Motorcycling Website** (www.adventure-motorcycling .com) has accompanied this book since 1997 but these days limits itself to classifying hundreds of trip reports, some of which you will find reproduced in this book.

In recent years **Horizons Unlimited** (www.horizonsunlimited.com) has grown to become the best web resource in any language for motorcycle-based travel. Run by Canadians Grant and Susan Johnson who spent over a decade on the road, their website has grown to many times the size of this book – and what's more it's free and up to date.

Their website has the most comprehensive selection of forums, ezines and stories or blogs as well as links that stretch in all directions. Just one weekend of surfing through the HU pages will provide enough material to delay your departure for months.

Oncoming travellers

Although too late to be of use in your pre-departure stage, don't underestimate the likelihood and usefulness of running into travellers coming from where you're going. You couldn't ask for fresher information unless you met the horse's mouth itself. They'll be able to fill you in on all your current anxieties about fuel prices, road conditions and the friendliness or otherwise of border officials, and likely as not, they'll be as keen to hear your news, too.

Paperwork

Collecting the right **documentation** and sorting out your money arrangements before and during your trip is a tedious but vital part of your preparation. Many prospective adventure bikers worry about carrying half a year's cash on them, acquiring motor insurance, whether travel insurance is worthwhile, or if they can get by without a carnet. All these questions and more are discussed below. Without just one of the several documents listed below, your trip will eventually come to a standstill, and even with them there's no guarantee that some recalcitrant border official will not turn you away.

Travel documents
With all the documentation listed below it is essential to establish early on:
- what papers you already have
- what additional ones you must get before you leave
- what others you can get once underway

It's also important to know:
- how long it will take to get all this stuff
- and how much it will cost

Do not leave things till the last minute (although with some visas starting from the date they're issued, this is easier said than done) and, as with any personal item, once on the move **keep all your papers with you at all times**. Some, like your passport or carnet, will be a headache to replace. With all these documents, **keeping photocopies** or duplicates, or at least a list of the vital details makes replacement quicker. Stash them somewhere secure or put the information on a **CD** or even a private **webpage**; failing a complete robbery or loss, you'll be able to retrieve the details or print them off, and start on the long road to replacement if necessary. Another good idea is to carry 'spare' originals: ownership documents can be duplicated, either officially or by 'losing' the original and requesting a replacement.

Note that you will accumulate a whole lot of **additional paperwork** at various borders, mostly to do with temporary vehicle importation (in places where carnets are not required) or temporary driving permits. Keep it all until you're in the next country, even if you don't know what it's about. Now is the time to invest in a wallet that expands like an accordion.

Passport
If you don't yet own a passport, get on the case straight away. If you already own one, make sure it is valid for at least **six months**, if not a year **after** your anticipated journey's end as many countries won't issue visas for passports that have less than six months left to run. As ever, by ensuring that your passport has plenty of use left in it, you're one step ahead of some awkward official.

If you're heading around the world and expect to visit dozens of countries consider getting a 'diplomatic' passport which has extra pages. Passport visa stamps tend to fill a whole page and anyone who's travelled before will know how police roadblocks (in some African countries posted on either side of every town) or immigration officials love to slap their little stamp in the middle of a blank page. Still others will quibble about sharing a perfectly usable page with that aforementioned stamp.

Once you get your passport check all the details; discrepancies between it and your other vital documents, even just the misspelling of one word can be all the excuse someone needs to bring your day grinding to a halt.

Although they don't exactly shout it from the rooftops, in Britain at least, it's possible to get a **second passport**. In applying the Passport Office will want to know what you are up to, and the easiest way to explain your need is that certain visa applications en route will take weeks during which time your passport will be unavailable or, most commonly in the case of Israel versus the Moslem world, the fact that one country won't issue you a visa if there is evidence of a visit to another. If your reasons are sound a second passport will be issued without a fuss.

Some hotels (in Iran, for example) keep your passport on registration as security or for police registration. Unless customary, resist this and instead offer to pay up in advance, or hand over a spare expired passport. Never give your passport away to anyone other than a uniformed official, and even then be wary in suspicious situations. They know as well as you do that without this vital document you are trapped.

Visas

Visas are a temporary permit allowing you to visit another country and are a pain in the neck, being little more than an entry tax. Not all countries require them in advance – the stamp you get on entering a neighbouring country may be regarded as an 'instant visa' – but it's those that do which make up the bulk

of your bureaucratic headaches. Brits will have few visa hassles riding though South America, but across Africa or Central Asia anyone might end up paying hundreds in visa charges. For all visitors, the complex visa regulations in these places add up to part of the challenge.

Applying for visas On a trans-continental trek applying for several visas will be a tricky game of timing and anticipated arrival dates; something that will hamper the spontaneity and mould the plans of an overland trip. Even if you're 'just' crossing Africa, don't expect to get all your visas nicely sorted out before you go. Instead, work out where you'll pass a consulate for your next country (besides that country's embassy in your own country, travel guide books are a good source of addresses). This simple fact will have a crucial bearing on your overland itinerary and govern the duration of your stay in certain countries. You may find yourself racing across a country or taking a thousand-mile detour just to be sure you can cross into your next destination.

Before you leave, consider using **visa agencies**. Usually located in your capital or nearest major city, they make their money by providing a speedy postal service while doing the queuing and applying for you. Though pricey, their couriers can make getting visas from consulates not represented in your country much easier, especially if you're busy working or live out in the sticks.

Some visas start from the moment of issue while others insist on a set date when you expect to arrive at the border – something hard to pinpoint when there's 4000 miles of desert, jungle and crocodile-infested swamp between you and that place. All you can do is give yourself plenty of time for problems, expect those problems to crop up and trust in your ability to deal with them. Remember that countless others have succeeded in traversing the same route; they've all worked it out – by using your wits and being flexible, so can you. As a rule, avoid **business visas**, they're more expensive and risk awkward questions on arrival. Stick to simple, innocuous tourist visas.

Before applying for any visa find out the answers to these questions:
- At what point does the visa start: from issue or from a specific date?
- What other documentation (besides your passport) must you present on application? Besides a handful of passport photos, this might also include bank statements or other evidence of funds, letters of introduction or onward travel tickets.
- How must you pay? Some countries are very specific.
- How long do you have before you need to use the visa (typically from one month to a year)?
- Is the visa renewable and if so for how long?
- Is it 'multiple-entry', enabling you to return to that country on the same visa, or just 'single-entry'?

In some countries visas are **extendible**, so that even though you may only be issued with a two-weeker for Iran, for example, renewing it is easily done at any police station. It must be remembered that having a visa will not guarantee you entry into that country; if they don't like you for whatever reason, the rules have changed or something is wrong with your paperwork, you'll be turned back. And being turned back to a country which has just officially waved you goodbye can be tricky.

Then again, on some borders where a visa is considered essential, just turning up may get you one issued on the border. Although what appears above might seem like a rigid set of rules created to discourage international travel, these rules get a bit mushy once on the road: expired visas need not mean a firing squad at dawn (but could mean a heavy fine).

Take visas seriously but recognise that once on the road, the further you are off the beaten track anything goes. If you happen to stumble into a country via an unmanned back route, present yourself at the nearest police station unless you're leaving soon in the same clandestine manner. A word of warning: most of the countries with which this book is concerned are paranoid about their security and have tense relationships with their neighbours. Accusations of 'spy' may be absurd to you, but will be taken very seriously, especially if you turn up in a country without the proper documentation.

Travel and medical insurance

Another possibly costly but recommended piece of documentation is travel insurance; something that everyone from your bank, post office or travel agent is keen to sell you should you dare to put just one foot on a deadly foreign shore. Ordinary travel insurance will probably not cover you for the hazardous activity that is motorcycling. Instead insurance companies who specialise in expeditionary cover will take on the job, and at not much greater cost. A recent quote from a UK specialist, for a four-month trans-African trip riding a bike came to £300/$540 or around £2.50/$4 a day.

Whoever you end up insuring yourself with, make sure they're crystal clear about the nature of your intended trip. As well as covering you for all the mundane stuff like robbery, cancellation, lost baggage and alien abduction, travel insurance also includes **medical cover**. For this, the worst-case scenario would be getting yourself evacuated by air from some remote spot and requiring intensive medical care.

Anything involving **repatriation** to the US, even from neighbouring Mexico may run up to six figures. For this reason it's vital that your medical expenses easily cover the above figures: £500,000/nearly $1m may sound like an astronomical sum but is just a starting point, £1m/$1.85m is better. Make sure that this figure covers everything to do with an accident, including medivac, ambulances, hospitalisation and surgery.

This is one good reason to go straight to a specialist; your credit card may give you 'package holiday' cover for nothing, but it's unlikely to cover a fraction of the cost of an evacuation from the middle of a Siberian swamp. If you're a European in somewhere like Africa, most medical emergencies involve repatriation, which is where the greater expense can lie. In Central or South America, the US might end up as your ultimate destination if you need urgent medical treatment, and no one needs reminding about the expense of medical care in that country.

Remember too, that to get a rescue underway you must first make that **all important phone call** to the country where the policy was issued. When you receive your policy, find this telephone number and write it clearly somewhere like the back of your passport or on your bike somewhere; this way you can direct someone to ring the number if you can't do so yourself.

Vehicle documents

Just as you need a passport, visa and medical insurance, so does your motorcycle. Of these the **carnet** presents the biggest problems in financial terms, while getting **third party insurance** that's worth much more than the paper it's written on is simply an insoluble problem.

Driving licence and International Driving Permit

Like your passport, your driving licence must show correct (or, at least, consistent) information with other documentation and be valid long after your trip expires. If your licence does not show the bearer's photograph, it should be supplemented with an **International Driving Permit** (IDP). These multilingual translations of your driving licence can be picked up over the counter by presenting your licence and a small fee plus a photo or two at your local motoring organisation's office. In Asia IDPs are especially useful.

Once on the road you may never have to show your IDP (though China demands them), but be on the safe side and get one; with their official-looking stamps they can double-up as another document to present to a semi-literate official. Note that there are two IDPs which cover the whole world. If you're going for the Big Trip you'll probably need both. In the UK your driving licence lasts till you are 70, but elsewhere in the world they are only valid for 12 months. If you expect to be on the road for longer than that and renewing it is not possible by post, making a good facsimile is the way round it.

Vehicle ownership document

Your vehicle ownership document is **much more important** than a driver's licence and will be inspected so many times you may want to laminate it before it wears out. In the UK it's called a 'logbook' or, officially, a vehicle registration document (VRD); the US has a state registration document as well as a 'title' or ownership document (retained if a bike is under lien). However, every border will want to see some sort of document and compare details with your passport, your carnet, your Blockbuster loyalty card and anything else they can think of. Perhaps more than your passport, it's crucial that the details on the ownership/registration document, particularly the **chassis and engine numbers**, match those on your bike and carnet, if used. Outside Latin America **photocopies are not good enough**, but a duplicate is always handy.

Having a vehicle ownership document that is **not in your name** is not always that great a problem as long as you have a good story and letter of explanation from the actual owner (plus an official-looking stamp or two). What is vital is an official-looking document to match the machine.

The reason for these elaborate checks is to ensure you've not committed a cardinal sin against humanity by selling your vehicle, or part of it, in the country concerned. Even slightly-damaged engine or chassis numerals (aka 'VIN' see below; easily done) may be grounds for raising complications. The evasion of tax on imported vehicles is what the fuss is all about; in developing countries these can be many times the value of your machine. If your bike has had a replacement engine or other substantial mods, check those numbers or risk losing all to some nit-picking official down the track. Check these numbers now while you still have a chance to easily correct them.

I also find that it helps to **highlight** your Vehicle Identification Number (VIN, usually the same as the chassis number) on your vehicle ownership document. This is what the customs guy will be looking for amongst all the other details so it helps speed things up. It also does not hurt to **sign** your ownership document somewhere, even if you don't need to.

Carnet

Just about every first timer's overland trip comes to a near standstill when they learn about the need for a *Carnet de Passage en Douane* and the need to indemnify the value of your bike, if not a whole lot more. It is this huge, if temporary drain on your funds that makes carnets such a pain, and can make you decide to do a trip on an old SP370 instead of that lovely 1200GS you promised yourself. If you're just riding around Central and South America, the good news is you can get by without a carnet as well as a whole lot of other hassles which help make this a great riding destination. More on p.190.

Written in French and English, a carnet is an internationally-recognised **temporary importation document** that, in the words of the *Alliance Internationale de Tourisme* (AIT; www.aitgva.ch), which administers the scheme is 'still required in many countries around the world [being] a customs document that identifies your motor vehicle. The Carnet allows travellers to temporarily import their vehicles without having to leave a cash deposit at the border. ... [It is] in essence an international guarantee for payment of customs duties and taxes to a government should your vehicle not be re-exported from that country.'

A carnet is issued by your national motoring organisation like the AAA in Australia or the AA or RAC in the UK. It lasts one year and, if necessary, can be renewed or extended from the motoring organisation in the country where it's about to expire. (Make sure this extension is noted on every page and not just the front cover). There is a list of which countries require a carnet but, to cut a long story short they include: **central**, **east** and **southern Africa** plus **Egypt**; the **Middle East**, **west Asia** and the **subcontinent**, and it will help in **Australia**.

The name of all motoring organisations licensed to extend your carnet are shown inside the front cover of all carnets. As you can imagine, making this country a Western, or at least an English-speaking one, is bound to be less hassle than contacting the Automobile Association of Vanuatu. If you lose a carnet, you must apply to the original issuing authority for a replacement.

Sure, you can **travel without a carnet** as long as you don't mind depositing the value, plus duty, that they slap on your bike when you enter a country: in west Asia this duty can be from **two to four times** the value of your bike.

Once you provide your local motoring organisation with details of your bike and every country you expect to visit, they estimate the value of your bike and the highest level of duty payable of all the countries you plan to visit. For a £5000/$9000 BMW heading overland from the UK to India, this bond might total £15,000/$27,000, i.e. the bike's value plus the maximum possible duty of 200% which Iran charges. A recent figure for a well-worn five-year-old XT600 heading down Africa's east side was just £1800/$3250.

Ways of underwriting a carnet Coming up with this money is usually a big problem for most overlanders but it can be done in three ways:

- Pay an insurance premium to underwrite the cost of your carnet.
- Get your bank to cover the amount with your personal collateral (eg. stacks of money, property or shares).
- Leave the required bond deposited with a bank in a locked account.

Most people either borrow the money for the third option or cough up for an insurance premium for the first. Your motoring organisation will put you in touch with approved insurance underwriters and what they charge depends on where you're going and the size of the bond required. Typically in the UK, they charge 3% of a bond under £10,000, so for the XT example above, that works out at £270, plus a 'service charge' of around £60, plus refundable deposits of another £250. As you'll be gathering by now, it's all adding up to hundreds paid out or thousands locked in the bank. Suddenly learning Spanish instead of Swahili seems like a good idea.

How a carnet is used Carnets come in a number of pages from five to twenty-five, each page is used for a country where this document is mandatory. A page is divided into three perforated sections, or vouchers: an **entry voucher** (*volet d'entrée*), an **exit voucher** (*volet de sortie*), and a **counterfoil** (*souche*).

When you enter a country that requires a carnet, the Customs will stamp your counterfoil and exit voucher and tear off and keep the entry voucher. When you leave that country, the counterfoil will be stamped again and then the exit voucher will be retained. When your travels are complete you return the carnet to the issuing organisation for discharging. What they'll want to see is a bunch of double-stamped counterfoils and probably a few unused but intact pages.

Should you sell your bike on the side, your carnet will not be discharged and you'll eventually be liable for the duty in that country – remember, they could have your money. Should you sell your bike officially you'll need all the permanent export and customs documents to prove that you've done so legally and paid all duties. In South Africa, where bikes are often sold at the end of a trip, the rates are around 7.5% duty plus another 14% VAT for a 600cc bike. By comparison, if you're hoping to sell your bike in the UK, you're looking at 10% duty plus 17.5% VAT.

Getting involved in **fake carnets** is not really necessary (or that great a saving for a pricey perfect copy) unless you plan selling your vehicle on the side; not something that most adventure motorcyclists get involved in. In Africa you might get away with it, but in parts of Asia an online database of genuine carnets makes it a risk.

Third party motor insurance

If you're boldly going where no one you know has gone before don't expect to be able to get third party motor insurance from your friendly local broker. Quite understandably, and despite the loss of some juicy revenue, your insurer won't touch an overlanding biker with the longest barge pole they could get their hands round. A UK company will cover you for Europe as far east as Turkey as well as Morocco and Tunisia, but even these latter two are becoming difficult. If someone does offer to insure you beyond this area, as in some cases I've heard, it's because they've not understood what they're getting themselves into or are just taking your money. It may be quite likely that you're not covered, even if you think you are.

What you do instead is **buy it as you go**, but don't expect to be able to buy it everywhere. In an economic confederation of states like Francophone West Africa, around £2/$3.70 a day will cover several countries, in Uzbekistan one rider paid £2-3 for two weeks cover. One rider even got his Triumph Trophy around the world without insurance. Indeed the only time he was asked to present evidence of insurance was on the Malay/Thai border where flashing his multi-stamped carnet was enough to be waved through. This is a good example of the '**library card effect**': any official-looking piece of paper covered with rubber stamps plus a photo of yourself will please a bored border guard. Latin America is a place where even asking about getting motor insurance is likely to either take you days and cost heaps of money for something of dubious validity, or paying a bigger sum to some corrupt officer who'll be happy to stamp an empty packet of cigarettes and send you on your way. Basically it's the same as with carnets: **if they don't ask don't offer**.

The dubious validity of Third World motor insurance or the impossibility of getting it at all underlines the fact that should you cause an accident such as killing someone's child or worse still, a breadwinner, the complications into which you'll sink may take years and large amounts of money to resolve. India is a place which probably has the most demanding riding conditions in the world. In this desperately poor and overpopulated country, people are not averse to throwing granny in front of a swanky-looking couple on a GS1150 and then nailing them to the floorboards for compensation.

Motor insurance is an unravellable quandary: rigorously enforced in your own country, out in the sticks it's mostly unattainable or of little value. The answer is to rest often, ride carefully and be alert.

Other travel and motoring documents
Additional motoring documents to those mentioned above include:
- Green Card insurance extension for UK riders crossing Europe.
- An International Certificate for Motor Vehicles: inexpensive multilingual translation of your vehicle ownership papers issued by motoring organisations for countries which don't accept the original.
- Motoring Organisation Membership Card. Remember that some enlightened countries (such as Australia) offer reciprocal membership to their own motoring organisations for free. Your membership card will also be useful when renewing or extending a carnet and may also have value as a 'library card'.

Local permits
What's been covered above is only what you must try and arrange in your home country. Additional documentation will be gleefully issued for any number of reasons (mainly to get more money out of you, or 'fine' you for not having it). Typical examples include registering with the police within 24 hours of arrival, photography and filming permits (at the last count, only Cameroon and Sudan required these, although ciné can be a different kettle of fish), 'tourist registration cards', currency declaration forms (see below), or permits to cross 'forbidden' areas such as China, Egypt's Western Desert or tribal homelands. As these are the sorts of places where police roadblocks are frequent, omitting to get one of the above permits when required may cost you more in the long run.

As much as following proper procedure (without which civilisation would clearly crumble), paperwork is a game of wits as well as an opportunity for corrupt officials to create difficulties which can only be solved with a bribe. By at least starting your journey with proper documentation you'll have a good chance to get well underway without unnecessary hassles until you learn the ropes and find out what can and cannot be got away with.

MONEY
Along with insurance, money and how to carry it is another thing that many adventure riders worry about before they leave. The cost of any major trip is likely to be at least a couple of thousand pounds and riding with that sort of

money through the insecure territories of Asia, Africa and Latin America is enough to make anyone nervous. For advice on changing money and dealing with the black market, see p.102.

Best currencies

Thanks in part to the far-reaching tentacles of the Coca-Cola culture, the desirability of the **US dollar** is well known in even the remotest corners of the world, places where other hard currencies might be stared at in incomprehension. Certainly, throughout South America and across most of Asia this would be the most readily-convertible hard foreign currency to carry. In Africa they're more used to the **Euro** and the British pound. Avoid using British £50 or US$100 bills: they are rarely seen abroad and the latter is often thought to be counterfeited. For the same reason don't do street deals for $100 bills, especially in the vicinity of Nigeria where they make them (along with a whole lot of other counterfeit stuff).

Credit cards

Credit cards are the most useful way of avoiding the need to carry large rolls of cash. While it may be a while before we see the familiar blue-white-and-gold bands of a Visa card along the Ho Chi Minh Trail, a compact credit card or two is definitely an item worth carrying on a long overland ride. One day, somewhere, you're going to bless that little plastic rectangle for getting you out of a fix, most probably to cover air freight to the next place or just paying for a restful night in a plush hotel when you're out of cash. And across North America, Europe, Australasia and South Africa you need hardly ever use cash at all.

Contrary to the reasonable assumption that credit card companies hit you hard for overseas purchases, they actually offer the best rates of exchange for the day of your purchase and no service charges (at least with Visa).

It goes without saying that you should keep tabs of how much you're spending on the card and, at the very least, get your minimum monthly payment sorted out (you can arrange this sort of direct debit with your bank before you go, assuming, of course, you have money in the bank to pay it off). Better still, build up your credit card credit before you leave.

A good travel guidebook should tell you which of the three main brands (Visa, American Express or MasterCard) are widely used in your destination, but with the negative connotation 'America' has in some countries or to some individuals, the anonymous Visa or less commonly seen MasterCard are more widely reliable.

Travellers' cheques and money transfers

A back up to hard cash are travellers' cheques, most useful in US dollar form: safer than cash but no more useful than credit cards. In developing countries don't rely on these troublesome forms of 'cash' – they might be virtually hard currency for holidaymakers in Florida but may prove frustratingly unchangeable when you need them most. And despite what you're told, don't put your faith in a speedy replacement of stolen items. First you have to declare them lost and a working phone, let alone reimbursement, might be days away. Travellers' cheques are merely a secure back-up which can be easily cashed (or in the States, used as cash) in Westernised countries. Furthermore, although issued in a rock-solid currency like US dollars, you may find that cashing them in gets a handful of local currency at the official rate, not something you necessarily want. Some countries even levy a tax on imported travellers' cheques. Short of cash, credit cards are much more useful.

Money transfers or cabling, are generally more useful to students caught short while InterRailing around Europe rather than adventure bikers pushing back the limits of two-wheel endurance. If you do end up using this service, you must state a nominated local bank where the money will arrive. Again, in most cases a poorer country will hand over **local currency** rather than the dollars you may have been counting on. Also, be aware that no matter what may be promised, changing back a local soft currency into a hard currency is either impossible, heavily obstructed or achieved at such a bad rate that you'll be depressed for days. When buying local currency, get only as little as you need; it's easier to top it up with a little black market dealing as you start running out, rather than hope to sell your excess local currency to another traveller.

Security

How or where you carry your stash is up to you. A good idea is to stash a portion on the bike (along with other small valuables) and keep the rest with you. Wherever you put it on your bike (use your imagination, but think laterally!) make sure you wrap it up securely against possible damage.

Another good idea is to secrete some more money on your person: there are all sorts of devices sold in travel shops; above all go for something that's comfortable and convenient so you'll never be disinclined to wear it. Ordinary belts come with secret zipped interiors; money belts go around your waist, your neck or shoulder-holster style à la Dirty Harry. You can velcro your wad to the inside of your trousers or keep it in an elasticated bandage around your shin. The rest can be put in a secure inside pocket of your jacket.

Keep your 'day cash' separate from that large, tempting-looking wodge; you don't want to be unpeeling a couple of dollars from a roll of $2000 to buy a kebab in a crowded market. Another general point about **pockets** is get into the habit of using the same ones for the same things, and be forever checking that the zips are closed as you walk into a crowded area. Stick to this habit religiously: wallet and passport here; bike keys there; small change in that one. This way when something goes missing or you need something quickly, you know where it is. It's one good reason for using a jacket with lots of secure pockets.

Credit card fraud is now common, so do **check your statements** carefully. There are stories from Africa and South America of credit card accounts being skinned alive – in fact it's surprising it doesn't happen more often. This is usually following a purchase like a night in a hotel where your number is retained and somehow abused. Where possible it's best to limit the use of your card to just withdrawing cash from ATMs or banks and then pay for all services and goods with the cash. Resist using your card as liberally as you might at home, even if it is possible.

Choosing a motorcycle

Motorcyclists have been up the road and around the world on everything from scooters to 2.3 litre cruisers, making trips from a little over two weeks to thirteen years, seven months and four days. Any machine that starts, turns and stops will do the job, but ask yourself would you be pleased to chug across the Bolivian altiplano pegged out while llamas and small children trot past, struggle over the Wahiba Sands on a full-dress tourer weighing half a ton, or ride a machine which they stopped making before you were born?

Important factors

If you need some guidance in choosing a bike here, in no particular order of importance, are some factors to consider:

- **Weight**
- **Economy**
- **Comfort**
- **Robustness**
- **Spares back-up**
- **Reliability**
- **Mechanical simplicity**
- **Solo or two-up?**

And here's another thing to remember: the bike you eventually choose is going to be loaded with up to 50kg (110lbs) of gear, more if you're riding two-up. This weight will reduce the machine's agility and braking performance as well as accelerate wear on all components, especially tyres and drive chains. So whatever bike you settle on, consider the worst-case scenario: riding it fully-loaded on a gravel road.

If you're not concerned about making an outlandish statement on two wheels then settle for a **single or twin cylinder machine of at least 600cc**. A 40hp engine of this capacity produces enough power to carry you and your gear through the worst conditions while not over-stressing the motor. It'll also give reasonable performance and fuel economy of at least 50mpg (which equals 17.6kpl, 5.7l/100km or 41.5 miles per US gallon). Multi-cylinder engines may be smooth but are unnecessary and, in case you hadn't yet guessed, **four strokes** are far superior to two strokes on a long trip, despite the latter's power-to-weight advantage.

Engine cooling and transmission options

Water-cooling is now the norm on modern, big-engined bikes, not because it's better, but because a water-cooled engine can be built with finer tolerances so producing higher performance. Water-cooling also reduces engine noise as manufacturers are compelled to make their machines and resulting emissions more environmentally friendly – and there is no doubt that because the heat dissipation is more even, water-cooled engines last longer between rebuilds.

Even though mechanical simplicity is desirable and water-cooling is another thing to go wrong, it's no longer a reason to avoid a water-cooled machine. But despite the impression, a machine with a water-cooled engine run cooler in extreme heat, though it will at least warn you when the mperature is getting very high, so giving you a chance to back-off, or stop and see what's wrong.

As long as it's in good condition and well maintained, an **air-cooled** engine is no worse than a water-cooled equivalent and with it you have no radiator or water pump worries. But maintaining an air-cooled engine while on the road (for example, by making regular changes with quality oil) can be more difficult than you think. These days air-cooled engines are really only still used on some single-cylinder bikes – most modern multis have liquid-cooling of some sort.

Transmission by either **shaft or chain** is a less cut and dry issue. Shaft drive transmission tends to be fitted on non-sports machines (in both road and a dirt sense), but due to its weight, rarely comes on true dual sport machines. As long as the system is reliable, its weight and slight power-sapping effects are balanced by reliability and virtual freedom from maintenance.

Chains and sprockets on the other hand are a very efficient, light and cheap means of transmitting power from an engine to a back wheel. Although they're exposed to the elements, modern 'o'-, 'x'- or lately x-y-z-ring chains can now last for thousands of miles. So when it comes to transmission settle for shaft drive on a heavier machine or use a chain driven bike with **top quality chain and sprockets**. There's more on chains on p.50.

And if you happen to be wondering about a kickstart-only or **electric start** model: go for the button. One hot day, when your bowels are in freefall and you're stalled on a one-log bridge, you will bless that button.

Carbs, fuel injection and catalytic converters

Electronic fuel injection is becoming more common on motorcycles, mainly because it offers smoother fuelling, superior economy and cleaner emissions at a price which today's electronics now make viable. As long as it works it's also maintenance-free, something that carb-balancing BMW Boxer owners may be pleased to hear. And don't think fuel injection is new fangled – all diesel vehicles are fuel injected (these days electronically) and no one complains about that.

An EFI management system is constantly measuring various parameters in the engine to deliver an optimum charge to the combustion chamber and this alone puts it miles ahead of any carburettor – once well described as 'a brick with holes in it'. Think of all the YIPS, YOPS and YAKS induction tricks they have been trying over years to smooth out carburation, especially on lumpy singles – well EFI fixes them in one go; ride an old Funduro alongside an EFI 650GS and you'll see the difference. Another advantage of EFI is that it's not so badly affected by **altitude** – the system merely compensates for the lack of oxygen by feeding less fuel; soon you'll be running up and down between Chile and Bolivia just for fun! Like water-cooling, EFI on motorbikes may appear unnecessary but it's a real step forward and has brought a new lease of life to a lot of ropey old engine designs.

Many EFI bikes now feature **catalytic converters** (or 'cats') built into their silencers to clean up emissions. Normally these must be fed unleaded fuel which is not always available in the sticks. However, you can run a cat on leaded fuel for 'a few months' before it stops cleaning emissions properly. When this happens it won't alter your bike's performance, but it will affect the engine's emissions when it comes to your next roadworthy test.

On all bikes fitted with a cat, you can replace the stock silencer/cat with a no-cat aftermarket pipe for your trip. The bike's electronic emission sensor will adjust the fuel injection accordingly, meaning the machine *should* run fine.

Touring bikes – the comfortable compromise

Touring bikes have one huge advantage and one huge drawback when used for adventurous motorcycle travel. Even when loaded up, they can be supremely **comfortable and stable** over miles of highway, with fat tyres on small wheels and big torquey engines making this sort of riding a pleasure. When you're averaging a couple of thousand miles a week, comfort is an extremely important factor which doesn't just mean the size and thickness of the saddle.

Comfort means multi-cylinder vibration-free engines and smooth power delivery, supple suspension, powerful brakes and protection from the wind. It allows you to relax while riding so defers the inevitable fatigue; and when you're not tired you can cope better with the 101 daily challenges long-distance riding throws at you. Comfort also means an effective silencer, the clothes you're wearing, and your state of mind: these latter two subjects are covered on pp.80-3 and pp.95-103. And comfort means the space and power to travel with a pillion passenger for an extended period.

It's when a big touring bike has to face unsealed roads that things can turn pear-shaped. What ran as if on rails becomes an unwieldy dog that devours your energy and can jeopardise your entire trip. I first crossed the Sahara with a guy on a BMW R80. I made it, his bike ended up in flames halfway across. Even at less than walking pace, soft sand and especially mud are misery to ride on a road bike, as effectively bald tyres slither around to dump you again and again. Road bikes were not built for this sort of riding, and components will clog up, wear quickly or break, as will your own resolve to take spontaneous excursions or vital short cuts on dirt roads. Smaller road bikes of 600cc or less will be more manageable, but anything over the one-litre class can be near unrideable in tough off-road conditions.

Still, you can have incredible global adventures on a road bike as long as you think about where you're going and the type of riding you expect there. If you're going to cross the Americas, a road bike is fine most of the time, as it will be for most of the overland routes to Singapore. And of course Australia can be ringed and bisected without leaving the blacktop (although you'll miss the best of the Outback this way). Only a true trans-Africa trip demands a dual-purpose machine to cope with the sands of the Sahara and the mud of the equatorial rain forests.

However, anywhere in the world a main road can be cut by flooding or landslides and in this situation traffic either waits or finds another way through, which usually means getting messy. Furthermore, anyone who's travelled much will know that the best adventures are waiting for you in the rarely visited places far from the beaten track and smooth sealed roads.

Dual sport or trail bikes

The best characteristic of trail or dual sport bikes can be summed up in one word: **versatility**. There's nowhere you can't go on your trailie that a flat-six Gold Wing can get to (albeit without a six-speaker airbag), but the whole thrilling realm of unsealed roads (or no roads at all) becomes open to you.

Dual sports don't only mean singles like KLRs and XTs, but also the very popular '**big trailie**' option of which the BMW GS series and Honda's Africa Twins are best known. It's no surprise that these two models in their various incarnations have become the most popular bikes for adventure riders. They may not be great in the dirt, but they ride as well as all but the plushest ABS-moulded road tourer and evoke a spirit of adventure that is the icing on the cake.

Trail bikes have genuinely **useful features**, such as folding foot controls, bigger than average front wheels to roll over the bumps better, long travel suspension to absorb them and more ground clearance than average when the suspension runs out. And, to a certain extent, they're designed to be dropped without suffering critical damage.

Because they're trying to be the best of both worlds, some of the disadvantages of these bikes are what makes them trail bikes; they include:

- **High seats** make them intimidating for shorter riders although some manufactures have been getting to grips with this in recent years.
- Some have poor high-speed **stability and cornering** due to long travel suspension, high ground clearance, seating position, 21"front wheels, trail-pattern tyres and 'wind-catching' front mud guards.
- **Narrow saddles** give poor comfort, especially for passengers.

Enduro racers

If weight is such an important factor (it's the one thing that 'big trailie' riders complain about most often), a four-stroke enduro like KTM LCs, Honda XRs and Yamaha TTs must make a great adventure bike, no? Well, they could be if your adventure is purely off-road. While it's true that, unloaded, these bikes are much more functional off-road than trail bikes, they differ in some key ways. The engines can consume more fuel and require more attention due to their higher state of tune. Because they're designed for regular maintenance, the **engine oil capacity** of these machines is very small. That's fine if you change it after every couple of rides as you're supposed to, but left for a couple of thousand miles is not so good for enduro engine longevity.

This no-frills nature also extends to **basic lighting** and a **narrow seat**, designed for standing up and shifting body weight rather than day-long support. **Rear subframes** are also a weak point on these kinds of bikes; they were never meant to carry a load greater than a number plate. The truth is a machine like this would be all but wasted on a long touring trip. You must remember that by the time any bike is loaded up, **all traces of nimbleness will be largely eradicated** so think twice unless you're committed to off roading, or like your enduro bike too much.

Still having trouble deciding what to take for your big ride? Here follows my list of **Top Ten Overlanders**, a mildly-informed personal selection followed by a pick and mix of other machines. Maybe yours is in there somewhere.

KTM ADVENTURE 640R

Manufactured From 1997 (originally 620)

Engine 625cc watercooled single

Dry weight 154kg/340lb

Fuel capacity 28 ltr/7.4 US gal

Max range 530km/355mls @ 19kpl/45mpUSg

Riders like Suspension, power, big tank, build, light weight

Don't like Vibration, seat pre-2003, engine reliability

Even after eight years in production and improving all the time, the Adventure R is still in a class of its own; an off-the-shelf overlander appealing to uncompromising riders who value the KTM's single-minded design and performance. The build-quality, components and attention to detail set 640Rs apart, as does the tough frame when compared to mushy Jap examples. On 2003 and later models, the switchable CDI to run on low octane fuel is another a neat touch.

Crisp, responsive power and quality suspension makes Adventures a gas on the dirt, even loaded up, but the high compression adds up to vibration through the famously uncomfortable seat (much improved since 2002). Get used to it and fit bar weights off a Duke plus foam grips. Oil leaks can be either unbearable or tolerable. Reports of unreliability (a run of cheap Eastern European head/gearbox/main bearings, and broken electrical wires) also vary. Learn to live with engine noises but, where fitted, check sidestand welds, fit steel sprockets, replace control cables, use stronger/cheaper Honda mirrors and fit a second fan. Also, go for the more economical and better-built Mikuni CV carb'ed models from 2001 onwards which on the highway can return up to 700km/460mls at a 50mph cruise.

Alternatives A KTM 640 LC (right) costs about £1000 less, is easier to source but has the same suspension and components. You won't get a fairing or trip computer but the big tank off the Adventure will fit once you add a fuel pump. Or, for the price of three 640s you can go large with the Dakar-ready 660 Rallye. An XR650R needs a lot of accessorising to bring it up to 640 Adventure spec.

BMW R100GS

Manufactured From 1987-1997

Engine 980cc air-cooled flat twin, shaft

Dry weight 210kg/463lb

Fuel capacity 24 ltr/6.3 US gal

Max range 410km/270mls @ 17kpl/40mpUSg

Riders like Shaft drive, mechanical simplicity and accessibility, suspension

Don't like Unreliable electrics, shaft problems, brakes

Love them or hate them (many feel both) the Paralever GSs were and still are a hit for those who are wary of the heavy, electronic 1100/1150s. Among the many improvements on the preceding G/Ss was better suspension, though

the Paralever rear link has been described as an engineering solution for a problem that doesn't exist; expect a shaft to last 50,000km – not that bad. Other features include a small wind shield (always handy) and a rather exposed oil cooler, rim-mounted spokes (for tubeless tyres) and a much bigger battery.

The Paris-Dakar version came with a huge 35-litre tank and a fairing with crash bars but weighed in at 236 kilos while from the airhead grave came the R80GS Basic, part G/S (the original model) but with White Power suspension on a Paralever back end and a distinctive blue frame. A 'Kalahari' version came with a handy 35-litre steel tanks, hand guards and the small windshield of the early Paralevers.

Things to know: the alternator/rotor can fail; so carry a spare (plus the tool) or get it rewound with a better diode board from Motorrad Elektrik – though a simpler fix is increasing the gauge of some of the electrical wires to reduce loads. Subframes need bracing, but no more than any other mono-shocker carrying an overland load. All these 'weak points' are relative when one considers how hard GSs get used: loaded up like vans to head RTW two-

up. All it takes is some owner involvement which is part of the satisfaction of owning a BM.

For model history go **to www.mica peak.com/bmw/gs**; webchat is at **www.ukgser.com** or for North America, **www.airheads.org**.

Alternatives The more sophisticated fuel-injected GS twins or an Africa Twin.

HONDA XRV750 AFRICA TWIN

Manufactured From 1997-2002

Engine 742cc water-cooled inline V-twin

Dry weight 208kg/458lb

Fuel capacity 23 ltr/6.1 US gal

Max range 415km/276mls @ 18kpl/42.5mpUSg

Riders like Tough, reliable, smooth V-twin power

Don't like Weight, fuel economy (RD04), fuel pump, basic rear shock (RD07)

The Africa Twin is the big overlander for riders who want something other than a BMW GS. No other multi-cylinder Japanese adventure motorcycle gets close in popularity, though many come and go. Based a bit more loosely than Yamaha's Ténéré rally replica on the Dakar-winning V-twins of the late 1980s, the XRV is actually closer to the much less fashionable Transalp which remains in production.

By far the most common praise is the unswerving reliability, not something that could be said for BMs, while in Europe plenty of equipment and know-how has evolved over the years to make the AT ready for the big trip.

The dodgy electric **fuel pump** on the RD07s from 1993 is the only regular complaint. Contacts on the original Honda pump on earlier models weld up. Later pumps were said to be fine and some riders fit a Mikuni vacuum (non-electric) pump as found on KTM Adventures – but still have fuel starvation problems which suggests vapour lock in hot conditions. Travel with a spare pump or, if necessary, eliminate the pump with a bit of hose to get you home. Rear shocks can also cook, especially two-up, which an AT does not manage quite as well as a BMW. But they are tough at surviving multiple crashes: one rider even rode his through a deer at 85mph – he remained upright if a bit shaken, the deer was in two halves. In English the best website is **www.xrv.org.uk**.

Alternatives An XL650V Transalp costs less, is 10% lighter and less powerful but still carries 19-litres of fuel. Other big Jap trailies like TDMs or Valadero have not caught on though Suzuki's fuel-injected 650 V-Stroms twin is a contender even if it's perceived as a road tourer. At 25kg lighter and with knobblies and a bashplate, how bad can it be on a gravel road?

YAMAHA XTZ600 (3AJ) 'TWIN LAMP'

Manufactured From 1988-1991

Engine 595cc air-cooled single

Dry weight 147kg/324lb

Fuel capacity 23 ltr/6.1 US gal

Max range 460km/306mls @ 20kpl/47.3mpUSg

Riders like It's the best Ténéré, fairing

Don't like Weight, gearbox wear, no kick start

In the ten-years of production, the first and last (both pictured) of the air-cooled Ténérés were the pick of the bunch, launching an enduring biking cult among European riders who valued the virtues of simplicity and function. The

bike was named after an especially gruelling stage of the original Paris-Dakar rally after which the field was usually decimated by half – but Yamaha XT600-based desert racers won this rally five times.

The legend came to an end in 1991 with the twin-lamp faired 3AJ model – it may have been 20 kilos heavier than the original, 30-litre tanked, kick-start model, but in an unsophisticated package, it was all there – a bombproof 'Jap-reliable' engine, acceptable suspension, a decent tank capacity and bash-plate, plus a fairing which stopped the long ride becoming the long neck. Avoid the electric/kick 'IVJ' models which came in between.

Heaps of kit and know-how as well as several European websites keep the XT-Z name alive (including a lively forum on **Horizons Unlimited**, see p.16), with an answer for every trick in the book and even downloadable parts fiches. In the UK, **David Lambeth** (see ad in the back) is Mr XT Ténéré and can fix your fifth gear pitting blues – not as bad as it sounds, but ageing 3AJs tend to lead hard lives so need looking after.

© KARIM HUSSEIN

Alternatives Yamaha diluted the Ténéré name on inferior models and lately seem to have given up on it altogether. The air-cooled ones are what you want; you can pick them up in the UK for around £1500. If you can't, try Ténérising an XT-E, or why not treat yourself to that KTM Adventure 640R – a tricked-out Ténéré with power, suspension and long-range stamina.

KAWASAKI KLR650

Manufactured From 1987

Engine 651cc water-cooled single

Dry weight 154kg/337lb

Fuel capacity 23 ltr/6.1 US gal

Max range 460km/306mls @ 20kpl/47.3mpUSg

Riders like Know-how and aftermarket goodies, price

Don't like Seat, minor engine issues

Surely one of the longest-running motorcycles in Japanese production history; all they do these days is change the paint scheme (for 2005 it was Aztec Red) and all for a bargain US$5150 or £2800! KLRs are very much the Ténérés

© TOM GRENON

that North America never got – slightly less functional but no less refined and improved by amateurs and small-time engineering houses who between them have fixed every last crease that Kawasaki didn't iron out. On a run fuel consumption can easily top 21kpl (50mpUSgal) – if only your butt could outlast the tank. Corbin seats are available.

The big tank, small fairing and the 650cc water-cooled engine gets the KLR off to a great start but unless you like steering with oars, brace the front forks. Balancer chains are said to be a weak point: to get an idea of the condition of the balancer sprockets, take a look at the mesh oil strainer behind the right-hand engine cover: if it's full of bits of rubber, you're better off replacing the balancer chain sprockets and guides. A more common problem is the stock idler shaft adjustment lever but you can buy a re-engineered replacement for just $40. And disconnect the sidestand and clutch cut-out switches before they do it themselves. Any other questions will be answered at **www.klr650.net**.

Alternatives Realistically, KLR adventure riders are exclusively based in North America and true alternatives that offer what the KLR does for the price are few. A Honda XR650L is similarly well known in the US and costs about the same. It's a much more dirt-oriented machine but needs fiddling with the jetting to run right and of course a big tank. A new Suzuki DR650SE is also a (less-loved) option.

© CRAIG HIGHTOWER

BMW R1150GS

Manufactured From 1999-2003

Engine 1130cc oil/air-cooled four-valve flat twin

Dry weight 249kg/549lb

Fuel capacity 22 ltr – 5.8 US gal

Max range 418km/278mls @ 19kpl/45.6mpUSg

Riders like EFI fuel consumption, ready for RTW

Don't like Weight

BMW's ground-breaking GS series gets better with every new version. When the fuel-injected Telelever 1100GS came out in 1994 it was a hit, but the 1150,

© Bob Goggs

was a whole lot better. To sum it up, despite its daunting bulk the giant GS is amazingly easy to handle loaded up, even on gravel roads.

Apart from the distinctive assymetric front lamps, the telelever (which adds up to dive-free forks) was lighter, the gearbox was six speed the clutch was hydraulic.

They took the chance to improve the well-known gearbox-subframe weak spot from the 1100s but though less show stopping, the footrest brackets will easily break in a tumble. But you get an adjustable seat height, ABS and a replacement chip to enable the engine to run on 87 octane (it needs it). If you must fiddle with something, a set of custom-tuned Ohlins shocks greatly improve the suspension.

In 2001 the 1150-based 'Adventure' was released with a lower first gear, knobbly tyres and switchable ignition for poor fuel. Suspension travel is 20mm longer on a White Power shock, the tank is 30-litres, and there are hand guards, crash bars and other protective features and rather tinny OE luggage.

© Bob Goggs

They seem to have thought of just about everything with the 1150s. Fuel injection or other electronics has never been a problem apart from the same surging as on the 650s when the EFI gets into a loop – the twin plug head fixed that and not all bikes suffer from it which suggests it depends on tuning. For **web** see the R100GS page. See also Helge Pederson's 1150 dvd on p.269.

Alternatives By now the 1200GS will be making an impact, 30 kilos lighter and with a host of other refinements (but also teething problems on early models), it will be carrying the GS legend on to the next generation.

ENFIELD BULLET 350/500

Manufactured From time immemorial

Engine 346- or 499cc air-cooled single

Dry weight 164kg/361lb

Fuel capacity 14.5 ltr/3.8 US gal

Max range Potentially 364km @ 26kpl/62mpUSg

Riders like Retro charm, cheap, can be fixed anywhere

Don't like Needs to be fixed everywhere, brakes

Derived from the forty-year-old casts and dies Royal Enfield left behind, Indian Enfields have been going ever since. In recent years riding around the subcontinent on rentals or even buying and riding back home has become a subgenre of adventure motorcycling (see p.156); the adventure is: will you make it? Things are moving forward though: 2004 Electra models featured gas shocks, electronic ignition, disc brakes and CV carbs – but the original Bullet is still available and some say, better.

Buying new in India (**www.royal enfield.com**) will give more teething problems than a croc with gum disease; go for reconditioned secondhand. Whatever happens, Indian roadside mechanics know Bullets better than their own families. Spares are also widely available and astonishingly cheap.

These machines suit a type of laid-back rider who sees the 50mph cruising speed and regular delays as a bonus. It must be remembered that, unless badly maintained or repaired, they never actually fall to pieces. A Bullet will give you a journey to remember and plenty of roadside encounters which is what travelling is all about. On the road carry cables, a chain link, rectifier and a coil, and try to buy original Enfield spares: cheaper imitations have an even shorter life than the originals! Expect regular carb cleaning and loose fittings too.

Don't think they are complete turkeys – it's all relative – Dutch guy **www.ronaldcolijn.net** rode his Bullet 50,000km round the world. It took him five years but he wasn't in a rush anyway.

Alternatives For the price, nothing matches the Enfield esprit evoking your grandad motoring up the Khyber Pass to quell native unrest, although you might consider some of the many locally-built 125s.

© Chris Bright

BMW F650GS DAKAR

Manufactured From 2001

Engine 652cc water-cooled single

Dry weight 192kg/423lb

Fuel capacity 17.3 ltr/4.6 US gal

Max range 400km/250mls @ 23kpl/56.5mpUSg

Riders like Amazing economy, smooth EFI engine, comfy seat

Don't like Weight, surging and stalling issues, water pump leaks

There was nothing wrong with the old Rotax-engined F650 Funduro until the EFI 650s came out: a GS model (bottom picture) with a 19" front wheel and the slightly longer legged 'Dakar' with a 21" wheel (left). The lumpiness of the carb-engine Funduro was eradicated, fuel economy jumped and the whole machine, though very heavy for a single, felt ergonomically sorted.

Enduring issues with **surging** and **stalling** are the only fly in the ointment; worse with the early models and possibly on 'leaner' North American versions. Surging around 3500rpm is annoying, but cutting out at a road junction can be truly alarming. Software updates to the CPU (v.10 to date) along with new injectors fixed many, though the 'twin plug' 2004 models suggest they've still not got on top of it. Some early bikes never had the problem or had it fixed after a couple of upgrades.

The tank may only be 17 litres but that's equivalent to a 20-litre 'carb' tank. Still not huge, but people get carried away with big tanks when you think of the cost of a 10-litre fuel can. The plastic bashplate is hopeless; Touratech make a carbon fibre one which looks nice but alloy works best to protect the hoses and water pump (some leak). You'll find a mass of detail (if not so much on overland prep) on the Chain Gang website: **www.f650.com**.

Alternatives Don't write off the old Funduro. In the desert I found it snatchy and lacking in low speed torque but Acerbis did a 27-litre tank and Slovenian Benka Pulko rode hers round the world for a few years. Otherwise Yamaha's EFI XT660R could be worth a look, though it's built down to a price, is no lighter, has huge, low-slung pipes and lacks the 650's long-range comfort.

HONDA XR650L

Manufactured From 1990

Engine 644cc air-cooled single

Dry weight 147kg/324lb

Fuel capacity 10.6 ltr/2.8 US gal

Max range 201km/125mls @ 19kpl/45mpUSg

Riders like Suspension, proven engine, still available new, my dvd (!)

Don't like Seat, seat height, cheap build

You're off to a good start with an XRL. A 15-year-old design, it's still available new: an NX650 engine in an XR chassis sitting on CR suspension. All simple, long-proven technology, it adds up to a great all-terrain tourer that's cheaper and less temperamental than a KTM and a better traveller than an XR650R. Originally sold in North America, they offered better dirt manners than KLRs but with the same range of after market know-how.

In 2002 XRLs reached Australia and Europe (sort of) where in a short time they've taken off where XTs, NXs and other discontinued singles have become hard to find. The engine still survives in the FMX650 supermoto. Out of the crate they're well known for needing attention to jetting, gearing and plumbing (you'll find my mods on the AM website: ...**com/desert-riders**), but once that's done they're ready for adaption.

We crammed on a 37-litre tank off an XR6, but a smaller 25-odd litre version will make the bike easier to manage. Ours ran well on low octane and never exhibited the NX's starting problems. If you're running heavy racks and boxes the rear subframe needs bracing, along with a heavier rear spring. An XR650R bashplate fits and a windshield is also a good idea – and try and get the hang of reading the oil level right; it's a very awkward system. One rider who covered thousands of African and outback miles on an XRL and a snazzier XRR said he'll stick with the 'L'; the 'R's' extra poke offered no particular advantage once loaded up.

Alternatives For half the price new you can either downgrade to a well-rebuilt XT or NX Dominator (20kg heavier!) if you can find them, or stay kind of level with a new KLR650 or Suzuki DR650SE.

YAMAHA XT600E

Manufactured From 1990-2004

Engine 595cc air cooled single

Dry weight 156kg/344lb

Fuel capacity 15 ltr/4 US gal

Max range 285km/190mls @ 19kpl/45mpUSg

Riders like Price, XT heritage, simplicity, electric start

Don't like Fewer frills than a cue ball in the snow; no kickstart

Production of the classic 600cc Ténérés wound up in Europe and Australia in the 1990s, but the water-cooled XT660Z which replaced them never caught on as an adventure bike. Since that time, with the original air-cooled Ténérés get-

ting thin on the ground and going for premium prices, riders were forced to turn to the ultra basic XT600E. Someone must have forgotten to hit the 'STOP' button on the production line as it was still on sale in early 2004 when the new fuel-injected XT660s came out. (In fact the E still survives as the relatively expensive TT600RE though who knows for how long.)

And so the 'Ténérésing' of E's caught on, adding at the very least a decent-sized tank, a bash plate, plus alloy wheels, an oil cooler and braided steel brake lines for improved feel. After that you might want to think of some suspension and somewhere to go, but by this stage you could have bought something decent in the first place. Depending on how far you go, the package doesn't quite add up to the charisma of a true Ténéré, but the E gets on the job without complaining; it's a popular rental in many places round the world.

A 600E is a bit like an ultra-reliable Enfield, a simple, old-fashioned cheap and cheaply-built machine that won't have you committing Yamhonduki when it falls off its stand and gets scratched. Technology was from the early-80s, with the Ténérés twin carb set-up returning good economy and, like the

3AJ, you get a reliable old nail with an 8.5:1 compression ratio that will happily run on yak piss (if you ask nicely).

Alternatives Honda's mildly more sophisticated NX650 Dominator or the TT600RE with the alloy that the E never got, though still managing to weigh nearly as much. Or if an E is all you can afford, think wide and get yourself any old shed (see overleaf).

BMW R80 G/S

There are not many bikes suitable for long RTW rides; maybe four or five stand out. But I'm convinced the BMW R80 G/S (and possibly later GS models) are head and shoulders above the rest. So much so that as you read this I'm somewhere in the world on my '85, already on its second time around the clock, while my 1200GS looks after the house.

- a G/S is tough – you can hurl it into rivers, bounce it off the scenery and lob it down a mountain with impunity; it just carries on.
- The shaft is virtually maintenance-free and doesn't break like the Paralèver GSs.
- It's low-tech – anything that breaks can be mended by a bush mechanic and only a few show-stopping spares need be carried. Many police forces around the world still use air-heads, providing a source of help.
- It's been around a long time with no unnecessary modifications. BMW still make parts for it (all easily and quickly obtainable),

and companies like Touratech make all sorts of goodies for it.

- It's light and low enough for even a small person like me to pick up (once QD luggage has been removed).
- The standard alloy-rimmed 21- and 18-inch wheels are very strong, and can be shod with tyres obtainable almost everywhere. I've yet to experience a loosened spoke.
- Maintenance is simple: new engine oil every 8000km (any old 20W50 will do), gearbox/shaft/final drive every 16,000km. Tappets now and again (takes 20 minutes). The standard toolkit is enough to virtually dismantle the bike and is not made of plasticene. The hand pump which lives inside the frame top tube will pump up a tyre to a reasonable pressure without working up a major sweat.
- It may not be very powerful but has great low down torque. When it comes to sticky situations the G/S has the grunt to claw its way up a rocky slope or through a muddy morass with a minimum of gear-changing or clutch-slipping.

Let's face it, the pedigree is impeccable. It was originally designed for the Paris-Dakar, and has all the characteristics necessary to fulfil its obligations as a long-distance bike. I'll give mine up when they pry it from my cold, dead fingers!

Cynthia Milton

BUYING AND SELLING ABROAD AND BIKE SWAPPING

Thanks to the internet and particularly the Horizons Unlimited Bulletin Board (**HUBB**; see p.16), selling your bike or buying someone else's in a part of the world which you want to get to has become possible. Scan the Hubb Buy/Sell forum and see what's on offer.

Besides renting a bike or getting a 'buy back' deal (both possibilities become more prolific) there is also the option of 'bike swapping'. Wherever you live can sound

pretty exotic to someone from the other side of the world and with an informal agreement and transferred insurance, neither party should pay much at all. If you can connect with another traveller who wants to swap, this could be the least expensive option of all, as long as you can arrange insurance to cover it.

There is a Bike Swap Forum on the HUBB at www.horizonsunlimited.com.

Grant Johnson

Other machines and other strategies

Less common among adventure riders are **Suzuki DR** singles. Since the original DR400 of the early 1980s, capacities have gone up and down from 600cc rally clones to the odd and overweight DR750/800S. By Japanese standards some Suzukis had a comparatively poor record for reliability and build quality and this, along with being unfashionable, is why they've never caught on.

Versions of the **DR600/650** have been around as long as XTs and XLs, but early ones had dodgy electrics and later ones had problems with blowing head gaskets and output (engine sprocket) shaft wear – though this is a common ailment with many big singles (KLRs) whose lumpy engine characteristics give the transmission a hard time (the Yamaha 3AJ gearbox problems are partly attributable to this). Nevertheless, riders have reported long overland trips on the 325lb **DR650SE**s with no major problems; it's still sold in the US from around $5000, offering solid, no frills technology.

The better regarded **DR-Z400S** is a more common choice: having used DR350s on their RTW Mondo trip in the mid-nineties, Terra Circa (see dvds, p.269) used 400Ss to cross Russia, though not without engine problems. Nevertheless a small DR is light enough to be good on the dirt, easy to pick up

DESERT DIVERSION

Now being well into middle age, I decided it was high time I experienced the Sahara on a motorbike. The only problem was that I wanted a simple and reliable off-road bike, but with shaft drive and preferably four cylinders.

With nothing fitting that description, I had to build it myself. Modifications based on a 1996 Yamaha XJ900S Diversion included removing the fairing, extending the suspension to give 150mm travel at both ends, so increasing ground clearance, plus motocross handlebars and mudguard. A scrapped fuel tank was increased to 45 litres, I added engine and hand protections, a rear tubeless 130/80 tyre was mounted backwards on the front 17" rim and I made a comfortable home-made seat and an enduro front light with a mountain-bike speedometer.

Two 36-litre alu-boxes were specially made including a holder on the back for a pair of off-road tyres under a lockable cover. Inside there was room for a tent and sleeping bag etc.

On the sand it was not too bad, no worse than a BMW, but the real challenge were the muddy trails leading in to Mali, alone with a fully-loaded bike. With the track being waterlogged the only alternative was to drive off into the bush, around all the flooded areas. This was an unexpected desert and savanna adventure with the average speed down to 10kph. On this trip the bike gained 17,000km but I lost 12kg!

Ronnie Skårner

and to air freight without costing a packet; it's just the long highway miles that can be a drag. For the right sort of gnarly ride they would be ideal.

Although it's a bit early to say, the 190kg **DL650 V-Strom** featuring a 90° V-twin fuel-injected engine and a 20-litre tank could be the new Transalp. It's commonly regarded as superior to the one-litre V-Strom and, with an alloy bashplate to protect that pipe and some better tyres, it would make a great adventure cruiser for mixed roads.

© HEIKKI LUKKARI

'Two wheels and an engine'
In the end of course **anything** that has the above two characteristics could be the bike for your adventure. It's possible to get fixated on my Top Ten and think that anything else will be less good.

17,000 MILES ON A 225 SEROW

For shorter folk, finding the right bike for the Big Trip can often prove tricky as the seat heights and fully-loaded weights of the traditional overlanding machines can be intimidating to the 'vertically challenged' rider.

Clocking in at 5'4" in warm weather, I found myself faced with this quandary when planning my year-long ride from Alaska to Argentina (see p.207). After looking around at several machines the answer came in the form of Yamaha's XT225 Serow.

Serow Good
Once I'd got used to the idea of riding nearly 20,000 miles with a top speed of a Trabant, the Serow (named after a stocky Asian mountain deer) appeared to be the ideal mini adventure motorcycle – a simple, rugged trail bike weighing in at just 108kg/238lb with a reassuringly low seat height of 31".

Its basic construction and lack of fancy gadgets made for easy tinkering, parts were widely available and the nippy 225cc motor returned excellent fuel consumption. Despite the small nine-litre tank, I only needed to carry jerry cans on the most remote stretches.

Another thing worth considering is that small tatty trail bikes are commonplace all across the developing world which makes blending into the background a little easier.

Serow Bad
The lack of power never bothered me until I got high up in the Andes. Here the stocky deer proved to be no mountain goat as the altitude took the Serow's breath away. Despite meddling around with different jets, the bike struggled painfully above 10,000 feet, at times barely able to pull away.

Another downside of small-capacity bikes like this is the eradication of their nimble qualities if loaded too much at any altitude, turning them into unwieldy *and* gutless slugs.

But if you keep your kit to minimum, give yourself plenty of time and keep out of the stratosphere, the Serow is more than up to the job.

Lois Pryce

AG BIKES FOR OVERLAND; MILKING THE POTENTIAL

In South Africa and Australia (and maybe in other markets too) you can buy yourself a Japanese 'ag' or 'agricultural' bike.

With barely a go-faster acronym between them, these are cheap, no-frills but functional farmers' machines usually around 200cc. The technology is Flintstone era; your average ag sled is a parts bin special not unlike the BMW Basic/Kalahari (itself a bit on the 'ag' side some might say). Old production lines have been quite literally farmed out to overseas factories where labour is cheap so development of this year's crotch rocket is not disturbed.

The Honda **CTX 200 Bushlander** is one good example, costing just 24,000 rand or AUD5000 (around £2000) plus on the road costs. For that you get what looks like an old XL185 (or XR200 come to that) with electric start and a back-up kick. They don't waste alloy on ag bikes; rims and swingarm, bars and racks are strictly ferrous for extra ballast. The CTX is heavy at 127kg (280 lbs) – an XR400 weighs 117kg, but then again it costs nearly double and is probably twice as good.

Crude handlebar lever protectors come as standard, part of a frontal rack which is matched by a similar sheep rack on the back. There are also rudimentary engine protection bars and a tinny bashplate; tyres are 18- and 21" MT21s. Along with the weight, oversized mudguards and 9:1 compression help keep the speed down, and what other bike comes with *two* side stands: with a couple of rocks or a ditch you've got a centre stand!

Downsides (besides the whole idea altogether!) are a rear drum brake and the small tank. Cruising speed is in the Bullet category but without the roadside repairs.

Yamaha produce the broadly similar **AG 200E** (electric/kickstart, 10-litres, enclosed chain, 119kg/262lbs and Suzuki have a **DR200SE**; same weight but with a 13-litre tank and an oil cooler, no less.

All of these bikes make a rugged, low maintenance, crashable ride, best suited to Indochina, Central Africa, Darien Gap and other low-speed, short-range, low altitude environments where transportation by or across rivers will be an option.

Only across Africa would the need for off-road utility be desirable; unless you're purposely seeking off-road challenges for trans-Asia or the Americas a **road bike** will be fine just about all the time. If you like the idea of transgressing genres you'll find that dual-purpose rather than full on motocross knobbly tyres will make your road bike more stable on dirt roads while still keeping it steerable on the highway – though it's amazing what you can ride with knobblies. Sjaak Lucassen has been riding round the world for a living on an Yamaha R1 with an aluminium shed on the back (he upgraded from a Fireblade) and Ronnie S modified a Yamaha XJ900S Diversion for a trip to West Africa and back (though he did lose 12kg on the way – see previous page).

Another machine worth considering is the four cylinder, fuel-injected **K100** series of BMWs produced from 1983 and which became 1100s in 1991. The engine is still found in 1200 format on some full dress tourers, but a K from the mid-1980s can be a bargain. On these bikes clocking up 100,000 miles or more is not a problem; the early EFI never gave trouble (apart from vapour lock in very hot conditions) though a new starter, alternator and maybe a clutch would not be a bad idea for a long trip. The only other thing that needs attention is checking for wear in the splines where the rear bevel/drive fits on to the swingarm. If it's not been greased regularly worn splines could fail, meaning an expensive repair. Drawbacks are of course the machine's weight at around 240kg/527 lbs and the fact that it is not so happy on dirt road compared to the flat-twin GSs.

© BRADLEY DISHER

If you are new to this game sticking to the well-known or proven machines makes things a lot easier – you know you have a proven set-up plus know-how and equipment will be easier to come by. If you like to be different or have experience and know that the Top Ten selection is rather conservative and self-perpetuating, the only limit is your imagination, your budget and the Laws of Physics.

Still agonising? Then think about **buying a new bike abroad**; it may help narrow down your choices. For example in the UK right now (early 2005) a Suzuki V-Strom 650 costs £5150; in Australia the same bike will cost you AUD10,000 or £4000 and in the US it's just $6600 or £3500. In the US less fashionable bikes like KLR650s or XR650Ls are incredible bargains by European standards and with plenty of kit and know-how too. In Brazil you can pick up a new, locally-built Honda NX4 Falcon 400 (a mini Dominator) for under £2200 (though check you can leave the country with it first). If you're European and wanting to ride the Americas or start your RTW there, it makes sense to buy there, saving money on a bike plus a whole lot on shipping costs.

Bike preparation and maintenance

Whether you're buying at home or abroad, **thorough preparation** of your machine is just about the best insurance you can get to guarantee yourself a mechanically trouble-free trip. And because long-range adventuring will require modifications, the more time you spend riding your modified machine before you leave the better.

Better still, if you're heading overseas with a new set up like metal boxes and racks, try to fit in a short **test run** beforehand to see how the bike handles and if everything works. Again, the fewer surprises you encounter in the nerve-racking early days of the actual trip the better. In somewhere like Africa or Asia you'll have enough on your plate without finding that the suspension bottoms out on what sometimes pass for roads out there.

For a trip to either of the two continents listed above, you want to start getting your machine together about **a year** before departure. Try and do as much of the work yourself, or under close guidance so that when something gives trouble, you have a clue how to fix it. Complex things like engine rebuilds or welding can be (or have to be) left to competent mechanics, but elementary repairs like changing tyres and oil, or cleaning an air filter are things you must be able to do before you go.

As a general rule, if you doubt whether any component will last the entire length of your planned trip, **renew it** and finish off the partially-worn item on your return. This applies especially to things like tyres, chains and sprockets which wear faster on fully-laden bikes ridden on bad roads. Alternatively, on longer trans-continental trips, these are the sorts of spares to be taken along, or arrange to have sent ahead if they're unavailable locally.

If you're buying a **new bike** especially for your trip, get it well in advance of your departure so that any teething problems can be sorted out. Lastly, bear in mind that modifications other than those recommended here may be necessary or useful on the machine of your choice.

Fuel quality

Most modern, single-cylinder engines have a relatively high **compression ratio** and can run terribly on the **low octane fuel** you'll sometimes be forced to fill up with in outback Africa or Central Asia. An XR650L runs 8.5:1, an XR650R has 10:1 while a KTM Adventure runs 11.5:1. Multi-cylinder engines

can use a slightly lower compression ratio but air-cooled engines in particular should always run on the highest octane fuel available.

Signs of an engine suffering on low-octane fuel are a light tapping from the cylinder head (known as **detonation**, 'knocking; or 'pinking') – worst in higher gears and under heavy throttle loads. The fuel charge is igniting before the piston has reached the top of its stroke at which point the spark plug fires. Low power, overheat-

Clean as a daisy, honest! © Trui Hanoulle

ing and feeling that your engine is about to destroy itself are also evident, and this may well happen if you keep pushing a motor running on low octane fuel in power-sapping conditions.

Only if you're off on a very long trip of six months or more is it worth **lowering the compression** (most easily, by fitting an extra base gasket), with the consequent alteration in ignition timing (something easier said than done on bikes with electronic ignition). These days bikes like big GS BMWs and KTM Adventures have switchable **electronic ignition** with an alternative 'map' to run on sub-90 octane fuel. On a few of the latest EFI bikes custom re-mapping may be possible and would have the same effect. Some electronic fuel-injection systems (R1200GS but not the preceding models) have 'knock sensors' which retune to suit the fuel used as well as the engine's state of wear.

An alternative is to change the position of the engine position sensor, thereby changing the timing as you would do with a distributor and points (rarely seen on anything besides Bullets these day, of course).

Unless you're planning on spending weeks in a low octane environment, a temporary solution to messing around with compression or altering the timing manually or electronically is using **octane booster**; a potent fuel additive in cans used for racing. A litre of this stuff (available to off-road competition shops but probably not from the souk in Kashgar or the roadhouse at Punto Gringo) is enough to last up to 660km/1000 miles on low-grade fuel, assuming you put in 10cc per litre and do around 17kpl or 40mpUSg.

Engine temperature

An **oil cooler** is not an essential addition to your air-cooled motor unless, broadly speaking, you expect to be riding through the summers within 30° north or south of the equator. If you do decide to fit a cooler, **dry sump engines**, that is those with separate oil tanks, lend themselves more easily to this modification as any of the external oil lines can be cut and a cooler spliced in with extra hosing.

Fitting an oil cooler reduces the oil pressure and increases the capacity a little. However, having an oil cooler does not mean that important things like oil level, valve clearances and carburation can be neglected if the bike is to run well in hot and demanding conditions. Mount an **oil cooler** up high and in front of the engine: under the head lamp or cut into your fairing is an ideal place. Accessory manufacturers may make kits to fit your bike, but a good-sized unit from a crashed sports bike or car like a Citroen 2CV can be picked up from a breaker's. Mounting on the front of the bike may mean chaffing hoses around the headstock. If you're not using expensive braided hose with proper fittings, tough 5mm-wall rubber hose with jubilee clips will do. Wind wire around the chaffable sections and then cover in duct tape. If you move into a colder climatic zone wrap up the oil cooler with tape or bypass it altogether – something easier done on home-made jobs. An over-cooled engine wears quickly and runs inefficiently.

Water-cooled engines which are now the norm should not need an oil cooler; if they're **overheating** there's something wrong with the cooling system or quite simply the conditions are too hot: most likely in desert sand where you're revving the engine hard at low ground speeds with a tail wind. In this case stop and **park into the wind** to let the running motor cool down.

Keep the engine running at tickover and watch the needle drop. Unless it's parked into the wind, when a bike stops moving the lack of airflow over the motor or through the radiator causes the temperature to rise a little. Turning the engine off at this point causes the temperature to rise dramatically which could send it over the edge. By keeping the engine running during brief stops on hot days the oil [and water] is kept pumping around, cooling the engine. Should your radiator boil over, refill it gradually, a little at a time. Pouring cold water into the baking radiator and barrel could crack something.

Although most water temperature gauges are pessimistic you shouldn't get into the habit of running close to the red zone unless you can face changing a blown cylinder head gasket with a smile.

On air-cooled bikes it is good to know your engine temperature. You can buy **oil temperature gauges** for XRs and the like which screw in, in place of the cap/dipstick, in the frame in front of the tank. Although not really essential, these gadgets are a handy way of gauging the *relative* temperature of your engine. Better still is a proper **oil temperature gauge**. Touratech make a sender that replaces the drain plug on many bikes and which wires into an IMO computer. I once tried to wire it into a regular car-type oil temperature gauge but, although the needles flapped about a lot, it never worked right.

In-line fuel filters work best but if near the barrel it's worth shielding them with foil tape to avoid problems with vapour lock.

Fuel filters and vapour lock

Whatever time of year you expect to be riding, it's a good idea to fit an **in-line fuel filter** into the fuel line(s) of your bike. The inexpensive translucent, crinkled-paper element type (left) work better than fine gauze items, which most bikes already have inside the tank as part of the fuel tap assembly. Make sure you fit it in the right direction of flow – there should be an arrow moulded into the filter body. These filters can be easily cleaned by simply flushing in a reverse direction with fuel from the tank. In desert areas dust is always present in the air and even in the fuel, and in Iran or Pakistan (see photo p.46) it's common for roadside fuel to be dished out from a drum using an old tin. The fact that they pour it through an old rag draped over the funnel is little compensation.

Fuel-injected bikes need to have very good fuel filters built in as standard; an additional fuel filter should not be needed and may disrupt the sensitive fuel induction process. Experiment but expect problems.

In hot conditions in-line filters can create **vapour lock**: evaporation of fuel in the filter body before it flows to the carburettor; this leads to fuel starvation. When the engine dies and cools down, the fuel will eventually condense and run into the carb again and the bike will run until it gets hot again. Vapour lock is worse when your tank fuel level is low and the filter body itself gets hot. We're talking temperatures of over 35°C here. To get round it, top up your tank and pour water over the fuel filter – you should see it fill up with fuel instantly. Wrap it in a damp cloth and think about some more permanent insulation.

I had vapour lock on a Funduro in Libya once and taped a piece of cardboard alongside the barrel to keep the heat off the in-line filter. It worked fine for the rest of the trip even when the temperatures got more extreme.

HIGH-ALTITUDE ATTITUDE

Carbs work best mixing consistent levels of fuel and air. At anything above 3000m there is increasingly less air and your bike (especially smaller-engines) will run 'rich', which actually means 'run very poorly indeed'.

Fitting smaller jets inside the carb can be a fiddly roadside job; lowering the carb needle is a bit easier. Both tricks reduce fuel flow

so lean out the mixture to balance it with the reduced levels of oxygen in the air. More air is easier still: temporarily removing the air box lid or even the air filter (if not dusty) will go some way to rebalancing the mixture.

All these steps will have to be reversed once you lose height. Bikes with EFI have much reduced problems at altitude.

Air filter

Air filters will require possibly daily cleaning during high winds, sandstorms or if travelling behind a dusty convoy. The **reusable multi-layered oiled-foam types** such as those by Twin-Air, Multi Air or Uni Filter are best. Carry a ready-oiled spare in a plastic bag that can be slipped in as necessary while the other gets cleaned when you get a chance. Make sure that the airbox lid seals correctly and that the rubber hoses on either side of the carburettor are in good condition and done up tightly.

Dust storm in the Sahara; most air filters prefer to stay at home on days like this.
© Jeff Condon

Greasing all surfaces inside the airbox is messy but catches more airborne particles and keeps the air filter cleaner for longer; a stocking over the filter is another way of keeping it clean. If you're *pushing* your turned off bike through deep water put a plastic bag around the filter and then refit it to keep water out of the engine.

Some bikes have poorly positioned air intakes that will cake the filter in one sandy day. Check your bike's snorkel/air intake and which way it's pointing. After modifying the

Although dry, this exposed paper filter is not such a hot set up. Reusable oiled foam filters work best if maintained correctly.

seat on an XR650L I found that sand spinning off the back tyre would have got shovelled straight into the airbox – an alloy baffle plate and some duct tape, kept it out.

You can rinse a re-usable foam with petrol and then soak it with engine oil but proper **air filter oil** does the job much better, remaining sticky and not draining under gravity. But if you run out, engine oil is better than nothing.

If you are careful, a small amount of air filter oil can last a few changes.

A freshly-oiled XR foam filter. Disposable latex or thick rubber gloves are handy.

CHAIN AND SPROCKETS

Enclosed from the elements, **shaft drives** are virtually maintenance free – at the very worst a drive shaft on a Paralever BMW might require changing at 30,000 miles. In this respect they're ideal for overland bikes, though they're usually fitted to heavier machines which can bring about their own problems on rough terrain.

A cheap chain ruined this sprocket in just 4000 miles – stick to the well-known brands.

Sealed chains – making them last

Most bikes are fitted with roller **chains and sprockets** which are more efficient when correctly oiled and tensioned – although cheapness and lightness compared to shafts is the main reason why they feature on most bikes.

O-ring chains have grease between the rollers and pins, sealed in with tiny rubber rings between the rollers and side plates. Only when these rubber seals begin to wear out after many thousands of miles will the chain begin to wear out like an ordinary chain. Manufacturers have since come out with somewhat gimmicky 'X-' and 'W-' ring chains (effectively, multiple seals), some of which are guaranteed for 12,000 miles. For *Desert Riders* we were testing various systems; the other two guys fitted DID 'gold plate' x-rings while I tried out a similarly-priced RK 'XW' ring, also made in Japan. Result: the DIDs barely needed adjusting while my OK RK needed about three or four adjustments in 5000km. I've used DIDs before which lasted incredibly so, to cut a long story short, fit **DID gold plate** sealed chains, or whatever brand is said to be as good.

Chain tension and maintenance

Your bike's manual will give instructions but in most cases a chain should be adjusted to provide **40mm** (an inch-and-a-half) **of slack** measured midway along the bottom run of the chain *with your weight on the bike*. On most trail bikes with long-travel suspension, this will give an impression of an overly slack chain when the machine is unloaded and at rest, but this slack will be taken up once the suspension is compressed to the correct level when the bike is on the move. I've found you can expect a certain amount of tightening and polishing of the chain towards the end of a hot day; this will slacken off to the correct tension as the chain cools during the course of the night. Make sure you adjust it correctly: remember, an over-loose chain is better than an over-tight one but keeping the adjustment correct is best. Realistically, with a quality chainset and moderate riding habits, you can expect to have to make adjustments every few thousand miles.

Chains are obviously vulnerable and external lubrication will attract grit and accelerate the wear faster than an RD350 with a jammed throttle. Automatic chain oilers (like the well-known Scott unit) are ideal for long road rides but in sandy conditions they should be disconnected. I've found sealed chains cope very well without any oiling, but oiling can only extend life in grit-free conditions. If you don't use aerosol chain lube (a bulky and possibly messy item to carry), a bottle with a small nozzle full of gearbox oil or proper pushbike chain lube is much more efficient. Lubricate at the end of the day when the chain is warm: start the engine, from the left side pull the bike over onto the sidestand (or on a centre stand), click it into gear – even with your hand holding the clutch in for safety the back wheel will spin. Now run some oil along the rollers – you'll hear the chain sigh with pleasure.

Although **enclosed chain cases** are a better idea, as far as I know only old-time MZ ever managed to make a sufficiently robust item. If anyone still makes them, after-market versions are only up to urban riding; on rough roads they will eventually fall apart as well as make wheel changes horribly messy.

Sprockets

Good quality **steel sprockets** are essential to get the best from an o-ring chain. Avoid lighter alloy versions – they won't last no matter how hard they say they are. And beware of buying cheaper, pattern 'chain and sprocket kits' from some mail order suppliers who sell obscure brands of chains and inferior steel sprockets.

Original equipment (OE) sprockets matched up with a good chain will give you at least 10,000 miles of trouble-free use and maybe even double that with regular oiling on the road. Both items are worth the extra expense for a longer service life. High sprocket wear and loosening sprocket retaining bolts used to be a problem with some KTMs.

Gearing

The good thing with chains is you can easily alter gearing; in general bikes are often too highly geared anyway.

For a long highway run you'll want high gearing, but when the going gets tough it's easy to swap the front sprocket with one that's say, one-

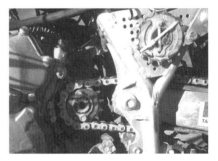

'Highway' sprocket zip-tied to the frame for the ride home (which never happened...).

tooth smaller so lowering the gearing. You'll be rewarded by better control on rocks as well as better response from the lower gears when you most need it.

CARRYING EXTRA FUEL

Without fuel you're going nowhere but first ask yourself, does your bike really need an **extra large tank**? There are few places in the world where a fuel range of more than **300km** is needed on a sealed highway, and that translates to just 16.6 litres or 4.4 US gallons if riding at 18kpl (51 mpUKg, 42.5 mpUSg). Long off-road routes where fuel consumption can rise unpredictably such as those found in the Sahara, are another matter and supplementary fuel will be required.

For most riders a range of about **400km or 250 miles** is ideal and that adds up to 22 litres at the above mentioned consumption levels. Besides the expense

This 5-litre plastic can was empty most of the time. It sat on the box lid with inner tube straps, made a useful stool and was used for measuring out fuel in increments from cans and drums to keep track of fuel consumption.

Taking the time to mark your big tank with an estimated capacity level is a good idea.

A 45-litre tank on a lightly-loaded 100GS.

KTM 650 in southern Algeria fitted with an Adventure tank and also a pair of side tanks – only really necessary for the Sahara.

(some special tanks from Germany go for €2300!), think about the extra weight of carrying 45-litres which is a maximum practical capacity for most bikes. On *Desert Riders* we were lucky enough to source relatively inexpensive '40'-litre XR600 tanks for our XRLs but they made the bikes very unstable in some off-road situations even though we actually needed that range and a whole lot more (we set up fuel dumps in advance).

Buying a bike like a KLR650 or a KTM Adventure with good-sized tanks in the first place is one reason why these machines are popular; it's one less thing that you need to adapt or spend money on, and on the odd occasion where you might need extra fuel, a **plastic fuel can of 5- or 10-litres** will see you through and weigh next to nothing (see top left).

Big plastic or alloy tanks

Although a major expense, if you need it, a bigger tank holding up to 40 litres can be preferable to taking up valuable space with 20-litre jerricans. **Plastic tanks** combine the best in strength, lightness and durability, as well as providing resistance to vibration damage and, if necessary, being easily repairable with glue. Alloy may look nicer but needs to be thick to be strong and so ends up being heavier than you think.

The good thing about a big tank is that it places the heavy weight of fuel close to the machine's centre of gravity where it has a less-pronounced effect on the balance of the bike – though you won't be thinking that when you first ride off with a full tank.

Acerbis makes a number of large plastic tanks to fit many of today's popular dual-sporters, with IMS and Clarke taking up the slack in the US and Australia. Most come in moderate capacities of around 20 to 25 litres, but a couple of examples are much bigger; the 45-litre tank for GS BMWs costs an incredible £500 in the UK, but can be made to fit some other bikes where there's a will (and probably a fuel pump).

Side tanks (opposite page, bottom left) are a neater solution to clanking jerries, coming at around 10-litres a side. But they are expensive for what they are and fitting them is not so simple though they don't both have to be used for fuel of course – one can be a water tank.

If there is room on your bike for a **jerrican**, don't discount it: for the price and utility you can't beat them. Available in Europe unused from military surplus outlets for around £5/€8 or new for not much more, they make reliable and robust fuel containers.

A jerrican holds 20 litres (4.45 UK gallons) when filled in the upright position. This leaves an **air gap** just below the handles which should not be filled (by tipping the can backwards) unless really desperate. The air pocket, as well as the X-shaped indentations on the sides, enable the can to cope with the pressure as petrol

A pair of 10-litre under-jerries on a 100GS at the Algerian border. Low mounting makes sense when they are full, but they'll only be full for a day or two, unless you run the main tank dry.

Bernd Tesch makes these 12-litre tanks which slide neatly into his panniers – good for fuel or water.

41-litre African Queens alloy tank for an XR650R – that will be €2300 please.

expands. Once warmed and shaken, take care to open the cap very slowly (the cap's clamp design makes this easy) to avoid a spurt of fuel.

A **clamp-on spout** should make topping-up while holding a heavy can easier but I find these spouts are slow and often don't seal so well, leaking fuel all over the place. A wide-bore **funnel** takes half the time but rigid plastic

Nifty vinyl funnel folds flat (www.zoelzer.de)

versions are awkward to stow. If not using a cut-down water bottle, I prefer 'collapsible' vinyl items (see left) with the end snipped off for faster pouring.

Jerricans themselves can be knocked about for years: I've never seen a welded seam leak, though **cap seals** do leak. You can buy spare seals or chop up an inner tube and clamp it across the mouth.

Building your own tank
Though expensive when done well, **aluminium** is popular in custom tank manufacture only because it's soft and easy to fabricate into complex shapes that make the most of a bike's capacity needs. Designs have improved since a custom-made alloy tank brought my first Sahara trip to a premature end, but alloy still copes badly with vibration, from both the engine and the terrain. Fractures can be repaired with glue or braised with blowtorch alloy welding rods (alloy tank users should carry these as a matter of course as high-temperature alloy welding facilities are rare in the bush). If you end up using an alloy tank, be sure that it's well supported underneath with heavy-duty mounting plates locating it securely with foam pipe lagging around the frame's top tube to help carry the weight. I've met people using home-made **kevlar** tanks, but not for a few years. Though light, they too are expensive to construct well.

An inexpensive alternative to increasing your fuel capacity is to replace the original with a big steel tank from any old bike and bashing it in the right places. A fiddlier option is to **enlarge the standard steel item** by welding on additional sections, or even welding another tank on top of the cut down original. The XT600 on p.34 has had half a 20-litre jerrican welded to either side of the standard 23-litre tank, upping the capacity to 40 litres.

This latter method is an award-winning real bodge but has the advantage of keeping the original mounting points, although **extra or strengthened mounts** should be considered and any welding will, of course, have to be fuel tight or sealed with resin.

Extended bashplate with integral toolbox from Overland Solutions.

Sump guards and other protection
The longer your planned ride the better it is to protect your motorcycle from small tumbles, loose rocks and bottoming out. Many trail bikes feature sump guards or bash plates from the factory, but some of these are not worthy of the name; the plastic items on BMW 650s, V-Stroms and Transalps spring to mind and yet the Dominator and Africa Twin had excellent OE bashplates. Especially if you expect to be riding off-road, but a

A FEW MORE TIPS

● **Trail bike seats** are not only narrow, they're often made of foam that feels nice and cushy in the showroom but is agony to sit on after a hundred miles. Older bikes too, will have sagged-out foam.

Without getting the whole thing re-upholstered, here's an easy way of firming them up. Remove the vinyl cover carefully (it's usually stapled on to the plastic seat base), disclosing the bit where you sit. Then cut out as big a block of foam as you can without severing the original piece. Get an offcut of firmer foam from an upholsterer and fit it into the hole. You might also want to cut down the seat height while you're at it. Then re-staple the vinyl cover and hopefully enjoy your new 'full-day' saddle.

Or, as is popular in Australia and Germany, cover your seat in a soft **sheepskin**: either properly fitted, or slung over like a rug. If you're heading for Tunisia you can pick up a nice fluffy one for 20 dinars.

● **Weld a wider foot** onto the end of your side stand. A three-inch square piece of steel will support your bike on soft ground.

● A **small perspex screen** bolted to your bike's plastic headlight cowling weighs vir-

tually nothing, keeps the wind off you and, unlike a fairing, doesn't get in the way of visibility.

First make a template from cardboard or bendy plastic, tape it in place and take the bike for a blast. Resist the temptation to cut yourself a big screen which has a greater chance of cracking 3–5mm thic... lip on its u... air up and over ...

Experiment wit... heights now so your h... Now comes the tricky part: so... spex over a naked flame to give it t... curves which provide rigidity and limi... bulence. Take your time, do it slowly and wear gloves. Once you've got the right vertical curvature, add a gentle top lip which has the effect of adding several inches to the screen's height. Smooth off the edges and make any last-minute bends before carefully drilling mounting holes.

● A good way of keeping an eye on your **throttle's position**, and thereby your general fuel consumption,

is to inscribe a mark on the throttle housing on the left along with an adjacent mark on the actual rubber grip. Make one of the grip marks with the throttle closed and another when fully open.

Especially on smaller-engined bikes, riding into a head wind or up a long incline, you'll find yourself inadvertently winding the throttle right open in an attempt to keep moving. It doesn't make you go any faster but it sure wastes fuel.

XT600s have two carbs, a slide unit for low throttle openings and a CV carb which cuts in at bigger throttle openings. Again by marking the grip at the point where the second carb cuts in – you can just feel it if you open the throttle slowly – you can keep the bike running on just one carb.

● Caught short in a rainy or cold climate? Knock up some handguards from 5-litre (1 gallon) plastic bottles (it works better if you have lever guards). The spout end fits neatly round your h a n d l e b a r s . Result: warm hands and dry gloves.

Touratech kevlar bashplate for GS BMW 650s – better than the original but then so is a wet paper bag. This one is already showing signs of damage on this lower, non-Dakar model. An alloy plate is best.

This is all the under-engine protection a BMW twin needs. Note the recessed location bolts – anything else will be knocked off or damaged on rocks; all bashplates take quite a hammering.

CRD bashplate on a watercooled XR650R offering good side protection as well as ventilation – amazingly it fits an air-cooled XR650L too, without any modification.

good idea anyway, an **alloy plate of about 4mm thick** is advisable. These can be easily fabricated or modified from other machines. On one desert trip two bikes sustained cracks to the engine from kicked-up rocks; one bike even had a good, broad plate. Make sure yours covers the width of the engine, including possible frontal impacts to water pumps and hoses.

On BMW twins the cylinders and downpipes are fairly immune to low-flying hits though, as on any bike, the sump certainly needs protection – a suspension-bottoming bounce onto a rock will easily poke a hole in the sump. On a BM this might be easier to repair than a vertically split crankcase of a typical Japanese bike. In the field I've fixed cracks with Liquid or Chemical Metal hardening paste – it's worth carrying some with you.

Lever protectors – a better idea than self-breaking levers [inset] as found on KTM950s.

Hand and lever protectors are a good idea on any bike – a broken lever mount can really ruin your day. Again don't rely on OE plastic items which won't help much when a fully-loaded overlander tips onto a kerb. Thick alloy bars which clamp solidly onto your handlebars from Acerbis or Barkbusters are one less thing to worry about. Around these bars, plastic wind deflectors can be fitted to keep the weather off your hands (see previous page). Without lever protectors, keep your lever mounts a little

loose on the bars. This way the mounts will have a chance of turning on the handlebars rather than snapping the lever when you fall off.

Engine crash bars are more a matter of personal preference and depend on your machine. Across-the-frame engines no longer have the alternator sticking out the side like they used to and cracking the rocker boxes on a BMW twin is not too serious. **Radiators**, water pumps and hoses, and oil coolers are a worry though, as are damaged foot levers and protecting these items (as well as carrying rad sealant and a spare gear-change lever) is worth considering. Some riders do get carried away with protecting their machine from all possible damage though usually it will be your luggage and handlebars which take the brunt of a fall, which is why metal boxes are preferred.

A chunky set of aftermarket engine bars on a BMW 650 add some protection to the tinny OE sump guard.

Wheels – spoked or alloy?

Modern dual sport machines are built with spoked wheels on alloy rims to reduce unsprung weight and improve road performance. Some rims may not be up to the heavy beating they'll encounter over potholed tarmac and corrugated tracks and they'll certainly need checking after rough sections. Rear wheels will be carrying maximum loads and are especially prone to damage.

Unless you're competent at rebuilding wheels and tensioning spokes correctly, you can save yourself a lot of bother by fitting **heavy-duty spokes** or, better still, uprate your wheels altogether with quality rims (Akront, Excel or DID are as good as they get), and getting the work done by an accredited wheel builder. The benefit of having this work done is the difference between having to check and tension your standard wheels regularly or ignoring the strengthened items for the entire trip. Then again, on *Desert Riders* I was the only one who got my XRL's stainless steel spokes replaced with supposedly better galvanised items – and I was the only one to experience broken spokes (though we all had *loose* spokes after the very rocky sections).

Most overlanders shy away from **cast or alloy wheels**. On sports bikes they are built for lightness, but tourers – the type of bike you will probably be riding – will have more robust items. Like everything else, cast wheel technology has improved in recent years and cracking rims seem to be a thing of the past. The new R1200GS is said to have cast wheels as strong as spoked rims though spoked rims are offered as an option and there is still something to be said for the inbuilt flex of spoked rims when absorbing road impacts.

Wheel sizes can be misleading. Trail bikes have 21" front wheels because they roll over bumps better than smaller wheels and cut through the dirt better than wider wheels. But on any bike it will be the **tyre pattern** that dictates how well a machine performs on different surfaces. Which brings us to...

TYRES

No other item gets prospective overland riders in a stew. And quite right too as tyre choice is vital. Punctures will probably be the most common breakdown you'll have to deal with; the tread pattern will be the most likely reason for you falling off; and worrying about finding replacements may be the most frequent service item short of where to fill up next. Choosing the right tyre won't have you dancing from the rooftops, but buying a sub-optimal tyre could be galling for all the above reasons.

In this section only **dual-purpose tyres** are discussed in detail as that may be what you're considering. Choosing a full-on knobbly tyre for your KTM 640 or a road tyre for a big touring bike is less difficult and less prone to poor choices if you pick one from the brands recommended below. The benefits of **tubed or tubeless** are discussed on pp.61-2.

In the end of course any tyre whose characteristics include being **black and round** and that keeps your rims from clattering along the road will do the job and across parts of Africa, Asia and Latin America there are brands you've never heard of waiting to wrap themselves lovingly round your rims. But at the outset, choosing a recognised **quality brand** will give you the best start: for motorcycles that adds up to tyres by Bridgestone, Continental, Dunlop, Metzeler, Michelin and Pirelli.

Tyre speed ratings (letters) and load index codes (numbers)

Speed symbol	K	L	M	N	P	Q	R	S	T	U	H
Speed (kph)	110	120	130	140	150	160	170	180	190	200	210kph
Speed (mph)	68	75	81	87	93	99	106	112	118	124	130mph

Index	lbs	kg	Index	lbs	kg	Index	lbs	kg
36	181.7	125	50	276.2	190	64	407	280
37	186.1	128	51	283.5	195	65	421.5	290
38	191.9	132	52	290.7	200	66	436.1	300
39	197.7	136	53	299.4	206	67	446.3	307
40	203.5	140	54	308.2	212	68	457.9	315
41	210.8	145	55	316.9	218	69	472.4	325
42	218	150	56	325.6	224	70	487	335
43	225.3	155	57	334.3	230	71	501.5	345
44	232.6	160	58	343	236	72	516	355
45	239.8	165	59	353.2	243	73	530.6	365
46	247.1	170	60	363.4	250	74	545.1	375
47	254.4	175	61	373.6	257	75	562.5	387
48	261.6	180	62	385.2	265	76	581.4	400
49	268.9	185	63	395.4	272	77	598.9	412

All road-legal tyres are speed and load rated by the manufacturer: a tyre branded with '58P' will be designed to work at maximum speeds of 150kph while carrying a load of 236 kilos. Travelling two-up will probably put your machine near its design limit and rear tyres and tyre pressures must be calculated carefully. The very least you can expect by choosing under-rated tyres is excessive wear and more regular punctures as the overloaded carcass flexes and heats up.

Having a bike shod with effective dual-purpose tyres greatly increases the **range** of your adventure because, according to the UN Counter Steering Directorate, there are at least ten times more unpaved roads on the planet than sealed. These tyres will work well enough on the highway but, by being effective on dirt roads or off road altogether, the places you can confidently explore are greatly multiplied. One day you may come to a junction: left takes you to your destination via the highway, right is a 100-km long dirt road through the mountains. Even if it's shorter it may well take you longer but that's not what your adventure is necessarily about. Along that road you may come to a breathtaking panorama, spend the night in a friendly village that rarely sees tourists, or even camp overnight in total solitude under the stars. You can do this on a highway too, but the chances of having memorable adventures are greatly increased by taking the road less travelled. You don't want to think 'Well, it looks interesting but I've already found this bike handles like a dog on gravel so I won't risk it'.

The right tyres can transform your machine – even something like a GS1150 (or a GSX1100R, come to that! see p.242) can make what lies ahead an adventure rather than a series of missed opportunities.

Tread patterns

Despite tyre manufacturers' proclamations about cunning, computer-designed knobs and grooves, to tyre manufacturers' marketing departments a tyre's appearance or form is as important as its true function. A cool-looking tread may sell better but may be no more functional than a boring-looking Avon Speedmaster from the late 1970s. What really matters in a tyre – the **construction** of its carcass – is impossible to evaluate just by looking at it.

Apart from the brand name raised on white letters, a snazzy-looking tread pattern is all that separates one brand from another. Construction technology to control flex while supporting the load and being as light as possible has evolved greatly, but tread patterns have not. A tractor tyre looks the same as it did 75 years ago and on a bike slicks work best on dry paved roads. But in the real world grooves are needed to expel surface rainwater and eliminate aquaplaning, while on the dirt tall, widely-spaced knobs dig in for longitudinal and lateral traction. It's as simple as that.

For adventure motorcycling the tread pattern is especially relevant to dual-purpose tyres on faster and heavier machines like BMW GS twins, KTM 950s, Africa Twins and the like. When new, these bikes must be marketed with a tyre that looks the part, but for safety reasons the machine must run a tyre that matches the performance on the highway where they will spend most of their time. Putting a Michelin Desert on a R1200GS will make it great in the sand but would be very dangerous on a wet mountain road.

Tyres like Avon Distanzia or Gripsters, Metzeler Enduro 1, 2 and 4s. Michelin Siracs and T66s and Pirelli MT90s purport to be dual-purpose tyres but on dirt roads they will be only marginally better than a road tyre and on the highway be only marginally worse than a street tyre. They will certainly **last** nearly as long as a road tyre – but then so will a road tyre. Many riders report that on gravel roads they are nothing special and in sand and mud they are hopeless. If you need a dirt tyre for grip, go for the dirt-biased road

From the left: on the gravel this tyre on a BMW 1200GS would be no better than a road tyre; the Metzeler Enduro 3 and Michelin T66 offer a bit more bite, especially at lowered pressures, while (right) the Continental TKC 80 (or a similar Pirelli MT21) are secure in the dirt – while they last.

selection listed below; otherwise choose a road tyre. Don't expect off-road performance from the dirt-looking road tyres listed on the previous page.

For most adventure riders, a typical unsealed road would be gravel or sand track, either graded smooth or more likely corrugated into a 'washboard' surface by the passing of heavy vehicles. Riding at sensible speeds in a straight line your tread pattern will not come into play much, any tyre will do as simple traction is driving you forward. It's on **loose surface bends** and in the soft ruts carved by trucks and cars where tread really comes into play and tyres without pronounced edge knobs (like most of the tyres pictured above) skitter about just like a street tyre on a Yamaha R1. Learning to ride on this sort of surface will be part of your adventure and you'll be surprised what even a regular street bike can manage – the only price being the fatigue in the early days as you correct minor slides again and again. (There is more on riding on these sort of surfaces on p.128).

In dry conditions on hard but loose surfaces a road tyre will work but things get even more critical when it **rains on an unpaved road** or a track becomes very sandy. Depending on your skill level, payload and experience, motorcycles with street or the above-listed 'dual-purpose' tyres can become utterly exhausting in mud, clay or soft sand (reducing tyre pressures helps) while something with pronounced knobs will be in its element.

Dirt-biased dual purpose tyres

If you think you'll need a dual purpose tyre or you have an interest in enjoying off-road riding and see highways as just a convenient way of linking one track with another, get yourself something that works rather than *looks* like it might. Names may change and new tyres come out by the time you read this but the Continental TKC80 (pictured above right) is a well-respected tyre in this category. There is nothing flash or ground-breaking about its pattern, just the usual spread of spaced out square knobs, though less high than a full-on motocross knobbly so your 950 KTM won't rip them off on rocks or squirm around as tall knobs distort on fast highway bends.

Other quality brand tyres that appear designed to genuinely perform as well include Dunlop 606s; Bridgestone Trail Wing TW52 and TW42 or better still TW302 and 301s; Metzeler Enduro 3s at a push (pictured above) or a

MICHELIN 'DESERT' TYRES

Names like 'Sahara' and 'Enduro' are irritating and misleading marketing tags, but I'm pleased to say Michelin's **Desert** tyre is the real thing, designed for rim-bashing desert use and once used by most of the two-wheel contingent of the Dakar Rally.

Riding on Michelin Deserts with heavy-duty inner tubes (again, 'Desert' tubes are available) and strong wheels is one of the best modifications you can make to your bike if you have a demanding, high off-road mileage in mind on a heavy or heavily-loaded machine.

These tyres were originally designed for powerful desert racers which, fuelled-up, travel two or three times as fast as you would with a pack of rabid hyenas on your tail. Because of this they can be **too stiff** for lighter machines, though despite this they can be fitted easily, provided you use good tyre levers, some lubricant and the right technique (see following pages). This may be the last time you will have to use your levers until the tyre wears out thousands of miles later; punctures with Michelin Desert tyres are rare.

Deserts can (and sometimes have to) be run **virtually empty of air** to allow the elongation of the tread footprint necessary for optimum traction in soft sand and mud. I have found on lightly-loaded desert bikers

Michelin Desert rear – too stiff for this lightly-loaded Funduro in the Sahara

like an F650 that I couldn't get enough spreading from the rear Desert to give me satisfactory traction in very soft sand. The revvy engine certainly didn't help, but I found myself struggling where a less rigid tyre would have spread out to create a larger surface area and so better traction. This is why we ran Michelin T63s on our *Desert Riders* XRLs, even if some of us suffered more punctures than we would have liked.

Michelin Desert are built to cope, but on any tyre running **extreme low pressures** (0.5 bar or 7psi) speeds should be kept down to avoid overheating which will accelerate wear and may induce punctures. See also 'Tyre Creep' on p.63.

Metzeler Karoo – though certainly not the Metz Enduro 1, 2 or 4s. The Michelin AC10 claims to be a highway legal enduro tyre but looks too radical for long-range overlanding unless you have a lighter bike. Michelin T61s or the 'Desert' pattern T63 would be much better for mixed riding as well as another well known classic in this category: the Pirelli MT21.

The price with all these tyres is **high wear** so it's not unknown to travel with a spare, dirt-biased rear while running on a street rear – and making do with a slower wearing dirt-effective dual sport front tyre.

Tubeless tyres

The trend for tubeless tyres on dual sports started as long ago as the Honda XLMs in the mid-eighties and continues with big bore trail bikes like the GS BMWs. The advantage of tubeless tyres is that they run cooler and so last much longer. Furthermore, they don't blow out suddenly as a tubed tyre can, but deflate relatively slowly and stay on the rim, giving you more chance to control the machine and bring it to a standstill.

Problems can arise when making your own roadside repairs. Assuming the tyre has not come off the rim, the normal method (outlawed in some countries) is to plug the hole from the outside with a ramming spike tool fitted with

RTW TYRES

Having gone RTW, I've settled on Metzeler ME88 (now ME880) on the rear of my R80G/S, and usually a Bridgestone Trail Wing 101 on the front. The pair wear equally.

We managed Africa on one set, and South America on another. Knobbly tyres aren't necessary on a fully-loaded tourer like ours: it was rare to need more traction, given our weight and power. The need *not* to crash in the middle of nowhere makes you careful.

Furthermore, a heavy payload can put a dual sport tyre over its load limit, even at max pressure. With the Metzeler, I've something like a 900 lb/410kg load limit at the recommended maximum of 49psi (3.4 bar). I find that running at 49psi, even at high speeds at 50°C keeps my max pressure under 60 psi (4.1 bar), an acceptable cold/hot pressure range. Running at around 38-40 psi bumps the hot pressure sky high due to the added flex of the tyre body. Note that the 'perfect' cold/hot range is around 7psi/0.5 bar. Also, remember that the hotter a tyre runs the faster it wears.

I've been asked many times about where to buy new tyres in Africa or Thailand or South America. It's always a problem, usually local tyres are too small or of poor quality, and shipping can be an expensive hassle. I think the best plan is to use tyres that will get you from Civilised Point A to Civilised Point B, with fresh tyres fitted at each point.

Failing that, you can ship tyres in via DHL or Fedex, although duties can double the price, so check carefully before shipping. Many travellers buy whatever is available locally and ride slower and carefully until they get to the next 'good' tyre shop.

As for the **tubeless-tyre debate**, I have had a number of flats in my 40 years' riding, all on tube type. After the last one – two-up, 70mph, 8000 feet in the Andes, exiting a turn with a 2000 foot drop about 10 feet to the outside of my lane, and no guard rail – I'm going tubeless! A three-inch screw instantly deflated the tyre, sending us into a not-to-be repeated series of lock to lock gyrations ending with the tyre off the rim and the screw going right through and out via the sidewall. The front conversion to tubeless is done now and I'm installing an R100GS swingarm and wheel, mostly so I can have a tubeless tyre.

Tubeless tyres don't generally deflate instantly like a tube type, and the tyre stays on the rim much better. Do carry a tube for roadside repairs – if nothing else, it makes it easy to get air in and the tyre back on the rim properly. And yes, it's generally ok to run a tube in a tubeless tyre for short distances.

Grant Johnson

a rubber bung covered in glue; unbelievably easy compared to messing around with tubes and levers, and reliable even off-road.

The problem with tubeless tyres (or tubed, so-called 'safety rims' as found on post '93 Africa Twins and late XTZs) is the bead is located in a **groove** in the

The sidestand bead-breaking trick works best with heavy bikes. © Bob; advrider.com

rim (see diagram p.65), and if the bead comes out of this groove (or you need to remove a tyre) you need a lot of force to 'break the bead', and some fast and high pressure to remount it. A tyre coming off a safety/tubeless rim is rare, but this will always be in the back of your mind if you have a puncture: can you repair such a tyre by hand by the side of the road?

The secret is, with **plenty of lube**, to use the bike's **sidestand** to lever and press down on the tyre wall and break the bead, and then the 'fast/high pressure boost' from a CO_2 cartridge (and yet more lube) to help remount it. Above all, **practise** the above techniques at home on an old tyre so you're ready for the big day.

Tyre pressures and tyre creep

Fitting a good tyre is not the end of the story. To get the best out of your tyre in varying conditions you must maintain the **correct pressure**. On the highway, carrying a regular load you may never have to meddle with pressures – but try and ride that bike on gravel or soft sand you'll find it barely controllable. On loose surfaces a larger footprint or contact patch is needed to maintain the levels of traction you get on hard surfaces and so keep your machine controllable. But low pressures mean a less rigid tyre, more flex in the carcass which creates heat build-up. A cheap tyre will delaminate in these conditions and all tyres will wear faster and become more puncture prone.

Running the right pressure on varying surfaces and with varying payloads is a matter of balance and experimentation; the guidelines given by manufacturers may be of some help. The lighter your payload and the softer the track surface, the lower pressures you can run; and you'll be amazed at the difference that low pressures can make in sandy or muddy conditions, even with a street tyre.

A **tyre-pressure gauge** is an essential item and you should get into the habit of using it daily to check your tyre pressures – ideally first thing in the morning when they're cold. This way you can keep track of slow punctures and get to know well what works best in what situation but remember the maxim: **as high as possible, as low as necessary**. Depending on the load capacity of the tyre and weight carried, **15psi/1 bar** is the optimum all-round pressure for a trail bike off-road, 10psi for soft sand, 20 psi or more on rocks. On a heavier tourer it's best to leave them as they are and just take it easy.

Besides causing a tyre to overheat, riding at the very low pressures necessary for traction in deep sand or mud can cause an 'underpressurised' tyre to get pulled around the rim, especially on the rear wheel of torquey engines (frontal tyre creep from hard braking is less severe). It's not a problem with tubeless tyres of course, but inner tubes can get dragged along with the turning tyre while the valve stays where it is and may eventually get ripped out, destroying the tube.

Therefore, for low-pressure use (typically, sandy deserts), it's essential to have **security bolts** (also known as rim locks) fitted to both rims, but definitely the rear, to limit excessive tyre creep. Security bolts clamp the bead of the tyre to the rim and, if not already

Keep an eye on your valves. If they begin to lean it means your security bolt isn't doing what it should.

Self-tapping screws drilled through the rim and just biting on the tyre bead are an alternative to security bolts.

fitted, require a hole to be drilled into the rim: an easy job. A slightly larger than necessary hole makes tyre fitting easier. I have found KTM rim locks on any bike are light and functional.

An alternative to security bolts which don't always work are **self-tapping screws** drilled into the rim so they just bite into the tyre bead and limit slippage. Two each side of the rim set at 90° intervals should keep the tyre in place. They make refitting a tyre easier though not everyone will be thrilled to drill holes in their rim. Carry some spare self-tappers as they can get lost easily.

Keep an eye on your valves. If they begin to 'tilt over' it means that your security bolt may need tightening or your tyre repositioning, as creep can occur even with rim locks. Always keep the nut at the base of your valve **loose**, or do not use it at all. They're only useful as an aid to refitting tubes.

Summary

Tyre choice can be difficult for a long journey which may include thousands of miles on all sorts of surfaces. Basically, it boils down to long wear, secure road manners but poor dirt grip from street or street-biased dual purpose/trail tyres, or faster wear but worse road grip and cornering (especially in rain) from dirt-biased tyres like TKCs and MT21s.

Whichever tyre you choose, make sure it has at least **four plies**; anything less is designed for light unsprung weight and will not be resistant to punctures on the potholed roads you will encounter around the world. Keep a regular check on your tyre pressures and the condition of the sidewalls. Mark any cuts to see if they grow (more likely at lower, flexing pressures). Take note of the load index ratings and bare in mind that your machine may effectively (if momentarily) exceed these on badly paved roads.

It's also as well to remember the Golden Rule: whatever works for someone in one situation, that's the best tyre for them, even if *you* can't get to the end of the street on it without falling over, puncturing six times or the tyre wearing out. In the end, it depends on your route, your riding style, your bike's power and weight, and your priorities, although conservative road riding and an alert and responsive riding style off-road (especially in rocky terrain) will mean fewer punctures, less wear and less grey hair.

PUNCTURES

Punctures are the most common breakdown you'll experience on your trip; you must be confident you can fix them yourself. The advent of 'lifestyle motorcyclists' has led to many riders calling out recovery vans to get their tyres fixed, but 'when I were a lad' we all knew how to fix flats ourselves.

Practise at home so that when the inevitable occurs you can be sure that the operation can be accomplished smoothly. Any emergency repair undertaken in a remote location can be a little unnerving; the better prepared you are to deal with them the less likely you are to make absent-minded mistakes, like forgetting to tighten a wheel nut or leaving your tools by the roadside (or in my last tyre change, somehow leaving a tyre lever *inside* the tyre!).

(Opposite) **Top:** Utah canyonlands. © Tom Grenon. **Bottom:** Fall colours on the Tombstone Mountains near the Arctic Circle, Yukon Territory. © Tom Grenon.

Avoid labour-saving aerosols which are messy, unreliable and usually explode in your panniers anyway. Although I've never used them, **puncture-sealing fluids** like *Slime* or *Ultraseal* (in the UK) are said to do an amazing job of plugging small pricks as well as balancing and cooling a tyre. They work by pouring in a given amount of fluid through the valve stem – then whenever your tube or tyre is punctured the pressure and centrifugal force squeezes the fluid out through the hole where it instantly solidifies and seals.

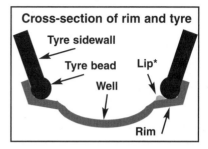

Cross-section of rim and tyre

By getting the tyre bead in the **well**, you gain the necessary 'slack' to lever the opposite side of the tyre over the rim.
*Locating lip and groove found on tubeless or 'safety' rims.

If you don't use that stuff the best way to repair a puncture is to fit a new tube without pinching it, though with some tyre and rim combinations this is easier said than done. Protect your pump, electric or manual, from dust and loss; it could be vital.

If you can't repair a puncture, try stuffing the tyre with clothes or anything else that comes to hand to vaguely regain its profile. If you do a good job, you can carry on without too much difficulty, but if the tyre is damaged or starts to disintegrate you're better off dumping it and carrying on on the rim.

Puncture-repair outfit

Assemble those items below which you need into a small lunch box. Depending on your tyres' sturdiness and the terrain, carry up to two spare inner tubes per wheel – especially if you intend riding on tracks through the sub-Saharan Sahel and the east African savannah where thorn punctures are common. One would think that the thicker the better but I'm told at low pressures the mass of a thick tube gets very hot, soft and so more puncture prone.

Right: Puncture-repair outfit
(From top left): 12-volt tyre pump with a valve extractor tool on top, digital and aneroid pressure gauges, levers, hand pump, tubeless repair plugs with reamer and roller/grating tool on the right, and tube patches in the middle. Some talc in a film canister is also handy for tube repairs.

(Opposite) Top: Ladakh high plains, northern India. © Trui Hanouille. **Bottom:** A jungle road through the Pygmy region of Cameroon. © Peter Kik.

1. If it's a cold day, heat up the tyre by riding around; it then becomes much more pliable. Find a flat place away from the road. If you have no centre stand, use a pannier or a U-lock opposite the sidestand, or just lay the bike on its side (taking the usual precautions).

2. Loosen the wheel nut (noting the chain cam position, if present), and push it forward. Unhook the chain and take out the axle retaining pins if present. Withdraw the wheel allowing the brake to drop away. Collect all loose parts carefully.

3. Remove the valve cap and valve base nut and loosen the security bolt or rim screws if present. Unscrew the valve core, releasing any remaining air and push the valve and security bolt into the tyre as far as they'll go.

4. Lay the wheel down and stand on the tyre, jumping up and down if necessary to push the bead of the tyre off the rim. (On tubeless rims pressing down/leaning on the sidestand works.) Check again that the security bolt is pushed into the tyre so it's not getting in the way.

5. Kick the bead around the security bolt into the rim with the front of your heel. Then, standing on the tyre to keep the bead in the well, push in the first lever to hook under the tyre's bead.

6. Getting the second lever in is hard until you release the first lever a little; hook the second lever under the bead, and then pull them both up in close succession.

7. Keep working round the tyre, checking that the bead is in the well until one half of the tyre is outside the rim. Now stand the tyre up, push the valve into the tyre, stick your other hand in and drag the tube out.

8. Lay the tube to one side and examine the outer tyre. If you can't find the cause of the puncture, pass your fingers over the inner surface to feel for any thorns or whatever. Taking the tyre right off may be necessary.

9. Refit the valve and inflate the tube to find the hole. If you can't hear the hiss of escaping air, pass the tube over wet lips or eyes where the pinprick will be felt as a cold jet of air. Or, if available, submerge the tube into a basin of water or a pool and look for bubbles.

10. Memorise or mark the position of the hole(s), release the air again and place the tube on a firm surface to roughen the area around the hole with sandpaper or a grater. The roughened rubber should have a scratched, matt appearance.

11. Wipe away the rubber dust with a petrol rag and apply a thin film of rubber solution over a broad area. Wait a minute until it's dry to the touch (test away from the contact area).

12. Choose an appropriately-sized patch. On most patches it is the **foil** side that is stuck to the tube. Press the patch down firmly, using a knife handle or roller to bond the surfaces together and eliminate air bubbles.

13. Sprinkle some talc over any exposed glue (ash will do) and if the tube was wet put some inside the tyre to reduce the chance of the tube snagging or twisting.

14. Stand the wheel up and push the tube into the tyre starting by pushing the valve through the hole in the rim. This can be tricky with stiff tyres – lever up the other side of the tyre to make room for your fingers to align the valve.

15. Now loosely attach the valve nut so the valve doesn't slip out during mounting. Make sure the valve is perpendicular to the rim by tugging the tube around. Refit the valve core and *partially* inflate the tube; too much will risk pinching the tube.

16. Standing on the tyre, position two levers at 10 and 2 o'clock and start levering them towards 12 o'clock. At 6 o'clock check the bead is in the well. As you move each lever on, stand on the tyre to make sure it's in the well and giving you the slack you need.

18. Check again that the valve is at right angles, if not try and drag the tube and tyre around the rim to line it up. Now re-inflate and watch the bead remount the rim. If it doesn't, keep inflating and deflating while adding in soap and levering if necessary...

19. ... but don't worry if it doesn't remount the rim. Once ridden about it'll work its way on. Check the pressure is not going down. If it is go back to #5. Otherwise, tighten the security bolt and fit the valve cap.

17. Wetting this last part of the rim with watery soap or WD40 helps. Take great care on the last moves not to push the lever in too deep and possibly pinch the tube. Gently lever the last 6-8" over with a satisfying 'pop'.

21. Reverse steps 1 and 2. Make sure the chain is correctly tensioned, the axle retaining pins are back in and the axle is tight. Re-store tools, wash hands (soap with sand works) and re-attach baggage. Recheck tyre pressure, pump up disc brakes and off you go.

Three ways to fix a puncture: let the bike sit on the swingarm (not so nice for the chain); sit the bike on a box (the blessings of q/d boxes, see p.74); or leaning it on its side. Inset: work on a tent groundsheet to keep bits from getting lost and grit out of the repair. If anyone is desperate for tyres there are a few half-worn Trailwings buried nearby at N28° 55.4' E 06° 22.8'.

Compressed CO_2 **cartridges** save pumping but eventually you'll run out. Get a **mini electric compressor** instead. Cheap Asian units (remove plastic bodies to save space) have given compressors a bad name, lasting an hour at best. The fully-enclosed Cycle Pump (pictured p.65) has been designed specifically for motorcycles and comes with fittings for car sockets, DIN plugs (as found on BMWs) or a fused pair of croc clips to attach directly to a battery (engine running is best). Keeping compressors dust-free and cool prolongs life, but for remote trips I'd still carry a **tough plastic hand pump** (metal-bodied pumps dent and lose their seal). Go for the old style with a floppy, screw-on stem (plus spare); I've found the lever clamp seal versions fail after a while.

Taking into account the variables of personal preference, in my experience a good **tyre lever** is a blade no more than 20mm wide, up to 5mm thick, and 200mm long. The crude wide, flat-ended types of bars with flattened 'spoon' ends are too wide and make lifting the bead harder which can lead to pinching a tube – one of the most depressing experiences in motorcycledom.

The ideal blade has a slender curved lip at each end which readily hooks under the bead of a tyre to lift it, but without pushing in too far and pressing against the tube. Kawasaki levers are said to be good, and I still use a little BMW lever from a long-gone R100. Whatever lever you use, take care in the last stages of tyre mounting (photo 17, opposite): avoid brute force.

Basic tubed (tubeless) tyre puncture kit (see photo p.65)

• One spare tube per tyre • Electric compressor and hand pump • Air pressure gauge • Two good tyre levers • Patches – *Tip-Top* are good • Tube of rubber solution, plus spare • Sandpaper or grater • (tubeless plugs, reamer and valves) • Valve extractor • WD40 for lubing the rim • Talc to 'dust' the gluey patch on a tube • CO_2 cartridges for emergencies.

Load carrying

His bike was packed up in a way that I'd never seen before. It looked like he lived on the fifth floor of a block of flats and packed his bike by dropping his stuff out the window onto it. **Phil McMillan**

As the Jack Nicholson character in *A Few Good Men* might have observed: not making your bike look like a war refugee's handcart requires **discipline**. The more stuff you have the safer and more independent you'll be, right? That's what you may think, but **the more you know the less you need**. You can either

A flotilla of alloy boxes prepare to set sail across the Sahara.

take my word for it now or learn from experience.

Riding, picking up or even just getting on an overweight bike can be demoralising and yet we're talking about a tiny amount of equipment – in volume it adds up to the typical allowance for an international flight – and all this to sustain you and your machine for possibly months on the road. Bikes being what they are, a 40-kilo or 88lb payload is probably at the modest end of the range, but with a full tank will be enough to make your machine handle like a piano and be barely possible to pick up singlehanded.

BAGGAGE SYSTEMS

On a bike there's not much choice about where the baggage can go: behind you and alongside the back wheel with a tank bag or tank panniers in front and a small backpack on your back. The most basic level of motorcycle baggage is a **rucksack** or kit bag strapped across the back seat – something that many a cash-starved motorcycle traveller has tried on a first trip – and what some worldly purists return to after many trips. Advanced basic high-volume packing involves two rucksacks hanging from the sides like throwover panniers with a kitbag over the back. It may not be secure in both a thieving and a fitting sense, but is as cheap as it gets and can easily be carried when off the bike.

For most people though the choice is between **soft fabric panniers** and plastic or **aluminium boxes** along with some kind of **rack**. Convenience of access, ease of removal, robustness and security are also important considerations. Ideally, no item wants to be buried so as to discourage its use, nor a bag criss-crossed with rope when one or two thoughtfully arranged straps will do the job. Everything that is used regularly should be close at hand. Also it helps if baggage offers enough room or is easily demountable so as not to impede wheel changes.

Fix boxes as low and forward as possible, while still giving room to paddle in deep sand or mud, swing a kickstarter and clear the ground in deep ruts. For hard dirt riding you'll feel safer with soft luggage.

When it comes to strapping things on the outside of your containers or on to your bike, don't rely solely on elasticated bungees – they will hold something down but not in place so are only good for very light items. Instead use **adjustable straps** (available in various lengths from outdoor shops) to secure gear on your bike. And make sure you carry lots of spares; they're easily lost, damaged or pilfered and are useful for many purposes.

Whichever way you decide to carry your gear, it's important to distribute heavy weights **low and as centrally as possible**. Doing this will result in real benefits in the balance and control of your machine, especially off-road. Light things like clothes, sleeping bags or empty containers can go on the back of the seat or even in front of the head lamp. If you're carrying extra fuel in jerricans, top up the tank regularly to keep the weight in that ideal location, or if you're carrying them low like the BMW on page 53, leave the fuel low until the main tank is nearly empty.

And don't worry about getting all this right on the day you leave. While a test run will iron out a lot of possible problems, a couple of weeks

Fifth floor, Sir? Nets are best used for catching butterflies, not wrapping up luggage.

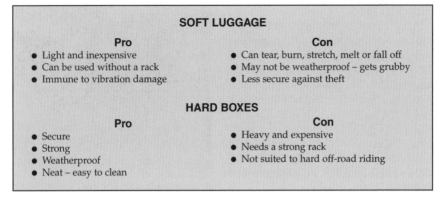

SOFT LUGGAGE	
Pro	**Con**
• Light and inexpensive	• Can tear, burn, stretch, melt or fall off
• Can be used without a rack	• May not be weatherproof – gets grubby
• Immune to vibration damage	• Less secure against theft

HARD BOXES	
Pro	**Con**
• Secure	• Heavy and expensive
• Strong	• Needs a strong rack
• Weatherproof	• Not suited to hard off-road riding
• Neat – easy to clean	

on the road will have your baggage and its contents ideally arranged for convenience and security.

Hard or soft luggage?

The Theory of Relative Space states that no matter how capacious your luggage, it will be filled to bursting point. Keep it small and you'll take little; use big containers and you'll cram them with unnecessary stuff and overload your bike. For a short trip (less than four weeks) or one where you don't expect to encounter bad weather or spend much time in cities (where most thefts occur), soft luggage will be adequate. On a longer trip or simply if you prefer it, hard luggage answers most needs while adding weight to the bike as well as time and expense to fit.

After years of making do with soft luggage, for *Desert Riders* we decided to try out alloy boxes from Touratech and Bernd Tesch on custom racks. The trip was a demanding cross-country ride, at times on barely rideable terrain. Even before it was over we all agreed that next time round alloy boxes were not for us. Their convenience is handy but at 30+ litres they're too wide on narrow mountain tracks and when the going got tough they were a danger to shins or roadside rocks. For that particular trip smaller boxes would have been better, or a much lighter rack supporting fabric panniers.

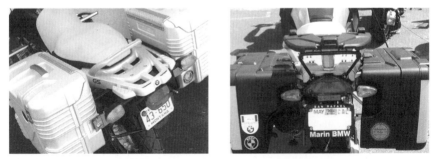

Moulded plastic Hepco & Becker Gobi boxes (OE on early 950 KTMs) feature a 3.5l water tank in the double-skinned wall – is that useful? OE BMW panniers from a 1200GS slide out to increase capacity. Nice for homeland touring but out in the world they will shake apart.

Hard luggage

The first thing to recognise is that regular motorcycle touring luggage from the likes of Givi or Krauser will not necessarily be up to the demands of bad roads and occasional spills unless you substantially modify the mounting arrangements – and even then the plastic cases may crack where metal would dent and fabric scuff or tear. One Africa Twin rider summed up his Givis hard luggage as 'panniers brilliant, racks dreadful'.

Small boxes on an old BMW. © Rainer Bracht

Aluminium boxes were originally hand-made by European riders until outfits like Därrs and Tesch in Germany started producing them. Lately the idea has caught on globally with people like Touratech, Metal Mule in the UK and Jesse Luggage in the US making their own versions to various designs.

Do you really need two 40-litre boxes?

At the very simplest level you get a box with a lid because curves and bends increase manufacturing costs. However, there's a lot to be said for a bevelled outer edge as found on Tesch and Jesse panniers when you come off as there is less of a corner to dig in and rip them off, and fewer corners to poke you as you slide alongside the bike.

Touratech get round the accessibility limitations by producing neat, **holdalls** which slip inside their 35- and 41-litre boxes – an idea well worth imitating on any box. Their mounting system is neat and simple, fixing in place inside of the box. This way you only need locks on the lid, although the current standard clasps are easily prised open – replace them with something chunkier.

A bevelled outer edge digs in less in a crash.

Fixed or quick-detach mountings?

Bolting an alloy box permanently to the rack is strong but not so convenient when you want to remove the rear wheel or squeeze the bike into a hotel courtyard (or get it stuffed it into

Jesse boxes are anodised – powder-coating is less durable. © Erling Foshaugen

Fully loaded on a rough road there will be a whole lot of stress on this Gobi's locking clasp and dust may clog the lock. The Därrs box has a similar system, but the metal would flex less.

an airplane hold, as we found out once). A strong, reliable and easy-to-use **quickly detachable** (or 'q/d') **system** is much more useful. Besides the example given above, easily removing your box to sit on or or use as a table, cooking wind break or bike stand is very handy.

The problem is that load-bearing q/d mountings can get damaged in a crash or even just on a particularly rough road after which they may loosen or no longer locate properly. In my opinion the most bomb-proof and fast, if not the lightest q/d set up, is to have the weight of a box sitting in a slim tray, with whatever types of attachments holding it in place from above. This tray need

A replacement rear subframe/pannier rack for a BMW from Overland Solutions.

All Jessed up and somewhere to go. Inset: stainless q/d clamps adjust for rough going.

not be the full-width of the box as pictured on the bottom right of p.78 (defeating part of the q/d ethos: slimness), or even as wide as the Overland Solutions subframe pictured left. Just a couple of inches of load-bearing shelf (with braced side pieces locating the box fore and aft) will be enough to take the vertical shock loads and contain the negligible forward/back forces, while the clips take the moderate outward loads. This way there is no twisting directly on the load-bearing mounts, as with the Därrs and Gobi systems, but instead an easily-absorbed force.

The advantage of this system is that if the box or mountings get mangled, you'll always be able to hammer the rack straight and lash the box back onto that tray: the tray will always take the weight. As mentioned elsewhere, it is anticipating and devising systems to work round these kinds of meltdown scenarios which are part of planning for a long trip.

Soft luggage

Soft luggage usually means some kind of throwover panniers or saddlebags slung over the back of the seat with a rucksack or kit bag across the back and other bags strapped on where they'll fit. This system has its drawbacks as listed earlier but is light, cheap and versatile.

Panniers or saddlebags

Throwover panniers come in Cordura, a tough woven nylon, canvas, PVC or can be made in leather. With Cordura, go for items made in at least 1000-weight (dernier) material which will be tough enough. The good thing with throwovers or saddlebags is that they **require no rack** as they just sling over the bike. They need fixing down of course and can stretch, burn, melt, fall off, tear, disintegrate or simply get stolen. I've experienced all but the last of these saddlebag woes in one eventful day!

Some of these drawbacks can be overcome with careful thought and planning but you should keep these limitations in mind. One problem particular to dual sport bikes is their high **silencers**. Even with heat shields, it's still possible for panniers to get pressed onto the pipe at high speed or when bouncing over rough ground. Nylon and plastic tends to melt while canvas actually burns – another soft luggage scenario I've enjoyed dealing with. The best solution is to hook the front edge of your bags securely onto

When the going gets tough you'll be glad of soft 'throwover' baggage: it's lighter, you don't need a rack and overloading is harder.

the frame or rear footrests to stop them sliding back and to fabricate a **proper guard around the silencer** so that there's no way they can come into contact. This is one reason why racks are a good idea, even with soft luggage.

In the UK, the Oxford 'Sovereign' series of throwover luggage (pictured on the Funduro on p.61) are toughly sewn, have useful pockets and zips that on my half-set are still hanging in there after several years. Plus they expand up to a potentially useful 56 litres by simply undoing a zip. Gearsack, and in the US, Chase Harper, Wolfman or Mags Bags are other brands of soft luggage.

Oxford 'throwovers' are actually individually removable with clips which themselves aren't up to the strain when packed to the limit on a corrugated track. With any fully-loaded bag swinging about – bought or home-made – something's bound to break, rip or get caught in the wheel. Avoid this by supporting heavy bags with a light rack (see p.76).

Frame-mounted Touratech Zega Flex fabric panniers – rigid enough to keep their shape but not break your leg. They zip together into a backpack too. © Touratech

Antipodean riders have a habit of loading their gear high and far out back – possibly due to the popularity of Ventura luggage systems. Aerodynamic they may be, but for stability, especially off-road, a worse set up is hard to imagine – the inset KLR is a disaster on wheels and it has to be said the Serow on p.43 looks about as stable as the Uraguayan peso.

The two Dominators above at least have pannier racks carrying heavy fluids low down. If you're expecting to ride on dirt, taking the time to arrange your baggage low will reduce crashes into just near misses. © Paul Jenkins

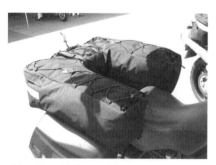

Mags Bags GT bag suddenly makes the back seat rather desirable.

Besides a tank bag, saddlebags over the tank are handy – easy to keep an eye on.

Other materials

Relatively new to touring are PVC bags like the Ortlieb Dry Bag and QL2 Side Bags which clip onto a rail. The Dry Bag is a standard tube-shaped kit bag of 60-litre capacity, but with a full length opening that rolls over and closes with a rainproof seal although, unless you live in a rain forest or the basement of the pawnbrokers in *Pulp Fiction*, there is something unappealing about PVC.

Less expensive and developed for canoeing are similar-shaped tubes like Cascade's SeaLine range. However, the end opening makes access a little less easy. PVC also suffers from limited resistance to abrasion, melting as you slide down the road, stampeding bison, UV rays from the sun and of course hot exhaust pipes.

RACKS

Hard luggage appeals to most riders taking on a big trip, being secure, strong and neat, but this system needs a **strong rack** to support it.

If you happen to possess unusual self-restraint and travel light, you might just get away with using soft luggage without a rack. But even with just a 10-litre jerrican on the back seat, the rear subframe can flex, possibly inducing a weave at speeds over 50mph/80kph on loose surfaces, especially if you're running road- or trail tyres. And if your baggage is much heavier or the ground rough, subframes can bend or crack.

Most overland bikers accept that a rack is a good idea because of the relative flimsiness of contemporary single shock subframes. These days just about all alloy and plastic box manufacturers supply racks for GSs, Africa Twins and the main singles, many of them suitable for overlanding. Tesch racks are heavy but sturdy – suited to

BMWs while Touratech-style racks (similar to the old Krauser design) are thoughtfully designed to minimise weight while distributing loads evenly. Anyone who produces alloy boxes and a rack to go with it, is aiming at the adventure motorcycling market so the rack should be up to the hammering, but don't count on it – alloy boxes have finally become fashion accessories and manufacturers are now capitalising on this.

Rear frames have a hard time when loaded up. A rack must add to the frame's strength, not stress it. Disconnect the battery *completely* when welding directly on a bike; sensitive electrics could get fried. © Trui Hanoulle

Building a rack

My first Sahara rack was made out of pieces of Dexion – industrial shelving – and my boxes were sawn-off jerricans with hinges. As explained, these days you can buy a complete overlanding luggage system with a rack to fit most bikes. But if you like DIY or have special baggage-carrying needs or an unusual machine, you can easily fabricate something yourself. The crux is not to end up with your luggage looking like the Brooklyn Bridge – and that takes more skill than you think. Here are some points to consider:

- Construct in easily re-weldable mild steel, not aluminium.
- Think about how the maximum weight will affect the rack and where the stress might lie.
- Weight for weight, tubes are stronger than a same-sized square section; avoid curved sections in either.
- Bolt the rack to your bike in four to six places. Don't weld it on.
- Make sure there's enough room for wheel removal, chain adjustment, suspension compression and the swing of a kick-start.
- In most cases a strut across the back is essential to stop inward flexing.
- Don't get too hung up on complete rigidity – it's better for things to flex or bend than to transmit that shock to your bike's frame.

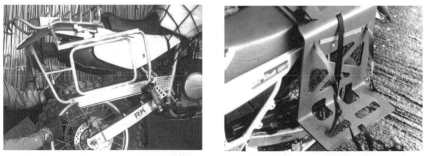

Left: Custom rack from Overland Solutions – strong, easily demountable but could have been lighter. On the back the upside down 'v' worked well as an alternative to a regular cross brace and the XRL's subframe was also strengthened in key areas – vital on many trail bikes.
Right: An unusual but very light rack made of heated and bent PVC sheet and 'Swiss-cheesed' for added lightness. Adequate to help locate bags and keep them out of the wheel. © Adrian Jowlett

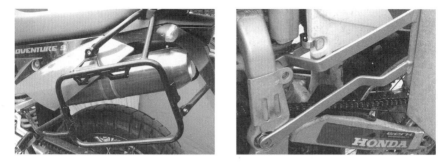

Why weld when you can buy this well-designed and light rack off the shelf? **Left**: DIY-ers can buy the central rectangle in 18mm tube from Touratech to base around your own design. **Right**: Bent strips on this XR650R are easy to fabricate and weld but are less rigid than tube and not much lighter. Think carefully where some racks attach to your bike – especially one's with alloy frames: where will the force be transmitted in a heavy crash?

Stronger rear subframe

The last point listed on the previous page is something where the function of 'off-the-shelf-racks (with optional adaptor plates)' is compromised. There's no way they can afford the R&D to anticipate the weak points on every model they're made to fit and, as mentioned above, attaching steel racks to slinky **alloy subframes** is tricky and may have been one thing which stopped the KLR650 catching on in Europe. Cracks on the subframe, steel or otherwise are not uncommon on arduous trips: usually at the bottom of the tube running back and up from the front footrests (to the top right of the sprocket picture on p.51). This tube is taking an excessive downward thrust – made worse by the jarring when your suspension bottoms out (a good reason to fit heavier springs, even for non-aggressive riders).

The custom gusset pictured on p.51 (not part of the XRL frame) is one easy way of adding strength, but all it really does is move the stress somewhere else. Because of the complex forces going on here, forces that were not necessarily anticipated when the bike was designed – the simplest answer to making sure a rack – home made or otherwise – does not lead to frame problems as listed at the top of this section is: **keep it light**.

Why weld II? **Left**: This minimalist Jesse rack works with the GS12's improved subframe – for a long time a weak point on GSs. (Jesse also make underseat silencers to reduce width.) **Right**: This home-made shelf rack will securely hold a dead sheep – it does not have to be this wide.

DIY rack essentials

Unless you have your own ideas, the basis of a bike rack is a beam from around the rider's footrests to the region of the rear indicators. It can be a tray rack or incorporate the box-mounting rectangle based around the 18mm rectangular loop supplied by Touratech that has become the standard for box mounts, at least in Europe. Based on this arrangement supporting the bike's subframe, further attachment points can be fitted to other frame lugs, spreading the load over several mounts. Use the same sized bolts for all mounts, check for tightness regularly, especially in the early days, and carry spares in case they sheer.

There's no real advantage to sitting heavy metal boxes in a full-width tray rack as pictured opposite below. As described earlier a couple of inches to take the weight of a box is all that is needed and keeps the back end slim when unloaded. This done, it's easy to think up a quickly-detachable way of locating the box securely to the rack so that it doesn't rattle or jump off. Touratech sell their mounts as spares but adding a backplate to their thin gauge boxes is not a bad idea if riding with heavy loads on rough roads.

Finally, it's crucial to **brace** both sides of the rack against inward flexing by fitting a supporting strut across the back, beneath the number plate (see subframe photo p.74). This strut must be far enough back so as not to interfere with the tyre on full compression of the shock and must be easily detachable to enable rear wheel removal.

Testing your system

Take your *fully-loaded* bike for a test ride to see how it holds together. Sitting a friend on the back and getting them to jump up and down a bit is not the same thing! Riding in this state for the first time will be alarming and you'll wonder how on earth you're going to ride it from Anchorage to Zanskar as you wobble down the street. This may be your last chance to consider cutting down on the weight. *Many riders end up sending stuff home in the early days.*

While loaded up, lay the bike over and **try to pick it up**; if you can't it's too heavy and unless you're certain there'll always be someone around to help you, you must consider reducing the weight – or joining a gym.

Clothing for the long ride

No matter how tropical your destination, on a bike it will be colder than you think. Dress well, it's easier to remove clothes than start chasing sheep for their wool.

As much as any of the advice given in this book, clothing is a matter of personal taste but, whatever image you decide to cultivate, you'll need to protect yourself from wind, sun, heat, cold, dust, rain, stones and falling off. **Comfort**, **lightness**, **utility** and **quality** of construction are all important features to consider as you'll probably end up wearing the same kit most of the time.

In fact, forget about taking excessive amounts of spare clothing at all and instead just make do with one change and wash what you wear every few days until it wears out. Save space by opting for multi-functional items that are light and quick-drying and resist the temptation to pack a spare pair of shoes, jeans or a jumper 'just in case'. In the unlikely event of an invitation to an embassy soirée, you'll create much more of a stir in your weather-beaten leathers than crammed into a crumpled shirt and tie.

Jackets

Any jacket should seal up snugly around your neck, wrists, waist and hem for cold days while being adjustable with zips and air vents as days or climates warm up. The **waist drawcord** or belt feature is particularly useful as it seals off your torso, so keeping the core of your body warm on a cool morning, while being easy to release on the move.

A good jacket needs to have all the qualities mentioned earlier and should also have enough pockets to carry valuables. Overland biking being what it is, keeping these items on your person is the only way of ensuring their security, so look for **big zipped pockets**, at least one of which is internal. Make sure the ones on your chest are not so high up that you can't easily get your hand in.

Probably the best jacket to fill all the above criteria most of the time is a **Cordura touring jacket**. Cordura is a tough woven nylon that is light, looks good, abrades well as you slide down the road, is easy to clean and forms a tough shell for a Gore-Tex liner. In the UK, Hein Gericke, Frank Thomas and Belstaff all make jackets from light but strong synthetic materials that are thankfully a long way from the crappy nylon products of two decades ago. For something around £250/$400 you get a lot for your money.

The German-designed Hein Gericke, in particular helped drag British manufacturers out of the primeval waxed-cotton era. BMW clothing is also considered high quality, but you're paying extra for the logo. Finnish firm Rukka have also hopped on the Cordura bandwagon. Twenty years ago just about every London despatch rider, myself included, wore Rukka's durable and compact PVC rain gear and their current range of jackets appear to be just as functional, if a little short and over-designed with gimmicky features and panels (often a warning sign). All these jackets feature some kind of protective padding along the shoulders and elbows as well as Kevlar patches on high-wear areas, and some include vents so you can keep cool while still being protected. When it comes to choosing a jacket, look out for the 'CE' logo – a European Union standard that relates to many safety features like armour. Try a jacket on while sitting on your bike, not in front of a mirror so you can be sure it's long enough in the arms and back when in the riding position.

In the US, Aerostich's two-piece **Darien outfit** or one-piece **Roadcrafter** suit have become firm favourites with long-range touring riders. They're not cheap but are considered an investment with a long line of satisfied customers. Quality construction and attention to detail is where most of your money goes, as well as an after-sales alterations and repair service. An Aerostich suit will last you many years and, it has to be said, the relatively plain design inspires confidence in a product which is not trying to be something it's not.

Out here you want reliable wet weather gear (if not a back up umbrella). © Andy Miller

Leather jackets have good wear properties and age nicely, but can be uncomfortably heavy when the going gets physical. And because of the properties of hide, they can only have a few and often awkwardly small pockets. Still, many riders do not like wearing waterproof clothing all the time, even if it is Gore-Tex. For them lightweight PVC waterproof will keep off the rain as well as Gore-Tex while taking up little space when not in use.

Trousers – alternatives to jeans

With trousers the accent is on comfort and protection, pockets are not important. Here a good pair of **leather trousers** is an advantage: they're hard-wearing and still look good when caked in filth. Avoid cheap thin leather; look for soft supple cowhide and one piece legs (no seam across the knees) – a factor which jacks the price up. Bare in mind that leather trousers will sag and stretch over the months and because they're heavy, you'll need a belt or, better still, strong braces to avoid the crotch eventually splitting in the countless times you swing your leg over your machine.

Leather trousers are unsuitable on a hot trip, especially in humid, jungle areas with plenty of river crossings. Wearing nylon in these conditions is not ideal, but a pair of **motocross pants** is still a good all-round choice, offering proper dirt-biking protection, padding and durability, while being light and quick to dry. Fit plastic **knee protectors** which slip into inside pockets on most brands. Even if you don't crash in them, it makes kneeling on the ground and working on the bike a whole lot more comfortable.

Your choice of sober colour schemes will be limited of course, you'll need

BREATHABLE FABRICS

The efficacy of wonder-membranes like Gore-Tex is much discussed when applied to motorcycling – and some think it's over-rated. The micro-pore membrane that you'll never see is sandwiched in the layers of your jacket and releases water vapour – condensation formed by sweat – while miraculously resisting the ingress of water (aka, rain).

The thing is, for breathable fabrics to work, a certain amount of 'thermodynamic pressure' and heat must build up inside the jacket for the vapour to reach 'escape velocity'. This heat energy will be easily generated jogging up Nanga Parbat carrying a baby hippo, but not when clinging to the bars of a motorcycle at 70mph.

So they may not always work, some condensation may be present, and leaks do occur if the construction is not so good or the membrane has been damaged.

One thing's for sure: it's important to keep breathable clothing **clean** and **treat the outer shell** with a water-repellent coating like ScotchGuard or Nik-Wax for it to be effective. This stops water soaking into the outer shell so 'clogging up' the evaporative pores of the membrane

On balance, even if it only works partially, compared to oilskins or PVC rainwear, do-it-all breathable clothing is a real benefit to the adventure tourer, even at the price you have to pay.

to flick through a few catalogues to find something that won't frighten the horses. Get a quality pair of pants fit for riding into the ground. Alpine Star's AST-1 or ST-5 pants come in a looser fit than close-fitting MX versions while still having the same construction and provision for padding.

Boots and gloves

Invest in a tough pair of boots that will last the trip and protect your feet and lower legs in the frequent low-speed tumbles. The better you're prepared for these small accidents, the more you'll be able to enjoy your riding without fear of injury. **Full-on motocross boots** are as valuable as a good helmet and gloves; made to take a beating while protecting your legs. The trouble is they're not great for walking; ex-army or high-shinned work boots will cost a fraction while still giving your feet and **ankles** some protection.

Wearing a pair of padded palm motocross **gloves** is the most comfortable way to protect your hands on the dirt while giving good feel at the bars. At other times you may find inner gloves or overmitts useful. Fingerless cycling gloves are also cool and comfortable to wear when the weather and pace really warm up, but however hot it gets, *always wear some kind of gloves*. To a certain extent **handguards** keep the blast of the wind and rain off your hands allowing you to wear a lighter and more comfortable pair of gloves.

Helmets

For riding on the dirt a full-face motocross helmet and a pair of motocross goggles are the most convenient; light and comfortable MX goggles will seal-off your eyes from dust, wind and glare better than a full-face road helmet's visor, whether tinted or used with sunglasses.

Bell and Arai are well known for their quality MX helmets and Arai make the particularly useful Tour-X series which can be used either with goggles or with the visor for highway or town riding when a quick flip up of the visor is handy. While costing a packet, they come in plain colours, have a washable lining and offer a level of comfort and ventilation you'll appreciate.

COLD-WEATHER CLOTHING

All year-round bikers are familiar with the misery of riding in cold weather wearing inadequate gear. Little wonder most adventure bikers head south and east towards the sun. But some perverse individuals will still choose to head in the opposite direction while round-the-worlders will eventually run into a cold season or high altitude.

You need to face riding in freezing temperatures with optimism rather than dread. **Retaining and maintaining body heat** is what counts. Fairings, **windshields** and handguards – temporarily bodged out of available materials if necessary – are the first stage in retaining body heat and are a good idea in any climate. Maintaining body heat means regular stops for **exercise** and refuelling with **hot food** and drinks.

Insulation is the next step as it is the **trapped, still air** heated by your body that keeps you warm, not bulky materials per se. The best of these create capacious air cavities so choose a thick fleece or even a down jacket under a windproof outer shell. Seal off all the points where heat will be lost like cuffs, the waist and neck, and wear a thermal or silk balaclava on your head.

One-piece under-garments or even outer shells (like the Aero' Roadcrafter suit) are extremely efficient and also very comfortable to wear because they eliminate the gap or compressed waistbands in the kidney area where vital core body heat can be lost. Plus they avoid that 'stuffed dummy' feeling when wearing several layers. The drawback with one-piece clothing comes in the palaver needed to get it off, when things warm up or when nature rings the bell.

Your engine produces electrical power so using **electrically-heated clothing** makes eminent sense. As your body cools blood is drawn from the limbs to the core to sustain vital organs; by externally warming your trunk, blood can then be spared on frigid limbs. Many riders swear by **heated grips**; they work best with *thin-palmed* gloves.

And if you happen to get caught out in a cold area, converting your water bag into a hot water bottle and stuffing newspapers under your jacket and against your shins will help conserve your warmth while giving you something to read once you've dug your snow hole. You'll find a good link on cold weather riding at www.adventure-motorcy cling.com/cold/.

© ANDY MILLER

While not as quiet as a full face lid, many long-haul riders choose **combination helmets** like those from BMW, Shoei or Nolan. The front hinges up to reveal your face, and if that doesn't go down well you can just open the visor in conventional full face mode. Many developing countries don't have helmet laws but, while being very agreeable, riding without a helmet invites sun stroke within a couple of hours, or spilled brains in the event of an accident. Then again, it's polite to take your helmet off when talking to people, especially grumpy officials.

Blending in

A word about looking flash. Being an adrenalin sport to some, motorcycle apparel manufacturers produce a lurid range of riding gear. Plodding round the world at 50 miles per hour is a different game, just about every country you visit will be poorer than your own, and initially people's attitude towards you will be governed by your appearance. Although it's obvious you're hundreds of times richer than the locals, a low-key dress sense and muted-looking machine at least avoid underlining this fact. Furthermore, the poorer (i.e. more normal) you look, the less chance there is of getting ripped-off as a rich tourist or turned over by an unscrupulous border guard. Painting your bike a plain matt colour may be more than most want to do, but it does make your machine less conspicuous.

Shipping overseas

Grant Johnson

If you're going to travel long distances on a motorcycle, eventually you'll encounter either a large body of water or a 'no go' area. Either will require you to arrange transport for the bike. There are two main options and a number of creative alternatives.

Sea shipping should be less expensive than by air, but port charges at both ends can actually add considerable amounts to the cost. I know of cases where shipping relatively short distances was more expensive than flying. Then there is the question of risk – ports are more prone to theft or damage than airports. Finally, how much will you spend during the 3-10 weeks before your bike arrives; one thing many people overlook is the time and cost expended in waiting for your bike to arrive or be released. It can work best at either end of a big trip when you are back at home earning money while your bike is at sea.

Creative alternatives to shipping include leaving your bike overseas to wait until your next vacation. Werner Zwick has done this in several South American countries over the past couple of years, coming back months later to pick it up when he gets more vacation time. Peter and Kay Forwood left in 1997 for an RTW trip on a Harley Davidson, but periodically left the bike behind and returned to Australia to replenish funds.

One thing to consider is that some countries (such as Malaysia) accept the Carnet de Passage, and others (such as Thailand) stamp the vehicle information into the driver's passport on entry, so the driver cannot leave without the vehicle. One rider had to ride from Thailand into Malaysia in order to fly back to England temporarily without his bike.

Sea freight

The decision whether to use air or sea is often made when you do the first check on price – an airfreight company will quote say US$900, and by sea freight it's only US$400. Sounds like an easy choice.

However, where it all goes badly wrong is when the bike arrives at the destination and you find out that there are 'port charges'. To unload the container from the ship is US$50, to move the container to the other end of the dock is US$75, to unload the container and get your crate out is US$100, to move your crate to the shipping company is US$50, and paperwork costs for customs, agriculture and fumigation all add up to several hundred more. All of a sudden it's not such a good deal anymore.

It's worth appreciating that sea freight is best suited to low-value bulky commodities like oil or ore or livestock. Even cars can be considered low-value and bulky. But a motorcycle is a small, high-value item that may not amount to much volume, yet is a single consignment liable to the same series of charges as a quarter million tons of coal.

Moreover, the money, in our experience, is the minor aggravation – what's worse is when the bike doesn't arrive as promised. One traveller shipped out of the UK by sea to Ecuador, planning on three months travelling around South America. As a former RTW traveller she was experienced so left lots of time to get the bike there. On arrival 'que moto?' was the response from the port authorities. A quick call to the shipper in the UK revealed that the bike was still waiting for a ship.

Riders' shipping reports

My story is kind of a nightmare. I shipped my bike with plenty of time from Rotterdam to Perth, flew there but my bike was not there. Because there was no room in a container for Perth, they put it into a container for Sydney though it still was not even in Australia. Very annoying, so I asked the handling agent in Australia to put it on a road train to Darwin where I finally picked it up.   Fulco S, Netherlands

We met one rider who shipped from Kenya to Mumbai and got as far as riding along the docks, but could not get a release for two weeks, and only then after he'd lined a few pockets. And a British couple who flew their bikes into Delhi spent a solid week of twelve-hour days chasing officials. Few people realise that Franz Kafka actually wrote The Trial *after trying to import a CZ250 ISDE Replica into Mumbai.*   Colette S, UK

I shipped my bike from Surabaya, Indonesia, to Durban, South Africa. I paid US$270. On arrival in Durban, I had to pay another US$250 just to get the bike from the agent. There was an agent fee, clearance fees, and the most significant was a wharfage fee, which is worked out by the value of the bike. I wasn't aware of this, and the value they used was what was on my carnet, which was its new value. It probably would have worked out cheaper for me to fly it.   Chris A, Australia

Shipping from St Gallen, Switzerland, to Buenos Aires was just $500 for two bikes – but to get the bikes out the port of Buenos Aires we paid another US$650…   Dieter Z, Switzerland

We shipped the bike to Mombasa and this was the most stressful part of the trip due to delays. We employed HC Travel in the UK as our agent who in turn employed a company called Quintrans to arrange the shipping and packing. Quintrans packed the bike and employed a shipping line called Rohlig UK to transport it to Kenya. One of those two arranged for a Kenyan company, Kenfreight to be the receiving agents in Mombasa. Apparently Rohlig didn't have enough freight going to Mombasa to fill a container so they placed the bike with another shipping firm resulting in the change of ship.   Stephan and Chenda S, UK

The sea freight for Stephan and Chenda ended up taking over six weeks from the UK to Mombasa. This story also illustrates the risk of dealing with small companies and agents versus dealing with larger shipping companies who have their own staff at both ends.

I've heard of loads more horror stories like this, but the lesson here is that sea shippers do not give you the full costs. No matter what they promise, it's not a guarantee.

DON'T LEAVE BEFORE THE BIKE!

Don't leave before the bike! I made a big mistake by leaving Nairobi two hours before my bike. I was going to end my eight month trip gently by riding back to London from Rome rather than just arriving at dreary Heathrow.

When I got to Rome, my bike wasn't there. The local agent knew nothing of my shipment. The airway bill number didn't register at all. I called my cousin who luckily lived in Nairobi. The freight manager, knowing I'd already left, had decided he wanted a bribe so he stopped my bike leaving. When Anne contacted him he said I'd been quoted the wrong rate and that it had now doubled.

It took another three days to arrange for it to be shipped by another airline and I ended up sending it directly to Heathrow. But it was still nice to visit Rome.

Jeremy Bullard

If the bike isn't there when you are, you can spend a lot of time on foot, not enjoying the planned trip on your bike, and a lot of frustration dealing with shippers and forwarders and customs.

As mentioned above, it's safest to ship the bike home after a trip, when it doesn't matter so much how long it takes. Ports in Europe and North America aren't usually as expensive as most of the rest of the world.

Air freight

Shipping by air is much more reliable even if some countries' airlines are increasingly reluctant to put these 'dangerous goods' inside their passenger airplanes. You might have to look for an air cargo company. The USA is especially difficult to ship a bike in and out. Many travellers are finding it is much easier to ship in or out of **Canada** when travelling to North America, and in fact one of the major shippers to and from the USA, *Motorcycle Express*, based in the USA, primarily ships via Canada. You'll find a directory of air freighting agents at: www.azfreight.com.

Most other countries aren't a big problem, but you will often find that the airline doesn't want to deal directly with you; they prefer you to use an agent. Where possible, you can do the paperwork yourself, but it can be a lot of work, and often the agent's fee is money well spent.

Crating versus uncrated

Whether you ship crated or uncrated, you will usually only be required to drain the fuel from the tank, and possibly disconnect the battery or not be allowed to take it at all. Some, however, will require the bike to be crated, which will involve either building a crate or preferably, finding a friendly motorcycle dealer who has crates to throw out.

Air freighting uncrated is great and is quite common on some routes such as the Panama–Colombia/Ecuador leg over the Darien Gap. Girag ships hundreds of bikes every year uncrated and so far I have only one report of a problem, a couple of items stolen that were only strapped on. Lufthansa also ships uncrated anywhere in the world that they fly. Out of Frankfurt is the common route for European traffic.

Air freighting tips

You may be able to get away with leaving the battery in the bike, but they may

insist you remove it, even if it's a sealed item. This means you'll have to buy a new battery at your destination. Some travellers have carefully packed the battery in a box and attached the box to the crate floor, with other gear (that won't get damaged by any acid fumes) covering it. Or you could just stash a sealed battery in your baggage, after thoroughly insulating the terminals with melted wax or tape – at least it looks like you tried to be safe if it gets discovered.

A compacted HPN BMW ready to fit through mum's letterbox. © Jeff Condon

We usually leave the front wheel on when shipping as we're lazy – it can be an advantage to be able to just wheel the bike out of the crate and drive away, particularly in places like Nairobi. All I usually do is take off the mirrors and windshield, but it does cost a little more. Sometimes the warehouse where you pick up the bike will insist you take the crate away. We've always been able to get around this, but it's taken some persuading in the USA and other areas where unions and safety regulations are strong.

A metal frame crate with a Serow inside.
© Lois Pryce

Get crates from a local bike dealer. **Wooden crates** are the easiest to deal with but these days most are metal frames (pictured above) with a cardboard wrapper which are harder to customise. They are lighter, which is good, but usually the problem with a bike on an aircraft is volume not weight.

Weight versus volume

If the weight is over x kg/m^2 you pay the weight, if under you pay based on volume. Bikes are bulky, and you have to work hard to get the volume down in order to pay the weight price and you'll have to really squeeze hard to get down to the weight price. Also, you'll sometimes find that there's a big price break over 300kg, enough to make sure the weight is *over* 300kg and not under. Ask many questions about price breaks, and what happens if the weight is more or less, and the breaks on volume if any.

Other packing tips

Don't fully compress the forks. The bike should be tied down on its suspension, about halfway down. It should not be resting on centre-stand or side-stand, only on its wheels, and vertical. This will not harm the springs (unless you leave it for a couple of years). Use up to six good tie downs and don't skimp on the crate.

If you really want to squeeze the volume down, take the front wheel off, rest the bike on the sump or forks, and tie it down securely. If you're energetic, you can also take the rear wheel off, front fender, panniers, and the handlebars. Just unbolt the handlebar clamp(s), leave the cables and wiring attached, and turn the bars sideways, wrap up and secure. Always remember that the goal is to make the crate smaller.

By small boat, RoRo ferry, etc

As the front cover of Helge Pedersen's *10 Years on 2 Wheels* demonstrated, there are many other ways to ship a bike in certain areas, such as the onion boats from Melaka Malaysia to Dumai Indonesia, ferries to Iceland and North Africa, ferries from Japan to Vladivostok or across the Caspian Sea, and small boats between Panama and Colombia. With this trip, just be sure you won't be dropped off after midnight on a quiet beach!

Get the latest information on shipping at: www.HorizonsUnlimited.com/tripplan/transport

Women and adventure motorcycling

In the following two accounts, Nicki McCormick and Lois Pryce give their impressions and advice on riding in Asia and across the Americas.

RIDING IN ASIA

Nicki McCormick

Half a day's drive west of nowhere, three rusty oil drums by the roadside revealed themselves to be a petrol station. As fuel was being filtered through a scrap of cloth, the inevitable crowd gathered. Faces pressed closer and the questions began:
  'You lady? You man?'
  'Lady.'
  'LADY?! Alone? No husband?'
  'Uh huh.'
  'But madam', my interrogators demanded, 'Who drives the motorcycle?'
  This was Pakistan: an unaccompanied young woman riding from Delhi was so far removed from people's concept of 'female' as to be impossible. My gender established, I was shown to the only hotel in town which was way outside my meagre budget, so I said I'd camp instead. The manager suddenly became animated.
  'No, madam, you can't possibly camp round here! It's far too dangerous!' I silently agreed with him, and was relieved to see the price tumble as I half-heartedly insisted I'd be fine in my tent.
  The only guest, I spent the evening on the veranda listening to tales from the days of the Raj. Charming and well-educated, the manager was the perfect host, until he casually slipped into the conversation, 'Do you need your own room tonight, or would you prefer to share mine?' I acted suitably horrified and haughty, demanded my own room and barricaded the door, just in case. But the manager had already forgotten the incident.
  Next day I entered the notoriously dangerous state of Baluchistan with trepidation, but luckily instead of baddies I found only friendly restaurateurs who invited me to meet their families and insisted I devour extra chapattis (for strength).
  Climbing into the mountains, storm clouds threatened, dusk was approaching, and the road became a muddy track. I felt insignificant and alone, and I wasn't quite sure how far the next town was. Then, just as I thought I was getting the hang of riding in mud, I suddenly found myself pinned under the bike in a pool of muck. A group of camel drivers, looking every inch the ferocious tribesmen I'd been warned about, ambled round a corner. Masking my fear with a forced grin and a nervously friendly wave, I appealed for help. Realising I was female, they rushed to my aid as I righted the bike. 'Very strong. Very brave,' they gestured but, concerned for my safety, they commanded a passing motorcyclist to stay with me till Ziarat, where I arrived at dusk.
  'Come and meet my family' someone insisted. In a courtyard sat 60-odd women in their Friday finery. I was flabbergasted. So were they, and the whole crowd froze as this mud-encrusted foreigner was led into their midst. Then questions came flying from every direction.

'Where are you from? Where is your husband? How did you come here?' Like a visiting celebrity, women and girls fought to shake my hand, others looking on shyly from the back. Meanwhile, my host had arranged for me to camp for free in the hotel grounds. All too soon they had to leave, and a matriarch tried to press a leaving present of cash into my hands. Instead, I accepted her phone number in Quetta and promised to come for dinner in a few days. The manager of the hotel clucked sympathetically at the state of the bike, boasted approvingly of my adventures to everyone within earshot, arranged for several buckets of hot water and then rustled me up the best biryani on earth.

And that was the end of another good day in Pakistan. In fact, most of them were good days. The ones that weren't were more to do with bikes and bureaucracy than being a woman alone. It was a pleasant surprise as I'd been apprehensive about the idea of a long motorcycle journey alone and possessed only basic mechanical knowledge.

Personal safety

A more important consideration is personal safety. Many of the events of that one day in Pakistan could have become problems. The ideal solution is a tricky balance between maintaining a strong, brave, capable woman image which projects the respect you need to avoid hassles, while at the same time being feminine enough to allow a bit of chivalry and protectiveness. If you know yourself fairly well and are prepared, many of the potential disadvantages and risks of travelling as a woman can be eliminated, or even turned into advantages. It is possible to have the best of both worlds.

To stay safe, you must be respected. The bike is your biggest asset here – the concept of a woman travelling on a 'male' form of transport is often so incomprehensible that you are treated as an honourary man. A woman with a motorbike does not come across as vulnerable but fearless, slightly crazy and intrepid, someone not to be messed with. People are shocked, but you are far more likely to encounter admiration than hostility as a result.

When I walked through the bazaar of one town, even fully robed, I was stared at, catcalled by giggly young men and felt a little vulnerable, a shameless foreign women unaccompanied in male territory. The next day I rode to the same market. No giggles. No lewdness. Previously disapproving old men decided I was worthy of a nod. Young men approached to make intelligent conversation and ask about the bike. Suddenly I became a person, I had respect again. A bike takes the focus off you and your marital status, opens doors and is a great conversation starter.

The most common stress-inducer when travelling alone (even in Europe) is sexual harassment. Mostly it's low-level stuff – propositioning or the odd furtive grope. If you act cautiously, more serious harassment is very rare and paradoxically, the further you are from touristy areas, the safer you'll be.

Incessant 'romantic' offers can be more irritating than threatening. It's usually more a case of 'well, we've heard what these Westerners are like – you never know if you don't ask'. Reacting angrily can often provoke laughter and more teasing, especially among young men. Ignoring the comment entirely works well, and it can help to act shocked and disappointed that someone so friendly, in such a hospitable country, could think such shameful thoughts.

Declaring yourself to be the daughter or sister of the potential suitor usually stops all offers dead by putting the guy into a protector role. A calm appeal to another, preferably older, man nearby can often shame someone into desisting.

In general, the safest accommodation is a room with a lock (preferably your own) in a full-ish hotel, or with a family. Camping near people is normally OK if you ask someone senior-looking for permission first, thus making them your 'protector'. Free-camping is only really safe if it's somewhere totally isolated, where inquisitive passers-by aren't likely to spot you and pay a nocturnal visit.

Male companions

Travelling with a male companion doesn't necessarily reduce harassment, but if you are travelling with a man, make sure he calls you 'wife'. Women travelling with male partners can expect to be ignored in conversations and treated as invisible, especially in Moslem countries. It can sometimes be hard to keep your cool, but it's worth bearing in mind that in many places low-level lasciviousness is par for the course, and the creeps aren't worth ruining your trip over. It's not all roses travelling with a man of course: in sticky situations they love to take charge – for better or for worse.

In many countries, contact between the sexes is strictly limited, and men's media-fuelled image of Western women is that they are all promiscuous and available. But riding a bike doesn't fit too well with the perceived bimbo scenario. Mentioning your father as often as possible also helps, as does a stash of family photos to prove that you too, are someone's daughter or sister and not just a foreigner. A chaste, high status profession, such as teacher, gives credibility and respectability. If you are a topless dancer, it's good to lie!

Some women find it useful to invent a husband. This can, of course, pose the question 'Well, where is he, then?' ('dead...?', 'arriving any minute now...?'). A well-received reply to the innumerable questions was to tell people jokingly that I was married to my motorcycle. 'It's just as much trouble as a husband, but I can sell it if it gets tiresome!' Humour can defuse most situations.

Dressing and acting discreetly

In Moslem countries especially, clothes showing the shape of the body or expanses of flesh are seen as shameful or provocative. It can be difficult to conform to local dress norms while keeping protected for riding, but a long, baggy shirt is usually enough to cover any curves.

Actions that seem natural at home, like shaking hands or walking alone with a strange man, can often be seen as a huge come-on. Instead of shaking hands, salaaming with the right hand on the heart and a slight nod of the head is acceptable. Giving lifts to men is risky, as it is anywhere, and if accepting a guide, it's wise to let someone (a hotel manager, for example) know who you're with, and to subtly make sure your companion knows they know. Sometimes this might not be possible, but the most important thing in any potentially risky situation is to act calmly and confidently, and never show fear. Trust your instincts, without being paranoid.

The distressed damsel ploy

Not speaking to anyone because they might harm you takes away the enjoyment of the trip, but it pays to be wary. If and when you need help, the most common reaction to a maiden in distress is chivalry – you're far more likely to be treated sympathetically than a man might be. Both men and women feel the need to look after a lone woman. This can mean cars stopping to offer assistance when you're stranded by the roadside, a mechanic giving your bike extra special attention

Distressed? Who are you calling distressed?
© Nicki McCormick

because he wouldn't want to feel responsible for you breaking down somewhere, or priority at border crossings. Rooms may be found for you in full hotels, and in many countries, as a woman you'll be welcomed into a side of family life that male travellers never see.

Throwing feminist principles to the wind and playing the helpless girlie when necessary can work miracles in getting your way. (Freya Stark once said that the biggest advantage of being a woman is that you can always pretend to be more stupid than you are and no one will be surprised). Women have a greater chance of successfully pleading ignorance and charming their way out of difficult situations, flattery gets you everywhere, and it's often a lot simpler than wounding a vulnerable male ego and creating an enemy.

And finally

Your perception of yourself affects other people's perception of you. If you manage to act as if it's the most natural thing in the world for you to be trundling your bike across Asia or wherever, chances are the people you meet will accept and respect you for it. The reaction from home may often be along the lines of 'Oh, you're so brave! We're so worried about you'. Things can go nastily wrong for a woman alone on a bike in Central Nowhere. But they can also go wonderfully right.

TRANS-AMERICA MUCHACHA

Lois Pryce

'Where ya headin', little lady?' came the voice over my shoulder. It's guaranteed, anywhere in the world. Get out the map and within seconds there'll be a helpful native hovering around, ready to offer a convoluted verbal version of the printed information in front of your nose. My latest self-styled guide eyed my home-made UK licence plate curiously. After all, this is Alaska and young British ladies on dirt bikes don't come through these parts too often, especially in the middle of a snowstorm.
'Argentina', I replied.
'You're riding this little modasickle from Alaska to Argentina?'
'Er, yes'.

'Jeez!' he exclaimed, rolling his eyes, 'I dunno why women wanna do that kinda thing.
I guess it's just so they can say they done it'. My new friend sneered disparagingly.
Slightly taken aback, I attempted to clarify my motives.
'Well, to be honest, I just fancied a bit of an adventure'.
He raised his eyebrows sceptically.
'And...' I continued, before he could get a word in '...I'm upholding a good British
tradition, after all, we are a nation of explorers.'
It seemed this was the wrong thing to say.
'Goddam! You Brits!' he spluttered. 'Still obsessed with colonialism and conquering
the world.'
Realising I wasn't on a winner, I buckled up my helmet, ready to leave.
'Hey girl!' he said hastily, suddenly all smiles. 'Here's my number, give me a call, we
could get together...'
But I was already gone, leaving him standing in the snow waving his business
card, his offer of good times drowned out by the roar (well ok, splutter) of 225 throb-
bing cubic centimetres.

I'm happy to report that this gentleman's response was by no means typical. In fact, his was the only negative attitude I experienced in my entire nine-month ride through the Americas. During the remainder of my journey, in every country, my heart was repeatedly warmed by displays of immense kindness, generosity and encouragement from men and women alike (if you exclude officers of the law, of course). There is definitely a hearty dose of goodwill out there for female adventure motorcyclists. And for the record, there was not one moment that I ever felt my personal safety was under threat.

It's a man's world

By choosing to include Latin America in my route, I did wonder if I was potentially throwing myself to the wolves. Upon leaving the USA, although there's no official sign saying 'WELCOME TO MACHOWORLD – YOU ARE NOW ENTERING THE LAND OF THE LATIN LOVER', it's obvious that from here on, you're playing by a different set of rules. Masculinity reigns supreme and the division of the sexes is abundantly clear.

As a general rule, men do the drinking, smoking and lifting of heavy objects; women look after the home and have babies. This is, of course, normal life for *chicas* south of the border, but it can be a bit of a culture shock to the independent Western woman arriving on a motorcycle fresh outta California.

Bear in mind though, that in their world you yourself are a one-woman, two-wheeled, travelling culture shock. As the *muchacha en la moto* you'll be a novelty item everywhere you go, so expect to be stared at, pointed at, quizzed and (hey, if you're lucky) even poked and mauled. While this can be intimidating at times, it is generally borne out of genuine curiosity, so if you can grin and bear it with a friendly smile, and brush off unwanted overtures without bruising your suitor's ego you should manage to ease your way out of most situations, leaving everyone's pride intact. Remember, a Latin loverboy's ego is about as fragile as his country's economy.

Unfortunately, 'machismo' is as much a part of the Latin American culture as dictatorships and civil war, and this is simply a fact that one has to accept. Travelling solo in this part of the world does require some re-adjustment of your behaviour and at times, severe gritting of the teeth, but there's no use in allowing it to wind you up as this only provides extra entertainment for your 'admirers' while spoiling your day to boot. It's tough, but any feminist principles are best left at the Mexican border in the special bins provided.

Now for the good news: as a motorcyclist you already have a massive advantage over the average gap-year backpacker trudging her sorry way along the 'Gringo Trail'. This is alarmingly apparent as soon as you get off the bike and change into your flip-flops for a wander around town, only to find yourself accompanied by the hissing and catcalling of the over-attentive local *hombres*. Although you're not totally exempt from harassment while riding – filtering through grid-locked, rush-hour traffic in Lima in 100-degree heat while being barraged with wolf-whistles and lewd suggestions from the stationary cars was one particularly memorable day for me – the bike will almost always help in gaining you respect. Arriving in a town on a motorcycle invariably raises you to 'near-male' status from the men's viewpoint, while promoting you to a super-heroine in the eyes of the women, who never having even contemplated leaving their country, let alone on a motorcycle, will proclaim you to be *muy valiente*. Just don't tell 'em how easy it is!

Get married – fast!

Family and married life feature heavily in Latin American society and you'll frequently find yourself being quizzed about your own personal situation. It's often a good idea to invent a husband who has just nipped off to buy some bike parts (or another suitably manly pursuit). Throughout Latin America I wore a fake wedding ring, giving me instant respectability and helping me out of all sorts of tricky situations, including negotiating my way through a Mexican roadblock with a hastily concocted tale of my devoted spouse awaiting my arrival in the next town. But where my imaginary husband really came into his own was at police and military checkpoints where I was regularly met with the two standard questions: 'Are you married?' 'YES!' and 'Do you have any drugs?' 'NO!' Get these answers the wrong

Him indoors – Her on the road.
© Lois Pryce

way round and you could find yourself on the receiving end of a marriage proposal from a Nicaraguan prison warder.

Latin lovers to the rescue

While all the Benny Hill-style pestering is undoubtedly annoying, it's usually harmless and often tempered with a gentlemanly regard for old-fashioned chivalry. God forbid that a woman should adjust her chain tension or even check her oil unaided! Maybe some of you female readers are expert motorcycle mechanics, but my skills in that area are rudimentary, and let's face it, men do seem to know more about this stuff. So when José (who was pinching your bum in the supermarket a few hours earlier) spies you by the roadside miserably watching oil pouring out of your crankcase, any unsavoury thoughts are banished from his head by the gleaming opportunity that has presented itself to him. The chance to be a knight in shining armour! Tools, pick-up trucks, friends, brothers are all rounded up and an unholy cacophony of banging and clanking ensues until you are up and running again, with not a pinched bottom in sight. There is only one rule in this situation which must be heeded: do not offer any advice. Even if you absolutely know they're doing something wrong, or they've picked up the wrong size socket, or they haven't replaced the washer or whatever. Just don't try telling them. As far as they're concerned, you know *nada*. And more importantly, they don't want you to know anything – it'll only offend their sensibilities. So just sit there, let them over-tighten the bolts and make precise adjustments with tyre levers, because y'know what? They'll fix it a whole lot quicker than you will. Once again, a feminist stance has about as much use here as a Russian thesaurus.

If in doubt, break for the border

If you find that your exciting adventure is under threat by being either patronised or molested at every turn, you could do worse than hop over the nearest border and see how the land lies there. The lecherous Latino stereotype is certainly alive and well, but to varying degrees depending on what country you happen to be in. Harassment hotspots in my experience were Baja Mexico, Colombia and Peru. Havens of respect and gentility were pretty much everywhere else, with Ecuador, Bolivia and all of Central America taking the top spots. A striking example of the cultural differences between two neighbouring countries took place at the Ecuador–Peru crossing at Macara where I was courteously invited into the inner sanctum of the Ecuadorian exit point to be fed, watered and provided with detailed information about my onward journey. Five hundred yards down the road at the Peruvian entry station I was smarmed over by a slew of unctuous immigration officials.

Of course you don't want to go around shunning contact with every swaggering moustachioed man you see (unless you do). But there's that fine line between common sense and paranoia. Intermingling with locals is all part of the experience. Your common sense will naturally find that correct level of wariness while still satisfying your urge for adventure. Just remember to be patient and genial while retaining an air of confidence, even if you don't feel it at the time. Some of the people you meet may not see things the way you do, but for the brief time that your paths cross, it doesn't really matter.

Y finalmente...

In the run up to your departure you will be inundated with tabloid-fuelled horror stories from well-meaning friends and relations. 'You'll get raped!' I remember one panic-stricken acquaintance of mine declaring hysterically. These people must be ignored at all costs. Of course, one can't deny that bad things can happen and that there are nasty people out there. But this is as applicable to Tunbridge Wells as it is to El Salvador. It may be worth pointing out to the doom merchants that good things can also happen and there are nice people out there too. Alternatively, you can save your breath and get packing.

Sure, you'll have some tough days, miserable days, and days when you wish you hadn't got up. But you'll never wish you hadn't set off.

Life on the road

The Big Day is approaching and the nation's media, or just your friends and family are gathered to see you off. Then again, maybe you're slipping off quietly at dawn. One thing will be certain: you'll be chewing your lip and your throbbing hangover won't help.

If you've had the chance to prepare thoroughly pat yourself on the back; you've done well. But if you're like most mortals, you're bound to have overlooked something. This is normal – accept it and deal with the customary moment-of-departure crises, large or small.

SETTING OFF

You start the engine, heave the bike off the stand (don't forget to flick it up!), click it into first and wobble off down the road, appalled at the weight of the machine. Once out on the open road you wind it up and allow some faint optimism to creep in to your multiplying anxieties as passing motorists stare at you with what you hope is envy.

Finally on the move after months, if not years of preparation, the urge is to keep moving, especially if you're heading out across a cold continent. Try to resist covering excessive mileages in your early days even though movement will probably be the best tonic for your nerves. Better still, don't make any crazy deadlines to quit work and catch a ferry the same night and meet someone three countries away for breakfast.

If you've got a long way to ride, even to get to your port city, aim to spend the night near there before the ferry departs. The **early days** of a big trip, especially in unfamiliar countries with perplexing road signs and 'wrong-side' driving are when most **accidents** happen. If an estimated 75% of all overlanders achieve hospitalisation through *accidents*, rather than commonly-dreaded diseases and banditry, you can imagine what that figure is for motorcyclists.

Culture shock

Alone on your first big trip into foreign lands it's normal to feel self conscious, intimidated, if not even **paranoid**. This is because you are exiting your comfort zone and entering the thrill of an adventure. 'Adventure travel' has become a tourism marketing term to distinguish active holidays from lying by a pool, but an 'adventure' is what it sounds like: indulging in an activity with an uncertain or dangerous outcome. The less glamorous aspect of this is the **stress** involved in dealing with strange people, languages, places and food. This can be exciting; your senses are sharpened and your imagination is stimulated. But the freedom of motorcycling also translates to vulnerability which can be manifested as an exaggerated suspicion of other people. Paul Randall's anecdote over the page strikes a chord: a debilitating neurosis compounded by bike problems and pressing deadlines which can look trivial in retrospect.

Recognise that it will take a couple of weeks and some stressful encounters before you acclimatise to life on the road. Wariness is a vital behavioural pattern found in all animals and these days 'rich people taking cheap holidays in other people's misery' can make us assume we're asking for it.

One of the most important lessons to learn on your travels is to get beyond this xenophobia, to recognise that it is in fact the people of the world, their humanity and generosity which will give you your most rewarding experiences and memories. One of the most frustrating scenarios is when you realise you've been rude to someone who was only trying to help or be friendly. This can be understandable when you have been pestered by hustlers urging 'mister, psst' for days. The trick comes with gaining the experience to distinguish one from the other, and very often it is in rural areas where people are more 'real' and less interested in flattering their self esteem at your expense (or simply ripping you off!). It's normal to see a journey as a series of trips from one urban centre to the next; often, as in Paul's visit to St Petersburg (see box below) it's a bureaucratic requirement. But try and plan your itinerary to ease these stresses. If you're heading for a big city, have a recommended hotel in mind for the **first night**. It will give you something positive to focus on and breathing space until you get the feel for the place.

Out in the country where pressures are less acute, make the most of **roadside cafés** for tea breaks, meals and rests. They are great places to mix with local people without feeling overwhelmed. The owners and customers will be regulars used to passing travellers and may well treat you like any other customer. Above all try to resist the mania particular to motorcyclists of devouring miles at the cost of gaining far more precious experiences.

CRACKING UP IN RUSSIA

Weblog; September 3rd 2003. I realise that things have been far too easy recently travelling around to Lithuania, needless to say Russia put an end to all of that. I was nervous about getting into Russia: visa headaches, no bike insurance, red tape – but I got in OK and stayed at Pskov. I had to get to St Petersburg to register (otherwise there would be trouble) and had to do it in three days.

Russia for me was tough – it's all very well knowing how to say 'Hello, my name is Paul – kak paniemajesh?' But that's not exactly a full vocabulary. I found the people very cold and felt too intimidated to buy food. Looking back on this I feel a bit daft but that's how it was – and I was in a rush so skipping meals seemed OK.

I got to St P cold, wet and miserable and found a suitably grotty hotel where I had to bribe the security bloke to make sure my bike was 'safe' at night. I tried to out tough him but I've watched too many movies – it didn't work. Next day I went to collect my passport from reception but it had gone missing; the receptionist looked everywhere but couldn't find it. I guessed the security bloke had nicked it for another bribe. I was starting to panic but the receptionist told me they did not have it – I must have it, check your money belt Mr Paul – so I did and there was my passport! What a plonker! Anyway I got very upset, I could not say sorry in Russian, so I just left feeling very small.

I went to register and then my bike wouldn't start. I managed to get it going somehow and tried to find a place to stay the night before registering. The bike kept breaking down, I had not eaten for a few days and then I started to lose the plot a bit...

Looking back I think I was having a bit of a nervous breakdown fuelled by lack of food. At this point an American guy said 'Hello' . We chatted, I told him what I was doing etc and he offered me a luxury flat for the night with free secure parking for my broken bike and dinner with his family. After that I got the bike going enough to get registered on the other side of town. **Paul Randall**

(Opposite) Approaching the Assekrem Pass in southern Algeria.

ATTITUDES TO SECURITY

Now that you're travelling deeper into the unknown, you'll be getting worried about your security. Four-wheel overlanders have it easy, but on a bike all your gear is out there for the taking and it's understandable to feel vulnerable, exposed and obsessed about security. This section could be filled with any number of canny tricks about secret pockets and booby traps, but the only knack you need to develop is common sense and vigilance (backed up by comprehensive travel insurance).

Accept that you're going to lose something or maybe even everything, either through carelessness or theft. Much has been said earlier about the need to keep your valuables safe, but in the end it's all just stuff that can be replaced, albeit at a price and great inconvenience. This is just a simple fact of travelling: riding motorcycles through distant lands is risky.

Fear of the unknown is an understandable self-protection mechanism and since man has travelled, others have preyed on him. The perils of travel are probably no greater than they were five hundred or two thousand years ago, and the need for vigilance has always been the same.

In a town, only let things out of your sight that you can afford to lose – and don't think that the fringes of your homelands are any less risky than Africa or Asia; petty pilfering in the developing world is as likely as outright theft in the West.

Cities anywhere are the lairs of thieves who prey on rubbernecked tourists and are one good reason to avoid them. In these crowded places keep any evidence of your wealth or your confusion under wraps. Wallets should always be zipped into an inside pocket and cameras not dangling temptingly around your neck. Markets, ports or crowded travel termini are favourite haunts for pickpockets. As you wander into these places check everything is zipped up and be alert. One good tip I read but have never actually used is having a **dummy wallet** with your day cash plus some expired credit cards and even an old passport. If you get mugged they'll be delighted with this and the more expired crap and other junk the better.

Avoid looking open-mouthed at maps on street corners; in heavy city centres plan your route corner by corner before you walk out of your hotel room and when you do walk, imitate the advice given to women walking alone at night: march with a single-minded motivation that emits the signal 'Don't fuck with me!' in a heavy Sylvester Stallone accent. Beware of pats to the shoulder and other distractions which are well known snatch-and-grab set-ups.

Coping with robbery

During the months preceding your departure, it's likely at least one person – an individual who watches a lot of tabloid television and doesn't travel much – will have expressed alarm at your adventurous itinerary. 'Africa/ Iran/Colombia [take your pick], are you *crazy*?' You might knock back some bluff reply, but underneath you can't help thinking they might have a point. While theft is usually an urban problem, robbery, or what's quaintly know as banditry, usually occurs in remote regions, and is as likely in the US or outback

(Opposite): Taking the high road in Baja. © Clement Salvadori. **(Previous pages):** Brew up on the Salar de Uyuni, Bolivia. © Martin Wielecki.

Australia as anywhere else. Again be wary of set-ups like broken-down cars needing help. In the very unlikely event that you ride into an ambush or are set upon by armed bandits in the middle of the night, the common advice is let them take what they want and live to tell the tale. If you're smart you'll have a stash of cash on the bike which itself is rarely an item worth stealing.

Weapons for self defence

For some people, usually from already violent societies, the prospect of riding into the world may raise the question of self protection? Most of us have never seen a **handgun** and would consider the idea absurd. I can't think of any situation, personal or otherwise, where a handgun would have not made things worse. In parts of the US (as well as mafia-dominated economies and areas of civil unrest) gun ownership may be widespread but make no mistake, in the rest of the world they are illegal and unnecessary. In the unlikely event of a hold up, will you have it at hand and know how to deal with a bunch of thieves who may also be armed? The very urge for possessing a gun on the road engenders an aggressive attitude that really should have worked its way out during adolescence.

Mace or **pepper spray** sounds like a more innocuous and compact alternative, recommended in some ursine habitats and sold elsewhere as an urban self protection agent. Again, on a bike ask yourself how often are you likely to come up against a sole assailant who can be dispersed with a quick blast? The reality is that, if you indeed are under an attack from which you can flee, you will be able to do it better using your wits (and if necessary physical force) than hanging around to use a weapon.

Knives, of course, are a genuinely useful tool, at home or on the road, and in extended lengths may be part of a 'bush master/hunter' persona we may aspire to in the wilds. You may be tempted to carry a big knife to 'skin rabbits', or even a machete 'to cut firewood'. In fact the best firewood lies loose on the ground and the most useful blade is on a Swiss Army or multitool that can be used to peel an orange without mobilising a SWAT team.

BORDERS AND CHECKPOINTS

The vagaries of border crossings and, to a lesser extent, getting past checkpoints, are perennial worries to travellers. This anxiety is understandable because it represents a complex challenge: the need to use their wits to overcome a hurdle to their progress while dealing with possibly obstructive officials, hustlers, forms and demands in foreign languages, and all followed by the latest stretch of 'unknown' which lies beyond.

STREET WISE MANIFESTO

- **Trust your instincts** – if a situation or a place does not feel good, get out of there.
- **Camp discretely**, out-of sight of the road or stay in the security of settlements.
- **Ride sensibly** Be alert, rest often and stay together if in a group.
- **Don't ride at night** unless unavoidable.
- **Keep a low profile** in hostile areas.

- **Leave M16s**, mace and machetes at home.
- **Keep your valuables** on you at all times.
- **In towns park out of sight**. Many hotels let you park inside or round the back.
- **Avoid exposing cash or valuables** in crowded places. Someone is watching.
- **Learn and use the local language** – you'll be amazed at the positive response.

GETTING PARTS

Messrs Honda, Suzuki and Yamaha may sell motorbikes in every corner of the world but that doesn't mean that parts for your Euro/US model, not to mention BMW, Aprilia, etc., will be available or even obtainable in far flung places.

Having witnessed a Thai parts supplier stuff my piston in his pocket, hop on his scooter and disappear off into the Bangkok traffic in a trial-and-error search for some piston rings that 'might' fit convinced me to forget the expense and have parts couriered out from the UK. The resulting series of catastrophes, by people who really should know better (it is their job, after all) remains the most frustrating part of my trip. How can it take *two months* to get a gudgeon pin for Honda's ubiquitous XR400?

Should you want to get parts from home, to minimise the risk of waiting weeks or even months for them to arrive try the following:

● Before you leave, try to find one, or preferably two, parts suppliers who specialise in your bike; make and model. Big multi-franchise dealerships often carry plenty of parts for the latest whizz-bang plastic-fantastics but very little for old, trusty overlanders. The bike press, owners' clubs, motorcycling organisations and Yahoo groups are all good places to start looking.
● Phone them up and tell them what you're doing and where you're going. Ask them: will they ship parts abroad and if they have done so before.
● How much stock they actually carry. Some companies who claim to have every part available often don't.
● If they don't have a part in stock where would they get it from. Some UK dealers, for instance, get their parts from mainland Europe which takes longer and the savings aren't always passed on to the customer.
● Get contact details, especially email address, phone and fax number and a contact name.
● Do a little research on your bike. Are there any parts notorious for failing and/or being difficult to obtain? Dependent on cost, you might want to pre-order a part or maybe leave it with a reliable friend.
● If you do order parts from abroad, use a courier; DHL, FedEx, etc. Regular postal services may offer a 48-hour international parcel service, and indeed your package might reach the destination country in that time, but when it hits customs it will probably just stop dead.
● Couriers usually offer a customs clearance service, and although more expensive, if you consider the cost in time, money and sheer frustration of hanging around for weeks, they represent good value.
● Expect the worst. Sadly, it is highly likely that someone down the line will mess it up. Never assume that the person or company you are paying to provide a service will actually perform.

Think about what could go wrong and plan accordingly. Always give detailed instructions and information and keep track of all involved. Remember, 'Assumption is the mother of all cock-ups'.

● Make sure the shipper provides you with the courier's tracking number. Most couriers offer a web-based tracking system – use it! As soon as your package has landed get in touch with the nearest courier office, preferably in person and with all your documentation. Keep the pressure on. The slogan 'every second counts' doesn't always apply in some parts of the world.
● If second-hand parts are being sent, make sure they are completely free of oil, uranium, anthrax or any other substance that could be deemed 'hazardous'. Airlines can get funny about what's in a package. If in doubt, check with the courier or airline first.
● Ask your supplier to reduce the value of each item on the invoice and therefore the amount of duty you will have to pay. But don't get too carried away; customs aren't stupid.

If it all goes wrong, don't get stressed. Try to remain calm, smile and remind yourself that you're having the time of your life. Ranting and raving may make you feel better for a while, but it will certainly make your situation worse.

The above may seem excessive, but it's all based on real life incidences which have left people tearing their hair out. A few hours' pre-departure preparation could save a lot of time on your trip.

Richard Virr

What you must remember is that, in almost all cases, what you are doing has been done before, several times. If your documentation is in order – something that is nobody's responsibility but your own – eventually you will get through. If you've been pulled over for speeding (the most common traffic infraction), simply accept you've been nailed, just as you would do back at home where it is also seen as an integral expense of independent mobility. It's very common for motorcyclists to be able to talk their way out of these situations: you'll soon learn to tell if the guy is professional, devious or just wants to ascertain your bike's top speed and say 'Manchester United'.

After a few countries, you'll have the hang of crossing frontiers, or at least be resigned to the inevitable hanging about and the power games which sometimes need to be played to win the day. Nevertheless, adopt this Platonic strategy at any official barrier:

- Remain calm and polite.
- Switch off your engine and remove your helmet if they mean business.
- Be patient and smile a lot.
- Never grumble or show unnecessary irritation, even in the face of provocation.
- Obey all the petty instructions for searches and papers.
- Accept delays and sudden, protracted 'lunch breaks'.
- Be suspicious of strangers wanting lifts or deliveries over borders.

If you're being given a hard time, stoicism and good humour may diffuse a tense situation. Try to remember that the glamorous benefits of a uniform and a machine gun soon pale when you're living in a tin shed far from your family and haven't been paid for six months. Read the situation. If there's a request to make some untoward payment or 'tourist tax', stick up for yourself, ask for a receipt, negotiate, but in the end pay up. Remember that, no matter what many overland travellers assume, they're not just picking on you.

Bribes aren't daylight robbery, but a way of life in many developing countries. You may resent this custom – and many travellers boast that they've never paid a penny – but that's just what it is, a custom. A couple of dollars can save hours.

It may look cool in the movies but never smugly hand over your passport with a wink and a twenty folded inside. This is not how the game is played and could land you in big trouble (or just waste money). You'll know when you're expected to pay. If an impasse has been reached ask if there is some kind of official tax (or, if you're in trouble by the road, a fine) that can be paid and to whom it should be paid. Perhaps they can arrange for the payment to be forwarded to the correct department? Accept payments as part of travelling, but don't think you have to pay your way through every border or tricky situation.

Some official tariffs are negotiable; often it's just winning the game by getting something off you that counts. It doesn't have to be money, but money is the ultimate compact commodity which partly explains its widespread popularity. On a bike you won't have the room to carry a disposable stash of last year's mobile phones, Madonna cassettes or even lighters and pens.

EQUIPMENT CHECKLIST

These are some of the basics you'll need on a long overland trip. It's unlikely that you'll take just these items, but consider them as part of a useful checklist to give you ideas on essentials you may have overlooked.

Documentation
- Passport
- Vehicle ownership document
- Carnet
- Photocopies of all essential documents
- Cash, credit cards, travellers' cheques
- Travel tickets
- Travel insurance
- Green Card and/or Third Party Insurance
- Driver's licence (including IDP)
- Passport photos
- Address book/list or personal organiser

Camping and sleeping
- Tent or treated mosquito net
- Sleeping mat
- Sleeping bag with stuff sac
- Clock or watch
- Collapsible stool
- Ear plugs
- Head torch

Cooking
- Stove and fuel (if not petrol)
- Spares for stove
- Tea towel and pan scrubber
- Lighters
- Spoon and fork
- Cooking pot(s) and pot gripper
- Swiss Army knife or multitool
- Washing-up liquid
- Mug
- Water container plus water bag/bottle

Toiletries
- Soap, flannel and towel (or sarong)
- Razors
- Detergent
- Toothbrush and toothpaste
- Toilet paper
- Sun screen and skin moisturiser
- Insect repellent
- Universal basin plug
- First-aid kit (see p.108)

Navigation and orientation
- Maps and GPS
- Guidebook(s)
- Compass

Clothing
- Boots and light shoes
- Socks and underpants
- Thermal underwear
- T-shirts or shirt
- Fleece jacket
- Gore-Tex riding jacket
- Gloves
- Leather trousers or riding pants
- Shorts
- Balaclava or sun hat
- Crash helmet (and goggles)
- Spare dark lenses or sunglasses
- Needle and thread

Bike spares and tools
- Spare keys
- Front and rear inner tubes
- Extra tyre(s)
- Puncture repair kit (see p.65 and 69)
- Connecting link(s) for chain
- Control levers and cables.
- Oil and air filter(s)
- Speedo cable
- Wire and duct tape
- Spare nuts and bolts for rack fittings
- Instant gasket
- Epoxy glue
- Diaphragm for CV carbs
- Jubilee clips
- Small tub of grease and small WD40
- Electrical wire, connectors and bulbs
- Radiator sealant
- Spark plug(s)
- Petrol pipe
- Spare bungees and straps
- Spanners, sockets and wrench
- Adjustable spanner or mole grips
- Allen keys
- Cross-and flat-bladed screwdrivers
- Pliers with wire cutters
- Spoke key
- Junior hacksaw with spare blades
- Top-up oil and rag

Miscellaneous
- Camera and film/memory cards
- Pen, notebook and envelopes
- Phrase books
- Spare batteries for electrical gadgets
- Solar calculator
- Mobile phone
- Waterproof bags
- String or rope
- Postcards from your country (as gifts)

CHANGING MONEY

Some borders have currency-changing facilities, others out in the bush don't. If you're lucky, the nearest town will have a **cashpoint machine** (ATM) and this is the simplest way to obtain local currency. If there is a good network of them in a given country, you only need withdraw a little cash at a time. This way you never have too much to lose and won't get stuck trying to change a weak local currency back into US dollars or whatever. Even if it's possible it will be at such a bad rate that it's hardly worth it.

If ATMs are unknown it may be possible to buy the local currency in the preceding country. Otherwise, changing money can take hours in some banks going from one counter to another; get used to it, it's the same for everyone. Currency exchange booths in large town centres need not be as dodgy as they look, can save hours and might even offer a better rate.

'Sorry, no change' is something you're bound to hear when paying for a local service with a high denomination note; newly born taxi drivers can mouth it even before they can say 'mama'. When you've got nothing else there's no way round it, but learn to hoard low denomination notes; they're useful for tips.

Currency declaration forms

Some countries try and undermine their black markets by insisting you complete a Currency Declaration Form (CDF). On it you fill out all the foreign currency you are bringing into a country and possibly other valuables too. Any further exchange transactions you make in that country must be matched by receipts or entries on the CDF, so that when you leave, the cash you brought in equals what you're taking out, less the money you officially exchanged. Half the time these forms aren't even checked when you leave, but don't count on it. Any money you don't declare on the form (i.e. smuggle in) must also not be discovered on departure.

Black market

The use of the black market to change foreign currency into local at an advantageous rate is an accepted part of travel in countries with weak or 'soft' currencies. It's also a popular set-up for naïve travellers and by its very nature illegal, leaving you liable to fines, confiscation of funds and even imprisonment. To many locals your hard currency represents access to desirable foreign goods which their currency cannot buy, or even a ticket out of the country.

Making deals

Use the black market by all means (sometimes there is no choice and some banks even encourage it to save queuing), but keep your eyes open and your wits about you. If you're a beginner here are some guidelines:

- Establish exactly how many dinars you're being offered for a dollar (for example). Repeat to them 'So you are offering me 300 dinars for one dollar?' and if they agree then spell out the total amount you want to exchange, i.e. 'So you will give me 4500 dinars for fifteen dollars?'
- Ask to see the currency offered and check that the notes have the right number of zeros. It is also helpful to learn to read the nine cardinal Arabic numerals if heading that way.

- If there's room for negotiation, go ahead. A wily black marketeer is going to offer as little local currency as he can for your valuable dollars.
- Deal one-to-one and don't get drawn into any shady corners or deals.

Watch out for sleight of hand. I'm sure I was diddled with the '**Romanian Hand Trick**' near the Libyan border once. There is some ploy in which they count out the money offered, give it to you to count, which you do, and find everything in order. At this point your guard is down and they *take it back* to check, and even though you're staring at their hands something happens and you get back less than you thought. If this 'handback' scenario happens, be on guard, try and resist it or count it all again. Obviously the black market rate will represent a major boost to your funds, but don't stick your neck out to gain a measly ten per cent. While you should never take them for granted, you'll soon get the hang of making these useful if illegal street deals. And if you're ever unsure, trust your instincts and walk away.

Two-wheel camping

On the road it's surprising how rarely you actually need to camp. Werner Bausenhart (*Africa: Against the Clock on a Motorcycle*), managed to ride a Funduro up and down the continent over several weeks without ever spending a night in a tent. In Asia and South America overnight accommodation is even easier to come by, although the motorised vagrants who called themselves *Terra Circa* spent almost every night out during their ride across Europe and Russia. Not taking camping gear should mean you need carry a lot less stuff though it rarely works out like that.

The truth is, of course, disregarding the savings in paying for accommodation, camping is *part* of the adventure. There will come a day when you either have to, or want to, park up in a nice spot and enjoy a night out. Sure it means a whole lot of extra gear, but that should really add up to no more then 5–10 extra kilos. In return to get the autonomy not only to ride where you like but also stay where you like.

Sleeping, **cooking**, **eating** and **drinking** are the basic elements of camping (washing too, I suppose). The greater the comfort and efficiency of these elements, the better will be the quality of your camping experience: on a long ride it needs to be. As with all biking gear, it depends how committed you are to saving space and weight. A tasty meal followed by a good night's sleep is important to allow your body to recover after an exhausting day's riding.

Tents, sleeping mats and sleeping bags

On my early Sahara trips I never carried a **tent** or even a mat; I just unrolled my sleeping bag on my clothes, dozed through the night and woke up aching. These days I usually carry just the inner bit. In still conditions a tent adds about 5°C to the ambient temperature though it also offers a psychologically comforting shelter. Crawling in and flopping out after a hard day's riding can be a real

Surrounding yourself with good gear makes the whole business less fraught.

tonic. On a warm, windless night you always have the option of simply lying on it like a groundsheet.

Don't waste your money on an expensive ultralight design ready to withstand a Himalayan blizzard: for most situations a simple two-pole crossover design will stand up without pegs or guy ropes and cost from £30/$55. With these tents you'll need to quickly anchor them down either with your baggage or rocks or a line to your bike. In windy situations without ballast (or guy lines) they take off like kites. A one-person design may be lighter but I prefer the space of a two-person dome in which there's room to do more than lie flat. If you're planning on spending several days in one place you'll also appreciate a bigger tent.

Sleeping mats and bags

Closed cell foam sleeping mats used to be bulky for the comfort they offered. Nowadays, though expensive for a piece of open-cell foam in a bag with a plug, the self-inflating Therma-Rest-type sleeping mats work amazingly well. I've managed for a few years with a three-quarter-length Ultralight model which rolls up to around two litres in volume; that much volume I don't mind using up for the comfort it gives. It hasn't punctured yet, nor have I had a problem with sand getting in the valve, though using it in or on a tent may help. On soft sand I have found digging a shallow **sleeping trench** greatly increases the comfort; vaguely replicating sinking into a soft mattress.

As for **sleeping bags**, compactness and warmth within your budget is what it's about. Get the best you can afford which can mean spending over £100/ $180. Manufacturers' seasonal ratings are subjective, aim for a three-season with a **boxed foot** and a 'mummy' **head cowling**: these two features alone are worth an extra 'season's' rating. If you can afford it, the lofting qualities of **down** are still unbeatable, best plucked from spoon-fed virgin white geese (and not to be confused with inferior *feathers* which are sometimes in the mix). Not only does down fluff out to fill a large volume (the key to insulation), it

Sleeping bags – invest in the best you can afford. © Karl Rees

compresses better than any man-made fabric and will do so for many years so it takes up less room (the weight saving is negligible). But down can get ruined when **wet** or even just damp; if it stays damp it may go mouldy and once wet it takes a long time to dry.

If you are heading into a wet environment or can't be bothered to worry about your bag's humidity too much get a **synthetic** bag; they are as warm, even when wet and – warmth for warmth – only a bit more bulky than down. With either filling go for a quality brand that will last you years.

One drawback that I've always found with sleeping bags is that, sleeping in a tube, you are unable to move your knees up which means you may end up with a stiff back in the morning. A few years ago I got an egg-shaped Yeti down bag which gave more knee movement and have lately acquired an ultra-compact synthetic bag with stretchable knee section for the same effect.

Air your bag out every morning by turning it inside out and letting it hang in the breeze on your tent or bike. Especially with down you want to stretch the washing cycles out as long as possible as it reduces loft in the long run.

Lighting
On short winter nights you'll need some lighting in the evening; a good spread of light around your camp makes life much easier. The bike's parking light is too weak and the main beam risks flattening the battery. A **head torch** is the solution; LED Petzl Zipkas are incredibly compact even if they don't burn holes in the night. A good head torch and a clear night sky is all you need.

Cooking, eating and drinking
Relying on firewood for cooking can be too much of a gamble in some places. A small **petrol (gasoline) stove** is the answer; you have a tank full of the stuff so if you ever run out, not being able to cook up a brew is the least of your problems.

The problem with petrol stoves is modern ones are designed to run on 'white fuel', a cleaner petrol than that which comes out of most outback fuel pumps. Lead-free is better but is only found in cities. Prolonged use of low octane leaded fuel may eventually clog your stove's generator (feed pipe) or jets with soot. I would guess this process takes a couple of months of daily use, so either take a **spare generator** (if applicable to the model you use) or take a gamble and hope the stove won't block before you head back. Taking a litre of white fuel defeats the object of saving space and weight. Better to fill your bike's tank with unleaded when you can and top your stove up at the same time before you get deep into the bush where ordinary leaded fuel is all you'll find.

Using local leaded fuel your stove may spurt and smoke a bit before it fully heats up, but once hot, petrol stoves put out much more heat than butane and, being under pressure, are more resistant to wind. The windshields which come with most stoves are pretty ineffective, so work out a proper wind break with your baggage to increase efficiency and save fuel.

Anything that claims to run on **multi-** or **dual-fuel** is either a play on words (ie: it runs on leaded *and* unleaded – big deal!), a compromise in the jet size, or requires fiddly changing of jets. On the road you need a simple petrol stove, not something that claims to run on diesel, kerosene, white fuel and Orangina.

Coleman 533. Though extravagant, I also find a flask saves boiling water for lunch.

The Coleman 533 I've used for years (renamed a 'Sportster' in some markets) claims to run on white fuel and unleaded, but I've always run it on African fuel with an occasional burn-through on unleaded when I get home. I'm still on the original generator and I've heard that if it blocks up you can take out the wire inside, try and clean it or eliminate it altogether to get a rougher flame. To start it you simply pump it up, turn on the fuel and light it. This sort of ease of use is the key for all sorts of overlanding equipment. Which brings us to what I call 'red bottle' stoves made by various manufacturers with the fuel bottle (usually red) attached by a hose or pipe to a compact burner. The idea I presume is it's more compact to pack but takes a bit of assembly. I've tried an Optimus Nova which squirted fuel from the jammed clip-on connection and watched new MSRs spluttering and then permanently blocking after a couple of hours' use, despite cleaning and replacing parts. Others have reported reliable results from red bottle jobs but they cost twice as much as a 533. They require fiddly assembly which can lead to leaks or blockages, as well as regular cleaning maintenance, the last thing you want to do when you're hungry. A seemingly petty drawback many also mention is the **noise** of some 'red bottle' stoves and poor heat control: either all or nothing.

Consider a stove's **stability**, both on the ground and for holding pots; there's nothing more frustrating than watching your half-cooked dinner tip over. In my experience Coleman models are ideal in this respect: the squat compact shape of the one-piece unit sits securely on the ground, and the wide burner gives off plenty of heat and support for a pot. 'Red bottles ' have very cleverly designed fold up burners but lack a large base for anything but a small pot.

Getting into camping takes some adjustment and clumsy accidents are common when you're tired or still getting used to the whole business. A reliable uncomplicated and stable stove goes a long way to minimising this.

One-pan cooking

It may sound extreme but a half-litre **mug** and a one-litre **pan** with a lid will do. A plate is unnecessary and a spoon and a penknife are all the cutlery you'll ever use. You can cook your rice/pasta, put it in the mug with a lid on top to keep it warm, and then, if you're not simply throwing it in with the pasta – cook whatever else you have, chuck the pasta back in and eat – leaving one pan and one cup to wash. Avoid pouring hot water away: use it for soup or washing up.

Don't get drawn in by trick titanium cookware from camping shops. A sturdier stainless saucepan with a spot-welded rather than rivetted handle from Woolies will take rough use and sand cleaning without getting grubby or bent.

Clean water

People tend to be very squeamish about drinking water from wells, rock pools and even rivers, but in my expe-

One-pan cooking means less washing up.

rience a **water filter** (see p.121) or even tablets are not necessary. In warmer tropical countries there is a risk from polluted well water or food due to the higher temperatures and denser populations with poor sanitation. In this case **sterilising tablets** like Katadyn's Micropur are worthwhile, leaving no unpleasant taste as chlorine- and iodine-based tablets do.

Remember tablets sterilise but they don't remove impurities. This may be just harmless silt but to get rid of it you need a filter. Even without a filter a packet of tablets will be useful.

Water containers

The best way to carry water while riding in is a **hydrator** in your backpack; basically a water bag with a hose that clips to your shoulder straps. This way the water is secure and it's easy to drink while riding – small regular sips are better than big glugs when you stop. Camelbak set the ball

Hydrators like this 3-litre Platypus, are a good way of making sure you drink enough while you're riding.

rolling years ago but seem expensive for a bag with a hose. Platypus are another brand but I've found their less pliable bladders can acquire pinprick leaks. With either you don't have to buy the full pack, but can just buy a bladder and hose which fits in your own daypack, cutting or melting a hose hole on the top of the bag to avoid having the hose pass through zips.

Off your back your main water container should ideally be around 10 litres, double that for remote desert sections. Ortlieb make nylon water bags in various sizes which can also make bulk water holders that will cram in and can be adapted to be a hydrator. The good thing about **water bags** is that they get smaller as they empty. Rigid containers are nearly as light but they take up space and can be awkward to lash down.

Water bags for your bulk water reserve save space and are easy to use.

Health and medical emergencies*

Paul Rowe

The key principle to avoiding illness and injury on your trip is that prevention is far better than cure. However, with some prior planning and a small first-aid kit you will be able to deal with most ailments which arise to keep you and your group riding.

First-aid kit
A small tuppaware box is ideal and should include the following:
- Paracetamol
- Strong painkillers (analgesics)
- Anti-malarials
- Antacids
- Anti-diarrhoea tablets (Loperamide 2mg)
- Laxatives
- Anti-histamines
- Rehydration powders
- Broad Spectrum Antibiotics (eg amoxicillin 500mg)
- Multi-vitamins

Equipment
- Latex gloves (good for oily repairs too)
- Tweezers (for tick removal)
- Sterile syringe set. Two hypodermic needles per person
- Sterile dressings, plasters, bandage
- Alcohol wipes ('Sterets'); can also be used to start fires
- Superglue
- Antiseptic cream
- Durapore tape
- Safety pins
- Thermometer
- Savlon antiseptic concentrate
- Steristrips

Good **painkillers** could make the difference of being able to carry on riding in an emergency, so see your doctor prior to departure and request a supply of Codeine Phosphate 30mg or Tramadol 50mg tablets. Also ask for some amoxicillin or similar antibiotic (beware of any group member with penicillin allergy) as wound infections, dental abscesses, ear and urinary infections are all more common during remote travel.

* For those travellers who may not want to cart their *AMH* around with them, this useful section is available online with all hyperlinks at: **www.adventure-motorcycling.com/medical**

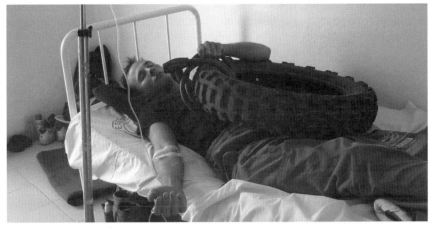

Illness, including malaria, is much more likely if travelling in the hot season. © Jeff Condon

Although contrary to the manufacturers' advice, a lot of space can be saved by removing tablets from their blister packaging and putting them into small zip lock plastic bags. Just remember to label them clearly.

Obtaining supplies

Between a friendly doctor and your local pharmacy you should be able to obtain most of the kit for your trip. For anything else, try these sites:

UK	BCB Ltd	www.bcb.ltd.uk
	Lifesystems	www.lifesystems.co.uk
	SP Services	www.999 supplies.com
	St John Ambulance Supplies	www.stjohnsupplies.co.uk
US		www.safetycentral.com
Canada		www.mec.ca
Australia		www.firstaidkitsqld.com.au

Minor injuries

Minor cuts and grazes are common ailments. Apply the following general principles:

- Stop the bleeding.
- Clean thoroughly to reduce risk of infection.
- Keep it dressed to maintain cleanliness.

Bleeding is stopped by simply applying **direct pressure**, elevating the limb and bandaging firmly to hold the dressing in place. Dilute some Savlon concentrate in clean water and clean wounds thoroughly, picking out any gravel or other foreign material. If the wound is gaping you can close it with either Steristrips or ordinary household superglue (Loctite). Hold the wound edges together and smear the glue along the surface, maintaining that position for one minute. It will flake off after a few days once it has done its job. Steristrips are sticky paper strips which are very good at holding wound edges together but are less effective in humid environments.

Foreign bodies should be removed whenever possible but otherwise can be left in place for removal by a surgeon once you return home. The exceptions are any organic material (wood, splinters, thorns, fangs) which are likely to become infected or anything embedded in your palm or sole which will become too painful for you to function normally. For these you will have to venture to a local medical centre for removal. Any spills which leave gravel in your face need to be cleaned meticulously or may leave permanent scarring.

Planning for serious injury, illness and evacuation

Most riders give little forethought about what would happen if they were to become incapacitated during their trip. Thankfully these events are rare, but some pre-trip planning will help things run a lot smoother if things go wrong.

A worst-case scenario can be broken down into the following stages:

Casualty event ➤ First aid ➤ Stabilisation ➤ Summon/move to help ➤ Casualty evacuation ➤ Repatriation.

Consider what you would do at each stage after initial stabilisation, which is dealt with later in this chapter. Go through some scenarios in your mind asking yourself questions about how you would cope with an emergency at different parts along your proposed route.

How will you raise help? Will there be a mobile phone signal or do you need to carry a satellite phone? Are there any dwellings or bases with VHF radio? **Who will you call?** Is there an ambulance service and if so will you have to pay cash? Can you leave your travel plans with someone who will come looking for you? How can you signal an aircraft? How long might it take to get rescued? A list of worldwide contact numbers for local police, fire and ambulance can be found at **www.sccfd.org/travel.html**.

If you're spending a significant amount of time in an area it may be worth identifying where the local hospitals are, roughly the level of care they provide and whether there are likely to be any English-speaking staff there.

In the event of a **serious accident** the involvement of an established international recovery agency can be a godsend. These 24/7 organisations are dedicated to the evacuation and, if necessary, repatriation of those injured or taken ill overseas. However, aeromedical transfer is expensive so you need to be sure that your travel insurance includes cover for this eventuality. Your insurance company will want to be involved from the earliest stages and can be a useful ally at this stressful time so should be contacted at the first opportunity.

First-aid training

Ideally, all members of a group should have some first-aid training. If you travel alone you take an accepted risk, but prior first-aid training could still save your own life. In the UK conventional first aid is taught by St John's Ambulance Service (**www.sja.org.uk**), the British Red Cross (**www.redcross org.uk**) or look for 'first aid training' in your region. However, as you can read on p.209, practising first aid in a remote environment with poor communications, adverse conditions and sub-optimal transport is challenging. Add to this that the responsibility may fall on you to straighten broken limbs, stem haemorrhaging and so on, it would be wise to undertake one of the more advanced first-aid courses aimed specifically at expedition first aid.

Aeromedical emergency transfer agencies

First Assist	www.Firstassist.co.uk
Aeromed 365 (UK)	www.aeromed365.com
Air Ambulance Network (USA)	www.airambulancenetwork.com
Swiss Air Ambulance	www.swiss-air-ambulance.ch

It is a good idea to keep all your **important information** and phone numbers together for use in an emergency. Write all of the following onto a piece of card, laminate it and keep it with your passport:

- Information about any medical conditions you have, prescribed medications and known allergies.
- Blood group if known.
- Next of kin with contact details.
- Contact numbers of insurance company, travel agency and some international medical evacuation agencies.
- One fallback number at home who can be contacted in any emergency to help you summon assistance.

First aid and basic trauma management

Significant injuries are rare amongst motorcycle travellers, despite the perception that it is a 'dangerous' form of transport. The key factor to improving survival in the event of a serious accident is prompt access to definitive care, i.e: a hospital with surgery and intensive care facilities. As soon as you have made the scene safe and performed a brief Airway, Breathing and Circulation assessment ('ABC', see below) your priority is to get help to the scene or, depending on experience, location and vehicles available, perform a rapid stabilisation and transport to hospital.

ABC

Although there follows a brief description of the ABC approach to trauma, it must be emphasised that a book is no place to learn such skills. Any group embarking on a serious motorcycle journey needs at least one person who is trained in first aid, for whom this should be an *aide memoire*.

A   Airway and Cervical Spine

The airway extends from the mouth down to the larynx and ends where the trachea (windpipe) divides into the left and right lungs. After trauma the airway may be obstructed by dislodged teeth, blood, facial bone fractures or, most commonly, the tongue falling back into the pharynx (back of the mouth) because the patient has been knocked unconscious. The signs of an obstructed airway include noisy breathing, gurgling and distress. A patient who can talk has a clear airway.

If you suspect airway obstruction you must carefully remove any obvious blockage from the mouth and then perform a **jaw thrust** which will lift the tongue clear of the back of the mouth thus opening the airway. To do this, approach the casualty from their head end, place your thumbs on their cheekbones either side with your middle fingers tucked in behind their jawbone (mandible) in the groove just below the earlobe. Now push the jawbone vertically up towards the sky and hold it there, checking again to see if air is now moving in and out of the patient's lungs. This manoeuvre is safe even in the presence of a possible spinal injury because the head is not tilted – only the jawbone is moved. Basic airway management of this type is the most important skill for any casualty carer. Without a clear airway the casualty will die in minutes.

Cervical spine protection is included with Airway in ABC because of its fundamental importance. What is meant by this is that the force of impact may have fractured neck bones (cervical vertebrae) or disrupted the ligaments which hold the vertebrae together. Any further movement such as turning the head or moving the casualty without proper stabilisation could push the broken bone fragment into the spinal cord thus permanently paralysing the patient from the neck down. However, a patient who is confused, has the distracting pain of a broken limb, or is buzzing from an adrenaline surge may not perceive the pain of a fractured vertebrae, so it is prudent to **assume that every trauma victim has a spinal injury**. Keep the patient still and their head supported in line with their body until professional help arrives.

B   Breathing

Management of specific chest injuries is beyond the scope of this book. However, you can help inbound medical personnel to guide you by exposing the casualty's chest and relaying to them the following information:

- Respiratory rate, i.e: number of breaths per minute.
- Whether there are any open or gurgling chest wounds.
- Whether one side of the chest is moving more than the other.
- Respiratory distress; i.e: is the patient talking normally or short of breath?

Repeat your observations every few minutes.

C   Circulation

Bleeding from open wounds may be easy to identify and stop but not from broken bones or internal organs. As an adult begins to lose some of their five litres of circulating blood, the body compensates by going into shock. This medical application of the word shock refers to significant blood loss not psychological fright.

Signs of shock

- Fast heart rate.
- Fast breathing rate.
- Paleness.

Signs of severe shock include:

- Reduced consciousness level.
- Weak pulse; may be too weak to feel.

At an **accident scene** there are several things you can do to reduce bleeding:

- Always remember scene safety; airway and spinal injury first, no matter how spectacular a wound initially appears.
- Apply firm pressure to wounds. If blood soaks through, apply more padding, always keeping the original directly pressed on the wound.
- Elevate injured limbs.

- Lay the casualty down and raise legs.
- Realign and splint broken bones.
- Internal bleeding into the chest, abdomen or pelvis can only be fixed by surgery. The best way to help here is to summon medical help as quickly as possible.

Fractures and splints

Broken bones are extremely painful, with most of the pain coming from the broken bones grating against each other and the jagged ends sticking into the surrounding muscles and skin at unnatural angles.

It follows that the pain can be greatly reduced by repositioning the broken limb into its normal realignment and holding it in that position. A comfortably splinted arm could make it tolerable to ride pillion on a bumpy track.

In addition to pain relief, the other major benefit of splinting fractured limbs is to reduce blood loss from the ends of the broken bones. To improvise a splint you will need something soft around the limb to provide padding, such as clothing or a sleeping mat, followed by something stiff to fasten to the outside to provide rigidity eg sticks or tent poles. Straighten whilst providing traction (pulling along the length of the limb) and have the splint ready to apply by testing it on the good side beforehand. For the patient this will be extremely painful but you will rarely do any more damage and the end result will be worth it.

Once a limb is immobilised it must be elevated, either in a sling for an arm or onto a padded pannier for a leg.

Other points regarding bone and joint injuries

Dislocations occur when a joint comes out of its socket, typically the shoulder, elbow, fingers or kneecap. The joint will be very painful, immobile and appear deformed compared to the other side. It needs to be located back into the socket by a medically-trained person as soon as possible.

Fractures where the overlying skin is broken are called open fractures. These are serious injuries and need urgent medical attention. Spinal, pelvis, and leg fractures require a stretcher and proper immobilisation so are impossible to transport by motorcycle.

A fractured **collar bone** (clavicle) is relatively common following a fall from a motorcycle. The treatment here is to hang the affected arm in a sling for four weeks. Although intensely painful, there are reports of people continuing to ride with this injury.

Helmet removal

It cannot be emphasised enough that **at the scene of a motorcycle accident, leave the casualty's helmet on until professional help arrives**. Attempts to remove a helmet by untrained persons can worsen a fractured neck and cause permanent total paralysis or even death. Even if you have had a little training or read the description that follows, the attending paramedics will have performed this manoeuvre many times, so leave it to them. This is true in all developing countries. However, a description of the correct technique for hel-

met removal is included here on the premise that in a remote motorcycling emergency where the casualty's airway is compromised, some knowledge is better than none at all. If you're heading on a long, remote trip, go on a first-aid course which covers helmet removal and practise at home until you can get the helmet off without moving the neck at all. Two rescuers are required.

• **Step 1** Rescuer 1 kneels above the patient's head. Grasp the helmet as shown left with fingertips curled around its lower margin touching the mandible (jawbone). Hold firmly to immobilise the head in line with the body.

• **Step 2** Rescuer 2 kneels alongside the patient's torso, opens the visor and checks the airway and breathing, then undoes or cuts the chin strap.

Rescuer 2 then places one hand so that the mandible is grasped between the thumb on one side and the index and middle fingers on the other side. The other hand is placed at the back of the neck with the finger tips reaching up under the back of the helmet.

The rescuer now clamps the patient between their forearm (front) and back (wrist) bracing the head, taking over in-line immobilisation.

• **Step 3** Rescuer 1 now pulls the sides of the helmet apart and rotates the helmet up and backwards by pulling the mouthguard over the patient's nose.

• **Step 4** Next the helmet is rotated the opposite way so that the back of the helmet slides up around the curve of the back of the head.

• **Step 5** Now Rescuer 1 can gently pull the helmet off. After helmet removal, in-line immobilisation must be maintained at all times.

Immunisations

Vaccinations need to be sorted out at least **six weeks** prior to departure as some may require several doses and also to allow time for your sore arm and mild flu-like symptoms to subside.

They're available from your doctor or travel clinic. Depending on where you're going and your prior immunisation status, your doctor will select vaccinations based on current state Health Department and WHO guidelines. Due to these variables your vaccination list might not exactly match that of your travelling companions – a source of anxiety for some but nothing to worry about.

Online you will find a useful vaccine recommendations generator at **www.fleetstreetclinic.com**.

Apart from Yellow Fever, which remains the only disease for which you must hold a WHO-approved certificate for entry into some two-dozen countries, mostly in **Latin America** and **Central Africa**, there is no legal obligation to have any of these jabs prior to travel.

Vaccination course notes

Hepatitis A	Single dose.
Hepatitis B	Three doses at 0, one and six months. Spread by sexual intercourse and blood. Advisable for a prolonged trip.
Japanese B Encephalitis	
	Three doses at 0, seven and 28 days. Recommended for Southeast Asia. Rare but fatal in 30% cases.
Meningitis	Single dose. Africa's 'Meningitis Belt' runs from Senegal to Ethiopia.
Rabies	Three doses at 0, seven and 28 days. Rare but 100% fatal. Prior vaccination only buys time and medical attention must be sought in the event of contact with source.
Tetanus	Single dose. Get up to date before any trip.
Typhoid	Oral or injection. Common in all developing countries.
Yellow Fever	Single dose.
Diphtheria, Polio and Tuberculosis (BCG)	Vaccinations are routinely given in childhood in developed countries. If you think you may not have had them, ask your doctor about a booster dose.

With all these conditions it is worth remembering that having a vaccination does not make you immune and it is always best to avoid coming into contact with the source of the disease in the first place. Having said that it is important to keep in perspective that all these conditions are incredibly rare and it would be a shame to let paranoia about contracting some exotic condition dissuade you.

There are many sources of information about travel vaccinations and other health issues on the internet:

Medical Advisory Service for Travellers Abroad	**www.masta.org**
World Health Organisation	**www.who.int**
Travel Health Online	**www.tripprep.com**
Travel Doctor	**www.traveldoctor.co.uk**

MALARIA

Malaria is endemic throughout the tropical world as far north as southern Turkey, down to the northern part of South Africa. It kills 1–2 million people every year, with travellers being more susceptible than those indigenous to malarial areas.

Since the disease can only be transmitted to humans by the mosquito, the simplest measure is to **avoid being bitten**.

Mosquito avoidance
● Wear long sleeves and long trousers between dusk and dawn when mosquitoes are active.
● Use DEET (50% is enough) containing insect repellent applied to all exposed skin.
● Use individual lightweight mosquito nets. Soak in Permethrin every six months to increase insect repellence.
● Use vaporising insecticides or slow burning mosquito coils in sleeping areas.

Antimalarial medication
There are two vitally important points here which cannot be stressed enough.
● Taking these medicines alone **will not prevent you from catching malaria**; they must be combined with the anti-mosquito measures listed above.

● The course of tablets must be **completed as directed** (i.e. four weeks after returning) even if you are symptom-free, as the organism can lie dormant in your liver.

The choice of anti-malarial drugs which your doctor will prescribe depends on geographical area, time of year and emergence of resistant strains in that area. The tablets will be either daily or weekly. Most of the drugs available will have some side effects, the only one worthy of mention here being Mefloquine (**Lariam**). The side effects of this have been well publicised and include stomach ache, diarrhoea, insomnia, loss of co-ordination and psychological changes, albeit in a minority of people.

However, it is effective against the most dangerous form of malaria (multi-resistant Plasmodium Falciparum strains) and currently recommended for high-risk areas in Africa, the Amazon and South East Asia. Due to the possibility of intolerable side effects occurring, it's advisable to start taking Mefloquine up to a month prior to departure to allow time to change drugs if necessary.

Useful malaria info websites
www.lshtm.ac.uk/malaria
www.malaria-reference.co.uk

Diarrhoea

Loose bowel movements occurs in up to 80% of travellers, usually simply from an altered diet or the stresses of an upset body clock, while infective diarrhoea is caused by contaminated food or water. It follows that the latter may be avoided by taking food handling and preparation precautions:
● Prepare your own food.
● Wash hands frequently.
● Protect food from insects and rodents.
● Keep food preparation surfaces spotless.
● Cook food thoroughly and eat immediately.

In addition be particularly cautious with:
● **Shellfish and crustaceans** As filter feeders they tend to concentrate whatever organisms may be in the local sewage outfall which may also contain poisonous biotoxins.
● **Raw fruit and vegetables** Although 'healthy', the locals may well use human faeces as fertiliser. Clean thoroughly or peel.
● **Dairy products** Boil milk before consumption.

Infective diarrhoea may be caused by viruses (which will not be helped by antibiotics), bacteria (E. Coli) or other parasitic micro-organisms (eg Giardia, Campylobacter, Shigella). Whatever the cause, the symptoms will be loose stools, abdominal cramps and loss of appetite with or without vomiting and high temperature. There may be bloody diarrhoea. These illnesses are usually self-limiting and will settle in a few days without treatment. One exception is amoebic dysentery (caused by an organism called Entamoeba) which is distinguished by a slower onset and bloody diarrhoea without fever. Medical attention with a full course of medicines for around two weeks is always needed.

Treatment

The most important aspect when treating diarrhoea of any cause is **adequate rehydration**. Powder sachets (eg Dioralyte) should be made up with clean water or you can make your own by adding **four teaspoons of sugar plus one teaspoon of salt and a little lemon juice to a litre of water**. Water which has been used to boil rice makes a good alternative.

Antidiarrhoea tablets (Imodium, Arret, etc) temporarily mask the symptoms but prevent the body from flushing the harmful bacteria from the intestines. As such they are best avoided unless you absolutely have to keep riding. The antibiotic Ciprofloxacin (500mg taken twice a day) is effective against most infective causes of diarrhoea but it is only worth considering obtaining a supply from your doctor if you're heading somewhere very remote or tropical.

Medical assistance needs to be sought if you have:

- Diarrhoea for more than four days.
- Diarrhoea with blood.
- Fever (temperature greater than 39°C/102°F) for over 24 hours.
- If confusion develops.

Spiders, snakes, and scorpions

Films like *Arachnophobia*, *Anaconda* and *The Mummy* have much to answer for. Apart from some non-venemous blood sucking/flesh eating spider species, none of the above has much to gain by running up and biting you; you're just too big to eat. They will only resort to doing so as a self-defence measure if they feel threatened.

Of the many **spider species** throughout the world that will give a painful bite, only **four** are actually dangerous to humans. The Sydney Funnel Web is the most poisonous, although no fatalities have occurred since the introduction of antivenom in 1980. First aid for a bite by this spider is similar to that for a snake bite (see below). The other notorious species include Latrodectus (Black Widow, Redback), Loxosceles (Recluse spider of North and South America) and Phoneutria (Brazilian Wandering spider), all of which caused fatalities in the days before the introduction of antivenom. Treatment of these bites consists of cleaning the site, applying a cold pack, giving a pain killer and getting the victim to a hospital.

Snake bites

Irrational fear of snakebites is common among travellers despite the fact that they are exceedingly rare and, with correct management, **hardly ever fatal**.

The most sensible precaution with snakes is simply to avoid the places where they are likely to be. This means wearing covered footwear in long grass or deep sand, stepping well clear of fallen trees and avoiding hollows. Never approach or provoke a snake.

When camping, keep your tent zipped up at all times, shake out your boots, helmet and jacket each morning if left outside, and be extra careful when collecting firewood. Snakes are attracted to your campsite for warmth (your cooling engine or warm body) and food, such as rodents feeding on your scraps. If any of your group is unlucky enough to get bitten by a snake, you will need to take the following action:

- Reassure the victim. They will be terrified and as such their heart will be pumping harder, accelerating the venom through the system.
- Calmly explain that a tiny minority of snakes are lethal to humans and of these, only 10% of bites inject enough venom to be harmful to an adult. You can also add that death from snakebite occurs after hours or days, not immediately as depicted by Hollywood.
- Cover the bite with a clean dressing. Never suck or wash a wound as it does not help and the hospital will need to swab the site to identify the venom.
- Bandage the limb tightly, starting nearest the heart.
- Immobilise the limb by splinting it, eg by strapping a stick to it as any movement speeds up the spread of venom.
- Give paracetamol or codeine painkillers, **not aspirin**.
- Transport to hospital immediately, moving the patient as little as possible.

If you're alone follow the same protocol but leave out the splint – you will still be able to ride. Move quickly but do not run. Never attempt to kill or capture the snake. Ignore local snake-bite remedies – it's the **antivenom** available from a hospital which will save your life should envenomation have occurred.

Scorpion stings

Although dangerous scorpions do exist in Africa, North and South America and the Middle East, the chances of a sting being life threatening are almost zero. The most common effects are severe localised pain, swelling and numbness which begin to subside after one hour, similar to an intense wasp sting. Signs of a more severe sting include sweating, shortness of breath, abdominal pain, high temperatures, progressing very rarely to death. Antivenom exists for these cases. Debate exists as to whether it is necessary to visit hospital after a scorpion sting at all. I would say almost certainly not unless the symptoms are progressive. First aid is as for spider bites (see p.117).

Back pain

Long days spent hunched over the 'bars (as opposed to *at* bars) makes back pain common amongst motorcycle travellers, even in young people and those who have never had any previous problems. Poor posture and relative inactivity cause the muscles of the lower back to go into painful spasm and can irritate the nerves where they run through the muscle causing pain down the back of the leg. This is called **sciatica** and symptoms can be quite debilitating.

The muscles in question do not work in isolation but rather in an important balance with other muscle groups, namely the deep abdominal muscles (Transversus Abdominis), deep back muscle (Multifidus), pelvic floor muscles and the diaphragm. The key to alleviating low back pain is to redress the balance by exercising these other muscles – something which can be done with a few simple exercises as you ride:

- Regularly tense your pelvic floor muscles gently and hold for ten seconds whilst breathing normally. These are the same muscles you use to stop yourself passing urine. If you feel your abdominal wall muscles tighten you are clenching too hard.
- Tilt your pelvis by pushing your hips forward so that your back is straight from top to bottom. Hold for fifteen seconds.

These principles and exercises are the fundamental basis of **Pilates**, a system of exercise which can be of great benefit to back pain sufferers. If you are prone to back pain when you ride you would be well advised to go to some Pilates classes prior to embarking on a long trip. The numerous subtleties are best taught by an instructor and you will learn a number of exercises which you can do while riding.

Exercise

Although motorcycling undoubtedly uses up more calories than driving a car or sitting at home channel surfing, it's important for your general wellbeing to do some **regular aerobic exercise** at the end of a day's riding. Anything which gets your limbs moving and heart pumping will make you feel healthier, sleep better and have more energy to cope with whatever the trip throws at you. Playing keepie up with a hacky sack or running after a frisbee are good sociable activities using items which take up little room in your panniers. Skipping with your tie-down rope is another good one.

Dentistry

The phrase 'prevention is better than cure' has never been more applicable when it comes to teeth problems on the road. A visit to the dentist several months in advance is an essential part of your pre-trip preparation for the following reasons:

- Almost all dental problems are predictable.
- Any small, previously unnoticed dental cavity can turn into a painful infection under the conditions of poor oral hygiene associated with overland travel.
- As Dustin Hoffman found out in *The Marathon Man*, toothache can become one of the worst types of pain and can be incapacitating.
- Dentists are few and far between in the developing world.
- Hygiene standards are not assured in such places. Transmission of HIV, Hepatitis B and C are possibilities.

Should a gum infection occur the symptoms can be subdued with painkillers, frequent teeth cleaning, hot saltwater mouthwashes and the antibiotics from your first-aid kit. **Oil of cloves** is a well-known remedy to numb toothache; keep some in your first-aid kit.

Altitude sickness

Humans can start to feel the effects of lack of oxygen over about 2600m/8500 feet, a height at which your bike engine will still be functioning without a problem.

Most people will feel unwell if they ascend above 3000m (9850ft), with much variation in individual symptoms and their speed on onset. Headache, fatigue, shortness of breath, dizziness and difficulty sleeping are the common complaints which develop within 36 hours and settle within a few days as acclimatisation occurs. They occur simply due to lack of oxygen and are nothing to do with your level of physical fitness or smoking. Acclimatisation is the process by which the body adjusts to the lack of oxygen with increased heart rate, faster breathing rate and more frequent urination. Vivid dreams are normal during this time.

Acute mountain sickness is the most severe form of altitude sickness experienced by mountaineers who climb too rapidly. It can be fatal and must be treated by immediate descent, although ordinarily would not occur at altitudes normally attainable by a motorcycle.

Heat-related illness

Heat-related illness describes a range of symptoms which occur as the body temperature rises; from heat cramps through to heat stroke which can be fatal. Humans need to maintain their internal (core) body temperature within a relatively narrow range of their normal temperature of 36.5°C/97.7°F in order to function properly. Heat acclimatisation is a process that occurs mainly during the first ten days after moving to a hot climate and is aided by exercising at cool times of day for an hour. The body adapts by gradually lowering its core temperature and making the sweat less salty, meaning that you actually have to **drink more** to stay healthy once acclimatised.

The important factors leading to the development of overheating are:
- High ambient temperature.
- Humidity: cooling by sweating is less efficient in high humidity.
- Heat production: exercise, feverish illness.
- Reduced heat dispersal: heavy protective clothing.
- Dehydration.
- Bodily factors: obesity, lack of acclimatisation.
- Alcohol: exacerbates dehydration, reduces perception and appropriate response to overheating.

Symptoms of heat illness include headaches, muscle cramps, nausea and fainting. Swelling hands and feet are common after travel to a hot climate but settle in a few weeks. Any reduced consciousness or confusion in a person with body temperature over 40°C means that **heat stroke** is setting in, requiring urgent cooling treatment and transfer to hospital.

Treatment of heat illness in all cases consists of **cooling and rehydration**. Stop all activity, find shade and lie in a place which allows air to circulate. Evaporation is an efficient cooling technique: undressing the patient, keep the skin moist while fanning. Bathing in water, application of ice packs or transfer to an air-conditioned environment/vehicle also help.

WATER PURIFICATION

Water is lost through sweating, urination and vomiting and in hot climates must be drunk constantly. Even then, it's common to be squeamish about water when on the road. A life lived off taped water makes you forget that this is a natural resource which falls from the sky. Along with **wells**, rivers in wilderness areas as well as shady rockpools in desert areas are most likely all safe sources of natural, clean water.

Polluted water is most commonly found around places of human activity, caused by poor sanitation and unhygenic practices. Luckily, **bottled water** is now commonly available throughout the world. Use it but check the cap seals as refilling empties is a well-known scam in poorer countries.

Eliminating bugs from water can be done in three ways:

- Boiling for four minutes (but see below).
- Sterilising with chemicals like chlorine, iodine or silver.
- Filtration.

Boiling uses up fuel and, along with tablets, does not remove impurities in dirty water. Furthermore, water boils below 100°C as altitude increases, so add a minute to your boil for every 1000 feet/300m above sea level.

Sterilising tablets (or liquids) are a less fiddly way of getting pure drinking water. Cheap and effective, their drawbacks include giving water an unpleasant taste (especially chlorine-based tablets), the need to wait from ten minutes to two hours to take effect, and the fact that they can't remove impurities. Iodine can be poisonous if overdosed and silver compounds are slow. For visibly dirty water pouring through a rag helps as it may remove cysts in which bugs like giardia or amoebic dysentery lie dormant.

BW Technologies

Manually-operated **filter pumps**, like the well-known Katadyns or MSRs are fast but expensive and if the Katadyn's ceramic core cracks as it gets thinner, it's had it. A lighter and more robust alternative is the Aquapure Traveller (right). Fill up the 500ml bottle, shake it and 15 minutes later you can squeeze out the water through the in-built filter cap which needs renewing after 350 litres.

TRAVEL HEALTH TIPS

- **Get immunised** against commonly-known diseases.
- **Avoid getting bitten** by insects, snakes, rodents and, of course, larger predators.
- **Take malaria pills** – better still use a mosquito net and repellent.
- **Take a first-aid kit** containing at least the items listed above.
- **Drink frequently** and if necessary rehydrate (see above).

- Be sure that your **water source** is clean.
- **Eat nutritious** freshly-cooked food and avoid re-warmed meals.
- **Travel insurance** is useful but in the end medical cover is more important than property insurance.
- **Back home**, if you don't feel well (re-adjustment often produces some ailments), consult your doctor and tell them where you've been.

Navigation and survival

Water = time   Fuel = distance

RIDING IN REMOTE AREAS

When riding in remote areas, these things should ensure that you reach your next destination safely:

- A reliable and well-equipped machine.
- Ample provisions for the route.
- Some company.
- Common sense.

Riding and navigating in a wilderness require a clear thinking mind aware of its own fallibility. It is very rare that you will become completely lost. You must use your logic and common sense to work out where you went wrong, and correct your mistake sooner rather than later.

NAVIGATION

Navigation anywhere requires knowledge of **where you are** as much as **where you're going**. Even on the tarmac highway where distances between settlements are vast, you should always take the trouble to know your position as accurately as possible. When on the dirt, landmarks such as major river crossings, distinctive mountains or steep passes should be anticipated with regular reference to your map, odometer and guidebook or route notes.

Anticipating landmarks becomes all the more important when riding in remote areas – generally deserts or mountains – when confirmation of your position adds much needed confidence. For example, stopping at a fork in the road, your map indicates a distinct turn to the south about 70km ahead where your route enters a narrow valley. Add 70 to your current odometer reading and memorise or write down the total figure 'turn south, valley, xkm'. As 'x km' approaches on your trip you should expect to turn south, allowing a bit of slack for your rough estimate.

Paper maps – much more usable than a 2" LCD screen.

Maps

A good map and knowing how to use it is of course essential to this sort of riding. As a rule, a detailed map with a **medium scale** of 1:1 million (where 1cm = 10km or 6.2 miles) is adequate for riding across regions with tracks but no signposts. A scale of 1:500,000 is better if you're looking to pick your way around sand seas or over indistinct passes. If you're trying to pinpoint some unmarked historical or archeological site, for example, a **large scale map** of 1:200,000 (where each centimetre represents 2km or 1.2 miles) or less will help you distinguish every valley, mountain and river. At this level of navigation a GPS unit (see next page) becomes very useful.

Don't count on getting large scale maps in the African or Asian countries you're planning to visit. They're usually hoarded by the military and may require complicated applications to buy while being more easily available in your home country. Note that in barren wilderness areas, the age of the map may not be so critical as in urban areas; things don't change much in the Sahara or the Hindu Kush. The French IGN maps of West Africa produced over forty years ago at the scales mentioned above are as good, if not better, for riding off the main routes than the commonly-used **small-scale** 1:4m Michelin map which gets updated every other year.

Trip meter and orientation

On a long route of a few days it's a good idea to note down the details of the complete itinerary such as distances, landmarks, forks in the trail, lakes and rivers, and stick them to your handlebars or tank bag for easy reference. Estimate your total fuel range conservatively and work out the mileage reading at which you expect to run out. Ensure that your destination is a maximum of 75% of your range allowing 25% leeway.

Reset your trip odometer at the beginning of a stage when all your reserves have been replenished, and only reset it at your next safe destination or when you totally refuel your tank. For this sort of riding the resettable trip is a far more useful instrument than your speedometer needle, and is why a spare speedo cable should be carried amongst your essential spares (although a GPS has a trip function too). Both tell you how far you've travelled and so act as a guide to your position and, crucially, your remaining reserves of fuel.

For quick checks on your orientation (south-east, west-north-west, etc) it's easier to use **the sun** rather than referring to an on-board compass or GPS. The fine degrees of accuracy a compass can offer are not usually necessary for ordinary navigation. Always keep half an eye out for the sun and get to know the directions of the shadows at various times of the day. After a while, a quick glance at your shadow and your watch will instantly tell you whether you are riding in the right direction.

Not getting lost

All these precautions are designed to mitigate the apprehensiveness of riding into a wilderness. Blindly following tracks without giving a thought to landmarks, orientation or maps is the most common way of getting lost. Sometimes a track can inexplicably begin to turn the wrong way or peter out altogether. If you're tired, low on fuel or your bike is running badly, these moments of uncertainty can lead to careless decisions, such as trying to take a short-cut back to your last known position. Correcting these sorts of mistakes in your navigation is where a bike's barely adequate fuel reserves are often used up. Off a track and in mixed terrain, getting totally disorientated is as easy as falling off your bike; and if you're pinned down by your bike just a mile off a track, but out of sight, you may never be found.

If ever in doubt, **stop and think** – never carry on regardless hoping that things will work themselves out. Look around you and consult your map and GPS carefully. Look out for stone cairns, traces of corrugated track or any other clues as to where you might be. Without a GPS, if you're lucky enough to have a major landmark such as a distinctive peak which is marked on your map take a bearing to help narrow down your position. It's a rare luxury to have two such landmarks in view but if they are sufficiently far apart you can accurately triangulate your position on a map and you're no longer lost. If this is not possible and you haven't a clue, turning back is the only answer.

Riding together

Getting completely lost is rare, but on or off the highway or in a busy city, losing sight of your riding companions is common. Before you set out, establish some clear rules and signals.

Out on the plains, bikes can ride side by side, but if riding in line on narrow tracks, one rider should take the lead and keep it, glancing back regularly for his companions. If the group is of mixed riding ability it's best for the slowest rider to lead, even if it becomes frustrating for the hotshots. The simplest **signal** should be flashing headlights: 'I am slowing down or stopping' – on seeing this the leader should stop and wait or turn back if necessary. For this reason it's worth retaining at least one of your **rear view mirrors**.

A common way to lose each other is when the leader stops to wait for the follower to catch up (there a real-time scene of such an event in my *Desert Riders* dvd). After a while of waiting and wondering, the leader retraces his route to look for the other rider. In the meantime the following rider, having seen the leader rider struggle through some mud (for example), has taken another route around a rise and races ahead to catch the leader, who by now is inexplicably out of sight. It is the responsibility of all riders to look out for each other – this should stop any arguments about whose fault it was. The leader should slow down or stop if he gets too far ahead of the rest of the group, who in turn should never stray from the route.

If you do lose sight of each other, ride to some high ground, turn off your engines, look around and listen for the others. In this position you're also more likely to be seen by the others. Failing this, an agreed procedure should be adhered to. For example, after a certain time out of contact, you should all return to the point where you last stopped or spoke together. If fuel is critical you should stop ahead at a clear landmark, such as a village or junction.

The whole point of riding together is to give each other much-needed support during a risky endeavour, so resist any individualistic tendencies and stick together while traversing remote tracks.

GPS

It is fun though, and I'd much prefer to have [a GPS] than not, but a paper map, sufficiently detailed, should be your main guide with the GPS offering valuable and time saving support. HU Forum

GPS receivers triangulate satellite signals to pinpoint your position anywhere on earth within minutes and to an accuracy of just a few metres. The size of last year's mobile phone and from around $100 so anyone can afford one.

Just three satellites are required to get a '3D' fix (longitude, latitude and elevation), ideally under an open sky with one satellite overhead and the others close to the horizon. Without local booster antennae, regular GPS signals are weak so cliffs and tall buildings may hamper acquisition. Heavy cloud should not impede signals.

Cross country out in the wide open spaces is where a GPS can become essential.

On turning on your receiver, the position and signal strengths of available satellites are clearly displayed on an LCD screen followed in a couple of minutes by your co-ordinates. These are displayed in traditional longitude and latitude or several other standards like UTM.

For most people the above function is sufficient, but receivers can also record 'waypoints' along your route and compute calculations including your orientation (bearing), speed, estimated arrival time to a given point, as well as a bearing towards a given point. They can do all this and much more as you move along, though this will reduce battery life (commonly 2 AA units). To run your GPS continuously either **hard wire** it to your bike's electrical system or use a DIN plug. The more common cigarette lighter plugs they are sold with are not good enough for rough riding. If contact is lost for just a split second your unit turns off and you lose the track and distance record.

GPS maps

The map data included on the latest GPSs have become useful for navigation in developed countries; places which already have a good infrastructure and signage, although easily reading the detail of GPS maps (as opposed to a big arrow in 'Go to' mode) while riding a bike is another matter. For most places in Africa and Asia the available GPS mapping information will only be useful for navigation along main highways to major cities (Latin America is reportedly better). If you are planning to get off the beaten track you'll need old fashioned **paper maps** (and if you want to translate your position, a paper map with long' and lat' grids – not all have them). Coverage is bound to improve with updated maps importable off CDs or websites.

Contrary to popular belief, a GPS has not yet replaced the need for conventional map reading and orientation any more than the Internet has replaced books. Knowing exactly where you are is academic if you've just run out of fuel or have broken a leg and distances can only be given in straight lines, the real distance along bendy roads will always be longer (and probably indicated on a paper map or on a road sign). GPS receivers won't get you out of trouble when lost, but they can quickly *stop you amplifying navigational errors* in the first place by confirming that you're off course.

They are of course useful for recording positions to pass on to those who follow. As another HU Forum contributor put it: '*All I used my GPS for was to record the co-ordinates of each night's camp. It's a nice gadget to have along but not essential*'.

SURVIVAL

Compared to cars, motorcycles are fairly reliable by virtue of their simplicity. The most likely causes of immobility are punctures, running out of fuel or an accident. A more serious situation might occur when you find yourself trapped by an immobile or irretrievable bike, or an unrideable situation, such as flooding or a sand storm. Once you're certain that riding your machine out is not an option, your next priority is to rescue yourself. Act in accordance with the '3 Ps' of outdoor survival:

Protection (shelter)

Arranging shelter from the elements, primarily heat, cold wind or precipitation, will greatly extend your ability to survive, now that you're solely dependant on yourself for mobility. In the case of an injured partner, shelter will be essential while you go to get help.

Depending on where you are, this means erecting shade or a windbreak if you're not carrying a tent. Get in the habit of wearing some kind of head covering to minimise heat loss or sunstroke; a crash helmet or a scarf will do if you've no hat. With protection secured you can now turn your attention to either recovering your bike, rescuing your partner, or preparing to walk out.

Position

If you've been regularly referring to your map, odometer and available landmarks, or you have a GPS and a good map, your position should not be hard to pinpoint. It may be just a short walk back to the last village, where someone can help you drag your bike out of a ravine, or it may be sixty miles to a minor highway. If you're sure no one will come this way you must be prepared to walk back to the last known sign of human presence.

Look on the map to see if there may be some place you could get help which you'd overlooked. Think about the easiest way of getting there avoiding steep gradients and other obstacles. Consider torching your bike, or just a smoky component like a tyre or a seat, but only when you can see someone who might see your signal. *Don't waste smoke and signals on the off chance that they may be spotted.*

Provisions

Establish the quantities of all your provisions, how much food and water you have and how many days it will last, including any emergency rations you may have stashed away. **Water** is by far the most critical aid to survival. Wherever you are you can survive a lot longer without food which you should consume frugally anyway, as digestion uses up water.

Staying where you are obviously uses less energy but might not be an option offering much hope. Think about what provisions you might find along the way. If there's a river, stick close to it, settlements or human activity usually accompany them.

Walking out

It's often said that staying with your vehicle and its resources is the key to survival but this usually refers to cars, which are more conspicuous. Certainly if you've checked out along a certain route, there's a chance that someone will come looking for you.

EMERGENCY EQUIPMENT

- Lighter or matches
- Aluminium space blanket or sleeping bag – for daytime shade and night-time warmth
- High energy compact rations
- Rescue flares: hand-held smoke or rocket. Use your rocket flares only when you are certain they will be seen by potential rescuers
- Compass and map
- Torch
- Binoculars. Useful when looking for lost companions or distant landmarks
- All the water you can carry

Use the comfort and facilities of your makeshift camp to prepare carefully for the walk out. You should carry as little as possible (see the box above), wear light and comfortable clothing and, most importantly, cover your head against the sun during the day and the cold at night.

As soon as you begin walking your water consumption will increase. Even on firm ground you're unlikely to average more than two miles per hour. If you've more than a few miles to walk in a hot environment, wait till evening or early morning when lower temperatures make distance walking less tiring.

The first four items listed above are best wrapped up in duct tape and stored in a secure place before you leave on your trip. Now they will be needed. To carry water efficiently, a harness should be made up to support this heavy weight on your back – a rucksack may now be useful. Avoid carrying heavy items in your hands. Follow tracks and avoid short cuts and/or steep ascents unless you are certain they are worthwhile. Conserve energy and, therefore, water at all costs.

Walking out should not be considered lightly; it's a last resort to save yourself when all else has failed. Attempt it only if you're certain your emergency situation could not be solved less drastically by staying put.

Rules of survival

The following rules will help ensure your well being in remote areas; they are not in any strict order of importance.

- **NEVER TAKE CHANCES** Keep on the track, carry adequate reserves of fuel and water, and ride within your limitations.
- **DON'T WASTE WATER** but drink as much as you need.
- **CARRY ENOUGH FUEL AND WATER FOR YOUR ENTIRE ROUTE** Recognise that difficult terrain and maximum loading may increase consumption of these vital fluids.
- **CARRY ESSENTIAL SPARES AND TOOLS** And know how to use them. You should at least be familiar with tyre removal and repair (see pp.64-9), oil and air filter changes and fault diagnosis.
- **NEVER CARRY ON WHEN LOST** Stop before you go too far, accept that you have made a mistake, and retrace your steps if necessary.
- **IF YOU CHECK OUT ON DEPARTURE, CHECK IN ON ARRIVAL** An essential courtesy that may prevent wasted searches.
- **KEEP YOUR COMPANIONS IN SIGHT AT ALL TIMES** Or tell them what you're doing and where you're going.
- **NEVER DRIVE AT NIGHT** Even on tarmac roads there is a danger of unlit vehicles, stray animals and potholes.

© ANDY MILLER

Off-highway riding

It's possible to traverse South America and Asia and rarely leave the tarmac, but if you're heading off the main highway or across Africa, gravel roads, sandy *pistes* and muddy jungle tracks are a fact of life. Wherever you go in the world, mastering the techniques of riding your heavy overlander off sealed highways will be one of the major elements of your adventure. When there's a trail of dust billowing off your back wheel (as above) you can't help thinking you really are abroad, far away from civilisation and heading into the unknown. Sealed highways are handy for shopping or getting to work, but the dirt is where it's at. It is here that adventures are ripe for the taking, from uninterrupted vistas across the wilderness to unexpected encounters with the people you meet out there in the back of beyond.

On the dirt, traction is unpredictable and constant reading of the terrain ahead is vital. It's this keyed-up involvement that makes off-roading so rewarding. Ever since Kenny Roberts rewrote the book on GP racing, it's common knowledge that today's top racers developed their rear-wheel steering and sharp reactions from sliding around on dirt bikes. And besides the improvements to your road-riding skills, off-roading provides the exhilaration of road racing at a fraction of the speed. By the end of the day you'll be parked up in some scenic and remote location, shagged-out, filthy, but satisfied. Unless I'm very much mistaken, it's what adventure motorcycling is all about.

(Opposite) Top: With a jerrican and a set of Michelin Deserts the Sahara is yours. **Bottom:** A shady spot in the Libyan Sahara – but watch out for thorns. **(Overleaf):** Black Rock Desert, Nevada. © Tom Grenon.

Gently does it

Riding off-road is fun, but until you get the hang of handling your loaded bike on various surfaces, you should take it easy. As a general rule you'll find **50mph/80kph** is a maximum cruising speed on any dirt surface. At speeds greater than this it's not possible to react quickly enough to the ever-changing surface – riding on dirt is never predictable.

Overland biking is not about smoking kneepads (but if you do, choose the filtered brands); it's about long-term survival, so never take risks, resist the impulse to show off and always ride within the limitations of:

- Your vision.
- The terrain.
- Your experience.
- Your bike's handling abilities.

And be aware of the consequences of:
- An accident.
- Getting lost.
- Running out of fuel or water.

Ready for a beating

Be in no doubt about the hammering your bike is going to get on dirt roads, or the just as frequent broken tarmac roads that you'll find beyond your home country. Much of the advice on bike preparation given in earlier chapters is concerned with limiting damage when riding over rough terrain. Lightly-framed dual sports with heavy loads, or cast-wheeled road tourers were not built for a beating on corrugated tracks and frame, rack or tank fractures are the second most common mechanical problem after punctures. Besides offering agility in the dirt, a lightly-loaded bike will put less stress on the already hard working wheels, suspension and transmission. Make sure it's up to it.

DIRT ROADS

Most of your off-roading will be on dirt roads of varying quality. At their best they're straight and flat, with a smooth and consistent surface requiring little

need for reduced speeds. But dirt being what it is, this won't last for long and most tracks will have been rutted by heavy traffic, washed-out by rains, blown over with sand, littered with rocks and, likely as not, corrugated.

Corrugations

Corrugations are another name for the washboard surface which an unconsolidated track develops as a result of regular, heavy traffic. The accepted explanations for these infuriatingly regular ripples of dirt are braking and acceleration, forces of passing traffic or the

(Opposite) Scene from the troubled *Desert Travels* tour.

'tramping' shock absorbers of heavy trucks with antediluvian suspension.

In a car you grit your teeth and pray that the shock absorbers won't explode; the best solution is to accelerate up to about 50mph/80kph and skim across the top of each ripple, so reducing vibration dramatically. On a bike, the same practice gives a smoother ride too, but at this speed your wheels are barely touching the ground and your traction is negligible. In a straight line this is not too dangerous, but on a bend it's possible to slide right off the track.

Wealthier countries grade their corrugated dirt roads once in a while but the honeymoon only lasts a few weeks. In the developing world, the passing of a grader is most likely an annual event.

The good thing is that on a bike you only need a tyre's width to get by and you'll often find corrugations shallowest or non-existent on either edge of the track, though rarely for more than a few metres at a time. You'll find yourself forever weaving around trying to find the smoothest path. On a plain it might be easier to avoid a corrugated track altogether and ride in far greater comfort and freedom alongside the track, but realistically this option is rare.

Corrugations do have one small saving grace. If ever you're lost or wondering which way to go, the most corrugated track is the one most frequently used and probably the one you want to follow. There may even be times out in the desert when, a little lost, the sight and feel of corrugations will be an immense relief, signifying that you've relocated a major track from which you may have inadvertently strayed.

But, overall, corrugations are just a miserable fact of dirt-roading and a good place to have knobbly tyres with slightly reduced pressures, a well-supported subframe, a comfy seat and a firmly wrapped kidney belt. Even on the spine-powdering ascent to the Assekrem Pass in Algeria's Hoggar mountains, the worst, denture-loosening patches last only for 20 minutes or so. Who knows why corrugations periodically flatten out, but it's a chance to rest before gritting your teeth for the next batch.

When the going gets rough, stand up

Standing on the footrests over rough ground is probably the most important technique beginners should master because when you're standing up:

- Suspension shocks are taken through your legs not your back.
- Your bike is much easier to control.
- Being higher up, your forward vision is improved.

Contrary to the impression that standing up makes you less stable it, in fact, has the opposite effect. It transfers your weight low, through the footrests, rather than through the saddle when you're seated. This is why trials riders and motocrossers always tackle tricky sections standing up on the pegs.

You don't have to stand right up, just 'weighting the footrests' will do. © A Miller

When standing up, **grip the tank** lightly between your knees to give your body added support and to prevent the bike from bouncing around between your legs. Padding on the inside of your knees or on the tank helps here.

As you get the hang of things, standing, just like sticking your leg out on a slithery bend, will soon become instinctive. You'll find it's not always necessary to stand right up; sometimes just leaning forward and pulling on the bars while taking the weight off your backside will be enough to lessen the jolt. In a nutshell: **sit down when you can, stand up when you must**.

RIDING IN SAND

Sand can be great to ride over if it's consistently firm, but in somewhere like the Sahara riding on sand requires a high degree of concentration – it's at its most demanding when riding through very soft fine sand or when forced along a track rutted by cars. Riding *along* rather than just across a sandy creek presents the most difficult condition that a desert biker regularly encounters. Here, fine waterborne sand is washed down by flash floods, and you can find yourself riding standing up in one- or two foot-wide ruts for miles at a time. Extremely tiring! You'll find more detailed guidelines on riding in deserts (and a lot more besides) in my other book, *Sahara Overland* (see p.180).

Low tyre pressures

By dropping the air pressure to as little as 5psi (0.3 bar), a tyre flattens out and its 'footprint' on the sand lengthens significantly (rather than widens, although it does that a little, too). Doing this changes your normally round tyre into more of a caterpillar track, increasing your contact patch and improving your traction dramatically, even with a trail or a road tyre. It can mean the difference between riding confidently across a sandy section or slithering around barely in control, footing constantly, losing momentum and finally getting stuck or falling over – every few minutes.

The trouble is that in this severely under-inflated state a tyre gets much hotter, due to the internal friction created by the flexing carcass (just as you get hot doing exercise). Softening with the heat, a tyre becomes much more prone to punctures. Keep your speed down on very soft tyres and be sure your security bolts or similar devices are done up tight as it's in just these low-pressure/high-traction situations that the dreaded tyre creep occurs.

Momentum and acceleration

These are often the only two things that will get you through a particularly soft stretch of sand, so don't be afraid to stand up and accelerate hard at the right time. A quick snap of the throttle in a middle gear gives you the drive and stability to blast assuredly across a short, sandy creek as the front wheel skims over the surface. No matter how much your back wheel weaves and bucks around, keep the power on and your backside off the seat for as long as it takes. So long as the front wheel remains on course you're largely in control. Keep off the brakes, especially the front. If you need to slow down

Lose momentum (or traction) and all you can do is push. © Andy Bell

use the engine to decelerate and be ready for the bike to become unstable.

Riding like this is very tiring, but in most cases even trying to slow down and stop will mean falling over or getting bogged. For those keen to ride to Timbuktu, note that the track from Bourem in the east requires riding like this for 200 miles/300km! Sand riding can be hair-raising stuff and you'll often come close to falling off, but the above techniques are the only way to get through soft sand short of paddling along at 1mph.

Try not to stop on this surface; you may find it hard to get going again.

Sandy ruts

About 25mph/40kph in third is the best speed/gear combination to maintain when riding along sandy ruts, the low gear and high revs giving quick throttle response to further difficulties you may encounter. Slow down through the gears not the brakes and don't be reluctant to rev your engine hard if necessary. It's in this situation where unreliable or ill-tuned engines begin to play up or overheat.

If you are in a deep rut, stay in it and don't try to cross ruts or ride out unless absolutely necessary. If you must change ruts urgently, hurl your bike and your weight in the preferred direction of travel while standing up and gassing it... but don't expect to get away with these kind of moves on a tanked-up 1150 with your missus on the back.

RIDING THROUGH MUD

Even on a 120kg competition bike with fresh knobblies, mud and especially bogs or swamps can present the dual challenge of negligible traction and treacherous suction. Coping with this sort of terrain on an overland porker is plain exhausting, and while sand riding responds to certain acquired techniques, the occluded consistency of water-logged terrain has no cut and dried rules, but if you can:

- avoid big mires if at all possible;
- ride in one muddy rut and stick to it, either attacking it standing up or, if you don't feel confident, paddling of even walking through;
- approach deep water-logged sections with caution; ride through slowly to avoid drowning the engine or coming off on submerged obstacles.

Some tracks crossing the Congo and Amazon basins and in far Eastern Russia are notorious riding challenges. Hundred-metre-long puddles stretch before you with vehicles sometimes backed up behind a bogged-down truck.

On a bike, tyres are critical: aggressive treads at low pressures make all the difference. Blasting into a huge puddle on an African track is a recipe for a muddy face plant. If you can't find a way around the side, recognise that it's going to be a slow and tiring paddle, and be ready to stop if the trough deepens. You're usually forced to ride through the trenches dug by the last truck's spinning wheels, but depending on the period since the rains ended these pits can drown an entire car. If you're not sure, **wade through first**.

Trying to ride through wet muddy ruts might be hard, but worse still is when they harden into concrete-hard trenches. In mountain areas, where you can't necessarily ride around these, manoeuvring a big bike or one with ordinary tyres will be sub-walking-pace torture. You'll have to drop into the ruts and paddle along, being careful that the sides don't deflect the wheel and dump you on the hard surface. It's the only way forward except for those skilled few who can style through on the footrests with a light front end and one hand on their hips.

With the right tyres you can chug steadily through muddy ruts. © Matt Ball

Bogs and swamps

The large expanses of water-logged wilderness found in temperate zones can be harder still to deal with, and no one in their right mind would push a track through this sort of terrain. Perhaps the best known example is the Kolyma Highway in Russia between Yakutsk and Magadan (see p.168), only rideable in summer by which time the tundra melts into a quagmire.

This is not a place to ride alone: in the desert you can extricate a bike from sand with a little digging and along the flooded channels of central Africa there are usually enough other travellers or villagers around to help out. Riding your bike up to its bars into a Russian bog may be the last time you ride it. Learn to recognise what sort of vegetation, be it reeds or moss, inhabits water-logged ground; keeping to high ground is not always the answer. Even with help, in terrain like this your mileages may drop to as little as ten miles per day while your ability to deal with this exhausting pace can be numbered in hours. Take on challenging new routes by all means, but be under no illusion as to how hard this task will be.

RIVER CROSSINGS

Who can resist the thrill of cutting a V-shaped shower of spray as you blast across a shallow river? The other end of this photogenic scenario is a bent crankshaft in an engine ruined by hydraulic lock: the consequences of a piston sucking in and trying to compress uncompressable water.

The first thing to do when you come to a substantial and unfamiliar water crossing is to stop and have a good look. Just because tracks lead down one bank and up the other doesn't mean the crossing is safe. In tropical or arid regions distant storms can raise an unfordable creek miles from the downpour in a matter of hours. And in a few more hours that river might be just a series of trickling pools. Furthermore, in recreational or farming areas 4WDs can churn up the river bed, creating mud or ruts which may tip you over.

Walk first

If in doubt about the river crossing **walk across first**: a wet pair of boots is less inconvenient than a drowned engine. Walking across establishes the strength of the current, the nature of the river bed and, of course, the maximum depth.

If you're confident or have walked it first,
ride through, otherwise play it safe and push.
© Craig Hightower

If you feel the combination of current, river bed and depth make riding possible – generally, if you can walk it, you can ride it – ride the bike through slowly, following the exact route of your foot reconnaissance. Still waters are usually deepest, so pick a spot just above some rapids; the water may be moving fast, but it's shallow. Keep the revs high in first or second gear. This helps run through any electrical spluttering, avoids stalling and keeps a good pressure of exhaust blowing out of the silencer. Resist splashing which sprays electrics and may kill the engine. Generally the 'plimsoll line' on most bikes is halfway up the barrel, below the carb, but wet electrics can snuff out an engine when blasting through a two-inch puddle.

Waterproofing your bike's electrics should have been part of your pre-departure preparation, but before you take the dive, spray in and around the plug cap and other vital ignition components with a water dispersing agent like WD40. Many singles like KLRs cut out when the **carb breather**, usually down near the right footrest, goes underwater – other bikes can suck water into the carb in this way. A **T-piece** spliced into that breather with an extension leading up under the tank will solve this.

Remember that the consequences of falling over are as bad as riding in too deep; keep your finger over the kill switch and use it the moment you lose control. Once on the far side expect your brakes not to work and a bit of spluttering as the engine steams itself dry.

Pushing across

If riding is too risky walk your bike across with yourself on the upstream side so there's no chance of getting trapped under the bike should you get pushed over. If your baggage looks like getting soaked, you may prefer to unpack it and bring it over on your shoulders. It may be a good idea anyway, lightening the bike if you have to push it across the river with the engine off.

Whether you walk the bike across with the engine running or not depends on the risk of the water rising about the air intake. If you go for a running engine keep your thumb on the kill switch in case you fall or it gets deep.

Truly, madly, deeply

Very rarely you might come to a river crossing which is way too deep to ride through but which, for whatever reason, you simply must cross; the aforementioned road to Magadan has several deep river crossings early in the summer. With careful preparation it's possible to totally submerge a bike providing the fuel, induction and exhaust systems are completely sealed off.

Doing this is no small job and you risk losing or ruining your bike, so make sure there's no alternative. Naturally the maximum depth you can walk through is limited by your height, but realistically don't attempt anything deeper than the height of the bars and don't try this radical procedure alone.

DROWNED ENGINE: WHAT TO DO

The worst has happened and your bike has taken a lung-full while running, or has fallen over and filled up. It's not the end of the world; this is what to do:

- Stand the bike on its end and drain the exhaust.
- Drain the petrol tank.
- Take out the spark plug and kick or tip out the water.
- Drain the carb and dry the filter.
- Remove the stator cover (on the left side of most singles), drain and dry it.
- If the engine oil has a milky colour, it's contaminated with water and needs changing.
- Once everything has dried out, test for a spark first and, if the bike runs, give it a full re-lube at the earliest opportunity.

Before you go ahead, establish the answers to these questions first:

- Is there a bridge or a ferry in the vicinity?
- Is there a shallower place to cross?
- Can you get the bike in a boat or the back of a truck?
- Can you leave the bike and swim across instead?
- Are there enough of you to carry lightened bikes across (on your shoulders or on sticks)? This will take *at least* three people per bike.
- Do you have the means to waterproof the bike and can get across without putting yourself in danger?
- Are you sure there are not more such rivers ahead – do you have the provisions to take them on?

If the answer to the first four is 'no' and the rest is 'yes' this is what to do:

- Remove as much weight from the bike as possible, including the tank.
- Kick over the engine so that it's on compression with both sets of valves closed (this only works with singles).
- Plug the exhaust securely.
- Disconnect the battery completely.
- Take out the air filter, wrap it in a plastic bag and reinstall it.
- Fold over all oil tank, battery, engine and carb breather hoses so they're sealed and tape them up.
- If you have some rope, set up a line from bank to bank, or to the bike so someone can help pull it through from the far bank.

Once you're certain the engine is watertight and you're all sure you can manage the feat, then push the bike in, at least one pushing from behind and one steering on the upstream side of the bike and another pulling the bike on a rope.

Now the bike's totally submerged there is no rush, take it easy; don't be distracted by bubbles rising from the bike; whatever's leaking it's too late to do anything about it now.

On the far bank let the bike drip dry – do not attempt to start it until you're sure it's fully drained. Pull out the exhaust bung and stand the

Walk first or drain later.

ROAD RIDING

Riding the roads of over-populated developing countries will be stressful in the extreme, nowhere more so than India where a collection of animal, vegetable and mineral hazards combine to give your brakes plenty of exercise (full list on p.153).

Basically, be ready for anything. Sudden stops without brake lights, cutting in, drunken drivers, things thrown out of windows, dead animals, live animals, holes in the road, a barbed wire road block, the list goes on and on. Anything goes on the highways of most of the world – just make sure those things don't get you.

Other traffic

You may complain about inconsiderate car drivers in your own country but you've seen nothing until you've ridden in **Colombia, Ethiopia, Iran** and, worst of all, **India**. Every year of motorbiking experience will stand you in good stead as you try and anticipate the hare-brained driving of most commercial drivers. Short of staying at home, alert, assertive riding and frequent use of your horn is the only way to deal with hazards posed by your fellow road users.

In poor countries ancient vehicles are kept running on a wing and a prayer. Expect not a shred of courtesy, instead be prepared for downright homicidal hostility. Don't count on insurance either, by and large other drivers won't have any and neither will you. All you can do is keep your speed down, your eyes open and ride to survive.

Pedestrians, carts and animals

What is it about animals and some villagers that makes them run out as you approach? They certainly wouldn't try it in front of a fume-spewing truck. As if dangerously driven cars and trucks weren't enough, most roads in developing countries are thoroughfares for anybody or anything on the move. Again, all you can do is give them a wide berth at slow speed with the brake levers covered.

Children and wild animals, like camels or kangaroos, have a habit of running startled across your path at the last second so always exercise extreme caution when nearing villages or herds of grazing beasts.

Potholes

Potholes are contagious. Once one appears, you can be sure that there'll be more ahead. You have to concentrate hard in these sections, as the mindless routine you have been used to on the smooth, empty highway is soon disrupted by hard braking, swerving and re-acceleration. A pothole's sharp edges can easily put a dent in a wheel rim so be prepared to manoeuvre to avoid this.

Luckily, on a bike you can squeeze through tyre-wide sections of solid tarmac where two holes are about to meet and generally you'll have an easier time of it than cars. In the end, if the road gets really bad, you may have the option of riding alongside, which may be no quicker but will prove more consistent than a badly damaged road.

bike on its back wheel draining any water which may have leaked in. Release the breather hoses, take off the carb and drain it, making sure there's no water in the inlet manifold. Take out the air filter, drain the airbox and reinstall the filter. Remove the spark plug and kick over the engine, hoping that no water spurts out of the plug hole; if it does check your engine oil over the next few miles of riding. If it's turned milky it has become contaminated with water and you should change it or continue slowly until you can.

Once all these procedures have been completed check for a spark and if all's well, fire the bike up and hope there's not another deep river a few miles further down the road!

PART 2: CONTINENTAL ROUTE OUTLINES

This section inevitably paints a picture about as broad as a V-Max in a mangle. Your opportunities are infinite but not wanting to jump in the deep end, most **first-timers** set out to follow established routes as indicated on the maps, venturing out off the beaten track as their confidence builds.

'Easy' countries are skimmed over: get a guide book. Detail here focuses on tricky but accessible areas like Central Asia and Central Africa, as well as shipping connections. This kind of information changes fast, though: it goes without saying that you should **seek more up-to-date information prior to your departure**.

Asia

From Istanbul eastwards for thousands of miles to a stone's throw from Alaska, and from above the Arctic Circle to below the equator and a short hop to Australia, the world's biggest landmass just about has it all. And for the overland rider it's easier than you think. Asia offers sealed road links from London's Piccadilly Circus all the way to Kathmandu and the Indian subcontinent (with a freight hop to Singapore) or, with a couple of thousand kilometres of gravel, rivers and mud as a finale, to Far Eastern Russia.

Part of the appeal of Asia is the **low cost of living** in the south (much less than Africa, for example); fuel prices here are among the cheapest in the world which adds up to longer travels for your money. Apart from obvious hot spots like Chechnya, Iraq and Afghanistan – Burma (Myanmar) and **China**, either forbid or severely discourage independent travel with motor vehicles. China requires exorbitant guide fees or expensive transportation on a rented truck which, time wise, is only viable between the Karakoram and Kyrgyzstan.

Principal overland routes; taïga, steppe or tropics

Trans-Asia is principally a lateral transit so, broadly speaking, you have three main routes. The **high route** runs across Russia between Japan/North America and Europe; easy in the west, potentially gruelling in the Russian Far East. The **middle route** also takes a northern passage via Turkey and the Caucasus through Central Asia with an optional dip into Mongolia. Finally the **low route** runs from the Middle East to India and Southeast Asia, but, until Myanmar eases up, requires freighting across the Bay of Bengal.

The routes' western termini are variable: Europe or North Africa, while around Turkey and Iran the high and low routes are interweavable with the middle route. On the east side the mass of China divides your options: taïga or the tropics, take your pick. On this side the mainland termini of all routes are more specific: Magadan and Vladivostok or Singapore/Kuala Lumpur, from where planes, ferries and freighters lead to adjacent continents.

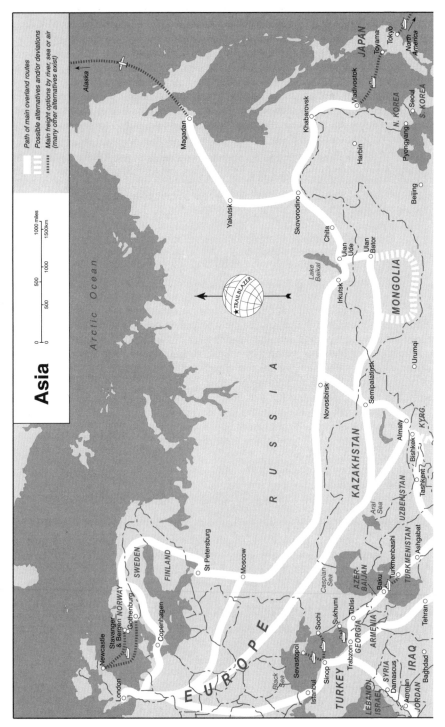

Asia

Path of main overland routes

Possible alternatives and/or deviations

Main freight options by river, sea or air
(many other alternatives exist)

1000 miles
1500km
500
1000
500
0
0

Arctic Ocean

Alaska

Magadan

Yakutsk

Skovorodino

Khabarovsk

Vladivostok

JAPAN

Toyama

Tokyo

North America

Harbin

N. KOREA

Pyongyang

Seoul

S. KOREA

Beijing

Chita

Ulan Ude

Ulan Bator

MONGOLIA

Lake Baikal

Irkutsk

Urumqi

R U S S I A

Semipalatinsk

KYRG.

Novosibirsk

Almaty

Bishkek

KAZAKHSTAN

Tashkent

UZBEKISTAN

St Petersburg

Moscow

Aral Sea

SWEDEN

FINLAND

NORWAY

Stavanger, Bergen

Gothenburg

Copenhagen

Caspian Sea

TURKMENISTAN

Ashgabat

Turkmenbashi

Baku

AZER-BAIJAN

Newcastle

London

E U R O P E

Black Sea

Sevastopol

Sinop

Istanbul

Sukhumi

Sochi

Tbilisi

GEORGIA

Trabzon

ARMENIA

TURKEY

SYRIA

LEBANON

ISRAEL

Damascus

JORDAN

Amman

IRAQ

Baghdad

Tehran

TRAILBLAZER

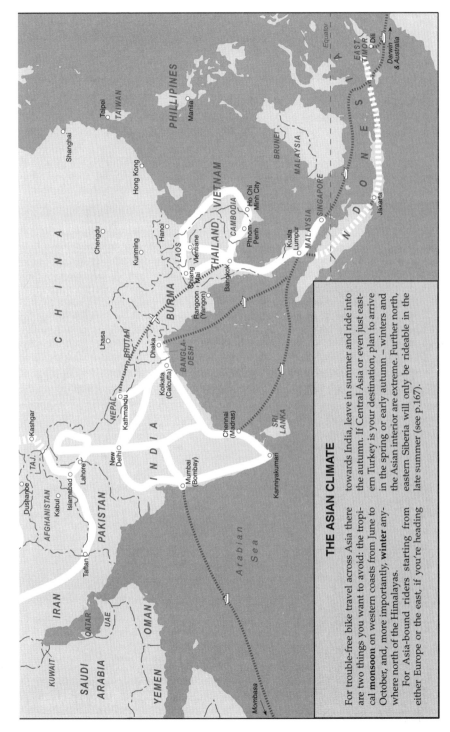

THE ASIAN CLIMATE

For trouble-free bike travel across Asia there are two things you want to avoid: the tropical **monsoon** on western coasts from June to October, and, more importantly, **winter** anywhere north of the Himalayas.

For Asia-bound riders starting from either Europe or the east, if you're heading towards India, leave in summer and ride into the autumn. If Central Asia or even just eastern Turkey is your destination, plan to arrive in the spring or early autumn – winters and the Asian interior are extreme. Further north, eastern Siberia will only be rideable in the late summer (see p.167).

Europe to India

Traditionally, coming from Europe, Asia begins once you cross from Istanbul into Asia Minor. **Turkey** itself offers few difficulties and plenty of amazing sights. The east and northeast regularly feature as highlights in trip reports, while in the oppressed Kurdish areas many riders have a positively great experience. Even then, gun emplacements and watchtowers are everywhere, as are police checkpoints every few kilometres. In east Turkey avoid driving or wandering off the road at night in these areas as you might be mistaken by the military for a smuggler or a PKK activist – or the other way round. A custom you'll have to get used to is rural children throwing stones at passing vehicles.

The main crossing to Iran is near **Dogubeyazit**, continuing to Tabriz. If you're having trouble with Iran or don't fancy the Georgia land entry border, there are **ferries** from Trabzon, Turkey, to Poti (Georgia) or up to Russia.

Iran

To some it may be part of the axis of evil and, at the time of writing, overdue for liberation, though as with Turkey, many riders have a great time meeting ordinary Iranian people. Farsi is the national language (not Arabic as some assume) but young people might speak English. Foreigners' movements within the country are not checked though Iranian friends might be checked up on so beware of putting locals in compromising situations.

The currency is the rial though Iranians commonly quote prices in *toman*: one toman equals ten rials which is a bit less than a euro right now. You can get by well on about £10/$18 a day. Bring **cash**; credit cards and travellers' cheques haven't caught on yet.

Don't be too irked if you discover you're paying ten times what locals do to get into museums and the like. It's official policy and anyway, it's still a matter of pennies. The same twin-price structure goes on in **hotels** where it can go a bit far; be prepared to bargain a bit (although hotels do pay higher taxes for foreign guests).

Visas

Getting a visa depends greatly on your nationality the general mood in the region and Iraq in particular, although it seems to have eased up lately. For Brits and especially Americans though, the process can still be tedious and slow in the extreme and if Americans manage to get a visa at all, they may have to pay for an escort at around $20 a day.

NOT THE ROAD TO 'DOGBISCUIT'

A couple of hours from Hakkari (southeast Turkey) we came to yet another checkpoint at the top of a pass where we had a chance to warm up and answer many questions including: 'Have you taken any pictures?' Our answer was, of course, 'no Sirree'.

We wanted to stop here as it was getting darker and colder, but we decided to press on. Two hours later after yet more stops, landslides and amazing scenery (observed in the dark, imagination helps) we reached Hakkari, a town sat in a bowl of mountains. The next day we crossed into Iran.

We were unsure what to expect coming this way but it turned out to be one of the best roads yet, one of those little 'Karakorams'. The normal route north through 'Dogbiscuit' we avoided because of the extra distance and uncertain weather.

Bob Goggs

TRIP REPORT
GREECE TO EGYPT ~ CAGIVA W16

Name	Zlatko Kampus
Year of birth	1950
Occupation	Professor
Nationality	Slovenian
Previous travels	Not many
Bike travels	Even fewer

This trip	Greece, Turkey, Israel, Egypt
Trip duration	Four weeks
Departure date	April 2000
Number in group	One
Distance covered	8700km (5438 miles)

Best day	Cruising Western Desert in Egypt
Worst day	Riding in Cairo
Favourite place	Sinai
Biggest headache	Leaving the bike unattended
Biggest mistake	Not getting the Syrian visa at home
Pleasant surprise	Some great people in Turkey
Any illness	No
Cost of trip	€900
Other trips planned	Tibet

Bike model	Cagiva W16
Age, mileage	5 years, 12,000km
Modifications	Changed motor (from Canyon 500)
Wish you'd done...	Centre stand, bigger tank, screen
Tyres used	Dunlop
Punctures	None
Type of baggage	Side bags

Bike's weak point	Unelastic motor
Strong point	Light and economical
Bike problems	None
Accidents	None
Same bike again	Yes
Any advice	Practise off road

TRIP REPORT
UK TO PAKISTAN ~ R80G/S

Name	Cynthia Milton
Year of birth	1954
Occupation	Technical writer
Nationality	UK
Previous travels	USSR, China, Vietnam
Bike travels	Round the Mediterranean
This trip	UK to Pakistan and back
Trip duration	Six weeks
Departure date	August 2000
Number in group	Two
Distance covered	12,000 miles (19,200km)
Best day	Nearly all of them
Worst day	East from Zhob – 68 miles in 12hrs
Favourite place	Peshawar
Biggest headache	Iranian driving: off the scale!
Biggest mistake	Can't take more time off in my job
Pleasant surprise	Pakistani people and officials
Any illness	None
Cost of trip	About £3000
Other trips planned	Got laid off – currently RTW
Bike model	BMW R80G/S
Age, mileage	15 years, 186,000 miles
Modifications	Small screen, heated grips, 45l tank
Wish you'd done...	Maybe a high-output alternator
Tyres used	Avon Gripsters
Punctures	A dozen? (but use UltraSeal)
Type of baggage	T'tech Zegas, tankbag on back of seat
Bike's weak point	Centre stand (broke)
Strong point	Easy to fix, bounces off scenery
Bike problems	Failed ignition coil
Accidents	Broke foot at 10mph on Zhob road
Same bike again	Absolutely
Any advice	Find someone to change your oil – saves getting mucky

Many travellers find using an Iranian travel agency speeds things up greatly (search Horizons – see p.16 – for addresses). Some New Zealanders got theirs the same day in Ankara (Turkey) while others waited for weeks in Istanbul. Some of these Iranian agencies use an honour system and ask you to pay for their services once in the country. The good thing is that Iranian visas are usually valid for **three months** before they expire, i.e. you have three months to get to the border. This gives you plenty of time to apply in a variety of places, hoping for the best.

Borders
A **carnet** is essential, though some riders have obtained an alternative transit document at the border for $150-200. The main crossing between Dogubeyazit in Turkey is at **Bazargan**. Border bureaucracy can be intimidating and certainly long-winded, but be patient and you'll get through.

Access to **Azerbaijan** is said to be by train only from Tabriz, but there's no reason you couldn't put the bike on the train and see what happens. Some travellers have got in from **Turkmenistan** (see p.165), but not so easily in the other direction, it seems, Turkmenistan access being what it is.

Riding and running a bike
Main (and most not-so-main) routes are pristine and empty tarmac highways. Asphalt is spreading rapidly across the country, but there are many desert routes. In the western and northern mountains there are networks of dirt roads through the hills of Iranian Azerbaijan. Driving standards amount to the same macho mania found in India, except speeds are much higher, but if you've got this far your chances of survival are good. One rider observed, 'I found it easiest to leave [Tehran] around 3am.'

Note that there are **few fuel stations** between towns so fill up in towns for long rides and plan for an

Tea-break trans-Iran. © Bob Goggs

autonomy of 300km. At about three pence or six cents a litre, petrol (gasoline) must be around the cheapest on the planet for 85 octane (and diesel is five times cheaper!). Multigrade oil is easy to find, 10-40W more so than 20-50W.

At the regular police **checkpoints** all they usually want to do is to shake hands and ask 'what'll it do, mister' to alleviate the boredom. Though sometimes officious, they are never threatening. Corruption towards foreigners is rare but if you get arrested, you might not have too many rights. There are no restrictions on travel, though border areas can be sensitive.

Pakistan
The national language is Urdu, which has many similarities with Hindi, though English is widely spoken except in the remotest parts. Travellers' cheques and Visa cards are accepted in larger towns, but be aware that most places on the Karakoram Highway (KKH) except Gilgit and Sost don't have banks.

PAKISTAN'S NORTHERN AREAS AND THE KARAKORAM HIGHWAY (KKH)

Though the northwest of Pakistan is tribal territory not always under state control, the wild scenery of the **Hindu Kush** and the Karakoram, as well as the 'untamed' tribal peoples, are what make a visit here special. Inter-tribal strife is common; the men carry guns like we carry mobiles, but in accessible areas at least, travellers are not in danger.

The **Karakoram Highway** ('KKH') runs from Islamabad to the Chinese border, a rise of nearly 4000m over 1000km, although most is in the last couple of hundred kilometres. The road is sealed all the way, surprisingly quiet and one of the engineering wonders of the world, carved out above the Indus and Hunza rivers. Landslides and rock falls are frequent, especially in the late spring thaw, or as a result of the frequent earthquakes.

The KKH has a few **branches** into side valleys and even though you must go back south, to ride through Pakistan and not come up here would lead to a lifetime of regret. You can do no worse than loop up from Islamabad or Peshawar to Chitral, over to Gilgit, up to the Chinese border, take a picture and roll back down to Islamabad. Late spring and early autumn are the best times to travel, but riders manage any time of year.

The KKH itself is open all year as far as Gilgit which is only at 1500m, though rain means rock falls. Further up it's snowy all year though the main road is clear. The branches often get blocked with rockfalls or snow, but on a bike you can usually get around. Lodgings are plentiful, a **fuel range** of 250–300km will do but expect carburation to get ropey (see p.48).

Peshawar to Chitral via Lowari Pass

West of the KKH, the **Lowari Pass** is just under 4000m; an amazing, winding, steep but beautiful route. In spring when the streams are flowing expect plenty of jet washes. Once over the pass and on flatter ground the road to Chitral is easy.

A must in this area are the **Kalash valleys** as described in Eric Newby's *A Short Walk in the Hindu Kush*. The Kalash practise their own religion and the women wear brightly-coloured orange and yellow beads and cowrie shells. Rumbur and Bumburet are the two motorable valleys with the former being more picturesque and culturally more interesting. The road in is quite rough, though spectacular, following a narrow track beside fast-flowing rapids.

Chitral to Gilgit via Shandur Pass

This is the highlight of any Pakistani off-roading with mind-boggling scenery. Head up the Chitral valley to Mastuj; coming from this side, the pass is not too difficult. The best part is the top of the pass; a plateau surrounded by snow-capped peaks. There's a lake nearby where you can camp. The far side of the steep pass is not for the faint-hearted. From this point to Gupis there are many very steep and tight sections and the occasional river crossing. From Gupis to Gilgit is fine.

Up the Indus to Skardu

Out of Gilgit a road branches off the KKH to Skardu, clinging to galleries blasted into cliff walls above the Indus valley. Beyond Skardu, the route to Askole is constantly being rebuilt with some very rough and quite daunting sections with extremely tight hairpins high above the river. The road from Skardu via Khapalu is sealed, beyond to Hushe has rough riding or blockages but astonishing scenery below the 7800-m peak of Masherbrum. There's a guesthouse in Hushe or you can camp.

To the Chinese border

The stupendous Hunza Valley is the highlight of the KKH. Most hotels are in Karimabad (Hunza), but Altit is friendly and cheap. The border post with China is at Sost where you leave your passport for the 80km haul to the **Khunjerab Pass** (4730m), an obligatory photo stop.

Babusar Pass – a KKH bypass

On the way back is a rough, summer-only route from Chilas over the 4195-m Babusar Pass to Mansehra back on the KKH, 100km north of Islamabad.

The KKH closes in.
© Iris Heiremans

Visas

Costs vary greatly according to nationality and in 2004 applying in Iran became no longer possible for non-Iranians so it's best to get them before leaving as they're valid up to six months. Otherwise **Letters of Introduction** (get used to the idea) from your embassy can help. Visa extensions are obtainable in Islamabad, but can take up to a week to sort out so go for the longest duration tourist visa (it costs the same) just to avoid the hassle of extending.

Borders, hassles and risky areas

Pakistani frontier officials are friendly, straightforward, seemingly not corrupt and lightning fast by Asian standards. A carnet is necessary for Pakistan, though vehicles have been allowed through without them in the past. There's one official border crossing to Iran, at **Taftan**, and one to India, at **Lahore**.

At the top of the Karakoram Highway (see box opposite) in northern Pakistan is the Khunjerab Pass at just under 5000m with the Pakistani border post of **Sost** leading to China. Once in a blue moon people have got permission to ride into China, but unless rules lighten up, don't count on it. Without a Chinese visa they often keep your passport way down the KKH to make sure you don't slip off somehow.

Men can expect homosexual overtures: a chance to find out what it's like for women travellers! Travellers are often warned of bandits in Baluchistan and especially in Sind Province (Karachi and Hyderabad) and to avoid travelling at night or in remote areas, something that's become more tense since Iraq and Afghanistan were invaded and OBL supposedly took to hiding in the area. Access to some sensitive border areas is forbidden by the police. The areas bordering Afghanistan, more or less between Quetta and Peshawar, are tribal areas that have never come under state control though and even near them gets edgy; it all depends on how the factions are warring.

Even the route down the west side of the Indus from Peshawar via Dera Ishmail Khan to Quetta (the centre of Pakistan's nuclear program) is officially closed though it's commonly travelled. At worst you'll be turned back by the police as your safety is again dependent on the caprices of local tribes people.

Riding and running a bike

Many people worry about riding the 'bandit lands' of **Baluchistan**, the 630km between the Iranian border and the first big town **Quetta**; all a bit close to Afghanistan for many people's liking. Ethnically the people are tribal Afghans though in fact robberies are rare and the dangerous reputation is exaggerated (global politics notwithstanding). Smile and wave to defer the odd thrown stone. Expect a rough, hot, dusty ride. The 'road' is in especially bad shape east of Dalbandin, with sand tongues and **steel ropes** or chains hung across the road near checkpoints; these are difficult to spot at low sun angles.

Depending on checkpoints and escorts, you can ride between Quetta and the border in about **ten hours**, but two days is considered normal and gives you a chance to enjoy the great Baluchi hospitality. There's a rest house at Dalbandin halfway along; camping out may be unadvisable or memorable!

Elsewhere you can rely on sealed roads between Iran and India, though motorcycles are not allowed on motorways for their own safety. Away from the Iran border, **fuel** is up to five times more than in Iran (still cheap), but as always it's advisable to fill up when you can in remote areas.

'India: you're standing in it'
Richard Wolters

After months of preparation, Charlie, Peter and I strap the bikes onto an aircraft pallet, just large enough to hold three BMWs. The bikes then flew from Brisbane with Malaysian Airlines and arrived in Chennai (Madras) a day later.

Our hotel there turned out to be a wise decision as in India chaos rules for at least 24 hours a day. We had no Indian rupees but, as usual, one does not have to look for the black market as the black market soon finds you. The official exchange rate was 27 rupees to an Australian dollar but we were offered around 30 which saved queueing in a bank. On the way back we passed a busy intersection and watched the traffic for about ten minutes, utterly horrified – soon we would be part of all this mayhem!

It was at this stage that I first noted Peter's excellent navigational skills. He must have spent a lot of time with pigeons as a young boy. I had no idea where we were, but he lead us straight back to the hotel via a few back streets. Peter displayed this skill many times on our trip and we were glad to have him along.

A taxi took us back to the airport where we checked in at the Air India office. Months before, friends of friends had warned me of what was likely to happen when attempting to clear Indian Customs – so we were ready for days of paperwork hassles.

As soon as the Air India office opened we were greeted by an Air India mamma, wrapped in a red sari and running an all-woman office. After a few minutes she announced that everything was in order.

'Please proceed across the road and get a gate permit.' We looked at each other and thought 'Stone the crows, that was easy!', as she handed the papers back. She continued in her pleasant Indian accent, 'By the way, who is your agent?' 'Agent?' we said, 'No worries madam. that's OK, we'll do the clearance ourselves.'

As if rehearsed for days beforehand, several of the nearby women looked up and mamma raised an eyebrow, giving us a very special smile as if to say: 'You fools...'

Ten minutes later we entered a dark building with offices decorated à la *Barton Fink*. Brown, grey and dark green were the predominant colours and few filing cabinets were to be seen. Instead, walls were pigeon holes crammed with files bound with bits of string, flapping in the gentle breeze caused by the creaking overhead fans. Computers were clearly a future fantasy.

'Please explain your business, Sir – what is your good name?' Pleasantries over, we were sold some forms and filled in another form in quadruplicate. It was now 11am. We went upstairs. 'What

'Be careful, I hear India is the worst driving in the world.'

'Be careful, thanks for that! Russia was bad at the time, Iran was controlled mayhem, Pakistan was all they could do, India is ... beyond all belief. No brakes – no problem ... no horn = accident, no end of smashed trucks/buses. Now I drive more aggressively and Danielle does not shout in my ear – perhaps she is speechless or her eyes are shut. I will miss this one day but for now it is sometimes over the top. You should try it!

Bob Goggs

T R I P   R E P O R T
LONDON TO SINGAPORE ~ F650 DAKAR

Name	Richard Shine
Year of birth	1969
Occupation	Lawyer
Nationality	New Zealander
Previous travels	Plenty of round the world by plane
Bike travels	London to Wales
This trip	London to Singapore via India
Trip duration	Four months
Departure date	July 2003
Number in group	Two to India, then solo
Distance covered	15,200 miles (24,320km)
Best day	Many, eg: Chitral–Gilgit in Pakistan
Worst day	50km of mud bashing in Laos
Favourite place	Pakistan: people and landscapes
Biggest headache	Chain wearing faster than expected
Biggest mistake	Waiting till I was 33 to do it
Pleasant surprise	Fantastic travel companion
Any illness	Hit a tractor and broke foot in Laos
Cost of trip	About £5500
Other trips planned	Yep, but dunno what just yet
Bike model	BMW F650 GS GD
Age, mileage	2002, 7000 miles
Modifications	Shock, springs, bash plate, pipe
Wish you'd done...	None
Tyres used	Conti TKC80, Metzeler Tourance
Punctures	Four
Type of baggage	Touratech/Ortleib hard and soft
Bike's weak point	None really. Did all I asked of it
Strong point	Bounces well, range, comfortable
Bike problems	Waterpump seals went in KL
Accidents	Two
Same bike again	Maybe, but variety is the spice of...
Any advice	Take good tools and a good mate if you can!

TRIP REPORT
DELHI TO KASHMIR ~ 350 BULLET

Name	Matt Power
Year of birth	1974
Occupation	Journalist
Nationality	USA
Previous travels	All over
Bike travels	Trans USA several times
This trip	Delhi–Kashmir round trip
Trip duration	One month
Departure date	June 2004
Number in group	One
Distance covered	2400km (1500 miles)
Best day	Near Leh. Briefly, no one else around
Worst day	Got run down and a fight near Delhi
Favourite place	Pari Mahal, Srinagar, at sunset
Biggest headache	Oil cap stolen, clutch cable broke
Biggest mistake	Not visiting Tso Moriri in Ladakh
Pleasant surprise	Friendly, fair mechanics everywhere
Any illness	Altitude at Khardung La (18,380ft)
Cost of trip	$750 plus airfare
Other trips planned	Alaska to Tierra del Fuego
Bike model	Enfield 350 5-speed
Age, mileage	One year old, 12,000 km
Modifications	Front disc brake (you'll need it)
Wish you'd done...	Knobby tyres
Tyres used	Stock
Punctures	Two
Type of baggage	Soft bags and metal toolbox
Bike's weak point	Spares for 5-spd left-shifter a pain
Strong point	It can climb cliffs
Bike problems	Changing clutch cable, flats
Accidents	One, no damage, just shouting match
Same bike again	Might go for the old 4-speed 500
Any advice	Walk the snow melt crossings beforehand!

INDIA PRACTICALITIES

You'll find English is widely spoken, even in the smallest village. Amex travellers' cheques are accepted in most banks and **ATMs** can be found in major cities.

The **black market** or licensed money changers might offer a slightly better rate and will definitely be much less tedious. Bureaucracy for anything from buying a train ticket to extending a visa is truly mind-boggling. It is often easier for a travel agent to organise tickets for you.

If you're heading away from big towns, have a stash of £, US$ or € and keep hold of small denomination Rupees. Petrol pump attendants always have lots of change, small shops don't. There's something to be said for not using the ubiquitous Lonely Planet if you want to avoid the tourist tramlines and ghettos; try the Footprint *India Handbook* using Nelles or LP **maps**.

Best riding seasons

The hyper-humid build-up (late March and April) and the subsequent **monsoon** (May–late September) are well worth avoiding. Riding into the cool post-monsoon season makes sense unless you're heading up to Kashmir and Ladakh. The **Himalayan** 'season' is June to October. After mid-October the road crews of the BRO (Border Roads Organisation) stop fixing/maintaining the roads or clearing landslides until the following summer.

Visas and borders

Visas are available in Islamabad (Pakistan) in three days with an LOI. Get the longer, six-month visa, even though it starts on issue.

The land border to **Pakistan** is at Atari, 40km from Amritsar, open 10am to 4pm, but arrive early and bring lunch. Vehicles are often searched for drugs. You must have a **carnet**. It's worth witnessing the daily flag-lowering ceremonies on either side of the border from the grandstands provided.

There are several crossings into **Nepal**, where you don't need a carnet if you're riding an Indian-registered bike. Sometimes there's a per-day charge if you stay more than two weeks. Good routes to Nepal include Sunauli in Uttar Pradesh to Bhairawa (south of Pokhara) and Raxaul in Bihar to Birganj (south of Kathmandu).

Riding and running a bike

There is only one road rule in India: 'Might is Right'. On a motorcycle you are down there with the pond life so ride accordingly. Defer to everything bigger and expect the unexpected (see box p.153). FYI, the world's highest accident rate is on the Bombay–Ahmadabad road. If you have an accident, the general advice is to disappear as quickly as possible, if you can still ride. Riding at night is risky.

For long sections putting your bike on the train is cheap and easy. **Chris Bright**

is your business? Your name? Three motorcycles? Please go downstairs and fill in one more form, then come back.'

Noon: we go back upstairs. 'Excuse me Sir, we have lunch break, please wait one hour.' Later a guy examines our papers. 'You have to pay import duty, what is the value?' We explain we have carnets. 'In that case you must go to the Harbour Customs House – better you go now!'

What followed was the first of several 45-minute dodgem slaloms across town in a three-wheeled taxi. The back seat was made for slender Indians and not bonzer-shearing champs like us. However, we managed to squeeze in without blowing the rickshaw apart and tried not to watch. Traffic clearance was measured with a feeler gauge.

Arriving at the Customs office we proceeded to another office called 'Preventive'. 'You need special document sir – here is one, please go to other floor to Xerox it.' We filled in the forms, showed carnets, made special hand signals and explained everything for the tenth time. Two hours later... 'Please come back at 10am so we can do it quickly. But first you must go back to the airport to get the 'xyz' document and bring that with you in the morning.'

INDIA ON AN ENFIELD

Built using the original casts and dies in Madras (Chennai), today's Enfield India is a virtually unaltered forty-year-old British Royal Enfield pushrod single. 'Export model' Enfields bought abroad are superior to the ones you can buy in India. Bullets have been described as 'always sick but never terminal': if you're expecting modern Japanese reliability, a Bullet definitely isn't for you. A tune-up (check plug, points, tappets, etc) every 500 km will go a long way to keeping the show on the road. Passing about one per hour, getting to know your local Enfield-wallah isn't difficult. An India roadside 'mechanic' knows the inside of a Bullet like the back of his hand and you can get a new piston fitted for the price of a Japanese indicator.

The unpredictable pace of life on Indian roads make things additionally interesting and mean your top speed is likely to be 50mph/80kph on any machine. Average *Enfield* speeds will be about a quarter of this. In this sort of environment the Enfield is perfectly suitable and will give you a journey to remember along with plenty of roadside encounters. The bike's poor reputation is somewhat exaggerated: if you treat it right, it'll last.

Enfield India also produces a **500cc diesel**, a rarity with the power of a moped but mind-boggling 400-miles per tank fuel economy! Can't say I ever saw one though.

If you're planning a Himalayan adventure a 500cc bike is best; the motor will chug over the world's highest rideable passes. On the plains and in the south the 350 is more than adequate. It's also more reliable, particularly if it has electronic ignition.

Some recent models now have the gear lever on the left and the foot brake on the right while incorporating a five-speed gearbox. The usual Bullet has the reverse arrangement, a throwback to the British Royal Enfield era. A popular crash scenario for inexperienced Bulleteers involves frantically stamping on the gear lever thinking it's the back brake,

New Enfields

350 Bullet Standard: Rs61,000
500 Bullet (with a front disc brake): Rs86,000
350 Bullet Thunderbird: Rs71,000
350 Bullet Machismo: Rs69,000
350 Bullet Electra: Rs65,000
These are approximate 2005 prices.

Buying used off travellers

Departing foreigners advertise in travellers' hotels in areas like Paharganj, or the New Delhi Tourist Camp. Standard price for a 350, regardless of age, is around Rs25,000; you'll rarely pay more than Rs35,000. Right now Rs100 = £1.20, US$2.20, €1.70.

Used dealers and rentals

The main Delhi bike market, Karol Bagh, has several dealers, the best known being Lalli Singh (www.lallisingh.com). Many people have positive things to say about him. I had a good experience with Soni Motors (www.soni motors.com) who rented me a very reliable 500cc Bullet, with toolkit and sale or return spares (very few needed) for just Rs300/day. Rental prices in Manali and Leh tend to be much higher and the bikes substandard.

Both the above offer guaranteed repurchase (no time limit) at 30% less than you paid. used prices are around a third higher than buying privately, depending on your bargaining skills. If you're planning on using a bike for more than about six weeks, it works out cheaper to buy/sell than to rent.

The owner of Nanna Motors, near New Delhi Tourist Camp, is an honest and good mechanic (highly recommended by owners of foreign machines) and can sometimes help with bike purchase (including new bikes). In the summer season his son also runs a garage in Manali.

Royal Enfields

The original British bikes are normally priced midway between new bikes and good second-hand ones. But beware, despite what is written on their documentation, they are invariably full of crap pattern Indian parts.

Modifications

To modify the standard 350 to be EU legal, budget on around Rs8000 to 14,000 for the bigger front brake off the 500 (or even a disc brake). A short pea-shooter silencer gives the best looks and sound. All important! Noisy, but India is a far cry from Switzerland.

Useful minor extras for Indian touring include: petrol filter, fuel tap lock, battery isolation switch, wider rear tyre, different handlebars and reshaped seat to improve handling and comfort, crash bars, luggage racks, superloud horns. None of these additions adds up to more than a few hundred rupees.

INDIA ON AN ENFIELD

Running an Enfield

Get used to the fact that you'll spend a lot of time nurturing your machine. Apart from regular carb cleaning, check nuts and bolts frequently – Enfields shake themselves to pieces on pot-holed Indian roads. As said before, a plug, points, tappets check every 500km will be time well spent. One item which requires frequent replacement are the **cush-drive rubbers** in the rear hub.

Before the diesel Bullet came a milk-powered prototype. Vast amounts of pasteurised 'fuel' were needed to attain even modest speeds and the project was abandoned. © Bob Goggs

Designed to reduce transmission shock, a Bullet's rear brake will heat up the rear drum during a long Himalayan descent, bringing the rubbers to melting point.

Spares are available in all but the smallest towns. Besides the usual items, carry cables, a chain link, rectifier and a coil. Always try to buy **original** Enfield spares, cheaper imitations have an even shorter service life. If you're heading up to Ladakh and Zanskar, it's best to carry all necessary spares with you.

Be prepared for roadside **repairs** everywhere and anytime, although most towns have a specialist Enfield 'metalbasher'. Note that it's worth supervising all work to check it's actually being done and that no old parts are being substituted. You have been warned.

Prices for common repairs are: puncture Rs30; carburettor clean Rs10-20; oil change with new oil Rs100; rebore and new piston Rs1000; fitting new clutch plates Rs250.

In India petrol prices average at around Rs50 a litre and a 350 Enfield will return around 80mpg or 25-35kpl.

Documents/regulations

Ownership papers: Not strictly necessary to get these in your own name as long as the owner on the documents has signed the transfer. Having said that, a sale letter from the seller stating you to be the buyer will do. If planning to sell the bike in a state other than the one it's registered in, you must obtain a 'no objections' certificate. Most dealers will organise a name transfer for a fee although being India, this can take a few weeks.

Third-party **insurance** is mandatory and worthless. It costs around Rs400 (£5) a year, and is obtainable at any insurance office. Any driver's licence will do. It is not the rule but in practice almost every foreign rider can get by in India with his own country's driving licence as the average policeman doesn't even know what an International Driving Permit looks like. However, if entering overland across the border it would be sensible to be armed with an IDP. **Helmets** are required in India.

Taking a Bullet out of the country

Since about 2000, it's only possible to ride your Indian-registered Bullet to Nepal. Under new regulations, riding one back to Europe or wherever is virtually impossible. The only realistic way to do it now is to buy a Nepal-registered 'export model' in Nepal, have your Carnet de Passage issued in your home country and ride it through India to Pakistan and back to Europe.

Chris Bright

When we left the office I cast my eyes on the sign in the hallway again, 'Preventive' it said. 'Preventive of us from getting our bikes!' I surmised.

Another white-knuckle ride in the tricycle taxi contraption and we were back at the airport for more documentation. We were kept waiting and although hungry and very thirsty refused the tea offered – organising a kettle would only slow things down. I was now dog-tired and a few hours later collapsed on the hotel bed after just two bottles of beer.

Next day. 'Please explain why your documents show one consignment of three packages and ours shows seven packages?' We explain that the pallet was a small one and we had removed the bags. They were placed on the floor individually. 'Ah, you might have to pay import duty on them.' 'No sir, they are part of the bikes.' New accessory forms are filled out. No wonder the

TRIP REPORT
LONDON TO NZ ~ KTM ADVENTURE

Name	Andy Miller
Year of birth	1967
Occupation	Engineer
Nationality	British
Previous travels	Caribbean, Maldives, Europe
Bike travels	Europe, Morocco

This trip	London to New Zealand via India
Trip duration	One year
Departure date	September 2001
Number in group	Three
Distance covered	25,000 miles (40,000km) or so

Best day	Going to Canada instead of UK from NZ!
Worst day	Guards on India–Nepal border
Favourite place	Too many
Biggest headache	Bike not at Bangkok airport
Biggest mistake	Riding in Delhi at night
Pleasant surprise	People in Iran after 9-11
Any illness	Just the Kathmandu Kwickstep
Cost of trip	Don't want to know
Other trips planned	Vancouver to Tierra Del Fuego

Bike model	KTM Adventure 640
Age, mileage	1998, 9000 miles
Modifications	Seat, 2-phase CDI, hydraulic clutch
Wish you'd done...	More space in the belly pan
Tyres used	MT90, Metz' Sahara 3, Mich' Desert
Punctures	1 blow out
Type of baggage	Hard

Bike's weak point	Time it takes to change the oil
Strong point	Strong and durable
Bike problems	Oil leaks from rocker cover
Accidents	Run off road in India – that count?
Same bike again	Got a 950 Adventure now
Any advice	At first packing, ask yourself do you need half of that stuff!

INDIAN TRAFFIC HAZARDS

Bovids

General Purpose House Cow (GPHC) Varying in colour from brown to black and white, they wander aimlessly through traffic. Dangerously limited ability to reason.

Buffalo Black with laid back horns – used for working the fields, pulling carts and obstructing traffic. Walks slowly and once moving keeps going in that direction no matter what. Make sure you're not coming the other way.

Brahmans or Sacred Mobile Roundabouts (SMR). Grey to white, smaller in the south, up to 1.8m tall in the north. Cocky, will not budge under any pressure. Creates its own roundabout with other Brahmans. Has eyes with 180-degree vision. Objectionable 'Holier than a GPHC' attitude. Immune to all intimidation; scoff at warp-factor air horns.

Goats

Commonplace and also contemptuous of traffic. Whole families cohabit in permanent squalor on median strips. The young ones are dangerous as they make sudden moves and lack respect.

Pigs

Have the tendency to cross the road in gangs and change course midway. Often seen stranded across median strips where they are able to disrupt *both* directions of travel. Highly intelligent, verging on conspiratorial.

Dogs

Most run away at the sight of big bikes. Less intelligent than a GPHC with learning difficulties. Minor hazard.

Monkeys

Very dangerous and unpredictable – jump out of the bush screaming and race along the road baring their teeth. Avoid braking hard on any Fresh Flat Monkey Formations (FFMFs), which otherwise have passed their most dangerous phase and are on the path to reincarnation.

Old men on pushbikes

There are two varieties: the 'I can't afford a hearing aid' type. Prone to making sudden right turns with perfectly bad timing.

The second variety usually wears sawn-down coke bottles polished with coarse sandpaper and held on by copper wire. These guys steer straight towards you with an 'I can't believe my eyes' attitude and change course just prior to impact (you hope).

Truck/bus drivers

The biggest threat to motorcyclists on a daily basis. Drip-fed on amphetamines and have adapted the Nietzschean axiom 'That which does not kill me and is not an SMR can be run at/run over/run off the road.'

Government vehicles and army jeeps

Attitude: 'We own the road so we drive in the middle – what are you going to do about it? I am too important/have a big gun'.

Yield or face the consequences, including several forms requiring stamping and countersigning by a Permanently Unobtainable Person (PUP).

Grain crops in need of thrashing

Can appear on the road in all arable areas up to one foot deep. Apply same caution as with FFMFs. Dry stalks can wedge against your exhaust and set you ablaze.

Everything else I forgot to mention

Whatever it is, it's out there on the road and heading for your spokes!

Richard Wolters

Indonesian rain forests are in jeopardy! 'Please explain your CB radios plus value, you might have to pay duty!'

'No sir, they are on the carnet.' 'I see! I will send you to another officer who will check the details. Your good names, why you are in India...'

Suddenly it's 11.30am 'Lunch time, please come back at 2pm.' We walked the streets for a couple of hours, then returned to the office – but no officer. He arrives at 2.30pm and must wait for his assistant.

'Please follow me. Passports please. Please go upstairs and Xerox pages one and two of your passports.' We go upstairs to the designated office and ask about the photocopy machine.

'Ah sir, you mean Xerox.' 'Yes, I suppose I do!' He looks at our papers and starts a conversation about our bikes, Australia, and Pauline Hansen. After ten minutes he says.'Gentillmens, I am only too pleased to Xerox your passports for you but our Xerox machine has broken down. Also, I would like to inform you that there no other Xerox machines in this building.'

We go outside and find a machine in another building.

At 3 pm: 'I will dictate as follows: 'Dear Sir, I have come to India for the purpose of... etc. I will not sell the above motorcycle as described in detail on carnet form. I will be in India for 'xyz'... I will not sell accessories, radios, etc...'

We offer him a bribe but he refuses. What are we doing wrong? We were hoping to have our bikes by the weekend. Although the bribe didn't work something else did and the officer went into a different gear. Maybe he thought that we judged him as being incompetent. Lord knows how he got this idea but things really began to move.

'Please wait while I get this stamped.' We now go back to the airport to complete documentation where there are more security checks, Customs checks, genetic fingerprinting and two more forms. We decide to employ an agent.

It's now 7.30pm, dark and the mozzies are out, probosces oiled for a night on the town. We go to the military guard and sit under the fan in his hut. A cow walks through the gate without documentation. Is this a good omen?

'Problem Sir, we only have one computer, the program for clearance can only handle six digits, your names have seven digits. I will have to get the forms and do it manually.' We are stunned but say nothing.

We have been at it for twelve hours solid. The compound is now almost deserted and we must now pay overtime for all remaining personnel. Calculations are made and after paying 3200 rupees we finally proceed to the bikes and quickly connect the batteries and mount the windscreens. We keep smiling and answer all the usual questions about the tank capacity, top speed, etc but keep working.

'Is this a double engine, a diesel, how fast?' 'Yes, yes, yes' we answer. We start the engines, the steel open and we're out! What did we learn from this? Use an agent and make sure if the cargo documents state three items there are three items. Unless you're a cow, that is.

ALL QUIET IN NEPAL

As we loaded the bike to leave the Chitwan National Park area we were told the Maoist rebels had called a strike – nobody could use the roads. We thought it was just another excuse to get us to stay one more night so we ignored them all.

As it happens it was true and the roads were 'Twilight Zone' quiet which did make for slightly nervous travelling. In the first town where we stopped for breakfast nobody dared travel because of the threat of being blown up or shot. They said that tourists were exempt, which was nice!

After a few kilometres we met this German on a Tiger (a Triumph... that is), the first overlander we'd met on the road. We asked about the conditions; perfect for riding he said, deserted roads and a piece of cake to ride into traffic-free Kathmandu. **Bob Goggs**

TRIP REPORT
NORTH INDIA ~ HERO HONDA CBZ150

Name	Neil Thomson
Year of birth	1972
Occupation	Podiatrist
Nationality	British
Previous travels	Lots of Indian backpacking
Bike travels	Enfielding around India, Morocco
This trip	North India
Trip duration	Six months
Departure date	November 2003
Number in group	One
Distance covered	5000km (3125 miles)
Best day	Every day in the Himalayas
Worst day	Rushing Agra to Delhi before dark
Favourite place	Himalayas
Biggest headache	The driving. Still wake up screaming
Biggest mistake	Took boots, forgot gloves. Doh!
Pleasant surprise	Finding an alternative to Enfields
Any illness	Nothing serious
Cost of trip	Around £5 a day once there
Other trips planned	Oh yes!
Bike model	Hero Honda (150cc 4-stroke single)
Age, mileage	One month old, 400km
Modifications	Furry seat, foam grips
Wish you'd done...	Foam grips before hands turned raw
Tyres used	MRF something
Punctures	None
Type of baggage	Soft panniers brought from UK
Bike's weak point	None. Beats a CB125 but only £650!
Strong point	It's not an Enfield Bullet
Bike problems	Fork seal (fixed under warranty)
Accidents	None (great brakes)
Same bike again	Definitely
Any advice	Enfields are from the 1950s... India is dangerous enough!

SOUTHEAST ASIA

Bob Goggs

Blocked off, as it is, by China and Myanmar to the north, and the Indonesian archipelago to the south, the five accessible countries of mainland Southeast Asia: Malaysia, Thailand, Laos, Cambodia and Vietnam (sort of) make a little sub group of their own and can be a great and not too expensive place to rest up after the rigours of India. The dominant Buddhist religion is relaxed, holiday resorts are plentiful and at the time of writing **fuel prices** ranged from around 25p/45c a litre in Malaysia up to 40p/75c in Cambodia.

Thailand and Malaysia

Thailand is a popular mainstream holiday destination and is regarded as a bit of a rest after India or Indochina; the cities are more developed than you'd expect and as usual the fun is to be had in rural areas or parking up on the islands and beaches. Carnets are not valid (avoid getting them stamped); motorcycles are allowed in with a temporary permit for four weeks at a time, possibly extendible for up to six months. If not, you may find yourself going in and out of Thailand, which is what many riders do anyway if they are exploring Indochina.

People say the traffic is dangerous for bikes (unless you've got some Indian miles behind you), but local bikes are everywhere and the best riding is in the **Chiang Mai** region up north where the humidity is less oppressive. With a good map there is plenty of scope for off-roading in the Mae Hong Son region along the Burmese border too. A great biking website for this area is Golden Triangle Rider: **www.gt-rider.com**.

Generally, travellers don't get too excited about **Malaysia**, an Islamic country with the traditional Moslem welcome you get elsewhere but that's often seen as a through port (see box opposite) to destinations like Thailand, Indochina or Australia. Whilst there is little of architectural interest, the natural beauty is no less stunning than Thailand. The roads are excellent and distances short although there aren't many possibilities for off-roading apart from logging tracks through plantations. Malaysia is tuned into motorbikers and you'll find basic wooden shelters for bikers built along all major roads and diversions around tolls.

After India and Thailand, riding is a dream. The only road hazards are boy racers on smelly strokers and reptiles. Motorcycle dealers in Kuala Lumpur and Penang stock parts and accessories for foreign bikes.

Heading south from Thailand **to Singapore** the most direct route is to cross the border at Sadao on the west coast. Pick up Highway 1 down to Butterworth and continue south to Kuala Lumpur, straight down to Johor Bahru and the Singapore border. This could be done in one long day. All other border crossings are straightforward on the Malay side and not subject to the nightmarish bureaucracy and scrutiny of western Asia.

Singapore

The cross-roads on the Asia to Australia overland route is anachronistically fast-paced, clean and modern and can be a shock to the system if you've ridden from the sub-continent. Bemused motorcyclists can often be found haunt-

SHIPPING IN AND OUT OF SOUTHEAST ASIA

As always your choice is between the speed of an airplane or the perceived inexpense of sea freight (more on p.84). From India, Madras/**Chennai** is the main port for shipping east, **Mumbai**/Bombay to Arabia and Africa (see p.189) and Delhi for air freight anywhere (see below).

In the last edition one couple described shipping from Madras to Singapore as the most stressful part of their two-year journey. Their BMW sat in a container on the docks for a month before finally leaving India; as Jeremy Bullard recommends on p.85, don't leave the country until you know the bike is on the way. In late 2004 another guy described a similar transit with Interfreight India as 'painless' (see HU), costing just £300/$500 (they did the clearing themselves in Malaysia, saving a few hundred bucks).

Others have proposed that a way of getting around the endemic Indian graft is shipping out of **Dacca** in Bangladesh to Kuala Lumpur (KL) in Malaysia – much cheaper than Madras to Singapore. But there's always a converse story of a guy who waited a *month* and paid off a lot of people to get his bike out of Dacca and on the road to Nepal. Your experience and attitude to the shipping game may have a lot to do with it.

Flying out of Delhi or Kathmandu

Other riders have had more luck flying out of Delhi – one guy even managed to organise his bike in one extremely hectic day (though this is not that unheard of with air freight, compared to shipping). The total cost to Frankfurt was around £800/$1500 – apparently flying to points east is less expensive.

Thai Air operate regular flights between Kathmandu and Bangkok, Some recent costs were $1.37 per kg for up to 500kg and $1.07 thereafter, plus handling, crate, etc. For a 400-kg BMW 1150 this was around $550. Compared to the agony of Chennai, this is bike-freighting nirvana.

In and out of Singapore or Malaysia

With the reputed bureaucratic complications of importing a bike into **Indonesia** (see box p.159), you need to make a short hop from the Asian mainland to, presumably, Australia.

Luckily, this is a relatively straightforward procedure and **KL** or **Singapore** are both major ports with worldwide links. Most ships from Malaysia go via Singapore, but KL makes for a cheaper and more pleasant alternative to spending time in Singapore. Your bike could be in **Darwin**, Australia, in as little as a week.

Once here though, a whole lot of buggering about commences with expensive fumigation; wherever you arrive in **Australia**, clean your machine meticulously beforehand, even mud under the mudguards, and dump any organic matter. (There's more on Australia regs on p.171).

Perkins Shippers (www.perkins.com .au) or their agents are the guys you want. A recent quote for sea freight out of Darwin to KL (actually Port Klang – which is also the noise your bike makes as they drop it into the hold) came in at just £130/$245. Another guy paid just £70 to get his bike to Singapore in about the same time, but ended up paying around three times as much once in Singapore, half of it in taxi fares.

Departure lounge in Kathmandu © Bob G

ing the offices of shipping agents because, for such a small country, bringing a bike in is a pain. Some riders recommend just ticking it off as a pedestrian and shipping out from Kuala Lumpur to Indonesia or Australia.

But if you do ride in, you'll find a major port shipping to most destinations worldwide (see box above). The good thing with Perkins is a bike can be wheeled straight into the container.

SOUTHEAST ASIA ~ TIGER 900

Name	Ian Foster
Year of birth	1963
Occupation	Architect/City designer
Nationality	British
Previous travels	Europe, USA/Can, China, Colombia
Bike travels	Europe, USA, China

This trip	SE Asia, Sarawak and Philippines
Trip duration	Three months
Departure date	April 1997
Number in group	One
Distance covered	10,000 miles (16,000km)

Best day	A new road in Chiang Mai, Thailand
Worst day	Borneo jungles with road tyres!
Favourite place	Beaches north of Phuket, Thailand
Biggest headache	Philippines: how long you got?
Biggest mistake	Trying to get into Indonesia in '97
Pleasant surprise	Singapore has nightlife
Any illness	No
Cost of trip	£2500
Other trips planned	Always... South Africa... USA

Bike model	Triumph Tiger 900
Age, mileage	1993, 8000 miles
Modifications	Higher screen
Wish you'd done...	Scottoiler
Tyres used	Metzelers
Punctures	One, right at the end in Manila
Type of baggage	Givi (it was completely crap)

Bike's weak point	Chain, high centre of gravity
Strong point	Speed, pose-value with the girlies!
Bike problems	None
Accidents	None
Same bike again	Not after Triumph Motors' attitude
Any advice	Keep it between the hedges!

INDONESIA

As with many difficult countries, getting in is tricky but once you're in you're rolling. Foreigners are exempt from the big bike ban; get a two-month visa in advance or a month at borders. Carnets are not asked for.

Getting in from Singapore or Malaysia is harder than you think; ferries are passengers only. Instead, head for any small port and put your bike on an 'onion boat' for around 400 ringgit. They don't let you on as a passenger to Dumai, so take a regular ferry from Melaka and then collect the bike.

How the customs and police will receive you depends on the weather but it can be done in a day, and riders reckon the further east you get (ie, away from congested Sumatra and Java) the better the experience. Bali is a Hindu 'enclave'; a 'costa' island popular Australians and a bit more expensive.

From here on you need to hop along to Dili in Timor (not Indonesia) from where Perkins (see p.157) ship regularly to Darwin. Irian Jaya and Papua New Guinea are considered going a bit far off the map.

Indochina

Indochina – or to be precise Laos and Cambodia but not so much Vietnam – has become an excursion loop out of Thailand or a stepping stone north to the Indian subcontinent, though coming *from* India, the indifference of the locals is a blessed relief. Shipping out of Indochina onwards is rare as Singapore or KL have more regular services. The Thai borders with Laos and Cambodia are open to overland travellers. **Vietnam**, it seems, has taken bureaucracy lessons from India, though is a great travel destination. Riding your own machine **over 200cc** will take some perseverance: one guy was advised to put it in the back of a pick-up, drive across the border, take it down the road and ride off.

It's all part of the 'overlanders' mentality'. Rules are plentiful but not as rigid as in the West; take advantage of it and be ready for anything. Having said that, **renting or buying** locally is by far the more common solution in Vietnam. Assuming you're in Thailand, the Bangkok embassies of the three Indochinese countries would be the place to check on entry formalities. Visas can be issued in a couple of days. If you're intent on exploring this area for some time, **November to February** are the coolest and driest months.

Laos and Cambodia

After the Americans had finished with it, Laos was the most bombed country in the history of warfare – and they weren't even directly involved! To this day large areas of the country are littered with what's become known as 'UXO' (Unexploded Ordnance) which includes mines as well as shells. The worst areas are in the southern arm of Laos because the Viet Cong's 'Ho Chi Minh' supply route once wove its way through here. The further from Vietnam you get the lesser the menace.

Banditry is also a problem along certain routes, with buses and bikes getting highjacked. But the roads are good: Laos comes across as less tame than Thailand but not as hard work as Cambodia.

The simplest way to get into Laos is from Nong Khai in Thailand across the aptly-named **Friendship Bridge** just south of the capital, **Vientiane**. At the border you'll get a visa issued on the spot – if only it was always so easy! From here it's a great ride through amazing countryside up to **Luang Prabang**. Otherwise, in the dry season only, the hills of the northwest are

---

'I'M NOT SQUEAMISH, BUT...'

I'm not squeamish about food, in fact I like to think I have a rather Marco Polo-esque pallet, I even tried fried locust once which tasted like chips with wings.

But in Cambodia my devil-may-care taste-buds met their match. This nation will eat anything, and the younger or even pre-born the better. Deep-fried chicks, eaten all in one go, bones and all, were stacked in neat pyramids upside down with their fragile necks gently swaying, fried black spiders with enormous hairy legs, and beady-eyed cockroaches still glistened in the residue of the oil they'd just been fried in.

Virna pointed out that even though we stuck to more recognisable dishes, they probably fried up the roaches in the same pan. My worst experience, mainly because it was only towards the end of it that I realised what I had just eaten, came when, in an attempt to stay on safe ground, I ordered a couple of boiled eggs. Cracking open the first one, I saw that the yellow and the white of the egg had mixed. I dubiously tasted it suspecting that it was stale and sure enough the taste didn't seem quite right.

Sign language and a handy prop allowed the lady who'd served me to explain it was a duck egg, something I'd never tried before, and she assured me that it was fresh and cooked to perfection. As I ate more I was intrigued by the taste, more like chicken than egg, but then I started to find bits in the egg that looked almost like tiny entrails and through the disbelief came the realisation that these eggs were fertilised. I had unwittingly eaten a duck embryo.

Andy Pag

Dug-out across the Mekong to Laos. Don't sneeze... © Simon McCarthy

accessible from Thailand's Chiang Mai district, as long as you don't mind balancing in a **dug-out canoe** across the Mekong river.

Cambodia has a reputation for landmines but we found it's also thought of as the most expensive and hassley place; too much 'Indo' and not enough 'China' for our liking. You can also expect some of the **worst roads in Asia** and some of the weirdest food. How does an entrée of freshly-plucked and still-beating cobra's heart appeal? You'll find this and other Kampuchean delicacies described in Anthony Bourdain's book, *A Cook's Tour*.

Unless you decide to dig a tunnel, there are three ways in, all currently unsurfaced. The main road from **Aranyaprathet** in Thailand to **Siem Reap** near the Angkor Wat temple complex is presently being sealed, but until that happy day could be difficult in the wet.

The route **from Laos** is rarely used so is neglected – or should that be the other way round? Either way it should only be attempted if you're prepared for a right old struggle, and even then, only in the dry season.

Along the coast a **southern route** runs through the mountains which brings you close to the beach resorts in Sihanoukville. It's a fun ride involving a few ferry crossings but again it's only really viable in the dry season.

(Opposite) Top: Getting high with Enfields in India. © Matt Power. **Bottom:** Iran; keeping up appearances. © Trui Hanouille.

(Overleaf, double page): World map.

(Opposite p161) Top: Roadhouse rendezvous, Western Australia. **Bottom:** Approaching the Tsaganurr Pass in western Mongolia. © Tom Bierma.

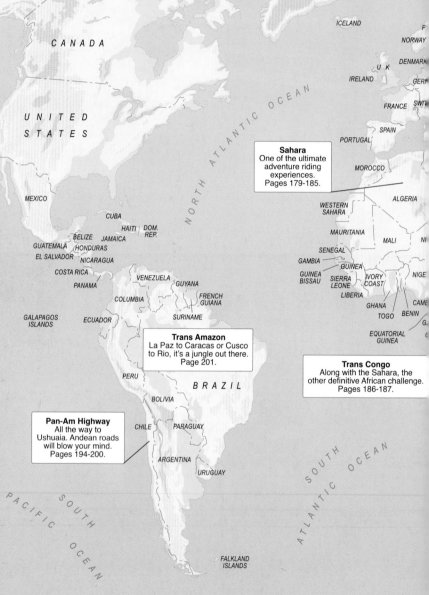

Alaska and Yukon
A sub-Arctic wilderness of mountains and big rivers.
Pages 204-206.

Sahara
One of the ultimate adventure riding experiences.
Pages 179-185.

Trans Amazon
La Paz to Caracas or Cusco to Rio, it's a jungle out there.
Page 201.

Trans Congo
Along with the Sahara, the other definitive African challenge.
Pages 186-187.

Pan-Am Highway
All the way to Ushuaia. Andean roads will blow your mind.
Pages 194-200.

ARCTIC

GREENLAND

ICELAND

NORWAY

DENMARK

U K

IRELAND

GER

FRANCE

SWIT

ALASKA

CANADA

UNITED STATES

NORTH ATLANTIC OCEAN

SPAIN

PORTUGAL

MOROCCO

ALGERIA

MEXICO

CUBA

HAITI   DOM. REP.

BELIZE   JAMAICA

GUATEMALA   HONDURAS

EL SALVADOR   NICARAGUA

COSTA RICA

PANAMA

VENEZUELA

GUYANA

FRENCH GUIANA

COLUMBIA

SURINAME

GALAPAGOS ISLANDS

ECUADOR

PERU

BRAZIL

BOLIVIA

CHILE

PARAGUAY

ARGENTINA

URUGUAY

WESTERN SAHARA

MAURITANIA

MALI

NI

SENEGAL

GAMBIA

GUINEA

GUINEA BISSAU   SIERRA LEONE   IVORY COAST

NIGE

LIBERIA

GHANA   BENIN

TOGO

CAME

EQUATORIAL GUINEA

G

SOUTH ATLANTIC OCEAN

PACIFIC OCEAN

SOUTH

FALKLAND ISLANDS

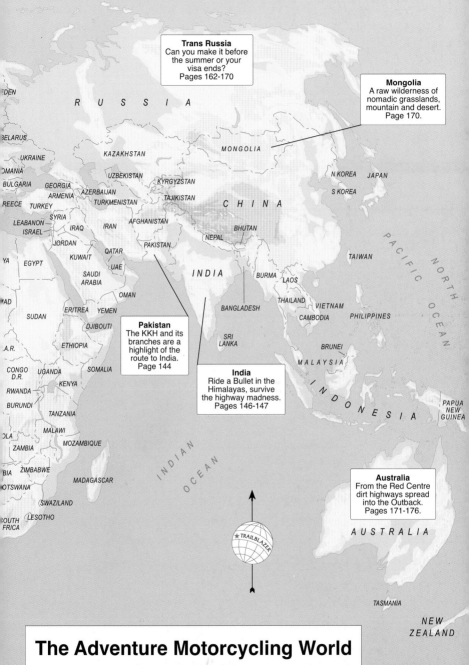

OCEAN

Trans Russia
Can you make it before the summer or your visa ends?
Pages 162-170

Mongolia
A raw wilderness of nomadic grasslands, mountain and desert.
Page 170.

EDEN

R U S S I A

BELARUS

UKRAINE

MANIA

BULGARIA   GEORGIA

GREECE   TURKEY

LEABANON   SYRIA

ISRAEL

ARMENIA

AZERBAIJAN

TURKMENISTAN

KAZAKHSTAN

UZBEKISTAN   KYRGYZSTAN

TAJIKISTAN

MONGOLIA

N KOREA   JAPAN

S KOREA

C H I N A

IRAQ   IRAN   AFGHANISTAN

JORDAN

YA   EGYPT

KUWAIT

QATAR

UAE

SAUDI
ARABIA

OMAN

PAKISTAN

NEPAL

BHUTAN

I N D I A   BURMA   LAOS

TAIWAN

P
A
C
I
F
I
C

O
C
E
A
N

N
O
R
T
H

AD

SUDAN

ERITREA   YEMEN

DJIBOUTI

ETHIOPIA

Pakistan
The KKH and its branches are a highlight of the route to India.
Page 144

BANGLADESH

SRI
LANKA

THAILAND   VIETNAM

CAMBODIA

PHILIPPINES

BRUNEI

M A L A Y S I A

CONGO
D.R.   UGANDA   SOMALIA

KENYA

RWANDA

BURUNDI

TANZANIA

India
Ride a Bullet in the Himalayas, survive the highway madness.
Pages 146-147

I
N
D
O
N
E
S
I
A

PAPUA
NEW
GUINEA

MALAWI

OLA   ZAMBIA

MOZAMBIQUE

BIA   ZIMBABWE

OTSWANA

MADAGASCAR

SWAZILAND

OUTH   LESOTHO

FRICA

I
N
D
I
A
N

O
C
E
A
N

★ TRAILBLAZER

Australia
From the Red Centre dirt highways spread into the Outback.
Pages 171-176.

A U S T R A L I A

TASMANIA

NEW
ZEALAND

The Adventure Motorcycling World

Selected Highlights

TRIP REPORT
SUMATRA ~ HONDA C100

Name	Sander Kaptein
Year of birth	1978
Occupation	Forestry
Nationality	Dutch
Previous travels	Poland, Norway, Australia, Canada...
Bike travels	Norway

This trip	Sumatra
Trip duration	Two months
Departure date	January 2003
Number in group	Me
Distance covered	3000km (1875 miles)

Best day	Through the paddies in W Sumatra
Worst day	None, I took it easy
Favourite place	West Sumatra
Biggest headache	Buying the bike as a foreigner
Biggest mistake	Not taking tools with me
Pleasant surprise	Friendly police, no problems at all
Any illness	No
Cost of trip	€400
Other trips planned	India to Holland

Bike model	Honda C100
Age, mileage	Who knows!?
Modifications	None
Wish you'd done...	Nothing for this trip
Tyres used	Rubber Rangers
Punctures	One
Type of baggage	Backpack

Bike's weak point	Shock not up to Sumatran roads
Strong point	Good engine
Bike problems	Nothing serious
Accidents	No
Same bike again	No, next time a GL100 for Indonesia
Any advice	Ride the same bike as the locals

CENTRAL ASIA, RUSSIA AND MONGOLIA

For just five words, that's quite an inspiring and exotic heading. The route to India and Kathmandu may well be a classic, but the northern highways across Russia and Central Asia which opened out after the fall of the USSR prove that global travel is not always becoming ever more restricted.

Visa-wise, the **high route** outlined earlier across **Siberia** is straightforward once you're in and you have the time; the tricky bit starts beyond Irkutsk and Lake Baikal where travel by railway, river or on winter ice is the norm. If you want to ride it all on a bike, the season is realistically limited to two or three months. This route would suit either riders wanting to keep the visa situation simple or dirt-loving, river-splashing desperadoes looking for a challenge in Far Eastern Russia.

Roadsign, Mongolia – about as rare as a one-humped camel. © Geoff Kingsmill

However, culturally (and in places, scenically) **Central Asia** offers the diversity that Russia lacks. It was through this region that the fabled 'silk roads' developed two millennia ago; a network of trade routes along which silk, paper and gunpowder shuttled west to Europe via places like Samarkand, before trade passed into the hands of the 17th-century European seafaring empires.

For the time being **China** sticks to its historic isolationism; only rideable if you organise the expensive escort though one day these regs will ease up. The good news is that a now usable border crossing in western **Mongolia's** Altaï mountains means this distinctive and undeveloped country – long a Timbuktu-like metaphor for the back of beyond – no longer needs to be visited in a loop out of Ulaan Bator, but can be satisfyingly transited. Can't face the schelp across the steppes? Then take the trans-Siberian railway from Moscow to Ulan: more on p.170.

The Caucasus and Central Asia

The Soviets may be history but their legacy of control and bureaucracy remains as fresh as Lenin's corpse. The good thing is, everything you've heard about Moslem hospitality is true and then some. As with so much of adventure motorcycling, the turgid grindings of officialdom will drive you nuts but ordinary human encounters will warm your heart. If there is a teahouse (*chaihana*) alongside the road, spend the night there for a few dollars room and board. They are much more fun and cheaper then hotels; you eat with the family and sleep on the floor. Support your local *chaihana*! If you overnight in the big cities though, make sure your bike is **securely parked** and out of sight.

Georgia and Azerbaijan

The Caucasus is the name of a mountain range in between the Black Sea and the Caspian Sea, but has also become a shorthand for the post-Soviet republics of Georgia, Azerbaijan, Armenia and, if they could have their way, Chechnya to the north. Most riders are making a transit **between Turkey to the Baku**

TRIP REPORT
CENTRAL ASIA ~ SUZUKI DR750

Name	Greg D and Natasha M
Year of birth	1969 and 1974
Occupation	Teachers
Nationality	Polish-Canadian, Russian
Previous travels	I rarely travel without the bike
Bike travels	Lots
This trip	Poland, Turkey, Uzbekistan, Siberia
Trip duration	Nine weeks
Departure date	July 2002
Number in group	Just us
Distance covered	20,000km (12,500 miles)
Best day	Every day
Worst day	Crashing on the Uzbek steppe
Favourite place	Greg: Bukhara; Natasha: Turkey
Biggest headache	Borders and checkpoints
Biggest mistake	Not getting Azeri and Turkmen visas
Pleasant surprise	Central Asia is a safe place to travel
Any illness	Nothing serious
Cost of trip	$7000
Other trips planned	Maybe Far Eastern Russia
Bike model	Suzuki DR Big 750
Age, mileage	1988, 38,000km
Modifications	A tin of black paint and a brush
Wish you'd done...	None to think of
Tyres used	Dunlop trail, rear: Shinko trail
Punctures	None
Type of baggage	Givi case, Kappa boxes, bags
Bike's weak point	Not enough poke two up with kit
Strong point	A real workhorse, simple + reliable
Bike problems	Just the usual things wearing out
Accidents	Two falls on the rutted steppes
Same bike again	Maybe. Looking for Super Tenere
Any advice	Take fast wearing spares

TRIP NOTES THROUGH THE 'STANS

As you will read, **visas** are a headache and places like Turkmenistan and Uzbekistan can be hard work. For cash, **dollars** are better than euros as a $1 note is a cheap tip. Turkmenistan has a 4:1 advantage on the black market which is virtually official.

Checkpoints are everywhere but with a polite 'Salaam aleikum, a handshake, smiles (and accepting tea) you needn't pay bribes. Motor **insurance**: if they don't ask, don't bother (but don't ram the president's limo either!).

Kazakhstan

Letter of Introduction (LOI) needed for a **visa**. I asked for a dual-entry visa and obtained my LOI from Khan Tengri Mountaineering in Almaty for $50 – **www.kantengri.kz**. Faxing the LOI to the Kazakh embassy in Berlin I was issued a visa on the same day for €110.

Entering Kazakhstan you have to fill out a customs declaration form similar to Russia, and you must register with the police within five days or face a $160 fine and a lot of hassle (the expectation is your sponsor registers your visa). I attempted to register my visa with the Police/OVIR at Semey but they insisted I have Kan Tengri do it in Almaty.

Riding tips Roads can be rough, especially around the Aral Sea. Drivers in Almaty are pushy and the police use speed traps.

Uzbekistan

LOI (not needed by Americans) from Kan Tengri for $50. It turned out to be issued by the Uzbekistan Olympic Committee. Make sure you get to the Uzbek Embassy in Almaty by 9.30.am and join the queue for a single entry visa on the spot for $50.

We entered from Kyrgyzstan near Karakol/Uchchorgan, not a regular border crossing point. The Kyrgyz soldiers let us pass after some paper work but the Uzbeks told us to go back, then allowed us through after some hours. Leaving Uzbekistan for Turkmenistan we had to show hotel receipts and match the money as stated on the customs declaration form. **Highlights** include the market in Tashkent and of course Samarkand and Bukhara.

Riding tips It turns out the direct road from Tashkent to Samarkand crosses Kazakhstan. After some arguing with the Kazakh guards we took a chance and carried on. Approaching the raised boom gates we enquired innocently 'Samarkand?', 'Da...' and kept moving. This technique worked getting back into Uzbekistan also, though it was a bit nerve wracking We managed to cross without showing our passports to any of them. Perhaps it's *normalnaya*.

The police in Uzbekistan are well known as unfriendly, especially in the east. In Namagan itself we were told to leave the city immediately.

Petrol is dirt cheap in Uzbekistan but getting it can be frustrating. I never saw a petrol station open and bought fuel from roadside cans. This fuel is as low as 72 octane and fuel consumption on our G/S doubled. I filtered the petrol through material catching plenty of rust and crud.

Kyrgyzstan

The least hassley 'stan. I picked up a visa in London for £80 but could have got it in Almaty on the spot for $30. LOI not needed.

Entering Kyrgyzstan from the eastern end of Lake Issykul via Kegen, I had my Kazakh visa stamped out but was not stamped into Kyrgyzstan so I was able to enter again later. When entering the Lake Issykul region you must pay a small national park entry fee.

Riding tips The roads in Kyrgyzstan are rough at times, the tunnels and passes around

---

ferry to Turkmenistan across the Caspian. There was a non-violent 'rose' change of regime in Georgia in January 2004 but it's not been all roses since then. Though safe, **Armenia** doesn't often get visited, mostly because its borders are only open (for overlanders at least) from Georgia. Unrest in Chechnya and less so in Dagestan and South Ossieta means you won't get through the **Russian Caucasus**; indeed the north of Georgia should be avoided and currently you might want to make a dash for Azerbaijan in one day.

Visas are not too hard to obtain for Georgia or Azerbaijan with a hotel reservation; the old trick of being allowed a five-day transit through one coun-

TRIP NOTES THROUGH THE 'STANS

Toktogul are particularly hair-raising. You'll come across a lot of roadworks so the future could be bright.

The road from Almaty to the northern shore of Lake Issykul in Kyrgyzstan is an extremely rough track that was barely rideable on a G/S. Three river crossings must be made early in the morning while levels are low. There was no border post.

To China via the Torugurt Pass

If you've not set it up **months in advance** (permits around $700; $100/day escort), forget it. The *Caravan Café* in Kashgar can help. In 2004 riders used the Irkeshtam Pass out of Sary Tash – an 'international' crossing – without escorts. A fluke or a sign of things to come? From either pass to Pakistan on the KKH is about 700km and three days.

Tajikistan

Not many riders make a visit here, but like Kyrgyzstan, it's comparatively easy to get in and not much hassle to be there. LOIs are needed, best obtained via tour operators.

Fuel can be hard to find, the police are conspicuous and the region round the Afghan border is well worth avoiding.

Turkmenistan

The grimmest of the 'stans for paperwork. Applying in Ankara or Teheran/Mashad is fast and easy, Tashkent slow: at least a week for the **four-day transit visa** for $31 with no LOI. If you wish to stay longer you will need a tourist visa and help for Stantours or the like.

Among other unpredictable and deranged actions, the despotic president has a habit of randomly shutting all borders. The Iran border had been closed in the months up to our entry and was to close again the day after we left, why no one knows.

Entering Turkmenistan takes hours. The process involves meetings with officials, each wanting an official fee plus a bribe for a speedy response.

There are other fees like 'petrol tax' based on engine capacity because it's so cheap (we're talking half a euro for 25 litres!). You're also given a wad of documents that includes a map of the country with your route marked on it. If you deviate you're breaking the law and there are so many checkpoints that leaving the route is difficult. We were stopped twice at the exit for extra payments while trying to deviate, then again down the road for another document check. Entry costs for crossing the border with one bike and two people exceeded $100.

Leaving the country was not much faster, with the guards even going through CDs I'd burned (to save digital photographs) on their computer. Turkmenistan was the only place I was stopped by suited secret service agents about taking photographs.

Frankly it was a fluke that we were able to get out across the Iranian border – it's been closed since so don't count on it. There is no land exit to **Kazakhstan** either (no road) but there may be ferries to Russia.

There's not much there now but the ruins of **Merv** (30km from Mary) will show you what happens when you get on the wrong side of a Mongol hoard.

Caspian Sea Ferry

Although services are regular, don't expect to simply buy a ticket (with an optional cabin) and ride on. The service is primarily focused on oil tanker trains. Once you work out departure times, expect to pay under $100 for the 14-hour crossing with a grubby cabin (the ferry is extremely slow). You may prefer to bring your own food and, coming from Turkmenistan, the services of a fixer could save you a day or two.

Alec Simpson with David Berghof

try if you had a visa for the other is no longer valid so it's best to let a visa agency do the work for you. Get your machine off the road in towns overnight or expect it to be stolen.

Roads are famously bad in Georgia, better in Azerbaijan. **Fuel** is easy to get, with hotels going for around $40. It's worth remembering that Georgia and Azerbaijan are Christian Orthodox surrounded by Islamic countries; some travellers have found that, particularly in Georgia, the spirit of traditional Moslem hospitality is rather thin on the ground, with a rise in mafia-like criminal activity.

Trans Russia and Mongolia

Shaun Munro

'It's the end of the road as we know it (1).'
(Vladivostok) © Simon McCarthy

For the adventure motorcyclist Russia can be broken up into three main parts: **Far Eastern Russia** from Magadan /Vladivostok west to Ulan Ude is tough going, with only the barest of necessities available; **Siberia**, large and spread out with a sealed-road network out of the cities and some access to modern conveniences. West of the Urals is **Russia**: Europeanised, touristy and the place you may encounter bent roadside cops.

From either end, it's a vast country that grows on the motorcycle traveller. What really stands out is **Russian hospitality**. It's rare to meet such warm and giving people who treat you as a friend with no suspicions whatsoever.

RUSSIAN PRACTICALITIES

Paperwork Checkpoints will want your IDP, bike papers, passport and Russian bike rego (supplied on entry) to copy into the log books. Carry photocopies as losing one item can mean a bribe or a spell in the salt mines. No carnet required.

Accommodation We paid about $10 a night for a sparse room. In cities finding a place can be difficult; stay in roadside *guestinistas* or camp outside the city. In Novosibirsk foreigners are only supposed to stay in certain overpriced hotels. Arrive as early as possible if you want to find a room without being stiffed. East of Ulan Ude you'll either be a house guest or camping most of the time so make sure your sleeping bag, mat and tent are up to it.

Visa Now simple (including intro letters) thanks to visa agencies. Hand them your passport, a couple of photos and up to $120. We've heard of a week but it took us two months so allow plenty of time. (Try for a multiple-entry visa if you plan to visit the 'Stans or Mongolia.) Register your visa with the OVIR (Immigration police) in seven days.

We were a month late and over 1000 miles out on our stipulated exit point but nothing was said. Others say expect problems, but it can be difficult to extend visas.

Fuel Fuel ranges from 80 octane to 93, cost is around 50c a litre. At petrol stations to stop runaways you pay first, then they turn it on. If the nozzle has no trigger you can get petrol spraying everywhere when your tank's full, as Ewan McGregor found. In the east aim for a 400-km range.

Learn the alphabet English or German will get you by in the west, but not east of Baikal. At the very least learn the alphabet so you don't end up in Xandyga when you wanted Palm Springs. And as anywhere, learning a few choice phrases greatly enhances your trip so carry a phrasebook.

Vodka One of the most common phrases you encounter in Russia is *'Davai! Malinka vodka'* which literally means 'come share a little bit of vodka with me and we will end up drinking for two days, departing the best of friends'. Initially this is a very enjoyable aspect of the Russian hospitality, but after months of people rushing up thrusting bottles of vodka in your face it gets a bit much. Just saying no thank you will not always help. We found that only claiming you had half a liver or no kidneys would stop further pleadings.

Shaun Munro with Alec Simpson

TRIP REPORT
FINLAND TO BAIKAL ~ CBR1000

Name	Pekka Salo
Year of birth	1961
Occupation	Pulp mill mechanic
Nationality	Finnish
Previous travels	Quite a lot
Bike travels	Spain, Turkey, Romania, Morocco...

This trip	Finland to Lake Baikal, Russia
Trip duration	Four weeks
Departure date	August 2001
Number in group	1
Distance covered	15,000km (9375 miles)

Best day	When I came home
Worst day	Rainy day near Moscow
Favourite place	Livstjanka by Lake Baikal
Biggest headache	Rear suspension
Biggest mistake	Worn rear suspension
Pleasant surprise	Friendly people
Any illness	No
Cost of trip	$670
Other trips planned	Vladivostok and Magadan

Bike model	Honda CBR1000
Age, mileage	1987, 190,000km
Modifications	None
Wish you'd done...	None
Tyres used	Pirelli MT90 rear, front Conti TKV 11
Punctures	None
Type of baggage	Soft all round

Bike's weak point	Hagon suspension (twin shock)
Strong point	Reliability and power
Bike problems	Back shock
Accidents	None
Same bike again	Sure, while it runs
Any advice	Mirror – signal – manoeuvre

The easiest river crossing. © Shaun Munro.

We flew from Alaska to Magadan and took a week to acclimatise and sort out the necessary paperwork with the local motoring organisation. The three of us were on a world trip and expecting the most difficult stage with unmaintained roads and a range of insects that made Alaska seem like the Bug Show matinée for under-5s at Disneyland.

During winter Siberia is to 'cold' like summertime Sahara is to 'hot'; on the Road of Bones we'd pass right by the Met station which recorded the world's lowest temperature. However, by arriving in mid-June (2003) we timed our arrival to maximise the time we would have to cross all the way to Europe.

All in all 10,000 miles (16,000km), a few accidents and too many bottles of vodka separated us from our exit point, the Black Sea. The paperwork was not difficult and when greeted with a friendly smile the local authorities were surprisingly helpful and efficient.

Magadan to Yakutsk – 'The Road of Bones'

Once our bikes were reassembled we were ready to hit the road, with little thought that that would soon become a literal expression. For the first 100km out of Magadan the road was fairly well paved and we vainly hoped it would continue so. However, the potholes grew wider until they *were* the road. We slowly grew accustomed to what the next 4000km to Ulan Ude had in store.

Stretching 2000km from Magadan northwest to Yakutsk, the Kolyma Highway formerly known as the **Road of Bones** (RoB) was the toughest part of the trans-Russian leg, at times covering just 24km a day. It's said every metre of the road, built to link gold and coal mines with Magadan port or the Lena river system at Yakutsk, cost the life of a gulag prisoner.

Barge cruise on the Aldan River out of Xandyga.
© Matt Glitman

About 650km north of Magadan, days of dust brought us to Susuman. As is typical of the region we were invited into homes where we spent a couple of days. Several bottles and huge meals later we had to drag ourselves away from our generous hosts. Had we known what lay ahead we'd not have not been so eager to leave. In the mid-1990s *Mondo Enduro* found the RoB a cinch, but with every passing year the abandoned section gets progressively worse.

At **Kadykchan** the road splits. Straight on leads up to Ust Nera where the hard-frozen winter-only route reaches back down to the Kolyma Highway just west of Kyubume. Summer rivers are too deep on this route and bridges are incomplete. Left at Kadykchan is the original and now **unmaintained** line of the Road of Bones. Over the next 300km or so bridges are sparse and mud is plentiful. Often either side of the track is a water-logged swamp which at times covers the road. If dry (or frozen) this section would not have taken long, but we had to dismount continuously to push through water holes that in places would have covered our heads.

Near Tomtor you'll pass Oimyakon which recorded the coldest temperature north of the equator: -71°C. During the summer (the only realistic time for riding), you'll encounter mud holes and round-the-clock mosquitoes and horseflies. Mud and water are OK, but it was the relentless **insect torment** which made our RoB transit hell: plenty of full-strength bug repellent will make this section more bearable, a region that is spectacularly isolated, something that is aided by the poignancy of the hard-won and now semi-abandoned settlements.

Ural dudes on the prowl. © Shaun Munro

Like the *Long Way* crew, we hit the RoB too early. Later in the season it's drier, shallower and just plain less gruelling, but at least the 22-hour days gave us plenty of time to work it out! Around Tomtor is the most difficult section: fifty-year-old bridges have been washed away or are going downstream soon. Only one river looked too deep and required sloshing ice water over the local 'ferry man' to truck us over for $20. In the end it was only waist deep, but knowing the shallow route was the crux.

Xandiga is a vital fuel point and where you ferry down the Aldan River to **Ust Tata** (8 hours haggle for $50). After disembarking, the road was good to **Yakutsk** (accessible by ferry over the Lena River). South of here is 1000km on fast dirt to **Skovoridino** where you'll meet the road from **Vladivostok**, 2500-km away (see box below).

The road west of Skovo was described as 'impassable' in mid-2003, so we put our bikes on a wagon as far as Chita for eighty bucks each. Later we met

CHITA TO VLADIVOSTOK – THE FORMER ZILOV GAP

We heard there was a roadless section in east Siberia, the distance varied depending on who you asked, putting it into the same category as everything concerning Russian travel.

The detailed and accurate **Russian Road Atlas** (see picture p.166) had dotted and solid lines between Chita and Khabarovsk, even though in 2004 Putin 'opened' the road from Moscow and Vladivostok on Russian TV.

From other riders (including Gold Wingers!) we heard of rocks and a 50kph maximum speed for '3 or 4 days'. To ride or take the Trans Siberian? We decided to ride what was once the roadless Zilov Gap.

Chita to Khabarovsk (850km from Vladivostok) is 2264km. The first 110km was good bitumen. The last 800km into Khabarovsk is 60% good bitumen. The 1600km in between varied from good dirt to

deep sand, gravel and rocks, with river crossings where bridges were missing. Road crews were working round the clock.

There was no accommodation but camping was not so easy. The road is built up over the swamps and Armco stops you getting to good camping spots. There are a few truck stops but the drunken camaraderie can get a bit much. Petrol was usually 92 octane, sometimes 80. We needed a **400km range**. All the traffic was heading west; used Jap cars imported via Vladivostok.

It took us six days to reach Khabarovsk. It's hard to enjoy riding when you think you're about to fall off. You don't forget times when you're on the edge for so long, day after day. But we can all dine out on the fact that we rode *all* the way across Russia.

Phil McMillan

some Italians who did it in a regular van. From **Chita** another easy 1000km got us in **Ulan Ude**: the junction for **Mongolia** (see box below). From Ulan a beautiful road leads around Lake Baikal but from here the Wild East is behind you; we even saw German campervans outside Irkutsk.

Irkutsk is a wonderful city with a distinctive European feel. Continuing west the roads are all sealed or being repaired. Stopping off at Novosibirsk or Ekaterinburg provides a welcome respite from monotonous road riding. You're always welcomed like a long lost brother. In Ekaterinburg we were the guests of honour at a party for the Black Knives bike gang; a hangover I'm still recovering from! Further west we had enough and took the low road to Turkey, catching a ferry from the resort city of Sochi on the Black Sea to Trabzon.

MONGOLIA: NO FENCES

Mongolia is one of the world's great AM destinations; your 'golf course' fantasy made real and on an epic scale too. Accommodation is cheap in the few tourist areas but elsewhere a tent is a must – it's how most countryfolk live. Credit cards work in UB, elsewhere bring cash: **US dollars** are best but for fuel or shopping use the local tugriks. **English** and **Russian** are the most spoken foreign languages.

Visas, borders and getting there

Visas are relatively easy though less waiting costs more. Americans get a three-month visa at any border, most others will need to obtain it in advance. Closest consulates are Ulan Ude and Irkutsk or Beijing. No letter of introduction or carnets are required.

If not riding there consider putting your bike on the **Trans-Siberian railway** in Moscow. Direct trains to UB leave weekly, take five days and cost from £150 to £300 one-way with a cabin, plus meals. You travel with the bike and arrive fresh as a daisy and raring to go. Otherwise, the border at **Altanbulag** north of UB can be tedious. They may want a deposit of as much as ten percent

of the bike's value, though with smiles and patience we got away with it. It's also possible to cross via **Tsaganurr**, in the northwest corner and via **Ereen Tsav** in the northeast.

Riding and running a bike

There are two paved roads in Mongolia: Altanbulag to UB and UB west to the touristy Kubla Khan capital at Arvaiheer. Elsewhere is communal land with no fences, few signs and indistinct tracks. Pick a spot and you can usually ride straight there, so a **GPS** will be genuinely useful. **Maps** (some in UB) are vital, but don't assume a bold red line adds up to any sort of road: 1:500,000 'Tactical Pilot Charts' (TPCs) work well with GPS.

Most tracks are easy to ride though they tend to fade out. Not to worry though, as the steppes are easy too if they're dry (though not all dry lake beds are as dry as they seem). **Fuel** (both leaded and unleaded) can be hit and miss out of UB; fill up at any opportunity. The same goes for drinking **water**.

Mongolians are honest and friendly – you'll have some memorable encounters (and meals!) with the nomads – but it's not unknown for things to disappear overnight so sleep with everything in your tent.

The **Gobi Desert**, which covers huge tracts of southern Mongolia, is actually mostly grassy plains and also easy to ride. Actual sand dunes only cover a relatively small areas just north of the Chinese border. Western Mongolia includes the **Altai mountains** which are passable in many places and so offer the best riding and scenery.

Summertime temperatures are warm but never too hot, even further south in the Gobi, though in the Altai the temperature drops, so bring clothes for snow at any time. Winter is, of course, colder than a well-digger's ...

Cheeky Mongolian. © Tom Bierma

Shaun Munro

Australia

While on its fringes Australia may be a familiarly Western country, its barely inhabited core, the **Outback**, provides as vast a wilderness as you'll find anywhere. The world's most arid continent, you can ride for thousands of kilometres across Australia without giving a thought to all the administrative and political hassles which typify travel in developing countries.

Some find this absence of aggro, added to the sometimes monotonous terrain and dispersed highlights to be comparatively unsatisfying after the hard -won battles of Latin America or Asia. How fickle we humans are!

For **bitumen cruising**, a travel guide will see you right. The dirt road touring outline here focuses on the Central Deserts and the Kimberley. With a trip up to Cape York (see p.242), you'd get about the best 10,000km off-road tour the country could offer.

Importing your bike

Get a carnet or apply for a 'Vehicle Import Approval' **in advance** and pay the 24% deposit on the value of your bike; you'll get it back when you export. There's talk that carnets can't be renewed in Australia so check with your carnet issuing organisation.They're also hot on wing mirrors, indicators, forbid oil leaks and love to fumigate your bike at your expense so arrive with a machine **clean** enough to eat off. More info at www.aaa.asn.au/touring.htm.

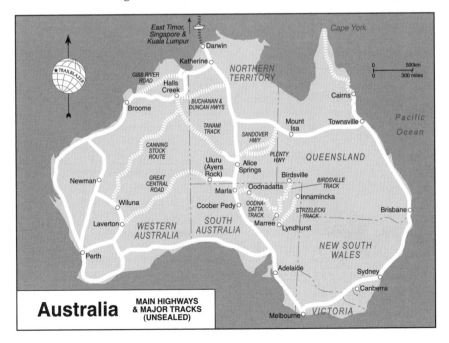

Australia — MAIN HIGHWAYS & MAJOR TRACKS (UNSEALED)

T R I P   R E P O R T
AROUND AUSTRALIA ~ KLR650

Name	Brian Canning
Year of birth	1950
Occupation	Self-employed
Nationality	British
Previous travels	Europe, Asia, America
Bike travels	A lot of Western Europe
This trip	Right around and into the centre
Trip duration	Six months
Departure date	March 2003
Number in group	1
Distance covered	22,239 km (13,900 miles)
Best day	Hitting a 'roo and staying on
Worst day	The day I flew home (grim)
Favourite place	Cape Le Grand NP, WA
Biggest headache	What's a headache? Get on with it
Biggest mistake	Not going earlier – and rushing it
Pleasant surprise	How attractive emptiness can be
Any illness	Felt sick when I had to come home
Cost of trip	£5800 with flights
Other trips planned	Got the atlas, just need the funds
Bike model	Kawasaki KLR650
Age, mileage	Seven years old, 17,590km
Modifications	None. Sold it back to the bike shop
Wish you'd done...	Bigger tank (range was 250km)
Tyres used	Not sure – cheap, black and round
Punctures	None
Type of baggage	Ventura tailpack and saddlebags
Bike's weak point	None (bigger tank would be handy)
Strong point	Cheap and reliable
Bike problems	None – just usual tyre/chain wear
Accidents	One close encounter with a 'roo
Same bike again	KLR was great – any bike is good
Any advice	Borrow luggage from bike shop

Major Outback tracks

Several former prospecting and droving trails have developed into corrugated cross-country 'dirt motorways' that converge in Central Australia. Most of them don't offer challenging riding unless it rains, but they all add up to agreeable short cuts between key areas.

Don't forget though, the riding may be relatively easy if you keep under 60mph/100kph but distances between fuel points can be up to 250 miles/400km and **summer** temperatures will require up to ten litres of drinking water per day. Don't take any chances – both experienced locals and urban, all-terrain thrill seekers die every summer on these tracks.

Birdsville Track: Birdsville QLD to Marree SA ~ 520km (325 miles)

Australia's best-known track is a much-tamed version of the once ill-defined stock route. All you'll get is dust storms, bleak, flat monotony, the Mungeranie Pub (fuel) halfway along and the Birdsville Pub at the end.

Old Ghan/Oodnadatta: Alice NT to Marree SA ~ 1050km (700 miles)

Historically and scenically much more interesting, this track follows the old Ghan railway and the Oodnadatta Track. The pick of the tracks in this area, it's a bit sandy from Alice to Finke but a good way of getting between Alice and Adelaide off the bitumen.

Strzelecki Track: Lyndhurst to Innamincka SA ~ 460km (290 miles)

A little-used and unexceptional track through very arid land that runs east of the Birdsville to Innamincka, a hotel in the middle-of-nowhere close to Coopers Creek where explorers Burke and Wills staggered to their doom.

Sandover Highway: North of Alice to NT/QLD border ~ 550km (345 miles)

A remote, little-used but straightforward short cut between Mount Isa and Alice Springs, possibly with a 400km fuel stage between the Aboriginal communities of Arlparra and Alpurrurulam close to the Queensland border.

Plenty Highway: Boulia QLD to Alice NT ~ 740km (465 miles)

Southern version of the above; a good way of getting west from Birdsville to Alice if you don't want to cross the Simpson 'against the dunes'. Marginally enlivened as it passes the Harts Range near Alice.

Buchanan and Duncan Highways: Dunmarra Roadhouse NT to Halls Creek WA ~ 750 km (470 miles)

A particularly desolate link if heading from Queensland to Western Australia without the detour north to Katherine and the Victoria Highway.

Tanami Track: Alice NT to Halls Creek WA ~ 1060km (660 miles)

Very handy shortcut to the northwest from Alice, the Tanami is a long flat 'dirtbahn' up to the WA border and a little rougher and sandier after that. A 400-km fuel range will do.

Great Central Road: Yulara NT to Laverton WA ~ 1140km (710 miles)

Often confused with the Gunbarrel Highway, this is a very useful link between southern WA and the Centre. Permits are easy to get in Alice but no one checks. Longest fuel stage is 350km if you use Avgas (which will ruin a cat' converter but is otherwise probably OK) or 816km for normal petrol/gasoline.

'Are you sure this is one of your Outback dirtbahns, Chris?'

Canning Stock Route: Wiluna to Halls Creek WA ~ 1860km (1160 miles)

Almost two thousand kilometres of sandy twin-ruts, this off-road trek across the Gibson and Great Sandy Deserts of WA is in a league of its own.

Fuel can be dumped in 200-litre drums at Well 23 by the Capricorn Roadhouse in Newman or bought from Kunawarritji Community (about KM1160 up, near Well 33), but this still requires a 1000+ km range.

The Gibb River Road ~ 710km (445 miles)

About the size of Ireland, the Kimberley is a flood- and fire-ravaged region in Australia's far northwest. The whole region gets washed-out from December to April. What makes the trans-Kimberley Gibb River's corrugations tolerable, especially in its western half, are the many gorges with year-round **waterfalls** or pools. Seeing as 'winter' temperatures are only a degree or two lower than the summer, they make a pleasant string of breaks between Derby and Wyndham. Bell Creek Gorge is probably the pick of the crop. Fuel and even accommodation is not the problem you might think.

Life on the Outback road

Apart from the risk of drunk or tired drivers, kamikaze marsupials and dehydration, Australia is a very safe country to travel in. You'll find surprisingly little evidence of rural redneck bigotry – in the north and west at least, and while common sense should never be abandoned, the desolate highway paranoia customary in the US is rare. The danger of **hazardous wildlife:** sharks, crocs, jellyfish and particularly spiders and snakes are all much exaggerated by yarn-spinning locals. Other road users and the heat are the real killers.

Along with everything else, **fuel** gets expensive in remote regions. At roadhouses like the Rabbit Flat in the Tanami, Mt Dare in the Simpson, or Warburton on the Great Central Road, expect to pay up to double southern city prices. Many of these places don't accept credit cards, so carry cash and note the restricted opening times.

AUSTRALIAN WEATHER

For the recommended areas of exploration, the summer months from December to March are the ones to **avoid**.

In the Central Deserts most days will reach 40°C or more, with an aridity that will devour your water supplies and energy. Even if accessible, these areas are little visited at this time and stranded without water, you're finished in a couple of days.

At the same time the north, more or less above the latitude linking Derby WA with Cairns QLD, experiences its **wet season**. Dirt roads become impassable and even sealed highways can get inundated. Cyclones usually occur at either end of the Wet. Rain can fall at any time in the Central Deserts too, but while patterns are erratic it's usually in the form of a brief torrential downpour.

Don't be fooled by the 'winter' in the far north – it's better described as the dry season with temperatures at 31°C every day. In the arid interior you might get the odd freezing night around July.

T R I P   R E P O R T
SIMPSON DESERT ~ 1150 ADVENTURE

Name	Tony Romanas
Year of birth	1965
Occupation	–
Nationality	Australian
Previous travels	Mainly Outback Australia
Bike travels	Mainly Outback – love the desert

This trip	Simpson Desert (SA–QLD)
Trip duration	Two weeks
Departure date	July 2004
Number in group	10
Distance covered	4000km (2500 miles)

Best day	Hitting the first dunes
Worst day	When the battery leaked
Favourite place	Desert, stars, campfire, mates, beer
Biggest headache	The bike was too heavy
Biggest mistake	Not paying attention in the dunes
Pleasant surprise	The big GS can take the big dunes!
Any illness	A cold went though us like wildfire
Cost of trip	$400AUD
Other trips planned	Canning Desert Run

Bike model	BMW GS 1150 Adventure
Age, mileage	1 year, 16,000km
Modifications	Stock – this thing has it all
Wish you'd done...	Gel battery
Tyres used	Continental twinduro
Punctures	None
Type of baggage	Backpack and 4WD

Bike's weak point	Heavy in soft sand, heavy to lift
Strong point	Torque, comfort, economy
Bike problems	Battery leaked when in its side
Accidents	1 heavy fall in dunes – no big deal
Same bike again	Absolutely
Any advice	Don't carry a 200kg load in the desert

GS1150s make ideal Outback cruisers and are easily rented.

One thing you'll have to get used to if you're cruising the Outback's highways is roadhouse food; a 'pie floater' is about as appetising as it sounds. If camped on the coast you're bound to meet recreational fishermen who'll have a fish or two to spare: gut it, wrap it in foil and stick it on some embers. On the other hand Outback pubs – often called 'hotels' and offering grungy if cheap rooms, will provide many memorable encounters as well as accommodation. Friday nights or pay days in 'welfare towns' are especially lively.

Which brings us around to the dangers of highway driving. Single vehicle rollovers (SVOs) are among the most common causes of death for young men in the Northern Territory, and Australia has a bad record for highway fatalities although nothing compared to Brazil or India. For the motorcyclist the chief dangers are other road users, drunk or otherwise, and more significantly animals, most especially wandering stock marsupials of various kinds which hop across the road, especially between dusk and dawn. A kangaroo is one tough animal to hit and you'll always come away worse. For this reason alone, it's not worth risking **riding in the Outback at night**, even on tarmac. It's the instinctive swerving to avoid these beasts (along with losing concentration or dropping off to sleep) that accounts for all those SVOs.

GPS is unnecessary on the tracks described here (not that that stops anyone!) as long as you pay attention to conventional navigational practice. Nevertheless, don't let the fact that 'it's only Australia' lull you into a false sense of security: if you are heading for the desert take all the precautions and preparation outlined in earlier chapters seriously.

RECOMMENDED BOOKS AND MAPS

There are several books on survival and motoring around the Outback, but one which puts it all together in a neat package is Lonely Planet's *Outback Australia*. Although biased towards 4WD, it's still an excellent guide to all the tracks described here and more besides. If you're from overseas, back it up with a conventional travel guide like the *Rough Guide to Australia* (Chris Scott writes the NT and WA chapters so you can be sure he looks after your unsealed needs!).

Some regional guides
Cape York, an Adventurer's Guide by Moon or *Cape York a 4WD Experience* by Lynn and Yvonne Fraser both offer detailed information on this classic ride.

Without a doubt the most detailed and practical book on the CSR is *The Canning Stock Route* by Gard. There are a number of excellent maps on the CSR. The **Royal Automobile Association of WA** (RAA of WA; 🖳 www.rac.com.au/travel) produces an excellent strip map of the CSR. Others include Hema Maps, Australian Geographic and Westprint (see below):

Map sources
HEMA Maps
🖳 www.hemamaps.com.au/
Westprint
🖳 www.westprint.com.au

Geoff Kingsmill

Africa

Most RTWers will agree, Africa represents the ultimate adventure overlanding destination. The combination of desert, jungle, unstable politics and crumbling infrastructure, along with the diversity and vitality of its peoples, make a visit to Africa unforgettable, if not always for the right reasons.

This vitality, when faced with many of the world's poorest and most misgoverned nations is something that will make you question the social value of wealth. Add to that the stamina required to cross the *pistes* of the **Sahara**, or the flooded trenches of the **Congo basin**, and you'll have an experience that'll swing your moods like a gibbon on pay day.

Regional explorations

Even when you can, you don't have to cross the whole continent to get an authentic impression of Africa. Indeed, such localised regional explorations can be more rewarding if somewhat less sensational than claiming a trans-continental trek.

North of the Sahara, **Morocco** is easily accessible from Europe and offers a perfect introduction to Africa plus, in the south, a great experience in its own right. **West Africa** offers a fabulous chance to experience the continent too; it needs greater commitment than Morocco but is also shippably close to Europe or even east-coast USA. At twice the size of Texas, **Mali** is a favourite, and you could easily spend three months exploring this region's dusty back roads and mud hut villages.The **Sahara** is now sealed all the way along the Atlantic route – how boring is that! Far more satisfying are the hardcore routes though the central desert: principally Algeria, Libya and Niger.

At the other end of the continent, **South Africa** makes an easier if unrepresentative introduction to the countries which lie to the north, notably the eastern states of **Tanzania, Kenya** and **Uganda** offering timeless images of African plains and celebrated wildlife parks. You can now take a good bite out of southern African without getting stuck in, but of course it's the continental transit that gives you the full picture and the ultimate challenge.

THE WEATHER IN AFRICA

Crossing Africa from the north, two climatic factors govern your departure date: **summer** in the Sahara, and the **equatorial monsoon**. The former (April to October) adds greatly to a motorcyclist's perils on account of the vast amounts of drinking water which must be carried. Off the easiest axes, don't even think about it in summer (see box p.183).

In central Africa the rains (up to ten months a year) bring all but river traffic to a standstill from June to September along the equator, and to a lesser extent from February to April. South of here the sealed road network makes the rains in southern Africa from November to April less of an issue.

If you're heading across the continent from Europe and want an easy time of it, set off around **October or November**, riding into the Saharan winter and the central African dry season.

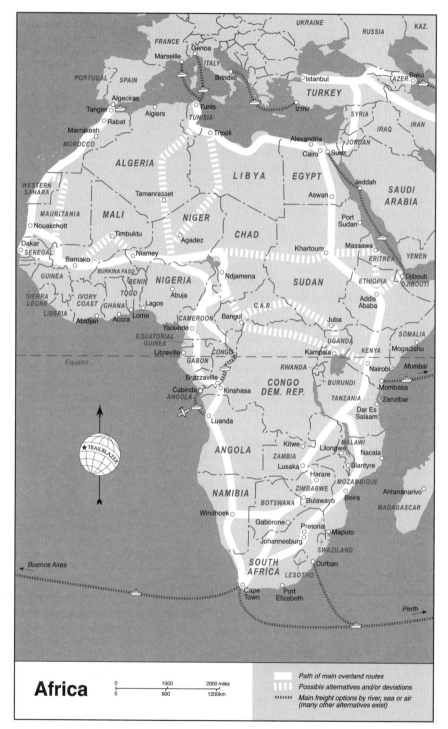

Africa

0	1000	2000 miles
0	600	1200km

Path of main overland routes

Possible alternatives and/or deviations

Main freight options by river, sea or air
(many other alternatives exist)

MAIN TRANS-CONTINENTAL ROUTES

Reading African travelogues of fifty years ago gives the impression of a Golden Age of African travel. European adventurers were saluted by border guards as they trundled across the French-controlled Sahara to British-controlled East Africa.

These days travelling across Africa is a game of snakes and ladders and it's not uncommon to change your itinerary on the eve of departure as another danger zone emerges. As a rule, political instability is **quick to develop and slow to subside**, while lawlessness at the remote frontiers of an ostensibly stable country are also a hazard to overlanders. Once in a while some brave or unhinged individual manages to cross a country thought to be deadly without any difficulties, the word spreads, others follow and the ladders shift. The unpredictable nature and logistical contortions of merely getting across Africa from one end to the other are what make this trip such a challenge.

The two traditional trans-African routes

Access permitting, the main way to experience Africa in the full has been to ride down from the Mediterranean to South Africa: traditionally ending at the continental toe of the Cape of Good Hope. Typically this is a 10,000km/6300-mile journey of at least two months.

Riders departing Europe are immediately faced with their first obstacle: the political and geographical challenge of the Sahara; a desert the size of America or Australia. Crossing it is easy via the Atlantic route to **West Africa**, a region which you can explore **without a carnet** (they have their own regional version). From here you can work your way through to Cameroon and **Central Africa's** feral republics like Gabon, Congo-Brazzaville and most especially the Democratic Republic of Congo (DRC, former Zaïre). Once you're in Angola you can scrape through to Namibia where the true difficulties end for the Cape-bound rider.

The other main route runs from **Cairo** via Sudan and Ethiopia into Kenya and then any which way south. Until 2003 these two routes were linked via **Chad** until the Darfur crisis developed in western Sudan. Unrest continues there, although oddly enough in early 2005 peace was agreed ending a much longer civil war in southern Sudan.

If stability actually develops here before Darfur, there could be a route through southern Sudan via the Central African Republic or even northeastern DRC – the old overland route of the 1980s.

NORTH AFRICA AND THE SAHARA

Easily accessible from Europe, North Africa provides a taste of Moslem Africa quite distinct from that south of the Sahara. Since the last edition of this book Algeria opened up – and then all but slammed shut again following the mass abductions of 2003 (see p.183). As this is written the sealed road from Morocco across the Sahara through Mauritania to Senegal nears completion, though the Algerians have been attempting to finish a similar project as long as I've been going there. This new **all-weather Atlantic Route** makes the Sahara crossable on a Honda Zoomer. It's also rather a dull route, unless you make some deviations inland from the Mauritanian coast to the Atar region.

There's also been talk of the long-closed and part-unsealed Layounne–Bir Mogrein route between Morocco and northern Mauritania opening up (see map), but as it crosses a strip of Polisario-controlled land, don't hold your breath.

High time to plug my 670-page *Sahara Overland* book (also published by Trailblazer) and the associated website: **www.sahara-overland.com**. You don't have to take my word for it, but between them they add up to the best English-language resource on travel in the Sahara, with an expanded section on desert biking plus seventy GPS routes across nine and-a-half countries.

There's plenty in there that it would be dumb to repeat here, so if you're interested in exploring the Sahara rather than just crossing it, get a copy or hook up with the website.

Morocco

Morocco is the best destination for an eye-opening experience of North Africa without committing yourself to expensive ferries or a desert crossing. Here you'll find ancient Moorish cities on a par with their counterparts in Asia, as well as a range of tracks (*pistes*) rising over the High Atlas to the fringes of the Sahara beyond. At many points on the southern edge of the Atlas ranges the drop from the scrubby high mountain pastures down to the oases on the desert floor will be a dramatic highlight of your visit.

One popular route idea that needs to be dispelled is **following the Mediterranean coast** from the Atlantic to the Red Sea. This plan often crops up on web forums, but for ten years or more the Algeria–Morocco border has been closed and there's little sign of it opening soon. You can only start the Med route from Tunisia eastwards through Libya to Egypt and as you'll read, you may wonder if it's worth the bother unless you're heading south.

Ferries leave southern Spanish ports for Morocco every few hours and cross in as little as 20 minutes. There's no need for a carnet or, in some cases, even a visa, making entry and paperwork relatively undemanding.

Dangers and annoyances include the **hustlers** in port areas and towns like Tangiers. I've met people fleeing Morocco after just a couple of days, so bad was their experience. And that's not including the hashish hard sell in the dope-growing area around Ketama. If you're tempted by a smoke, don't try and score here; set-ups are common.

Visits to southern Morocco are best in the **intermediate seasons** when it's neither baking at 40°C+ or freezing in the High Atlas, where snow commonly blocks the higher passes and lowland rain makes riding miserable. At any time of year in the mountains you can expect sudden **downpours** which quickly erode the Atlas's steep slopes and unmade roads. You'll find fuel prices in the north about the same as Europe (excluding the UK), but otherwise the cost of living is less, with food and lodging about half that of continental Europe.

The Grand Traverse of the Moroccan Sahara

While beach life around Agadir might be tempting (as well as being a place where southbound overlanders congregate), a good crack for the adventurous

T R I P   R E P O R T
MOROCCO ~ BMW R65

Name	Olivier Chartron
Year of birth	1965
Occupation	Computer scientist
Nationality	French
Previous travels	USA, Europe, Africa
Bike travels	Europe with Guzzi and K75

This trip	Western Sahara and Morocco
Trip duration	Five weeks
Departure date	September 2004
Number in group	Three then one after a week
Distance covered	7000km (4375 miles)

Best day	From Ouarzazate to Marrakech
Worst day	Rain in the Anti Atlas
Favourite place	Dhara, near the ocean
Biggest headache	Parking guards wanting fees
Biggest mistake	Too much gear
Pleasant surprise	People and the beauty of the Sahara
Any illness	No
Cost of trip	€1500
Other trips planned	Poland, Tunisia

Bike model	BMW R65
Age, mileage	24 years, 150,000km!
Modifications	Crash bar, windshield
Wish you'd done...	Enduro tyres
Tyres used	Macadam 50
Punctures	None
Type of baggage	Soft

Bike's weak point	Suspension
Strong point	Reliability, comfort
Bike problems	Weak front brake
Accidents	None
Same bike again	No, next time a R100GS
Any advice	Stop and speak to the people

TRIP REPORT
TRANS SAHARA ~ KTM ADVENTURE

Name	Gregg Flower
Year of birth	1959
Occupation	Journalist
Nationality	New Zealander/Danish
Previous travels	Most of the world
Bike travels	Africa, Europe, Asia, Australia, NZ
This trip	Tunisia to Niger and Benin
Trip duration	Three months
Departure date	October 2001
Number in group	Two
Distance covered	9800km (6125 miles)
Best day	Out of the Hoggar mts and into Tam
Worst day	Both endo-ing over a dune
Favourite place	The Ténéré, without doubt
Biggest headache	Arab boys with stones
Biggest mistake	Not enough care in the dunes
Pleasant surprise	The Tuareg people
Any illness	Bruises
Cost of trip	About $25 a day
Other trips planned	Trans USA via the hicktowns
Bike model	KTM Adventure
Age, mileage	2 years, 30,000km
Modifications	GPS, panniers
Wish you'd done...	Slightly lower gearing
Tyres used	Michelin Desert
Punctures	About 30
Type of baggage	Alu boxes
Bike's weak point	First gear too high in sand, economy
Strong point	Power and handling at speed
Bike problems	None really
Accidents	Don't ask
Same bike again	Yes, or maybe LC4 with Adv tank
Any advice	Get off the track

rider is the 1400km/900mile trail of tracks which stretch from the eastern border with Algeria to the Atlantic coast. You can't ask for a more satisfying, relatively easy and mostly dirt-track adventure. Range need be no more than 250km/150 miles so massive tanks or jerries are not needed, and even wells are fairly common. Thirteen routes in my *Sahara Overland* book cover this traverse where you'll also get the full story on Moroccan immigration.

Tunisia, Algeria and Libya

While the pricey 24-hour ferries from Marseille or Genoa don't put off central Europeans, **Tunisia** is a long way to go for not much reward. It has similar stability, lack of bureaucracy plus a well-developed tourist infrastructure as Morocco, but with much less hassle and, it has to be said, much less drama. Once you've got to Tunisia you might as well carry on to Libya, Algeria or the rest of Africa.

But southern Tunisia has plenty of something Morocco lacks – sand. The fringes of Algeria's **Grand Erg Oriental** flow over Tunisia's southern borders, creating the dunescapes which many expect in the Sahara. Trouble is, there are no meaty routes here and access without permits into the deep south can be limited. There's more in my Sahara book.

Algeria

As mentioned, Algeria, the best Saharan country by far, was coming out of the dark only to disappear again overnight when thirty-two tourists got kidnapped in early 2003 for up to six months, an event which we narrowly avoided thanks to a timely crash of mine while filming the *Desert Riders* dvd. Several motorcyclists were among the captives, including some guys we'd met just a week before they got nabbed. Despite its reputation, it was an unprecedented event in Algeria and hopefully the tourism situation will recover. When it does you can look forward to exploring the fantastic range of routes in the southeast of the country between the **Hoggar mountains** and the Tassili plateau by the Libyan border. It's all here: long, easy and spectacular routes over dunes, mountains and plateaux.

The classic **trans-Sahara route** from Tamanrasset to Agadez in Niger is still do-able and a great ride, even if you do need to follow the highway with an escort in Algeria.

HOT DAMN, SUMMER IN TUNISIA!

'...very hot, and pistes covered by moving dunes can turn easy routes into complete hell. Have to wait for others to ask. Got caught in a sandstorm in the Djerid which was a nightmare, making my face sore and stripping stickers off my tank.

The instant you stop you become soaked in sweat and you have to take off clothes. Simple digging becomes exhausting and sometimes you just can't drink enough. Getting stuck and ending up in featureless desert in the middle of the day is no fun, and you would be surprised, even if you are well-prepared, how hard it is. Scary.

I have a three-litre CamelBak bag which I fill up twice per day. I keep getting vapour locks in my fuel filter, even though it's as far from the engine as I could get it. Wrapping it in foil helps, but even so, I have to water it sometimes

There is nobody on the pistes, which is wonderful, but also a bit unnerving. Even local people often avoid travelling in the summer!

If you ever find yourself thinking 'it will be OK' you have to STOP and check again'.

Lewis Miller

DOWN BY THE RIVER

I rode the 200 or so kilometres from Nouakchott down to the Senegalese border at Rosso in a bit of a mood. I'd been in Mauritania for only four days and already I was sick of the place. Although the scenery in the Banc d'Arguin National Park was pretty decent, it didn't seem to make up for the relentless hassle from the desperate inhabitants of the towns we'd visited, nor for the grinding squalor of every inhabited corner I'd seen. Also, Greig, my travelling companion had started to get on my wick. He wouldn't speak to anyone, even though he knew a little French, and we still hadn't properly made up from the revelation two-weeks earlier that he'd come on our Scotland to Dakar adventure without a sleeping bag or a camping mat, though he had brought a flashy suit of motocross armour.

As such, he'd nearly caught hypothermia during our first night of camping in the frosty Moroccan Atlas. Since then, he'd bought some Berber blankets which he carried on the back of his XT600 in a brown paper parcel tied with string, but we'd never quite gotten over the bollocking I gave him.

Anyway, since the sleeping bag incident things had ticked along OK. After each great day's riding, things seemed to be looking up, but then there would be another little 'revelation', like he hadn't brought any food, or a stove, or any pans, and so on. Certainly,

on the ferry from Portsmouth to Santander, I'd been impressed by how efficiently he'd packed all his kit, and now I knew why: he didn't have any!

That isn't to say, of course, that he didn't have any reason to get mad at me. The night before we set off, for example, I'd gone to sleep worrying that the clutch on my XR600R would fry in the desert. I had therefore got out of bed at 3am and changed all of the clutch plates while still half asleep. Naturally I nicked the clutch cover gasket putting the engine back together, and it burst as we rode off the ferry in Santander. This had necessitated an unplanned and expensive 36-hour delay in Bilbao while the local Honda dealer got us a new gasket.

If we'd had some tensions in Spain and Morocco, the bizarre atmosphere of Mauritania had only made things worse. Since entering the country things had been pretty strange. We'd been in a minor car accident while out in a taxi in Nouadhibou. One of the wheels had fallen off the old Renault 4, causing us and the driver to all end up in the boot, as the seats weren't fastened onto the car's floor. Then we were offered the services of a 'renegade' guide for the run down the Atlantic coast. His rates had been much less than the official guides, but they got wind of the deal and kicked his face in. Then we'd got tied up in a deal where we shared an 'official' guide with

Libya

Forget outdated fears about Libya, it's now a favourite Saharan destination (especially with the current state of Algeria). The spectacular **Fezzan** of the southwest is the most popular region; out east it gets a bit dull, mile for mile.

While sealed roads lead south all the way to Ghat and Kufra (both dead ends) – and in a year or two, to the Niger border, riding the sands out here is the real thing (more in the other book).

All **roadsign distances** are in Arabic (it's worth learning the cardinal numbers at least) and checkpoints are common in the north. But at just a few pence a litre, **fuel** must be the cheapest in Africa. The only problem is they get you back on the cost of the visa, associated paperwork and escorts.

Alone in the Sahara. © Jeff Condon

DOWN BY THE RIVER

some nice German guys and a mad old Bavarian school teacher who had tried to insist that we drive round the clock as he needed to sell his old Mercedes and get back to class. This caused a mini-mutiny which resulted in the teacher and guide going off by themselves and us and the German guys continuing alone.

Since then, we had been the butt of one attempted swindle after another. The most recent had been when a policeman just outside Nouakchott had asked us to show him our 'other' yellow fever certificates, apart from the one's we'd just given him. He then announced that there was a hefty fine for not having this 'vital document'. Reasoning that he probably wouldn't shoot us and noting that he had no vehicle, Greig gave him an old pair of socks and I gave him the finger and we both tore off. Anyway, by the time we got to Rosso, I was pretty frazzled and really just wanted to be somewhere else.

Rosso itself was just as big a dump as anywhere else in Mauritania, only the hustlers here were even more obvious. As soon as we pulled into town, the garage mysteriously ran out of petrol and we were told by a 'friendly local guide' that our only hope was to get the last ferry of the day to the Senegalese side, where we'd find fuel. Of course, he wanted a small fee to assist us with the necessary formalities, so we decided just to sit it out and see what happened.

Unfortunately, it turned out that it really *was* the last ferry of the day, or so the local policeman told us and so, more in desperation than anything else, we took the guide's offer, but for a fee that was rather less than he'd prescribed.

Sure as hell, before we knew it he was barging to the front of queues, buying tickets, having our passports stamped and introducing us to various soldiers and policemen. However, just as we were completing a final passport formality, the horn of the ferry sounded. We looked up in time to see our bikes being pushed on board by our guide's 'brother' and a friend of his, and sprinted across the dock just in time to literally jump onto the ferry.

As we started to remove small children and youths from the bikes and detach our GPSs and stuff them out of the way of little fingers, a horrible thought crossed my mind. I raced to the back of the ferry. Looking back to the bank, I saw the guide getting into a pirogue and madly waving two small burgundy-coloured books at me. Just then, Greig yelled over to me, 'Andy, our passports!' 'Don't worry', I said, worriedly, 'they're coming across right now in a canoe'.

We looked at each other and then out to the Senegal River, where our guide was paddling furiously, and burst into hysterics. Suddenly things didn't seem half as bad.

Andy Bell

Currently the only way to leave Libya from the **south** is from El Gatrun via Tummu into the northeastern corner of Niger where you'll need to make your way to Dirkou (expensive fuel) and then east (possibly with guides) across the Ténéré to Agadez – around 1500km. We're talking desolate sandy desert tracks and fuel ranges of several hundred kilometres with few wells. This is not a route to be taken lightly – a GS twin will be hard work and 4WD support would be advisable. Nevertheless, unless the Libyans close this border (as they sometimes do), it adds up to the only moderately safe trans-Saharan crossing that gives you a real feel of being in the world's biggest desert.

WEST AFRICA

West Africa includes the sub-Saharan region from Senegal to Cameroon. Much of it was once a French colony and today **French**, and to a lesser extent English (in the Gambia, Sierra Leone, Liberia, Ghana and Nigeria) will be the languages you'll use the most. Another romantic idea many people have is **following the coast** around West Africa; the problem is, between Dakar and Abidjan in the Ivory Coast, there isn't one.

If coming across the desert from Mauritania to Dakar, expect heavy intimidation at the Senegal river crossing at **Rosso** (see box p.185) where you buy a **laissez-passer** (this is the local alternative to a carnet which is valid across Francophone West Africa). Senegal and Gambia are not especially interesting when compared to their more intriguing neighbours of Guinea and Mali. Wherever you go in West Africa you'll find not too much trouble obtaining **visas**, although **fuel** and accommodation will be expensive. The police here are not as 'demanding' as they can be in Nigeria and the more desperate Central African republics and as always, the people are great, a bit more lively that the less extrovert Berber-Arab peoples of North Africa (whose relative reserve you might miss after a while).

Timbuktu and Lake Chad

In the dry season from Mauritania it's possible to get directly into Mali along various bush tracks to places like Nioro and Nara and down to Bamako. Or from Senegal head via Tamba' to Kayes where they're extending the road that parallels the railway to Bamako – a nice run. This corner of Mali and the smuggling tracks leading in to Guinea (the source of medieval Europe's gold) is a great place for some 'off the map' adventures. If you're finding Africa a bit dull so far, the mountain tracks of **Guinea's Fouta Djalon** will perk you up.

Then again, **Timbuktu** is only a thousand kilometres northwest of Bamako. Go from Mopti to Goudnam (ferry), or get north of the Niger river's inland delta at Segou where gravel roads reach Niafounke. From here it could still be deep sand to the legendary oasis which is usually disappointing and hassley. Otherwise, from Bamako, sealed roads run via Burkina or Niger and around Lake Chad itself (a tough, sandy bush track on a loaded bike, see *Sahara Overland* p.605). Or you can take your chances crossing Nigeria into Cameroon. In Nigeria anything can happen (including good things!). Keep away from the south, but expect occasional trouble in the Muslim north too: go to Kano then east to Maiduguri and into Cameroon at Mora and on to Yaoundé for visas. Nigeria has the advantage of having some of the **cheapest petrol** in Africa, but also the biggest range of scams.

WESTERN ROUTE VIA ANGOLA AND NAMIBIA

From Cameroon this route, which had been hit and miss for years, seemed to be catching on in 2004, partly due to Sudanese visa hassles, the Darfur situation and the end of the hostilities in Angola.

Even then it's a tough one: pricey visas and **carnets needed**, mud tracks, heat, humidity, insects, bribery and disease. Joseph Conrad's *Heart of Darkness* was set here; you may not know the book but you'll know Coppola's aptly-named film version transposed to Vietnam: *Apocalypse Now*. As much as in the Sahara, it's common to **team up** with other overland travellers for this stretch, you'll need all the support you can get and speaking **French** is a big advantage.

Well at least it's sunny and dry.
Inset: sometimes it isn't. © Paul Jenkins.

From Yaoundé (the place for Gabonese, Congo-Brazza' and DRC visas) a direct route goes through **Gabon** and over the **equator**. Pick up Angolan visas here in Libreville, easier than Brazzaville city it's said). And if possible, get double-entry if heading via Cabinda and back into DRC (see below).

The Gabon overland route is the only option unless you can get from Yokaduma in east Cameroon to Pokola (40km south of Ouesso). Logging roads are being built to Brazza' but until that happens most travel by **barge** (actually, a floating shantytown) is down the Sangha and Congo rivers to Brazza'. Allow at least a week while feasting on on all sorts of endangered species.

From Gabon to Point Noire on the Brazza' coast, it's said a good road leads to **Cabinda**, an Angolan enclave north of the Congo estuary. Depending on how you're coping with the Central African Experience and the latest crime stats from DRC, you might want to put your bikes on a **ferry** or an Antonov transporter (unofficial, ask at the airbase) to either **Soyo** (ferry) or Luanda (ferry and plane) in Angola; both cost around $200. Then again, if you're untouchable, continue on a good track (if dry) into DRC

Escape from Cabinda. © Paul Jenkins.

and a bridge over the Congo river into **Matadi** by the Angolan border. Or miss out Cabinda altogether and head inland to Brazzaville, cross the river on the daily ferry to Kinshasa and make a run southwest to Matadi and Angola. Beware though, street crime, scams and plain old armed robbery in Kinshasa and on the road to Matadi are why travellers like the Cabinda connection.

The news from Portuguese-speaking **Angola** is they're only just getting into overland tourists. Roads are tracks in the north or pot-holed/blown-up in the south and Luanda is in a right state. Fuel is cheap but not much else. However, bush camping is inadvisable unless you have a mine-proof thermarest, so take advantage of mission resthouses as you may have done up north. The route to Namibia is via Lubango and into Odangawa. And once in **Namibia**, a great riding country, the pressure is off and you're home and dry.

EGYPT TO ETHIOPIA

While anything more than short excursions off the highway in Egypt are more hassle than they're worth, a ride down the east side of Africa to Cape Town is relatively straightforward; the equator is just four visas away where the worst is over. Brace yourself when coming into Egypt from north or south: the aggro, pedantry and vehicle importation regs are truly world class. They'll want your carnet (as do most countries on this eastern route) or give you their own, as well as a separate driving licence and number plate.

Getting between Sudan and Egypt entails traversing the length of Lake Nasser on a barge and disembarking at the Sudanese frontier post of Wadi Halfa; all in all an experience that can drive you round the bend. As long as this ferry keeps running (the vast land borders are not used), exit from southern Egypt remains possible. But first you need a Sudanese visa, famously

T R I P   R E P O R T
AMSTERDAM–CAPE TOWN ~ DOMMIE

Name	Meindert Baars
Year of birth	1972
Occupation	Telecoms engineer
Nationality	Dutch
Previous travels	Plenty
Bike travels	Oz and Maroc
This trip	Amsterdam to Cape Town
Trip duration	11 months
Departure date	October 2002
Number in group	Just me
Distance covered	About 45,000km (28,125 miles)
Best day	Any day anywhere on the bike
Worst day	Muddy roads in Gabon
Favourite place	Guinea, Gabon, DRC, Angola, Zambia
Biggest headache	5 days to get in Angola, but worth it
Biggest mistake	Not buying those croc-skin shoes...
Pleasant surprise	People on the road in rural areas
Any illness	Diarrhoea, malaria
Cost of trip	Don't ask
Other trips planned	Amsterdam–Russia–Japan–Oz
Bike model	Honda NX650
Age, mileage	Two years, 12,000km
Modifications	Bigger tank and better shock
Wish you'd done...	Bar raisers
Tyres used	OE whatever
Punctures	Loads on the bald rear
Type of baggage	Tesch alu boxes
Bike's weak point	Range, weight balance, 17" rear
Strong point	Strong, reliable
Bike problems	Top end in Namibia (watch the oil!)
Accidents	One
Same bike again	Nope, considering KTM Adventure
Any advice	Just go. Africa is easier than you imagine

unobtainable in London for Brits and probably Americans anywhere, but miraculously available in Cairo in just 24 hours (sometimes...), even without the necessary invite from a Sudanese travel agent. Not being American or British helps, but many lose heart and for them the answers add up to the demanding Angola or DRC routes, flying the bike to Addis or Kenya, or working out how to take a boat to Djibouti (near Eritrea). Unfortunately this is usually via Saudi, another tricky transit visa, especially for single women (and probably Americans). By now you're getting the picture, they don't call it 'Africa' for nothing!

From Wadi Halfa most follow the railway rather than the bending Nile to Khartoum and head east for Ethiopia. The southern marshlands of Sudan – war-torn since the early 1980s – may well become accessible again, but right now it's too soon to say. No one's been there for years.

There's general purpose unrest along the Eritrean border, though this does not disrupt access into Ethiopia, picking the right **season** is more important. **Ethiopia** has some of the most spectacular riding in Africa, although the hassle has an aggressive edge here and suffocating bureaucracy thrives.

This north–south axis through Ethiopia is relatively stable but the southwest and eastern border areas are still a bit jumpy. If you've read Wilfred Thesiger's books you'll know what the Danakil tribe like to do to strangers... Keep on the road south to Moyale and northern Kenya and you shouldn't encounter any untoward danger, although you might want to join convoys once in Kenya to get though the **bandit lands** of the northern provinces.

KENYA AND THE ROAD TO THE CAPE

Having crossed the Sahara and Ethiopia, or maybe even northeastern DRC or southern Sudan, trans-African overlanders customarily take a breather in **Kenya**, sub-Saharan Africa's most visited and touristy country after South Africa. Mombasa and its Indian Ocean resorts are the preferred hangouts for vehicle and body servicing and from Mombasa it's possible to ship to Mumbai in India on a Ro-Ro ferry for around £250 (plus around £100 for freight forwarders at each end and the usual Indian obfuscations and delays).

South of Kenya you can follow sealed highways all the way to the Cape, with road and official hassles decreasing with every southward mile. From Tanzania, whose game parks and natural spectacles equal those of better-known Kenya, the route continues via **Zambia** or **Malawi** and less securely through **Mozambique**.

After the drama and difficulties of the north, southern Africa can either be an anticlimax, expensive or a blessed relief. Both Botswana and Zimbabwe (fuel problems) can be crossed in a day or two, while to the west, **Namibia** is well worth a diversion if you have a few miles left in you. Other than that, southbound riders find little to distract them as they spin down towards the Cape.

'It's the end of the road as we know it (2).'
© Chris Bright

Central and South America

Like Africa, Central and South America conjure up their fair share of negative images: seasonal or corrupt governments, kidnapping by peoples' liberation movements and audacious banditry. As usual the reality is far more benign and, once you take the plunge, the experience is irrevocably rewarding. Compared to parts of Africa and Asia, the negligible demands on **documentation** are a big attraction, even if the cost of living is not always so modest.

If you're intent on a tip-to-tail run along the Americas, it's around 28,000km (18,000 miles) from Chile to Alaska. It's been done in five weeks, but if you're only going to do it once, allow **three months** at the very least.

As you'd expect, the **US dollar** is the most useful hard currency to carry. When it comes to changing into local currency, wait until you're in the country and then change just enough to get you to an ATM where you will get the regular exchange rate. Check out **www.saexplorers.org** and learn some **Spanish**: it will transform your trip and will help reduce 'gringo' taxes. A **Yellow Fever** certificate may be required in many countries.

MEXICO

Mexico is to North American riders what Morocco is to Europeans: a quick border crossing into a substantially different culture, a move which sharpens both senses and anxieties. **Paperwork** is straightforward, just passport and vehicle ownership papers ('title'), but don't forget a temporary vehicle import sticker for around $30 (something that you get one way or another across Latin America instead of a carnet) and make sure they check your bike out when you leave. **Fuel** is a bit more expensive than in the US.

Mexico may be a regular tourist destination, but tourists are also a regular target for robbery and rip-offs. Keep alert and advised of danger areas; if you're coming from the north you may be initially prone to wide-eyed innocence or more likely, bug-eyed paranoia. For all the rest, any good guidebook will fill in the gaps. Mexico's true highlights are the food, the Mayan ruins south of the capital, and the fact that it's emphatically not North America.

KISS MY CARNET

If you're just visiting Central and South America (rather than setting off on a longer world trip), you **don't need a carnet** (or even the Venezuelan *libreta*).

Bike details are stamped in your passport with a temporary import permit, though note that in some places the duration of the permit can be **shorter** than your visa. Don't get caught out! Always ask for the maximum allowed, no matter how short your visit.

Flying into Ecuador (as many do from Panama, to get over the Darien while missing out Colombia) can be an exception. Here you may still be asked for a carnet, but in September 2004 the law was changed (or corrected): no carnet. Tell the Customs to check up: Articles 82/83, decree 158/2082.

If you *do* have a carnet and use it, borders will be a bit cheaper and quicker, but it's not worth getting one just for Latin America.

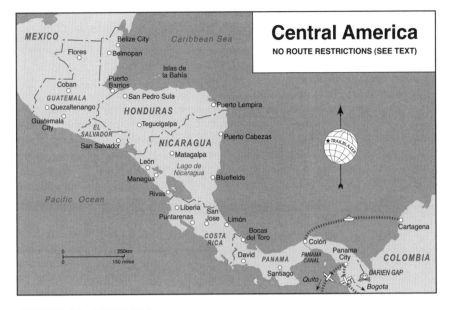

Central America

NO ROUTE RESTRICTIONS (SEE TEXT)

CENTRAL AMERICA

If heading south, a trans-Mexico trip will have prepared you for this compact isthmus of seven small countries, many of which can be crossed in a day or two. If you're coming up north you'll know what to expect: challenging border crossings and traffic 'irregulations'. Some riders sail through, others blunder across with a scowl. The officials you deal with are not without blame of course, but your attitude has a lot to do with it.

If you're running straight through and saving your strength and money for South America, **Belize** and **El Salvador** are often missed out. But Belize is no hassle; expect an almost normal border crossing with a $20 fee when you leave. Of the other five countries, Guatemala and Costa Rica cause few problems, while **Honduras and Nicaragua** seem the worst for undefined border formalities including the imposition of arbitrary fees like 'exit permits' on *entering* a country or even fees to search your baggage! As these demands rarely amount to more than $5-10, it's best not to be too bull-headed – it saves time – though you should certainly contest anything over ten or twenty dollars.

Some fees are for real though, and you may even get a receipt, typical prices are: fumigation in Guatemala $2; immigration fee $5 (exit fee 10 quetzals); $20 road tax in Honduras. **Insurance** everywhere is semi-optional for around $10.

For Nicaragua and Costa Rica have plenty of **copies** of your passport's and your vehicle ownership document's important pages (while of course

Paperwork! Heaps and heaps of paperwork. © Lois Pryce

GETTING OVER THE DARIEN

Once you get to Panama it's the end of the road, overland. It may be only 130km across but the Darien Gap is a lawless, roadless, tropical, disease-ridden impasse spanning the borders of Panama and Colombia. Ed Culberson's *Obsessions Die Hard* describes one of the few attempts to 'ride' across.

In early 2005 talk of the **Cartagena ferry** link was revived – otherwise some riders use private yachts or even smuggling boats.

Most **fly** to Colombia, or Ecuador: **Girag Cargo** at Tocumen cargo airport in Panama City are your guys, charging around $350 to Bogota or $650 to Quito, Ecuador, two to three times the cost of your own ticket.

In the words of one rider *'Turn up, no need to book, no need to crate, no need to deflate or dismantle, just disconnect the battery, pay $350 with no hidden extras and two or three days later bingo, the bike's in Bogota'.*

carrying the original) and even your **driving licence**. At the Honduras–Nicaragua border you're in the thick of it; see it all as a game of wits and try to remain good humoured.

Many riders report better experiences crossing **quiet, out of the way borders**, a practice which can work anywhere in the world. If you funnel down the obvious runways they'll be there waiting and wetting their lips for the next gringo shakedown. Don't all rush at once but recent reports suggest El Florido, (Guat) to Copan (Hon) is cool (and a great ride too) but avoid Agua Caliente. Elsewhere: Guat/Hon via Chiquimula; Hon/Nic via El Paraiso/Las Menos; Nic/CR via Penas Blancas and CR/Pan at Sixaola past Puerto Viejo.

Lois Pryce found that one way of getting in with the locals was to declare how much you disliked the previous country. Doesn't matter if you mean it, it works every time. The Mexicans don't like the Guatemalans, the Guatemalans don't like the Salvadorians, the Costa Ricans don't like the Nicaraguans and no-one likes the Hondurans, least of all when it comes to borders as you're about to read. As another Trans-Am rider put it '... *don't worry, almost everybody gets stiffed in Honduras.'*

Central American border strategies
Lois Pryce
The main features of these border crossings are the gangs of locals that besiege you as soon as you arrive; within seconds you're totally surrounded by them, offering to help you with the excessive paperwork, money changing, guarding the bike etc, all for a negotiable fee. Being surrounded by a group of swarthy gentlemen waving wads of currency in your face could hold a certain appeal in another situation, but in this case it's just plain annoying, especially as they grab at your clothes, touch the bike and generally, as Americans would say, 'invade your personal space'.

So at each border I would select a likely-looking candidate and agree a price for them to assist me with the necessary documentation. I would then spend anything from one to three hours following them from one dingy office to another on an endless trail of rubber stamping, paper shuffling, rain forest-depleting amounts of photocopying and of course handing over of money.

(Opposite): Dusk near the Nasca Lines in Peru. © Ben Lawrie. **(Overleaf) Top:** Cruising on Bolivian salt lakes. © Martin Wielecki. **Bottom:** Courtyard in Cusco, Peru. © Chris Bright.

T R I P   R E P O R T
Trans Americas ~ KLR650

Name	Michael Holton
Year of birth	1979
Occupation	Furniture maker
Nationality	Canadian
Previous travels	Bolivia, Chile, Japan, Europe
Bike travels	None

This trip	Canada to Tierra del Fuego
Trip duration	Six months
Departure date	October 2003
Number in group	1
Distance covered	38,000km (23,750 miles)

Best day	Riding through the Salar de Uyuni
Worst day	Peruvian coast: too many bad cops
Favourite place	Chalten, Argentina, Fitz Roy Range
Biggest headache	K&N air filter on the altiplano
Biggest mistake	Installing the K&N
Pleasant surprise	Armadillos and emu-ish birds in Arg'
Any illness	A bit in Nicaragua
Cost of trip	About $8000
Other trips planned	Africa, Med, most 'northern' roads

Bike model	Kawasaki KLR 650
Age, mileage	1 year, 20,000km
Modifications	Forkbrace, rad' guard, hwy pegs
Wish you'd done...	Suspension, pipe
Tyres used	MT21, IRC, MT60, Bridgestone TWs
Punctures	At least ten
Type of baggage	Touratech Zega alu boxes

Bike's weak point	Fuel valve
Strong point	Can take a pounding
Bike problems	New piston, valve guides, fuel valve
Accidents	None
Same bike again	Yes
Any advice	Ride with a partner if you can

This system, although tedious, worked for me, and all parties generally leave satisfied. The exception to this was the entry to Honduras. My 'fixer' on this occasion was a weasely chap with a gold tooth and a face with skin the texture of a sun-dried tomato. Patiently I followed him around the maze of offices, handing over more and more money for various 'services', never really understanding what they were, but totally at his mercy. Each time I would receive an official-looking piece of paper but still, I wasn't convinced.

In one particularly grimy office that would surely qualify as a victim of Sick Building Syndrome, we sat waiting under the glare of a bare light bulb, orbited by flies. I stared in miserable silence at one of those so-called 'motivational' posters that usually feature a picture of a dolphin and a message along the lines of 'There is no 'I' in team'.

After about twenty minutes of examining the faded, tattered poster I certainly felt motivated to get the hell out of Honduras – and I hadn't even got in yet! 'What's the delay?' I asked Tomato Face. He explained in resigned tones that the woman dealing with my paperwork had gone off to brush her teeth. For twenty minutes! I foresee a future of painful gum disease for that señorita.

Three hours later Tomato Face handed me a mountain of paperwork and finally announced I was free to go. Well, almost.

'The last thing you do now, you pay policeman' he announced.

'Oh yeah, and what's that for?' I enquired. 'To make everything go smooth' he replied, with a knowing smile. Sure enough a grim-faced, uniformed cop appeared and demanded five dollars from me. Cunningly, I asked him for a receipt, just like it advises in that AM Handbook. He just shook his head and walked away with my five bucks. Welcome to Honduras.

SOUTH AMERICA

When you add it all up South America is among the best motorcycling destinations on the planet. An extreme range of environments from barely-penetrable rainforests, hyper-arid deserts, the altiplano and the snowbound passes across the Andes tempt you in all directions. On top of this comes a half-decent infrastructure which does not require a knobbly-tyred bike with a mile-high saddle to get across (though the Amazon basin and a network of gnarly dirt-tracks await those looking for off-highway adventures).

South America is also a relatively stable place and as far as visas and documentation go, verges on European. Only the so-called 'Guyanas', the three small states of Guyana, Surinam and French Guyana (home of Devil's Island) sitting on top of Brazil, present accessibility problems to overlanders and with

POINTS OF ENTRY BY AIR AND SEA

If you're not starting your travels through Central and South America from the US, the following are points and methods of entry worth investigating. These connections also apply if you're leaving South America for other continents.

Coming from Australia or New Zealand, flying your bike to **Santiago** in Chile is much quicker than growing old and spending money while your bike steams across the Pacific. A recent price for a GS1150 from New Zealand came in at NZ$2500 (plus another $150 in Chile), while a 325kg bike from Santiago back to Europe cost $600.

Buenos Aires in Argentina is also accessible from Australia (with similar prices to Santiago) as well as on flights or ships from Cape Town and of course Europe.

South America

0 | 1000km
0 | 600 miles

Path of main overland routes

Possible alternatives and/or deviations

Main freight options by river, sea or air (many other alternatives exist)

THE WEATHER AND SEASONS

Stretching from above the equator to just a thousand km from the Antarctic mainland, and with several Andean summits peaking over 21,000ft/ 6500m within sight of the Pacific, the weather in this region is difficult to summarise.

Technically, the tropics stretch from the southern tip of the Baja to Rio de Janeiro. In lowland areas closer to the equator you can expect temperatures in the low 30°Cs year-round, with seriously heavy rains from April to July when overland travel comes to a standstill. In coastal regions near the equator, dry seasons last just a couple of months. Southern Panama is such a place, which is one of the reasons why crossing the Darien Gap remains so challenging.

If you're heading for Cape Horn from North America, try and hit the northern countries of Latin America in the early part of the year and plan to arrive in Patagonia for the southern spring when temperatures begin to warm up, but before the summer winds across Patagonia reach their full force.

A comprehensive tour around South America will demand a full range of clothing. Some rare days may see you sweltering along jungle track to end the day shivering over a 15,000ft/5000m pass. The only answer is to be prepared for everything.

TRIP REPORT
SOUTH AMERICA ~ XT600E

Name	Nik Mellor
Year of birth	1976
Occupation	IT professional
Nationality	British
Previous travels	Large amounts
Bike travels	Vietnam with Minsk; Bullet India UK

This trip	South America: the works
Trip duration	Ten months
Departure date	January 2004
Number in group	Solo
Distance covered	33,000km (20,625 miles)

Best day	Crossing the Bolivian Antiplano
Worst day	The gravel on Ruta 40
Favourite place	Colombia: friendly people, scenery
Biggest headache	Oiling the chain, *all* the time
Biggest mistake	Deciding to overtake that truck...
Pleasant surprise	Not meeting guerillas in Colombia
Any illness	Salad fever in Peru
Cost of trip	£8000
Other trips planned	Africa is next

Bike model	Yamaha XT600E
Age, mileage	6m, 5000km – bought/sold in Braz
Modifications	Ninja windscreen, leg protector
Wish you'd done...	Shock, better screen, bigger tank
Tyres used	Mostly Pirelli MT60s
Punctures	Five (all nails)
Type of baggage	Tank bag, backpack, panniers

Bike's weak point	15-litre tank
Strong point	Handled 5000m without carb adjust
Bike problems	Just a few broken spokes
Accidents	Three
Same bike again	For SA yes. Spares, strong, reliable
Any advice	Nope

nothing you can't see or catch elsewhere.

The biggest dangers, both of which are by no means unique to South America, are **street crime** in larger cities and ports, and other road users, especially on steep Andean roads and in Brazil. Here more than ever the line between 'your' and 'their' side of the road is academic. Just as in India, might has the right of way so ride alert and don't ride at all in poor visibility, heavy rain or ice or, of course, at night.

On the *cordillera*. © Chris Bright

Variations in **altitude** can also play havoc with your comfort levels (as well as your carburation): it's not impossible to rise four kilometres or 13,000 feet in a single day; dress for freezing temperatures, you can always take it off.

The Pan-American Highway

Most riders visiting South America arrive and stay on the Pacific side. Topography has much to do with it; between Colombia and Bolivia access into Amazonia is hampered by the huge run-off into the equatorial rainforest. There simply are no roads and as in the African Congo, transport is by riverboat.

But in the Andean rain shadow, most intense in northern Chile's **Atacama Desert**, the opportunities for great motorcycling are outstanding. The freight-carrying **Pan-American** or Interamerican Highway is not necessarily your first or only choice. Branching off it are deserted roads with mind-boggling views, mountainside routes with hairpins piled up like tagliatelli carbonara. Any number of back-road border crossings between Ecuador and Peru lead to the **Cordillera Occidental** and along the Andes' spine to the **Altiplano** of eastern Bolivia. Here the rarified altitude creates stunning blue skies bleaching salt lakes alongside dormant volcanoes. Moving south, take your pick: Andes oceanside or inland; Chile or Argentina, the former descending in an oxygenated rush to the hyper-arid north Chilean coastline.

Colombia – is it safe?

From Ecuador or Panama (and maybe Venezuela), the question arises: **Colombia**. If it was somewhere like Uraguay most would not bother fretting over it, but Colombia's reputation for armed robbery and kidnapping (hundreds annually) is balanced by the vitality of its people. Notwithstanding a decades-old guerilla war incorporating drug trafficking and corruption, no one who takes the risk with Colombia has anything but great things to say about the place and the people they meet there.

Some people just can't wait to get back on the bitumen. © Martin Wielecki

RUSH HOUR IN LIMA

I arrived in Lima during a combination of rush hour and political demonstration. Lima appears to be where American scrapyards send their surplus wrecks when space gets tight. Built-to-last pre-war trucks battle for space with gaffer-taped 1970s muscle cars and every vehicle belches plumes of filthy black smoke.

Firstly, one has to accept that an awful lot of white paint has been wasted creating lane markings on the roads in Lima. Secondly, traffic lights are simply guideposts to aim between; their colour is ornamental. Thirdly, using your indicators merely interferes with urgent horn operations, and you must use your horn at all times.

It took me a little while to work out these basic rules and initially my heart was in my mouth as I weaved my way daintily through this lunacy. It was only when I reached the centre of the city to discover a maze of twisty, narrow streets snarled up in furious gridlock that I realised if I was going to get anywhere I had to roll up my Highway Code and snort up a line of controlled aggression.

With my left hand alternating between thumb on the horn or middle finger in the air, I was suddenly riding as if possessed by El Diablo himself!

'Get OUT of the way!' I yelled as I rode onto the pavement, pedestrians flattening themselves against the walls. Through a red light; along the central reservations; slashing across lanes of traffic and through the park of picnicking kiddies. I was enjoying every minute and the great thing was, nobody batted an eyelid, it was all considered to be perfectly normal behaviour.   **Lois Pryce**

Tourists are a target so vigilance, common sense (as well as some luck) are needed. Ride only into the afternoon and then get off the road completely. Tensions in Colombia rise and fall. It's in your interest to assess the latest security situation and if possible get in touch with local riders for advice.

Ecuador, Peru, Bolivia
Collectively known as the Andean countries, in these three places the indigenous culture, both past and present, is more conspicuous, even if the standard of living is lower. Bowler hats, Inca ruins, llamas, they all add up to give a spirit of South America that's rawer, less familiar and in places, spectacular.

You've paid your border-hassle dues in Central America, down here it's more relaxed, Ecuador–Peru being as bad as it gets (but make sure you fill up with petrol in Ecuador: fuel is nearly twice as expensive in Peru.) The standard of driving is famously insane until you reach orderly and sanitised Chile.

Getting the GS blessed at Copacabana by Lake Titicaca in Bolivia. (A few weeks later it broke in half.) © Chris Bright

In southern Peru (considerably more pricey than other countries, as is Chile) you'll pass through the northern expanses of the Atacama Desert which leads to the even starker Chilean sections with no water or shade, let alone fuel, for up to 300km/190 miles at a stretch. This is the world's driest region, just a few hundred kilometres from some of the world's wettest jungles.

Bolivia
Landlocked between the mountains and the jungle, Bolivia should be top of your list. It's one of the least expensive South

TRIP REPORT
TRANS AMERICAS ~ DR650

Name	Bob West
Year of birth	1946
Occupation	Retired
Nationality	British
Previous travels	Lots
Bike travels	Europe to Dubai, 3 x around USA

This trip	Buenos Aires to TdF to Alaska
Trip duration	Five months
Departure date	December 2003
Number in group	Three then two
Distance covered	46,000km (28,750 miles)

Best day	Many: Calafate glacier was good
Worst day	920km in south Argentina (250 dirt)
Favourite place	Monument Valley
Biggest headache	Getting bike to Quito from Panama
Biggest mistake	Choosing the freight agent in Quito
Pleasant surprise	How cheap and good Argentina is
Any illness	The shits a few times
Cost of trip	About $10,000
Other trips planned	UK to Dubai

Bike model	Suzuki DR650
Age, mileage	2002, new
Modifications	Tank, Scottoiler, heated grips
Wish you'd done...	Better seat
Tyres used	Original Bridgestones then Kenda
Punctures	One
Type of baggage	Touratech Zegas on H&B rack

Bike's weak point	Seat over long distance
Strong point	Reliable, light, fast, handles
Bike problems	None
Accidents	None
Same bike again	Yes, what's wrong with the DR650!?
Any advice	Choose the right bike; you don't automatically need a GS1150

Drink of the gods, scourge of the innards. © Lois Pryce

American countries and one in which half the population remains indigenous Indian. And despite having grown into a major cocaine producer, Bolivia manages to get on with this illicit trade without the political or civil discord for which Colombia is famed. In Bolivia, the lesser routes across the desolate altiplano into Chile and Peru provide some great riding and spectacular scenery, but remember that this is a remote region with changeable weather.

Coming from Peru or Arica in northern Chile you cross borders at 15,000ft/4500m passes where *ripio* dirt roads lead to La Paz. Having caught your breath (unacclimatised people frequently pass-out on arriving at La Paz airport), an even more dramatic ascent continues across the 4700m La Cumbre Pass to be followed by a 3500m drop into Bolivia's humid Yungas region and an anaconda-infested route north to Venezuela.

This is a ride to remember not least because the altitude can play havoc with your carburation – and Bolivia's single-figure octane fuel doesn't help. But as long as the engine can turn the wheels, riding across the glaring, surreal expanse of the **Salar de Uyuni** salt lake is not to be missed. During the summer it may be under several inches of water; ride through that and the solution will eat your bike alive, but even then some reckon it's still worth it!

Patagonia: the Carretera Austral or Ruta 40

South of Bolivia, it's either Chile or Argentina for the road to the pointy end. After Bolivia, you'll find these Europeanised countries expensive but also rather comfortable. By the time you get to southern Chile (or northern Patagonia) the Pan-Am Highway grinds to a halt at **Puerto Montt**.

From here the unsealed **Carretera Austral**, completed less than a decade ago, continues south for another thousand kilometres to Puerto Yungay (Port O'Higgins) passing through the Chilean Lake District and several national parks. Winding through forests, past stunning glaciers and over rivers fed by ice fields, in places ferries make the connection across the fjords and although the scenery is wild, all the services you want are here.

'It's the end of the road as we know it (3).'
© Rupert Wilson-Young

Without ice axe and crampons, 20km north of **Cochrane** is your last chance to across into **Argentina**. From here it's 1000km down the notorious **Ruta 40**, not the place for worn trail tyres, not least because you'll need all the grip you can get to face the famously brutal westerlies which sweep across Patagonia, at their absolute worst in

December when they exceed 100mph (160kph). Riding down Ruta 40 is a challenging finalé to a trans-Americas run. At the end of the road, crossing the Magellan Straits onto the island of **Tierra del Fuego** brings you to **Ushuaia** which in the last few years has become an impromptu get-together for overland riders from all over. The town is horrendously expensive of course; it's often raining and always cold. From this point it's twice as far to the Argentine capital of **Buenos Aires** as it is to Antarctica, but you've reached one of the world's handful of continental extremes. Congratulations! Unless you're a penguin the way home is north.

Up the Amazon
While the Andean countries offer great mountain roads, the Amazon basin is the other definitive South American habitat, a humid, partially-depleted rainforest that spreads across at least half-a-dozen countries creating an untameable obstacle to overland travel. New roads are boldly carved, but one good monsoon (which in some places is continuous) and a few overloaded trucks churn up an unnavigable mire which is soon reclaimed by the jungle.

Up or down the Amazon, a different way (and west of Manaus, the *only* way) of travelling is using a series of **river boats**. These are not regular car ferries but cattle, log or vegetable transporters – there's always room for a bike.

You can cruise all the way between **Belem** on the Atlantic 3500km inland via 'road-locked' Iquitos to **Yurimaguas** in Peru, itself just 400km from the Pacific as the crow flies. RTWer Chris Bright recalls his travels downstream:

The road from Tarapoto to Yurimaguas was among the worst in the world; and it was dry. A day later it chucked it down so what am I complaining about! From Yurimaguas to Iquitos I travelled literally 'cattle-class' on the Rio Marañón for three days. Iquitos was great fun but just too hot for me.

I took several boats for the 3000km Amazon odyssey to Belem, including a dugout canoe. I've seen it all now; the GS has been dragged, winched, hoicked and a couple of times even ridden on and off boats. Spending two weeks in a hammock is something everybody should try once. It was fine when the boat was moving, but stopping every couple of hours took away the breeze and you can get cranky.

In Manaus I got thoroughly searched for drugs. Then they spotted my bike – kind of hard to hide really. Holy piranhas, my bike paperwork was not in order! Made it through though, after the boss's boss told the boss not to annoy tourists.

Elsewhere, the **trans-Amazon Highway** zig-zags south of the Amazon, passing below Santarem to Port Velho and Rio Branco (see below) west to **Cruzeiro do Sul,** right against the Peruvian border and alongside the aptly-named Serra de Divisor. Here it stops; the only way out short of getting into a 'Darien-style' scenario is back where you came or by small plane to Pucallpa in Peru.

Across the Amazon
North to south, the Amazon basin can actually be half-ridden. From south eastern **Venezuela** you cross into Brazil and **Boa Vista**. The road is good and takes you 1000km via **Caracarai** to **Manaus**. Allow two days to cover this stretch in the dry season (June to October). At other times it will take longer but it seems to be an all-weather route.

From Manaus to **Porto Velho** the first hundred miles may be OK but at the last count Humaita to Velho has been abandoned to the jungle like many other roads in this region, planned or built. Instead, find **river transport** up the Rio Madeira to Porto Velho – less than $200 for you and the bike – where potholed tarmac leads to **Rio Branco**. From here it's a short hop into **Bolivia** at Cobija via Brasiléia. Here a dry-season road leads to the Riberaita–La Paz highway. Or you can trace the Bolivian border west, past Asis Brazil (but check out at Brasiléia) to the Peruvian border post at **Iñapari** (dug-out river crossing) from where it's a rough road to **Puerto Maldonado** and another 560km of dust, mud and river crossings up to Cuzco for a shower and a fry-up.

NORTH AMERICA

You won't need much help from a book like this about where to go and what to do in North America; the highlights are well-known, information and impressions abound, just turn on a TV! What is more useful and harder to dig up are the practicalities of importing a vehicle and riding it around without getting sent to Guantanamo Bay. It's a whole lot easier than you might think.

Renting, buying or importing your own

The widespread availability of **motorcycle rentals** (and not just fantasy-fulfilling Harleys), as well as the low prices for motorcycles, new or used, may make you think twice before importing your own machine. Opinion is divided but, depending on what you're renting and where, for anything over **four-to-six weeks** it may be cheaper to freight your own machine over as there are no import penalties: **carnets** are not recognised in the US or Canada.

Importing bikes and motor insurance

Wherever you are, most find it simpler to *fly* a motorcycle over – **Canada** is less expensive than the US. From Europe motorcycle air-freight specialists like Motorcycle Express can sort out all the documentation to get you on the road across North America, Mexico (as well as Europe). Recent one-way DIY prices with other freighters include: a Serow from London to Anchorage for £500; a KTM from London to Newark NJ with UTI: $600. The rider arrived a couple of hours later and rode out the same day because the UTI shed is right by the Customs office. For various reasons, people advise avoiding JFK airport. **Shipping** just doesn't seem a great deal: sixteen days, also to Newark for £425.

Apart for your air waybill, vehicle-ownership document and passport, no other documentation is required to clear Customs – a temporary import document is issued enabling you to ride around the US and Canada for a year exempt from emission controls, local safety standards and taxes. Basic **motor insurance** for tourists costs from $50 a month and can be valid for both Canada and the US with an optional 'Yellow Card'. Of course additional insurance may be advisable as medical costs can be huge in the US.

Note that the new three-month visa waiver cannot be extended and does not expire and renew itself simply by nipping over to Canada for a day. If you expect to stay longer get a B2 visa.

Exporting from these two countries, by land, sea or air is even easier; just crate it up and get it out of there. Borders out of the US are simply drive through, they don't even stop you although your departure is recorded.

THE TRANS-AMERICA TRAIL

Travelling on a motorcycle, off pavement from one side of the United States to the other is an adventure that would have Lewis & Clarke signing up at reincarnation.com.

Following nearly eight years of gruelling research, a dozen sets of tyres and more nights in downbeat motels than I care to remember, I put together a route that is **98% pavement free.**

For your riding pleasure I've hooked up a network of gravel roads, dirt roads, old creek beds, forest roads, jeep trails, some single tracks; in fact anything I could link together that is suitable for a dual-sport motorcycle and won't put the rider at the wrong end of an irate farmer's shotgun.

The TAT's trailhead is just southeast of **Nashville, TN**. From there, the intrepid rider crosses Mississippi, Arkansas, Oklahoma, New Mexico, Colorado, Utah, Nevada, California and ends up at **Port Oregon** on the coast of the Pacific Ocean. On the way he or she will experience just about every dirt surface that man and nature could come with, and probably every type of weather too. Each day the rider will be rewarded with subtle changes in the people, the food, the culture and, of course, the horizon.

The Trail covers **4400 miles/7000km** and can be done in about three weeks at a push.

Navigating the Trans Am

I've created 105 detailed maps of the entire route which get updated annually as certain sections of the Trail get sealed. With scales down to 1/100th of a mile the maps are designed to be used in a roll chart holder in conjunction with your bike's odometer. On each map, the trail is highlighted in colour and includes both the turn-to-turn and the accumulative mileage. Each hand-made map costs around $5, depending on the state. Available from: ⌨ www.transamtrail.com. See you on the Trail.

Sam Correro

THE GREAT WESTERN TRAIL

The Great Western Trail (GWT) is a multi-use route lending itself to off-highway touring. It traverses mostly public lands, from Canada to Mexico for around 2400 miles through Idaho, Utah and Arizona, with some side roads into Montana and Wyoming. Still incomplete, it's already marked and mapped in Utah and parts of Arizona. The gwt.org website has been stagnant for some years so the project may have hit the stops, but what there is of it in Arizona and Utah is the best of the route and probably better than the parallel GDT (see below) which can be picked up around the Utah–Idaho border.

Current maps show the trail winding its way from Nogales up the middle of Arizona and Utah and along the eastern border of Idaho to the tip of the Panhandle,

The line uses existing National Forest and similar scenic roads with parallel routes designated for hikers, equestrians and cyclists. And while 'out there', it passes near or has side routes to communities for gas, food and lodging.

The GWT corridor crosses the east/west American Discovery Trail near Escalante UT, where the Golden Spike was driven in linking railroads from the west and east coasts.

⌨ http://gwt.org
⌨ www.utah.com/offroad
⌨ www.gorp.com/gorp/resource/us_trail/ut_great.htm

PAVEMENT ENDS

THE GREAT DIVIDE TRAIL

A few years ago the Adventure Cycling Association (www.adventurecycling.org, or get the book *Cycling the Great Divide* by Michael McCoy) worked out the Great Divide Mountain Bike Trail, 2500 miles of off-highway riding which parallels and crosses the Continental Divide along the crest of the Rockies, an imaginary line where rivers drain either to the Atlantic or Pacific. It runs west of the GWT through Montana, Idaho, Wyoming, Colorado, ending in New Mexico. Most of the route is on easy forest tracks and country dirt roads, do-able on a big GS, with occasional avoidable sections that are either rough or closed to motor vehicles.

Most importantly, the majority of the trail is legally ridable and is quickly becoming a classic North American dirt tour.

la and Alaska

Island, I can take my KLR out into the bush most week-
I'll head out to explore the coastal mountains of south
west British Colombia (BC), a compara-
tively civilised region of logging and
mining tracks leading into the Rockies
which themselves offer some of the
most spectacular vistas this side of the
Hindu Kush.

Cabin at Caribou Pass, NWT.
© Tom Grenon

If I've a bit more time, I'll head up
into the true wilderness in northern BC,
Yukon and the Northwestern Territories
(NWT) which stretch across to
Greenland. These are the barely-inhabit-
ed homelands of big rivers, early snows,
grizzlies, moose and caribou. Adventure
motorcycling is a serious business, with
a small climatic window of opportunity and the usual limitations of payload
versus range.

In the wilds

Rule number one in the remote corners of the northwest is that you are *not* at
the top of the food chain. Once this fact is appreciated everything else becomes
elementary. All wild animals instinctively avoid man and if an animal sees or
smells a human it will flee. For once it helps to smell like a stinking outlaw
biker as bears especially have an extremely acute sense of smell. Many incidents arise when the aroma of a cooked meal lingers around your camp-site
after you have retired into the tent. A bear approaches, you react in panic and
the bear is alarmed to suddenly encounter a competitor to his food and will
try to defend it.

Camp behaviour

A couple of editions ago *AMH* ran a story by Gregory Frazier, whose camp
and parts of his BMW were ransacked by a bear, while he was stranded without fuel on the Dalton Highway in Alaska.

Keep your camp-site clean of food scraps. Suspend food in a bag 10m
high between two trees and 100m downwind from your campsite. Cook 50m
downwind from the tent. When preparing a meal clean utensils properly, *not
on a sleeve or pant leg*. Burn all packaging materials thoroughly, tin cans should
be packed out after burning clean. If catching fish, clean the fish as far away
from the camp-site as possible, and wash up afterwards.

When buying food for an upcoming trip into an area with a heavy bear
population, get non-fatty type foods: avoid bacon, butter or margarine and
canned fish. Beef jerky should be consumed immediately and packaging
incinerated in a good hot fire. This is especially important in the Barrens areas
of the Yukon and NWT where there are no trees to hang up a food cache.

Other odours that will attract wildlife come from soap, deodorant, toothpaste and scented moisture creams. Have these sealed in zip bags, in with the food bag, which should be a roll-top dry bag.

It's easy to detect areas frequented by bears as they tend to defecate on roads and tracks. A pile twice the size of a dog's would be a timid black bear, but anything the size of horse droppings would be the more aggressive grizzly. On the North Canol the grizzly bear is dominant and once in the NWT, where grizzlies are protected, their numbers increase greatly.

When traversing back-country trails you might come across a strong smell of rotting: a very good chance you're close to a bear kill. A bear will feed on a large kill for many days so keep moving. Garbage dumps (every settlement has one) will attract bears that travel to and from the dump daily, so both the dump and the surrounding area are bad places to be on a motorcycle. Give a dump a 10km no-stop zone, and don't camp within at least twice that distance.

On the road

The risk of hitting animals on the roadways can be lessened by reducing speed. This is especially important at **dawn and dusk** when wildlife is most active. I've observed that even on roadways with lots of traffic wildlife feeding alongside won't give a car or truck a second glance, but when an unfamiliar motorcycle approaches they're liable to do anything, including jumping out in front of you.

Avoid camping on **game trails** and old roads or tracks in the back country. Just like you, wildlife would much rather travel from one feeding spot to another along a clear trail than beating through the bush. After a time, if a road is rarely used by humans it becomes a game trail.

Protection and precautions

Pepper spray (CS gas, Mace) is the best protection against an attacking bear: spray directly into the bear's eyes and nose (not all over yourself as one Japanese tourist once did!). Have several spare emergency flares, as these can be used to ward off an undecided attacker from a distance.

Making plenty of noise while going through the bush – especially into the wind – will alert bears and other large wildlife. Moose, elk and caribou can also become aggressive if surprised and cut off from their young.

Keep a **bear whistle** in your jacket pocket for those occasions away from the bike. If your bike is quiet, there are times on an overgrown track when it would be wise to sound the horn if you're solo or the first in a group of riders.

The weather

The 3700km (2300 miles) between the Canadian–US border and Inuvik in the Yukon Territory just 20° from the North Pole offers a diverse climate range.

Starting with the southern BC coast, the weather is mild enough to ride year-round. But this mild weather is limited to the *western side* of the coastal mountain range, anywhere to the east it will

Dry bags. Down periscope...

be a frozen winter wonderland that won't yield good riding conditions until somewhere around mid-April, when trips at lower elevations can be enjoyed in the southern interior of BC.

In the spring (April–June), BC, Washington and Oregon have the north west's equivalent of the monsoon rolling off the Pacific Ocean. This rain coupled with the melting snow creates flooding; not normally a problem on paved highways but restricting off-road exploration especially at higher elevations where the ground is saturated. In the far north the situation evolves very rapidly from winter into spring (June) and is much drier. At this time daylight lasts nearly 24 hours north of Whitehorse.

Another weather-related factor is the **mosquitoes and flies** of the north. The intensity will vary with the topography, but as a rule of thumb flat wetlands are bug activity centres, sloping mountain sides less so. The intensity also varies through the summer: up to early June the buggers haven't warmed up enough to hatch, but as soon as there's a five-day period of warm weather the infernal multiplication begins!

By early August wetlands produce clouds of blood-sucking bugs that will magically disappear with the first frosty nights in the last weeks of August. Not all areas in the north are like this but generally it's the norm. So the ideal time to explore north of Whitehorse is mid-August to mid-September, when the water levels are at their lowest, bugs are bearable and the fall colours will make you wonder what exactly *were* those mushrooms you just ate!

From mid-September backroad exploration becomes a gamble against early snowfalls while the fall (Sept–Oct) still offers great riding conditions  throughout BC: water levels are low, the weather is drier and there are fewer tourists clogging up the highways. And to turn it all upside down, snow can fall on any day in the Rockies, while Inuvik in the far north can get 30°C for days on end. Expect the unexpected.

If you're quick you might catch the last copies of Tom Grenon and Chris Scott fighting off the grizzlies in the *Call of the Wild* dvd (see AM website).

Lois on the Loose

Riding a 223cc Serow from Alaska to Mexico had had its moments, but **Lois Pryce** *found that getting to Tierra del Fuego nearly finished the little Yamaha off.*

The Pan-American Highway comes to a dead end about seventy kilometres short of the Colombian border in Panama, possibly making it the longest cul-de-sac in the world. It starts again in northern Colombia and continues south to Tierra del Fuego. This interruption is an area of dense jungle known as the Darien Gap and has long been a source of frustration for Pan-American road trippers. The ferry service between the two continents is no longer in existence, so in Panama City my only option was to put my bike on a plane to South America.

I had been warned off Colombia so I decided on Ecuador instead. As I flew south I regretted my lily-livered decision to avoid the kidnap capital of the world. After all, I thought, when would I be in this neck of the woods again? So I promptly went and bought a plane ticket to Colombia.

How bad could it be, I reasoned to myself. After all, if I'd listened to all the warnings I'd never have left home. Remember, doom merchants are everywhere and they must be ignored! And look on the bright side; a kidnapping would save on hotel bills and as for the torture and mock executions I'd heard of... well, there are people in London who pay good money for such services.

But one week without wheels anywhere in the world was enough for me, so I bid farewell to Colombia and flew over the equator for a welcome reunion with my Serow. Ecuadorian Customs was a two-day headache, or maybe that was more to do with the altitude. At nearly 10,000 feet above sea level, Quito can have a debilitating effect on visitors. But the real victim of these lofty heights was my poor 223cc motorcycle, spluttering up hills with the throttle pinned at a rather pathetic 25 miles an hour.

My stay in Ecuador was made particularly enjoyable thanks to the generous hospitality of Ricardo Rocco – fellow adventurer, rally rider and Ecuadorian ambassador for motorcyclists. He arranged for me to join a group of Quito bikers for a 300-mile ride to the southern town of Cuenca, where as I understood it, we would indulge in a weekend of hearty partying.

At 7am on a cold, rainy morning I arrived at the meeting point and my heart sank. Out of the thirteen other bikes, the smallest was a 750 – over three times the capacity of my slinky scoot. It occurred to me, not for the first time, that I might have got this power-to-weight malarkey the wrong way round. Along with my now rather tatty luggage and shabby, mud-spattered waterproofs, I felt like a two-wheeled vagrant against these immaculately-dressed, shiny-biked folk.

patient companions and I finally arrived in Cuenca to
with motorcycles, most of them emitting an ear-split-
t I hadn't heard since I left the States. It seemed I had
he Ecuadorian celebrations of the Harley Davidson cen-
into the proceedings with a vengeance. In for a peso, in
a while the fun had to come to an end.

Ricardo and the hungover Harlistas, a spectacular rocky
mountain ___ ne across the Ecuadorian Andes and deposited me on the
road to Peru where I was relieved to find a most orderly and efficient border
crossing.

We were poring over a detailed map when a young boy entered the room
bearing a tray piled high with slices of juicy watermelon. He was sternly
instructed to offer them to 'our foreign visitor' first, so under the watchful eyes
of three young uniformed soldiers I politely bit into a slice. Unfortunately, as
I took the bite, a large chunk of the fruit broke off and fell into my cleavage! A
few melon jokes passed quickly through my mind, but embarrassment won
out in the end. My face took on the rosy hue of the fruit itself, and I stared with
exaggerated rapture at the map in front of me, aware that they were studying
my own topography with equal fascination.

I was heading for Lima where I was due to meet my friend Amalia who
was flying in from London with her motorcycle to join me on the next leg of
my journey. The *Panamericana* in northern Peru runs parallel with the Pacific
coast through a stretch of bleak, arid desert. The road seems to go on forever;
a straight strip of hot black asphalt, shimmering with distant mirages under
the glare of the unrelenting sun. To the west are immaculate sand dunes and
the waves of the Pacific Ocean breaking far in the distance. To the east – more
sand and the peaks of the Andes like long grey fingers poking up through the
haze. Small towns line the highway, each one providing a scene from a
spaghetti western: shirtless men with their cowboy hats pushed back on their
heads trot on horseback through the dry, dusty unpaved streets. Ancient layers of paint peel off the sun-bleached wooden doors of the liquor store, where
grimy bottles of unidentifiable spirits are displayed behind barred windows.

And at a rare sighting of a stream or river, groups of women and children
gather to wash bundles of clothes and lay them out on the hot rocks where
they dry in minutes. But every mile or so, just to remind you that this is the
twenty-first century, huge billboards advertise Inca Kola, the national drink of
Peru; a nasty bubblegum-flavoured libation, appropriately coloured gold in
keeping with the riches of the nation's ancient tribe.

I couldn't linger on these sights for too long though, as my concentration
was required just to deal with the sheer insanity of the Peruvian driving tac-
tics. I eventually pulled up outside a hotel, unscathed but slightly frazzled and
in need of something a little stronger than Inca Kola.

Amalia arrived two days later and her bike followed shortly afterwards
and soon enough La Lima Loco was just a distant memory and we were out
on the road, riding through coastal desert before heading east for the Andes
and Machu Picchu and the famous Nasca Lines. Intrigued by their mystery we
took a flight to inspect the lines from the air but unfortunately this event coin-
cided with the gastro-intestinal upheaval following a plateful of Tacu Tacu.

Within a few minutes of taking off, half-digested Tacu Tacu was filling all available bags.

Half an hour later I staggered out of the cockpit with three quivering bags of Tacu chunder. The pilot, who had proclaimed Amalia and myself to be *'muy bonita'* before we set off, didn't seem so enamoured now.

The following day I was back on the bike, a little weak but ready to take on the 13,000 foot passes of the Andes and the accompanying altitude sickness.

As we hauled ourselves hand-over-hand up the hairpins the air became cold and thin. Then came the rain, which quickly turned to painful icy pellets followed by two hours of snow, nil visibility and the numb digits I thought I'd left in Alaska.

Half an hour later I staggered out of the cockpit with three quivering bags of chunder. The pilot didn't seem so enamoured now.

The land was sparse and barren at this altitude with no signs of human existence for miles upon miles. The only living creatures who could hack it up here were llamas, strolling about with smug grins in their thick woolly coats.

At last the road began to descend and we found refuge in a tiny Andean village. A small stone building advertising itself as a restaurant was the most welcome sight imaginable and here we stood, dripping and shivering, almost unable to speak. There was no electricity or heating and the toilet was a hole in the ground alongside a mangy dog. But we didn't care. The women in brightly coloured woven shawls and little black hats, plied us with maté, coca-leaf tea which supposedly countered the effects of altitude. We ordered everything on the menu and ate like savages.

Sunday 23rd November, 8.17am: the morning sun was twinkling on the deep blue waters of Lake Titicaca, and we had just ridden across the border into Bolivia. We had hooked up with an American motorcyclist, Robb and his BMW and the three of us set off along the beautiful curvy mountain road that follows the edge of the lake.

Half an hour after setting off, I was surprised to see Robb pulled over at the side of the road, enjoying the view on his own. 'Where's Amalia?' he enquired. 'I don't know, didn't she pass you?'. 'No' he replied, looking very concerned.

A speedy U-turn confirmed our worst fears. We were greeted with the most gruesome sight I have ever seen outside of the movies. Amalia was lying flat on her back in a pool of blood by the side of the road, surrounded by a group of concerned Bolivians. Her bike had fared better than she had. She was barely conscious, her teeth were smashed out and her face was covered in blood that poured from her nose, mouth and ears. Her chin was gashed open, her nose appeared to be broken and her right arm hung limply at an unnatural angle.

Robb leapt into action and sped off to raise help in the nearby town of Taquina. Meanwhile the crowd of onlookers swelled, and incredibly ended up including two English-speaking doctors who happened to be passing by, enjoying a day trip with their families. First aid was administered, and Robb returned with the news that he had mobilised the nearby naval base and that help was on its way.

Bolivia is the poorest country in South America, but while facilities may be limited, spirit and human kindness are in good supply. Amalia was patched up and injected before being carried into the 'ambulance'. The driver rather forlornly asked me for some money to purchase enough diesel to get us to La Paz, a three-hour drive away.

While her accident was indeed a shock to the system and a brutal reminder of the fragility of the human form, it never occurred to me to abandon my journey south to Tierra Del Fuego. Amalia's boyfriend arrived to take up the baton, and once I was sure she was on the road to recovery, I left La Paz with her blessing.

Still with Robb, we decided to ride south together, despite our respective motorcycles occupying opposite ends of the power spectrum. La Paz is the highest capital city in the world and the Serow was running worse than ever, despite experimenting with various sized jets in the carburettor. No matter what I tried, nothing seemed to get me up the hills any quicker than a trotting llama.

> **...the Serow was running worse than ever... no matter what I tried, nothing seemed to get me up the hills any quicker than a trotting llama.**

Altitude is not a topic that crops up that often back home but now I was downright obsessed with it. Each time Robb and I took a break I would be peering at his GPS or bugging him with questions: 'How high did we go today? How high up are we now? What altitude is this town? That town?'.

Having spent the last two months spluttering my way through the High Andes, the words 'sea level' had begun to take on an almost mythical quality – an oxygenated El Dorado where I could breathe, where my shampoo bottle didn't explode in my face and where I could reach speeds of, oooh... 55 miles an hour.

A hill start in the centre of La Paz was the final insult. Red light turned to green but the bike was barely breaking wind. A cacophony of irritated horns did little to spank the Serow into life and I was forced to push the bike over the hill. 'Let's get down to sea level! And sharpish!' I gasped at Robb. A quick glance at the map confirmed that the quickest route to the Pacific was a 300 mile ride west into Chile over the ominously-named 'altiplano'.

Fortunately the scenery was breathtaking as the bleak, windswept plains gave way to high desert, inhabited only by families of haughty looking llamas. At the Chilean border snow-capped volcanoes and deep blue lakes dotted with pink flamingos greeted us. The economic difference between the two countries was immediately apparent; here they had computers and everything! I filled in the usual forms and signed a statement assuring the Chilean authorities that my luggage didn't contain, among other substances, any animal semen. Well not the last time I checked, officer, but who knows what those Bolivian dogs get up to when I'm not looking.

Sure enough, the following day's ride was a swift and dramatic descent down the mountains to the coast. By the time the swathes of lush green valleys came into view, my bike was galloping along like the old times.

Chile turned out to be something of a culture shock. Suddenly, life was orderly and efficient again. This was good news in many respects, it just meant that I now had to be orderly and efficient too and, to be honest, I was a little out of practice.

We headed south for Santiago where we would meet up with Rachel, my riding companion from the Mexican leg of my journey. The Pan-American Highway in northern Chile follows the Pacific coast for some of its length but the major part of the road cuts across the Atacama Desert, a seemingly endless, featureless dusty brown landscape with the thirst-inducing claim of being the driest place on earth. This stretch made for some long hot days of riding through the hundreds of miles of stark desert scenery, with fuel stations few and far between and little respite from the fierce glare of the omnipresent sun. But welcome cooler evenings were spent camping on the deserted beaches and drinking local vino tinto.

'Phew, this is tough, this adventure motorcycling!' Robb and I would exclaim to each other, chuckling merrily as we kicked back in the sand, popping another cork and cooling our feet in the rock pools while watching the orangey-pink sun disappear slowly below the horizon.

If you're a certain Chilean traffic cop however, being posted to the Atacama Desert can't be much fun. The day we met him, his task was to escort a long line of trucks carrying huge pipes which filled both lanes of the highway while crawling along at 25mph. Robb pulled alongside the lead cop to ask if it was OK to pass. In reply he yelled and screamed from the car window, waving his white gloved hands wildly like a possessed Baptist preacher. Robb didn't understand a word of course, so continued to ride alongside, as he beat his fists on the steering wheel with uncontained rage, a torrent of Spanish expletives pouring forth. Robb's continuing presence only infuriated him further and he drew on his limited English.

"No! Fuck you! No! No! Fuck you! No!' he shrieked. I surmised they must get a lot of American cop shows on cable TV in Chile but a few minutes later his white-gloved hand appeared from the window and calmly waved us on. Too much sun can obviously do strange things to your head.

A few days later Robb, Rachel and I passed Christmas in the Lake District of Chile, renting a little log cabin with an outdoor hot tub and a backdrop of volcanoes. New Year came with just another 2000 miles across the wilds of Patagonia to Tierra Del Fuego and the end of the road.

Robb had technical matters to attend to in Santiago, so Rachel and I set off together, blissfully unaware that we were embarking on the most gruelling part of the trip so far: the Carretera Austral. This dirt highway, lined with wild flowers, winds its way passed hanging glaciers, cascading waterfalls and jagged snowy peaks at every turn. Despite the road, the Carretera still retains a frontier feel, similar to that of the Alaska Highway. So, not the kind of place you want to crash your motorcycle, right?

Riding on a dirt road, it's usually a good idea to keep your eyes in the direction of travel. I learned this the hard way when I glanced over my shoulder to check on Rachel's presence. In just a split second my front wheel hit a patch of deep gravel and the bike flipped over. As the dust settled and my brain registered what had happened, I knew I'd been lucky. After a few minutes staggering around while releasing a brief bout of Tourette's syndrome, I discovered my now-mangled luggage was scattered across the road. Still, nothing a few cable ties and gaffer tape couldn't cure. Of course the Mighty Serow started right up again as if nothing had happened.

We made our way a little more cautiously into Argentina, aware that worse lay ahead along the infamous Ruta 40, the godforsaken windswept gravel highway that cuts across the wilderness of Patagonia to Tierra del Fuego and the end of the world.

Ruta 40 folklore abounds; mainly concerning the howling 60mph winds that tear off the Andes across the bottom of the continent at this time of year. Motorcycles and their riders blown clean off the road; flying rocks causing untold damage; hundreds of miles without fuel stops; unavoidable crashes. The horror stories go on. Naturally, I assumed it was all wild exaggeration as so many of the 'road ahead' tales had turned out to be. On this occasion, I was wrong. A more unsuitable journey for a couple of fully-loaded, travel-weary 250s one can not imagine.

It never occurred to me that it meant 'Beware, Armadillo – The Creature of Doom!'

As our balding tyres crunched on to the first stretch of gravel, a lone armadillo appeared out of nowhere and scuttled across our path. I imagined this to be some sort of good omen. It never occurred to me that it meant 'Beware, Armadillo – The Creature of Doom!' We emerged around the corner of the last hill we would see for a while and sure enough, a furious gust sent me flying across the road. Rachel fared a little better with her bike's lower centre of gravity, but we both struggled onwards using every ounce of strength in our upper bodies just to keep moving in a forward direction. The bikes leaning at impossible angles, the engines flat out in second; it was the only way to go whilst battling the ferocity of the wind.

Without warning a violent gust would regularly whisk my bike round by ninety degrees, sending me careering off the road, sometimes dropping the bike, sometimes not. I soon adopted a technique for this by steering obediently into the wind for as long as it took until I could come to a controlled stop. This worked well enough until the wind spun my bike into Rachel as she passed by, the front wheel ramming her back wheel. I crashed. She looked around – she crashed. We crawled across the gravel, yelling, 'Are you OK?', the wind tearing the words from our mouths.

With the bikes upright, we attempted to decant my fuel can into our tanks, but to no avail. The wind sprayed the petrol all over us and the bikes. And then once again a howling gust slammed Rachel's bike to the dirt, the filler cap still open, precious gas spilling into the dry earth. Exhausted and aching, we lifted her bike as another vicious blast howled across the plain, this time sending Rachel herself flying to the ground. 'We've got six hundred fucking miles of this!' we shouted at each other above the roaring, laughing with adrenalin-fuelled hysteria.

There was nothing else for it but to continue across the desolate Patagonian landscape. Towns on the map became the source of fantasies but our hopes were regularly dashed when they turned out to be non-existent or at best, a house. The few crumbling settlements that did exist lamented the recent closure of the only hotel and restaurant and the shelves of their little grocery store stood half empty. Meanwhile, back on the road, ostriches out-numbered vehicles fifty to one. I felt very aware of being in the middle of a lonely and inhospitable land on the edge of the world and made a silent vow never again to refer to the outlying suburbs of London as being 'in the middle of nowhere'.

Four long days later we reached El Calafate, caked with dust, bruised, bat-tered and exhausted. Various nuts and bolts were missing, I'd got through a litre of oil every two days and my back brake appeared to have been blown clean away. But it was over.

Today I was greeted by glorious sunshine as I arrived in Ushuaia, the most southerly town in the world; eight and a half months and sixteen thousand seven hundred and ninety-eight miles since leaving Alaska. The bike and I were starting to fall to bits, but I think I'd feel a bit cheated if this wasn't the case! Now it's a mere two thousand miles up to Buenos Aires, then back home to Blighty for a decent cup of tea.

And so the adventure ended. Just the itch and scratch of a few mosquito bites to serve as a reminder of South America. And here I am once again in the real world of debt repayment, tax returns, insurance, MOTs, finding a job... hmmm... might be an idea for a new website – Lois on the Leash.

Lois on the Loose – the book: see www.loisontheloose.com

It Pours, Man It Pours

Andy Bell *hoped for a fast run home from the Algerian Sahara when a damaged tyre forced him to leave the Desert Riders Project.*

I was always told that there comes a time in every man's life when he has to put the greater good first. For me, it came some 40km south of Bordj El Haouas (BeH) when, after my fourth puncture in 24 hours, I bade farewell to my Desert Riding comrades and tottered up the piste alone. An earlier rock-strike had cut the beading in my rear tyre causing the wall to begin to split. As the split grew, the frayed belting would rub the tube raw, eventually causing a hole. As the tyre went flat, the split would grow... and so on. The upshot of this was that I wrecked my main and spare rear tubes in only 250km, and was now eating horribly into Chris's. To try to get through the Hoggar mountains in this state, would have been to court disaster and rob the 'Project' of its last spare 'chambre d'air'.

I left the guys with a feeling of mild shame, as if I'd somehow let them down, and rode gingerly toward BeH. Lacking Chris's route-finding instinct, I rode into town through the municipal rubbish tip, making it onto the road amid a flock of jeering urchins. As I was filling up with fuel, I began to hear the unmistakable 'stealth fart' sound of two Honda XRLs approaching. The Desert Remnants had decided to head north too and have a day's R&R in Djanet before heading west. I felt grateful for this second chance to bid them a proper 'farewell and bon voyage', and before long I was en route to Illizi with a happy heart.

It didn't last though. After a couple of hours of tripping merrily through the incredible scenery which bounds the southern rim of the Tassili-N'Ajjer plateau, the shadows began to grow longer and I was left to contemplate the fact that for the first time in a month I was totally without the comrades who I'd come to depend on for company, morale and occasional arguments. The road began to climb, becoming an Alpine-style pass with sweeping S-bends and nosebleed-inducing drops. It was here that I broke the First Rule of Good Karma, allowing myself to think 'This would be about the worst place you could possibly have a....', 'Aaagh!'.

The rear tyre blew pretty fast, sending the back end of the bike into a nasty weave. As it lurched across the road toward the crash barrier, I managed to jump clear, ripping the leather 'backside protection' out of my riding pants as I threw myself over the Armco. The bike, now on its side, began to slide slowly down the steep road, so after wedging it against some roadside boulders, I got busy fixing the flat.

As I set about re-inflating the tyre with a cheapo compressor that Chris had given me after I left my pump at home, a new silver Land Cruiser pulled up. The car was driven by a chauffeur and carried two soldiers and a small

chap in an immaculate brown suit. It was this guy who lowered his window and asked me in a perfect BBC-English accent if his men could help me. I explained that everything was okay, and that I would soon be mobile again. To this, he leant forward earnestly and said, 'May I ask you if everything is all right for you in Algeria?' When I replied that everything was fine, and I was enjoying my visit, he smiled and nodded as if he had laid on the entire country specifically for my amusement. He then told his driver to give me food and water, and bade me a 'pleasant evening'. In this barren wilderness it was a surreal experience.

Setting off again, my sole thought was 'please let this repair last until I get back onto the flat'. I must have asked the wrong god though, as 5km later and still on a steep climb, I felt the unmistakable 'duh-duh duh-duh' of knobbly tyre flapping against the rim.

By now, it was getting dark, meaning that my only practical option was to get a good night's sleep and attack the problem in the morning with fresh zeal. Unfortunately, however, Algerian mountain passes aren't widely renowned for their sleep-giving properties, with my entire available world consisting of a cliff face, a narrow road, a crash barrier, 18 inches of gravel and a 200 foot drop. Electing not to sleep on either the cliff face or the road left me with the option of a night in Hobson's Hotel – so I set up my sleeping mat and bag on the gravel 'shoulder' and hoped to hell that I didn't roll to the left while I was asleep. Unsurprisingly, the prospect of actually getting any sleep was wildly optimistic, so I needn't have worried.

As evening turned to night, I lay in stupefied boredom, listening for the sound of a diesel engine that might be my salvation. Every now and again, a truck did pass, though always heading south. The drivers, however, were fantastic: each gave me food and water and promised to collect me on their return from Djanet when his truck was empty. When morning came I had enough fresh fruit to open a market stall but also a decidedly more optimistic view of my trip. At least it was no longer freezing cold. I took care with my puncture repair, first glueing a layer of inner tube to the gash in the tyre wall, and then fitting my last spare tube. With no more tubes or patches, this one had to last. Setting off again through the brightening morning air, I reached the top of the plateau and swooped joyfully through chicanes bordered by red wild flowers and bare black rocks. I was going home. Oh no I wasn't…

Now I had no option but to await help, so I sat by the side of the road and tried to give myself a vitamin C overdose with my newly-acquired supply of citrus sustenance. After about half an hour, a ratty Land Cruiser came along. The Tuareg driver and his passenger were transporting a load of goats to Illizi and had no space left. They did, however, offer the promise that a truck would come along soon and the driver would help me. At the time, I took this to be some sort of mystical prophecy, completely forgetting that in all probability, they would have overtaken the truck in their relatively fast car a few kilometres back. After kicking my rear tyre and giving me three more oranges, the Tuaregs left with a wave, and I sat down again in anticipation of the lorry.

Sure enough, a high-bed truck of some unfamiliar French vintage appeared. I shook the driver's hand nearly off his shoulder and asked if he could take me and my bike the 80km or so to Illizi. The driver nodded and bade his 'son', who must have been in his late fifties, to help me load the bike. My heart sank as I realised the fantastic improbability of two people being able to lift a 222kg bike over their heads and into the small loading door. However, either Algerian lorry drivers' sons are immensely strong or I was immensely desperate, but within ten seconds, the whole thing was lying on its side on the bed of the lorry and quietly leaking petrol all over a case of Orangina.

In Illizi, the truck dropped me at a local tyre repair shop, whose owner was nearly killed by a falling XR650L. I thanked the father/son team and headed off to a local café for a 'crème' and pastry while the punctures were fixed. As I sat in the early afternoon sun, a mere 24 hours after leaving Chris and Jon, I reflected on the kindness that had been heaped on me in this short time and couldn't help but wonder whether I'd have got the same aid on the A74 at Gretna.

I couldn't help but wonder whether I'd have got the same aid on the A74 at Gretna.

Back at the tyre repair shop I picked up my patchwork tubes and tore out of Illizi filled with hope and wearing my 'adventure motorbiking' grin. At the checkpoint on the north side of town, however, I was emphatically waved down by the police and guards who detained me long enough for one of them to fetch a camera, so that they could have their photos taken with me and the bike. The plan was to reach In Amenas by dusk, so I settled down to a steady 80kph and let my attention wander across the vast Erg Bouharet. In this state, I was momentously unprepared for the next blow-out and took an unplanned excursion into the scenery which turned out to taste less good than it looked.

I changed the tyre in record time and almost burst into tears when the little Chinese compressor gave up the ghost at only 12psi. With no back-up pump, the tyre in a parlous state and the bike so heavily loaded, I'd be sure to run into more problems at such a low inflation and, of course, was now running on my last tube. Still, as other options weren't exactly throwing themselves at me, I made my way up the road at 30kph, hoping fervently for a friendly car with a pump.

The friendly car turned out to be a green Iveco wagon piloted by a young German couple with an 18-month-old baby in the back. As they told me something of the realities of 'family' desert travel I had to admit that it sounded fun, though I could practically hear the tutting of disapproving grandparents back in Europe. I finally reached In Amenas about an hour after sunset, wantonly breaking the 'don't drive at night' rule and grabbing a grubby concrete 'chalet' at the Hotel el Erg.

The next morning, sitting outside the only tyre repair workshop I could find, I kept thinking of the song, *I'm Waiting for my Man*, by The Velvet Underground, though the drug I was after was black and came in small rubbery pieces. After about an hour, a brand new Mitsubishi pick-up roared up. This clearly wasn't the puncture chap and I started to wonder if I'd maybe been singing the Velvet's song out loud. The driver was obviously the local 'geezer' and when I told him why I was waiting he grabbed an urchin off the street and told him to find the missing mechanic. Ten minutes later he returned with a somewhat shaken man still in his slippers who he deposited on the street before tearing off with a wave.

... the drug I was after was black and came in small rubbery pieces.

By this time, there was something of a Groundhog Day quality to my adventures and all I really wanted to do was get back to the tyres we'd buried just north of Hassi Bel Guebbour ('HbG') on our way south and now just a half a day's ride away. By half ten my spare tube was repaired yet again and I set off, determined to make the 700km up to Hassi Messaoud via the tyre dump in a single butt-numbing day.

The route from In Amenas took me north up onto the Tinrhert plateau via the steepest road I'd ever seen. Now heading directly west, my GPS informed me that I was only 300km from our buried tyres and freedom from pneumatic servitude. A few hours later I pulled up at the army checkpoint in 'HbG' feeling rather pleased with myself. The tyre had held out and a replacement was just up the road. The soldiers at the checkpoint remembered me from the journey south and gave me a mild grilling over what had become of my two companions. I was about to joke that I'd buried their bodies in shallow graves near Djanet when, out of the corner of my eye, I noticed my rear tyre going flat yet again.

Amazingly, however, HbG is a place which offers virtually nothing except a petrol station with – a compressor. Therefore, having thanked its owner for the use of the facilities, I set off again, now in a state of torment. As I rode toward the buried tyre, I reflected on the fact that I now had no way of changing it. Furthermore, if I rode back to HbG to use the compressor there and nicked my one good tube while changing it, I'd be even worse off than I was already! Still, this was a new and, in my opinion, better sort of stress than worrying about being late for work.

At the appropriate waypoint, I turned off the road and headed out across the sandy flat which formed the southern edge of the mighty Grand Erg Oriental. I located my buried Bridgestone without any problems and carefully reburied Jon's and Chris's in case a similar fate befell them. Given the lack of a means to change it, I simply lashed the thing onto my pannier rack and headed north towards civilisation.

My final puncture happened about an hour later. This time I was completely helpless, so I just sat and waited for some traffic. Eventually, a Land Cruiser pick-up with three Sonatrach engineers in the cab were persuaded that they wanted to take me and the bike the 200km to Hassi Messaoud. Because the bike was too long for the bed of the truck, we had to ride with the tailgate down. This didn't please one of the engineers who turned out to be a safety officer and insisted that I lie there wearing my crash helmet and gloves in case I fell out of the back!

This didn't please one of the engineers who turned out to be a safety officer and insisted that I lie there wearing my crash helmet and gloves in case I fell out of the back!

As we headed up the road, I sat wedged between the XRL and a drum of cable, watching the world go by in reverse. Proving that Algeria has boy racers too, a Toyota Carina started swarming over the tail of the pick-up trying to get past. Eventually its four moustachioed occupants tore past, dodging pot-holes on the dismal road as they did so; ten minutes later we found the Carina on its roof. We got the Carina back on its wheels, and its owners left us with much handshaking and cringing. As we watched it go, the safety officer gave a sermon on having the right vehicle for the conditions. I didn't understand much of it, but he seemed pleased when I patted the roof of the Land Cruiser and announced it 'plus solide'. I was still 100km from town after all and it was getting dark.

The engineers dropped me at a workers' hostel in the centre of Hassi Messaoud, full of young Muslim men who spent hours praying in the foyer. Most of them were about my age and I was glad when they offered to show me around town. We set off for a night on the tiles, which mostly consisted of drinking tea on street corners and them trying to convince me that if I liked Algeria, I would love the Gulf. That night, I lay on the thick woollen blankets of my hotel bed with my faith in humanity at a record high.

The next morning, I made my final journey to a *vulcanasiteur*. With the Bridgestone in place my troubles should be over. I bade a warm farewell to my new friends and made the 300km to the Tunisian border and next day devoured the 500km to Tunis, knowing the Genoa ferry would depart the following day.

As I rode towards the port, a light drizzle caused the diesel on the road to shimmer alluringly in the dawn light. Stopping at a roundabout, the front tyre carried on sideways and I landed on my shoulder in a jarring arc. The gendarmes ran across the road to take me to a nearby doctor, but no sirree, I was going *home*. Picking up the bike, I rode on grimly with a jabbing pain each time I pulled on the clutch. The port was deserted. The timetable had changed and the next ferry was not due for four days. I sat on the kerb, wallowing in pain and self pity while my nose bled onto my jacket.

> I sat on the kerb, wallowing in pain and self pity while my nose bled onto my jacket.

Four more days in Tunis: I couldn't face it, so I rode to the airport, sick with pain and, praise the Lord, managed to get the bike accepted as cargo to Edinburgh for just £200, even if I did have to dump the battery and 30 litres of unleaded in the airport car park. At the passenger terminal the only ticket going was in business class but my Visa card gave me a knowing wink, so that was settled.

The plane landed in Paris late and I had to run to make my connection, almost throwing up as each bound jarred my collar bone. I arrived at the gate to find the flight closed and the plane to Edinburgh pushing back. It was the last one of the day. I threw my ticket at the dispatcher and tried to explain that I could really really do with getting onto the plane. All that came out was garbled nonsense, but he must have heard it before as the plane stopped, came back to the stand and opened its door.

As I sat at the front of the little Embraer jet, eating roast beef salad and still clad in my bloody Aerostich jacket, MX boots and torn riding pants I tried to avoid the bewildered gaze of the suit next to me. Instead, I thought of the German family and their truck, of the oil engineers and the young men of Hassi Messaoud, of Chris and Jon, still at large in the Sahara.

In Search of Veal Veng

Cambodia's no different to anywhere else, **Richard Virr** *discovers.*
Get away from the main tourist areas and you discover the real people.

At last. After riding 19,000km from the UK to Cambodia on the narrow-seated Honda XR400R, the dirt roads of this little Buddhist country lay before me. Dunlop's finest knobblies were fitted front and rear and the luggage was pared down to the 3 T's: tools, tubes and a toothbrush.

The plight of Cambodia since the 1960s is well documented: the Vietnam War, US bombing, CIA infiltration, civil war, 10 years of Vietnamese occupation and of course, Solath Sar (or Pol Pot, his political name) and his band of extreme Maoist loonies, the Khmer Rouge. What is not so well known is the state of the country's roads. With the exception of Highway 1 running from the capital Phnom Penh down to the port of Sihanoukville, there is no tarmac.

Furthermore, the country's upheavals have resulted in dirt roads being completely unmaintained for decades. Sections of the main highways would put many a motocross track to shame. The 80km stretch from Memot to Snoul in the east of the country is not just canyon-sized dips and jumps but, being once part of the Ho Chi Minh Trail, actual bomb craters delivered airmail by Uncle Sam himself: in short, dirt bike heaven.

I had been dirt biking in Cambodia before. The previous year I joined up with *Angkor Dirtbike Tours* for their annual 'Extreme Rally Raid'. My first time both on a dirt bike and in Cambodia, it proved such a laugh that I decided to do it again, only this time riding my own bike over. The plan went horribly wrong when only eight days before the rally and just 70km from the start point in Phnom Penh, four water buffalo ran out in front of me. The resultant bike damage was minimal and was straightened out by a local bike shop for a few dollars; my broken arm was another matter.

After a terrifying experience in Phnom Penh's 'best' hospital whose plaster cast was so heavy that the sling was causing me to stoop, I flew to Bangkok for proper treatment and three months' recuperation. What a city!

So, back in Cambodia with XR and arm in good shape I was anxious to get out on those roads and trails. I joined up with American ex-pat, Al the Chef, for a four-day loop of the southwest. The highlight was to be the road from Koh Kong to Pailin. Running parallel to the Thai border and through the least developed corner of the country, it looked to be one of Cambodia's more challenging routes.

Navigation is the trickiest part of touring Cambodia. Outside the capital, the country has only a handful of road signs. Modern maps are based on surveys carried out decades ago and are hopelessly out of date. Asking directions is pretty risky too. The Khmer language, with an alphabet of thirty-three consonants and twenty-seven vowels, contains some extraordinary sounds to Western ears. Correct pronunciation is critical. With my limited Khmer I was

happy to be riding with Al who, having come to Cambodia two years earlier as a backpacker and never left, had picked up plenty of the language.

On the first day we rode the new dirt highway to Koh Kong which, built by the Thai army, is smooth and fast and the only inspiration came from the view as it cut through the virgin forest of the Cardomon Mountains. It was also completely empty which makes you wonder why it needs to be eight lanes wide. The answer lies in the fact that the cunning Thai army got to keep all the timber they cut for the road. Mature hardwood logs fetch a high price, making road building an extremely profitable business.

The only people we saw that day were the Cambodian army out on patrol. Four soldiers two-up on a couple of 110cc Honda Dreams, all tooled-up with AK47s and B40 rocket launchers. We stopped for photos, they stopped for a chat. We were told that a family had been car-jacked on that road the week before and they were out to guarantee our safety. I looked down at the four pairs of battered, lace-less shoes and hardly felt reassured.

We arrived in Koh Kong without incident and that night Al performed magic directing operations in the local restaurant kitchen; one would never normally go to Cambodia for the food. But the large quantities of Cambodian beer that accompanied our meal made the next day a write-off. We decided just to check out the road to Pailin; a quick 40km afternoon blast and all looked well. Quite muddy in places but definitely do-able. 'Should be there in eight hours,' said the Chef.

His prediction was looking pretty accurate the next day when we reached the village of O'saam, a little under halfway. The road so far had been better than I'd hoped for. Built purely for commercial logging purposes, there are no Alpine-style hairpins here. Instead the road goes straight up one side of a mountain and straight down the other along incredible gradients. Monsoon rainwater had cut deep gorges along the now abandoned highway leaving endless opportunities for playing in the mud.

My riding companion is one of those irritating people who can cross any terrain at lightning speed without so much as breaking a sweat. So it was some time before I caught up with him, sitting in O'saam's village shop drinking Thai Red Bull and looking very lively. Red Bull actually originated in Thailand, only the Thai stuff has seven times more caffeine and sugar than the European variety. It's something you appreciate more as you get older. And so we sat there with huge grins on our faces. Everything was going so well.

Red Bull actually originated in Thailand, only the Thai stuff has seven times more caffeine and sugar ... we sat there with huge grins on our faces.

We set off again and soon came to a fork in the road in the middle of O'saam. An old man standing by the road-side raised his arm to indicate right. Assuming this was the way all traffic went, we took his advice. But knowing the danger of assumption we decided to ask a few more locals if this was the road to Veal Veng, the next village on the route. Ten seemed a reasonable sample and we would follow the majority vote. Amazingly they all indicated frantically and smiled profusely. Off we went.

An hour later we'd only travelled 11km. Something wasn't right. By Cambodian standards, it was a reasonable road but several trees had fallen across it and we were forced to push through the jungle to get round them. That slowed us down considerably, especially as after each jungle diversion we had to stop to remove boots, socks and trousers to pull off the leeches we'd collected. With engine and body temperatures rising fast, we turned back to O'saam for more detailed directions.

We left O'saam for the second time cursing our ten strong sample for not mentioning the right turn we should have made about a kilometre outside the village. As we took that right turn it began to rain and within a minute the road was a river. Those giant potholes that had provided such fun earlier were now completely concealed under muddy water and were proving quite treacherous.

The road became increasingly narrow until we were riding along a foot-path which ended at an abandoned two-hut village. Now tired, soaking wet and less than happy, we headed back to O'saam again in search of a bed.

Nights in remote villages are not normally high on excitement but tonight was Khmer New Year, a festival that Cambodians manage to string out over twelve days. It was party time in O'saam. We joined the village fair and drank and gambled with the locals. I tried one game and placed a one dollar bet to gasps from the other players. The high-rollers were in town!

The next morning, armed with even more detailed directions, we left O'saam for the third time. The road to the two-hut village was correct, we just needed to go through it and keep going, apparently. I was so glad Al spoke good Khmer. Back at the two-hut village I picked up a hitch-hiker; a soldier carrying a 10-litre can of rice wine hooch. He was obviously keen to keep the party going.

On my trip the XR and I had tackled most surfaces; mud, deep sand, gravel, even snow, but not a swamp which faced us next. I stopped at the edge and peered into the murk. My pillion, no doubt anxious to avoid wasting valuable drinking time, tapped me on the shoulder and indicated to carry on. Eight clicks later my smile was back. Swamp riding was fun and my love for the XR reached new heights. Buffalo quartets apart, the old girl is just unstoppable.

At the next village I dropped off my grateful passenger and the usual crowd gathered around us. The village chief pushed his way forward. He took one look at me covered in mud and grinning inanely, and turned to speak to Al. I never found out the exact details of that conversation. I did ask Al but he just muttered something about going back to O'saam and swore a lot. In fact, we were in Veal Veng; just the wrong one!

I later found out that there is an explanation as to why Cambodia has two Veal Vengs. As part of the Khmer Rouge population relocation programme, they would sometimes move complete villages somewhere else. The new village would retain the name. At the end of their four years in power some inhabitants would stay where they were while others would return to the old site. Both groups would use the same village name.

As we rode into O'saam for the fourth time in 24 hours the smiles had been replaced by looks of pity and bewilderment – how can tourists be so rich when they are plainly so stupid?

We never went on to Pailin. When we got to the Veal Veng we wanted we took the new dirt highway to Pursat and checked into what was the best hotel in town, complete dodgy air-con, dodgier plumbing and over 40 TV channels of static. But at least it was still Khmer New Year. Their new year is timed to coincide with the start of the rainy season in April and, along with much drinking, Khmers celebrate with water fights and baby powder fights. Being chased around the hotel car park by gangs of young Khmer women intent on rubbing baby powder all over me was something I got used to very quickly. Fortunately, after the exertions of the previous days I couldn't run very fast.

Being chased around the hotel car park by gangs of young Khmer women intent on rubbing baby powder all over me was something I got used to very quickly.

During my many months in Bangkok I met quite a few overlanders who had few positive things to say about Cambodia. But then they'd all done the usual loop from Thailand via Laos, Vietnam and through Cambodia, stopping only in Phnom Penh and Siem Reap near the famous temple complex of Angkor Wat. These two places are the centre of Cambodia's tourism and some of the locals have not been slow to capitalise on the rich pickings from tourists. Harassing foreigners sure beats earning ten dollars a month as a policeman or soldier.

But, as with so many places in the world, once you get away from these tourist traps you get the true taste of a country. In these days of air-rage and supermarket-trolley-rage, it's humbling to witness a people who are so friendly, welcoming and so positive despite all they have been put through. And, if you're on a motorbike, it's a lot of fun getting out there to meet them too.

Deadhorse, Fish Story

Gregory Frazier's *been at it again, annoying the grizzlies*
up in the far north; all that's changed is the bike.

B
ear in camp!' When someone yelled those words my head snapped up, eyes opened and I let go of the bottle of beer I was holding. Forgetting the spilled swill, I quickly grabbed my cameras and ran from my campsite to the one across the road, hoping to get a picture. I had been in Alaska for nearly two weeks and had yet to see a bear. As it turned out this was the only bear I would see.

It was a 300-400 pound black bear that had decided to paw through the cooking dishes on the table of the campsite across from mine. The single woman in the tent at the site had become hysterical trying to get out and had snagged the door zipper making it impossible to open. The bear stopped its search for food when she screamed and dropped off the picnic table, moving towards her cooler.

I ran over to the tent, forced the zipper back, then forward and the woman zipped out, knocking me over. The bear was less than ten feet away and I was lying flat on the ground, half-beered and fumbling. I scrambled upright and followed the running woman as she scampered across the road to the safety of my campsite. I did not want to be bear food anymore than she did.

We got there at the same time, both of us winded and panting as if we had run a mile instead of forty yards. What a pair we made, both of us standing there, she flapping her arms and trying to speak, me frothing as my evening beer tried to come back up the way it had gone down.

With a combination of thrown pots and pans, whistles and camera flashes, I chased the bear from her camp. An hour later the woman had calmed down, but refused to return to her tent. I told her she could spend the night in mine. She chose me over the bear, but might not have had she known I had been on the road for weeks without having shared the pleasures of the night.

This was my first trip to Alaska since I had written my book, *Alaska by Motorcycle*. The publisher had decided to do a second edition, so I spent nearly two weeks doing research while wandering around Alaska. It had been interesting to see the changes, but after some twenty-two trips to the 'Last Frontier' some things had not changed.

Moose and fish were still plentiful. The roads seemed to be in better condition but traffic had become more congested, making travel time between points about the same. I noticed that Alaska roads had become filled with motorhomes and travel trailers, nearly all having been driven from the 'Lower 48' as they call the rest of the US up here. I also noticed a huge increase in the number of motorcycles that had either ridden the ferries or roads to Alaska.

Ten years ago I rode all day without seeing another motorcycle traveller.

This time I usually saw several riders each day, sometimes as many as ten. They were travelling on everything from heavyweight H-Ds to BMW R1200LTs, Goldwings, Suzukis and numerous dual-sports like KLRs and BMW F650s.

From the equipment I saw on the motorcycles, some riders had spent thousands of dollars preparing for their Alaska adventure. Some had expensive, extra-large gas tanks or had added spare gas tanks costing hundreds of dollars, thinking they'd not find gas. These seemed to have been foolish expenditures, especially when I thought of the wallowing behemoth motorhomes and trailers on the highways, some getting as little as five miles per gallon. Thirty years ago when I first rode to Alaska gas was a commodity of concern, but not these days. Gas was plentiful, but sometimes expensive, often costing a dollar more per gallon than in the Lower 48.

It was surprising to see how many tourists perceived Alaska as still being some kind of pre-1900 frontier. In the small town of Wasilla, just outside Anchorage, there was a Wal-Mart store that was identified as the busiest Wal-Mart store in America. This Wal-Mart was such a local attraction, some local couples got married there. In Anchorage I found shopping malls and food stores that rivalled those I'd seen in Los Angeles or Seattle. The big difference between shopping in Alaska versus shopping in the Lower 48 was the prices. For the $30 per night I paid in Oregon for a motel room I was quoted $90 in Anchorage and Fairbanks.

Getting away from the tourists was harder than five years ago. I finally managed by taking some extreme riding trails deep into the interior. One of those left out of Petersville and wandered into the southern part of Denali National Park. To get there I had to make numerous stream crossings, some with deep, fast-flowing ice water.

Crossing one stream I was hit by a fish. The clean glacial stream was about one foot deep and fifty yards wide. Near midstream my focus on the rocks and water ahead of me was shifted quickly to what looked in my peripheral vision like a log moving upstream towards me. Before I could analyse what I was seeing it ran right into my front wheel with a 'thunk' and started to thrash around in the water. I was so surprised I forgot to put my foot down to steady the motorcycle and both the Kawasaki KLR 650 and I flopped on our sides in the water.

A 30-40 pound king salmon swimming rapidly upstream towards its spawning ground had knocked me off my motorcycle.

A 30-40 pound king salmon swimming rapidly upstream towards its spawning ground had knocked me off my motorcycle. While I thrashed around in the water trying to keep my cameras from getting wet, the salmon got its bearings right, and swam around the downed motorcycle and on upstream. It was so close I could have grabbed it had I not had my dripping cameras in both hands.

Once I got the motorcycle righted I could not get it to start. When it fell on its left side it had been running, so sucked water into the engine, killing the

motor. Water had also gotten into the electrical system. I spent the next hour on the stream bank trying to get it to run, and slowing killing the battery with each unsuccessful attempt. After an hour I was reaching a high stress point because I realised it was salmon spawning time and I was on the bank where bears liked to collect their catch.

As I'd entered the area earlier in the day two miners on ATVs were coming out. One asked me, 'Do you have a gun?'

I said 'No.'

The older of the two said, 'I wouldn't go up that trail without a gun, and I sure as hell wouldn't go alone. We've just come from up there and have seen some huge bears.'

So there I was, with no gun, alone, and stranded on the bank of All-You-Can-Eat-Alaska-Salmon-Café for Bears.

Eventually I got the KLR dried out enough to start, repacked it and hurriedly left the area. As I rode down the road following the stream towards civilisation I started to feel better. Finally I was able to laugh at my situation, and myself knowing I was probably the only motorcyclist in the world who had been knocked off a motorcycle by a fish. As foolish as the *Guinness Book of Records* was, I thought I might petition for a record based on my fish story. Given what Guinness gave records for, like the most nails up your nose, my fish episode qualified as a special edition.

A quick run up the Dalton Highway showed just how different the weather could be on this treacherous road to Prudhoe Bay. Before entering the Dalton Highway I saw a flashing state highway sign that said the Dalton

Highway was closed due to forest fires and thick smoke. Fifty miles later I was riding through orange burning trees, coughing from the grey smoke.

Once I reached the Arctic Circle sign at the 115-mile marker the fire and smoke had been replaced by rain, which continued to Coldfoot. A hundred miles further north the rain had turned to snow over the Brooks Range.

I was mapping some waypoints for a possible motorcycle rally up the Dalton Highway, the Deadhorse Endurance Rally. Had it been run this year the riders would have had one day to ride the 414 miles through fire and ice. The upside would have been that since it was early July, sunset was around 3am with sunrise two hours later, so riders would have had plenty of riding in daylight.

The Dalton Highway paralleled the Alyeska pipeline south from Prudhoe Bay. I knew that the oil in the pipeline was heated to make the flow easier between pump stations when it was cold. At Coldfoot records had been set with 179°F temperature differences. The winter low had been minus 82°F with a summer high of plus 97°F. On my Dalton Highway day I walked over to the pipeline and put my hand on it. Even though it was close to 70°F

At Coldfoot records had been set with 179°F temperature differences. The winter low had been minus 82°F with a summer high of plus 97°F.

that day, I could still feel the heat coming through the protective outer shell of the pipe. Then I realised that in the winter animals probably gathered around the miles of pipe to keep warm. I wondered if the environmentalists who fought the pipeline when it was originally built appreciated that the heat pipe was keeping animals from freezing in the winter?

I finished my last days in the Kenai area south of Anchorage, stopping to take a photo and make a record of my having reached Anchor Point, the furthest point west one can ride on the North American continent. A night in Homer, eating fresh halibut that came from a 200 pounder caught that day nearly caused me to deviate in my travel plans. For $100 the captain of the boat told me next day I was 90% guaranteed to catch a halibut, and I pictured myself pulling in one of the giants. That evening the rain fell and wind started to howl. Camped on the Homer Spit, it felt like mid-winter in Montana which normally I try to avoid. I packed up in the morning and headed back up to Anchorage.

Several days before a local guide had taken me out for a night on the town. After a pleasant dinner with friends, he piloted four of us to what some call the 'best lap dance club' in Anchorage. We only stayed a short while but my time in the woods, days on the road and nights sleeping in a one-man tent compelled a return visit.

The Great Alaskan Bush Co II may have lived up to its reputation but I missed casting my vote. As soon as I walked in I saw another motorcycle traveller I had met a week before on the Denali Highway. He'd been riding a KLR similar to mine. We spent the next hour at the bar, paying for over priced beer and trading road stories about our travels in Africa, South America and Asia. Realising our pocketbooks were getting hammered we decided to go back to my campground, stopping at a supermarket for beer supplies at a far more favourable rate. At the store we paid one-fifth of what we had been paying in the bar, trying to ignore naked go-go girls and jabbering about life on the motorcycling roads around the world.

In the campground we spent several more hours comparing our tales of adventure and those of friends. By 11pm he decided it was time for him to ride to his motel. After he left I sat down to sip the last four bottles of beer in the grey twilight of the cool and quiet evening of the Anchorage Municipal Campground.

I was reflecting on my weeks in Alaska, the roads and trails I had ridden, people I had met and friends made. They had been long days filled with some of my best motorcycling in the last six months. Then I thought of how I had missed the one thing I had been thinking about for the last days, the go-go dancers at the Alaskan Bush Company. I remember that as my friend and I had been talking at the bar several of the ladies had nestled and rubbed against us attempting to sell lap dances, and in the mirror how hard it was to look at the reflection of the topless-bottomless dancers on the stage.

Then I closed my eyes, picturing one dancer that had exceptionally nice muscle tone and body movements. Both my hands were holding the beer bottle between my resting elbows on the picnic table. My head drooped and my chin rested on my chest while my mind replayed XXXX rated pictures of her dancing, an erotic memory that heated and sped up my male juices. Then someone yelled, 'Bear in camp!'

Over the page and far away

Maciek Swinarski *and a couple of mates set off for a high-speed run from Poland to Mongolia via some very vodka-sodden villages.*

Like all our previous departures this one was also quite tense: Przemek burned out his GPS when installing it, Pawel was working on his alu-boxes until the last minute, Michal had some problems with his new rally clutch and I'd had a nightmare installing the oil-cooler.

But just before the Russian border we felt that pleasant adrenalin charge – the fun is just going to start! The border-officer took Przemek's passport, looked at it, crumpled it, looked again and finally said:

'This passport is expired! Go back to Poland and get a new one.'

'But sir, is there no other way we can fix it?' Przemek pleas with an innocent face. Of course there is, Przemek's wallet becomes $5 lighter and we can happily continue.

Our plan is simple: full speed to Mongolia. During the day we're riding along the main Trans-Siberian highway. Sometimes I recognise places from *Mondo Enduro*, the movie that a few years ago had inspired me to travel on motorbike. We are in a hurry so we cannot enjoy too much off-road riding through Siberia. We are riding our butts off but when we look at the map; *psia krew*! Mongolia is still several pages away! At every gas station I've been asking 'How far is Irkutsk?' The answer is always the same 'My friend, Irkutsk is very, very far away'.

One day something strange happened to Michal's KTM. We all stopped and he kept on riding around us. It looked as if there was a problem with the clutch – when we pressed it the whole engine cover was moving. When Michal removed the engine cover I could see in his face that this was the end of his ride. Somehow he managed to limp back to Poland; we three continued east to Mongolia.

Because we are friendly guys we decided we would spend nights with local people. So when it was getting dark we would turn off the main road towards small villages and ask people could we sleep near their houses. Usually it worked and they prepared delicious suppers for us: grilled potatoes with bacon and mushrooms and of course a bottle of home-made vodka.

One night we arrived at a small village near the Trans-Siberian Railway. Everybody was completely drunk – even the kids! A ten-year-old boy staggered over with a cigarette in his mouth saying, 'Stay in our village. Nothing will happen to you. I guarantee.'

Everybody was completely drunk – even the kids! A ten-year-old boy staggered over with a cigarette in his mouth.

ially we felt quite comfortable but after one hour of hearing 'Nothing ppen to you. I guarantee.' – we started to worry. Nevertheless we decided to stay and Sasha, a very nice guy, invited us to his house. He prepared a great *bania* (Russian sauna), his wife Nadia prepared a huge meal and we got stuck in, drinking Sasha's vodka and listened to his Siberian stories. Unfortunately the house was situated near the train station and every time a train passed a very loud and psychedelic alarm went off so we did not sleep so much.

We woke up at five and by seven Sasha had already finished his breakfast (two beers and a bottle of vodka). Because of our restless night on the next off-road section we had a few crashes and destroyed two alu-boxes.

Near Kransnoyarsk, after a whole day of riding in heavy rain we stopped to eat something and warm up a little. Suddenly two big guys turned up – Polish missionaries who invited us over to their house. We were so happy we did not have to do any more riding that day and instead gave the bikes a check-up in their garage, enjoyed a hot shower and another monster feed. These tough guys told us a lot of hardcore stories about the life of Catholic priests in Siberia.

I will never forget the night in a village near Irkutsk. As usual we drove into a small village where one guy was extremely friendly and invited us to his house. While we were settling in our friend disappeared and turned up later completely drunk and in a totally different humour. 'Who are you!?

Where are you from?
Why are you here?
Who are you spying for?'

Where are you from? Why are you here? Who are you spying for?'

This didn't look too good but he insisted we eat supper with him and drink some vodka. He behaved very aggressively. 'Do not speak Polish at my table!' he yelled. He was a former soldier fighting in Chechnya, had been in some special forces and had probably done some awful things, and now felt forgotten and used by his country. We tried to cool down the atmosphere but with no success. Finally we managed to say goodnight and went to sleep.

Suddenly a woman woke us up at 2am crying loudly and shouting something about pigs. When we turned the torch on she started to laugh (while still crying) 'I thought that you are Chinese.' This was the wife of the Russian soldier who had been sleeping when we arrived. She told us that the Chinese are bad people and that they had stolen her mother's pig. Then she asked us to take our bikes and look for the Chinese thieves and the stolen pigs. Przemek and I jumped on the bikes with the soldier's daughters on the back to guide us. But soon I lost Przemek and started to worry, then suddenly I saw the drunk soldier – he was running in my direction and he tried to jump on my alu-boxes. Somehow I escaped. I told the girl to guide me back to her home quickly; Przemek was already there. I reported to the women that regretfully the Chinese pig-thieves had got away and was all set to leave this crazy house.

Near the Mongolian border we had a somewhat saner encounter. We met a Japanese girl Makiko on an incredibly over-loaded Enduro bike. She had started her trip a few weeks before from Vladivostok and was planning to go around the world in her aim to find a perfect man. Respect, Makiko! (Later she

spent a few weeks in Poland without any luck and the latest news is that she'd managed to cross Africa).

Finally we arrived at the Mongolian border. The land border had been open only for a month. Before that, travellers had to put their vehicles on the train. There were a few people there; some said they'd been waiting twelve hours. Nevertheless we figured out how the system works: the border officer showed up and opened the gate every half hour, allowing everyone to pass in. Then he yelled 'Stop!! Move back!' He would then look into the crowd and point his magic finger at the person who would be allowed to pass through; the same situation repeated every half an hour. After some time our main negotiator, Przemek, went to the border officer and tried to tell him that we 'really, really would like to cross the border.' He just smiled and only two hours later his magic finger descended on us. Another five bucks fluttered out of Przemek's wallet and we were finally in Mongolia.

We felt relief; after thousands of kilometres and three crates of vodka each, our dream had materialised. We prepared the bikes for two weeks of real off-road: changed tyres, chains, sprockets and left most of the luggage near the border. Now the fun began!

Mongolia proved to be even better then we imagined. Riding across mountains, steppes and desert among wild horses, camels, yaks, antelopes and with eagles flying above us was just fantastic. Although it was hard to communicate, the nomads were very friendly. Even in the middle of nowhere we always had some guests when preparing the camp. Their first love was horses but right after that came motorcycles, so they just loved our bikes. The most popular motorbike in Mongolia is the Russian IZ Planet and sometimes we could see a whole family riding on one creaking Planet.

GPS is a must out here. Apart from the region near the capital there are no roads and no signs. We managed to obtain 1:1m maps which were good enough to prepare waypoints each day.

There was only one problem: punctures. At the beginning it was funny, then annoying and at the end it was a real nightmare. Even asking a shaman to spill horse milk on our tyres did not help. By the time we arrived in southern Mongolia, the Gobi desert, Przemek's tyre was history, having been repaired so many times. A Planet's tyre did not fit his Yamaha, so Przemek jumped on the first plane to the north and returned after three days with one of the road tyres we'd left near the border. During this time Pawel and myself were riding through the Gobi desert. I had my share of punctures too and also damaged the tyre. But it wasn't so bad and a great Mongolian tyre specialist managed to fix it – he cut off part of a Planet tyre and put it between my tyre and the rim.

After two weeks of off-roading we were so happy to see tarmac again – no more punctures! We really loved this trip; both Russia and Mongolia were really beautiful but we had run out of time so from Irkutsk to Moscow we travelled by plane, covering three whole pages of maps in half a day.

See our photos at www.motomongolia.prv.pl

How did Pakistan get its name?

You'll find out later, but for the moment **Georgie Simmonds** *describes the last weeks of her trans-Asian odyssey, crossing Pakistan on an Enfield.*

Having avoided the monsoon and several sources of premature death in India, we wondered whether Muslim Pakistanis could really be any different from their Hindu neighbours. The answer was: thankfully yes!

The locals we met were worried that the whole nation was being portrayed as reactionary, Al-Qaeda-harbouring and anti-Westerner. What struck me so vividly in Pakistan was that you should not judge people by the politicians who represent them. The everyday Pakistani we met could not have been happier to see us. Respectful and polite, we never felt threatened when owning up to being British, even though the Iraqi war had only 'ceased' two months earlier. At the Pakistan Embassy in Nepal, an official had announced, 'I think you will enjoy our country'. And as it turned out, he was right.

Word on the street was that a sweetener was required to prevent a long drawn-out Customs inspection of our Enfield and BMW. The Bossman eventually turned up, apologised for the heat then asked us how the Carnet guarantee worked and why, when he put claims into various European Automobile Associations, they were never honoured. His speech and movement were laboured, I mentally diagnosed Parkinson's disease, so I helped him fill in the customs ledger and we were sent on our way – no inspection and no bribery.

Pakistan was our first really Islamic state and I endeavoured to dress accordingly. The shalwar kameez (cotton baggy trousers, long tunic and scarf) that I'd bought in India was an immediate success. I was flattered to receive compliments about my attire from young women.

We were equally astounded by the number of people who approached us wanting to welcome us to their country. Children would be sent to shake our hands and requests for us to appear in their photographs were at an all-time high. During a Sunday evening stroll in Lahore we met dozens of children inviting us to meet their parents. Though ridden with hair lice and suffering from skin complaints it was hard to ignore their gorgeous green eyes that reminded me of the famous *National Geographic* magazine cover of the Afghan girl.

Little did I know or appreciate that the liberal city of Lahore would be the last time I would see women wandering freely about and eager to interact with us. In the countryside we'd only see women working in the fields and desperately avoiding contact with foreigners.

Surprisingly a very common opening question would be 'Are you a Christian?' Simon, being a devout atheist, caused some offence and we came to realise it was better to call yourself a Christian than an atheist in the Muslim world, since a belief in some God is better than none at all.

The Pakistanis were huge in comparison with their Indian relatives. The fact that Muslims are not vegetarians like Hindus must have something to do with it. Pakistanis prohibit the consumption of meat two days a week, but as chicken is not considered to be meat, their high-protein diet goes uninterrupted!

In preparation for the imminent visit to Iran I realised I needed to buy myself another shalwar kameez outfit. Bagginess and modesty were a must in Muslim countries; T-shirts and standard trousers were out since the showing of skin or the mere hint of the shape of a woman's body is a big no-no. I would never claim to be a shopaholic, but choosing a shalwar was great fun. All I had to do was sit back whilst a group of boys ordered me a Coke and showed me hundreds of combinations; the choice was mind-boggling.

I settled for a bright red/yellow/black tartan-like outfit; I wanted to make a statement. A tailor was summoned to measure me up and the next day I picked my little number up. I was later mortified to read in the Lonely Planet that wearing red in Iran can be dangerous because it is associated with the enemy of Emam Hossein, Mohammed's nephew.

Time to leave open-minded Lahore and marvel at the contrasts of modern, structured Islamabad and its sprawling chaotic neighbour, Rawalpindi. Pakistan was another country lacking in road signs, even on the main road to the capital, but stopping to ask a policeman was a double-edged sword; they were helpful and knowledgeable ('the road you need is behind you'), but keen to show off their power ('Sir, if you turn to go in that direction I have the power to fine you'). When Simon explained we didn't have a reverse gear the policeman donned his white gloves, stopped the traffic and allowed us the illegal turn.

We had a foreign bike alert at the next checkpoint: a German-plated XR250; lo and behold it was Ulli who we'd met in Kathmandu. We agreed to ride into Rawalpindi together, but the presence of a slow-moving police car in front of us seemed to suggest we were being given an unwanted escort. We kept our cool and waited for them to get bored. They eventually allowed us to overtake them, but when I looked in my mirror I saw that they had pulled Ulli over. When he was eventually allowed on his way, he explained that he had been reprimanded for not driving to the left of the yellow line. Our monster bikes were supposed to follow the same rules as gutter-driving putt-putts.

Our only reason for visiting Islamabad was to obtain Iranian visas. They were the last documents we needed to allow us to complete the big trip. Our stress levels were kept high by making use of a travel agent in Iran; for a reasonable charge of $30 each, the agency made a visa support application in Tehran. This made the task of getting the visa in Islamabad a doddle; several frustrated tourists we met had to revisit the Iranian embassy for weeks on end. I will consequently plug the Pars Tourist Agency at www.key2persia.com.

Visas in hand we waved good-bye to Ulli and wished him well for his adventure into Afghanistan. We had been curious but never really tempted because of the dangers involved. A week earlier an Italian motorcyclist had been killed near Kandahar (fortunately Ulli survived).

We were now to embark upon one of our major goals: the Karakoram Highway peaking at the 4730-m Khunjerab Pass on the Chinese border. We were surprised at how quickly Rawalpindi disappeared. We followed the banks of an innocuous river most of the day until, with a roar it joined the mighty Indus. We could immediately see why the river was dubbed 'Mighty'. Its force was indomitable and not once during the seven days that we accompanied the Indus did we see any vessels trying to ride it.

The second day's ride took us to Chilas, a town we were warned to avoid. It was claimed the locals were hostile towards foreign women and the town was in the heart of Yagistan: Land of the Ungovernable. Even the colonial British had avoided it. But for us the waves from men and roadside children (the women had all but disappeared) were no less forthcoming than anywhere else. The only oddity was at the checkpoints along that part of the KKH. In other areas the police wanted date of entry and visa numbers. Around Chilas all they wanted to know was when we entered their region and when we would be leaving it.

> **The town was in the heart of Yagistan: Land of the Ungovernable. Even the colonial British had avoided it.**

With every hour the scenery became more spectacular. I could never describe it as pretty, just incredibly raw. The area was a collision zone of the Indian and Asian continents and the mountains were still being heaved up. There was very little traffic on the road so every time we stopped for water the sounds of nature were eerie. The geology was in motion; rocks tumbled towards us as we stood below the crumbling valley walls. As we moved further north, snow-capped mountains began peering over our shoulders and glaciers stretched down to the road. I wish I could adequately describe the colours; every imaginable shade of mauve, terracotta, brown and grey gave the impression the landscape could only be extraterrestrial.

Gilgit was the main tourist town on the KKH. Our guesthouse was a haven of tranquillity with travellers from all round the world congregating with stories of derring-do. It was obvious how 9-11 had affected the tourist industry in the struggling region, but even though money was tighter than usual we received an invitation to eat with Yaqoob the manager one evening. He'd laid on a sumptuous feast for seven of us tourists and never asked for a contribution. That act really summed up the innate hospitality of the Pakistanis.

The last Pakistani town on the KKH was Sost, a dire trading post full of anxious businessmen waiting for signs of their lorries crossing the border. It was there at 3000m altitude that I had the most vicious of headaches, which almost prevented me from riding my own bike to our goal at the top of the pass. We wanted to wave goodbye to China, the country we'd skirted around since Kyrgyzstan over a year ago. Numbed with painkillers and a couple more hours' sleep we set off for the border. It was a steady climb to the Khunjerab Pass and mercifully my headache dulled. The temperature dropped, golden marmots whistled playfully and the one-man border guard accepted our 'Manchester United pencil bribe' to allow us into No-Man's-Land for a photo. As we turned to head back down the pass, tears welled up as we realised we were really going home now.

We knew that the road beyond Peshawar was under construction and the political situation was changing daily, so we sought advice on the best route to the Iranian border from the tourist board. We chose to by-pass Darra, a 'wild-east' town whose inhabitants are famous for making and selling guns. Our route took us over the old mountain road to the garrison town of Kohat. The traffic police were shocked to see foreigners in the town and in no uncertain terms showed us the way out; no Pepsi from them!

We opened our door to be greeted by a soldier with a rifle (an Enfield, no less!)

The following two days were to prove a test of resilience and nerve. I can't actually believe what we got away with. We could easily have spent a few nights in jail, but instead we came up smelling of roses, and we started to realise how Pakistan managed to spend 70% of its budget on security.

It all started when we checked in to our hotel in DI Khan. I was surprised to be asked exactly what time we'd be leaving but I gave an estimate nonetheless. Next morning we opened our door to be greeted by a soldier with a rifle (an Enfield, no less!) who seemed to be guarding the hotel. We thought little of it until he marched into our room asking us for our departure time.

Riding at our genteel pace out of town we became aware that a police pick-up truck in front of us was maintaining the same speed. As a test, we pulled over under some shade and watched the vehicle stop and turn around. 'Is everything OK, sir?' they asked. We asked why they were escorting us. 'Ah, it is for your own protection sir.' Simon didn't want their protection so asked them to leave us alone. They seemed a little uncertain but agreed to give up. No sooner had we regained our freedom than another vehicle was on our tail. We spent the rest of the day playing cat-and-mouse with various marked and unmarked trucks, getting more frustrated and angry with them as they picked up our trail along each section of the main road.

Tensions grew when we furiously waved down yet another vehicle. A couple of burly man-mountains in civilian clothes stepped out. We demanded to see their ID. 'We don't have any ID on us, it is Sunday. But we are policemen. You can see we have 'POLICE' painted on our truck.' We said we didn't believe them; they could easily be Al-Qaeda terrorists targeting us! Simon got out a marker pen and wrote 'POLICE' on the BMW's white plastic hand guard. 'Now I'm a policeman, so bugger off.'

Things came to a head as we entered the similarly-named town of DG Khan. We were guided to a police station and after some chats, mangoes and a coke we were escorted twenty kilometres out of town just after a sign that read 'You are now entering the Tribal Areas', making us think this was where we needed an escort. It wasn't long before we got stopped again and told we needed to wait for another escort, but not before the Bossman commandeered a huge watermelon in our honour and ordered us off the bikes. 'For God's sake will someone give the hospitality a rest, we just want to find a hotel'. This time the police guide was mounted on a brand-new Honda CD70 Cash Deposit ('Cash Deposit' really is the name, proudly splashed across the tank!). He guided us up a valley along the scariest and narrowest of single tracks, clinging to a cliff face to Fort Munro, straight to the police station for more registration. The local policeman had no idea what to ask so a couple of posh boys were summoned as interpreters. I thanked them and commended their perfect English. 'Well, we're from Lahore you know. They're practically illiterate up here.'

We eventually settled into an overpriced hotel, full of partying Pakistanis, where the Chairman of the English Department at Lahore University offered us mangos and whisky. There we learnt why our day's journey had been so fraught: DG Khan is the home of the Pakistani nuclear industry!

Next day we sped deeper into 'The Tribal Areas', a lawless area of Pakistan that the government keeps out of. Many men carried Kalashnikovs, complimenting a long black beard and wide turban. We felt that we shouldn't mess with these guys, but putting a camera in front of them made their faces light up with a broad smile and shining eyes.

We followed a stony and sandy track that zigzagged across a ripped up road. As my suspensionless Bullet hit rock after rock, I dreamed of an F650. It only stalled once, just before a river crossing but it took ages to restart. As I sweated over the kickstart we could both hear gunfire in the distance.

We'd been storing a couple of dozen pencils in our tank bag for 'deserving kids', tending to ignore kids that shouted 'money, pen, sweet' with held-out hands. Fearing we might end up going home with a lifetime's supply of pencils, I jumped at the chance of off-loading them at a passing school. The open-air classroom contained a mixture of ages and sexes. The kids were dumbstruck on seeing us. As we rode away I suddenly realised that all teaching was being done on slates with chalk. Oh well, they seemed grateful.

Quetta was the last major city to visit, and a pleasantly organised and clean one at that. Simon serviced both bikes on the hotel forecourt before we set-off for a two-day ride across Baluchistan to Iran. Our last (sleepless) night in Pakistan was in Dalbandin. When we checked in we were warned that the electricity would be cut-off at 2am. As we sadly listened to our fan wind down in the early hours, our thermometer climbed to 38°C.

So how did Pakistan get its name? No, it's not 'Land of the Pakis' but is in fact an acronym referring to Punjab, Afghania, Kashmir and Sind with the suffix 'stan' meaning 'country' in Persian. So now you know.

Old Boxers Never Die

But they sure get a beating. **Simon McCarthy***'s Paralever endures thousands of kilometres of abuse from Central Asia to Indochina.*

If you're not interested in getting oil under your fingernails, you might want to skip this story. But if you want to know how rugged an old BMW can be and how it's important to be lucky as well as good read on.

In Chiang Mai I finally fixed a problem with the bike's engine that I'd caused about one year and 35,000km before.

I'd serviced the bike just before we set off on our epic ride. I always do it myself, mainly because I don't want to spend money on labour charges, but partly because I don't trust the ham-fisted kids who pose as mechanics in most bike shops.

Part of the service routine is to 're-torque' (loosen and retighten) the studs (big bolts) that hold each cylinder onto the crankcase. The re-torquing process is supposed to stop oil and gas leaks from the cylinders. Unfortunately, the torque specified by BMW is right on the edge of what the studs can take, so if you so much as sneeze during the procedure the studs start to tear out of the aluminium crankcases. If that occurs you have to take the cylinder off and repair the damage.

So just days before the off, guess what I did? Yes, I over-torqued one of the studs and I felt the metal starting to give way. Shit! What to do? My two options quickly boiled down to one as I considered all the million and three things we had to do in the next couple of days. I could strip the bike and get it repaired, or just ease the tension on that stud a bit and see if I'd get away with it. So this 'ham-fisted kid' took the easy way out and loosened off the nut.

And the bodge worked. The stud held all the way to Kyrgyzstan where we filled the engine with water and wrecked the starter motor, ignition unit, piston rings and cam-chain. I fitted my spare ignition unit on the spot, which got us going again, and used the Internet to order a second-hand starter motor from Motorworks in the UK. It was delivered in four days by DHL to Almaty. Once fitted the now rattling and smoking bike survived right across Kazakhstan, across half of Russia and around a very arduous run into the Mongolian deserts and valleys. What a bike! I had damaged it at home, all but wrecked it in Kyrgyzstan, and it had still taken us all the way to Japan.

But I get ahead of myself and the broader story. In Mongolia we stayed at a guesthouse in Ulaan Baator where Vincent, an Internet friend of mine, had also stayed with his BMW R100GS (the same bike as ours). He had had a terrible time with his bike when a serious rattling noise started in his transmission. These old GSs are infamous for drive-shaft failure at about 35,000km and he of course diagnosed the problem immediately, ordering a new drive shaft from BMW in Germany. It had taken BMW over a month to locate and deliver the part to Vincent in UB. He was most annoyed when he found out that our starter motor had taken just four days from the UK. To cap it all, when his shaft arrived and a local mechanic pulled the bike apart, he discovered that the noise wasn't caused by a failed drive shaft; it was actually coming from a worn-out gearbox bearing! So then he had to find a new gearbox bearing. The incredibly helpful Mongolians did lots of things for him; they found him a decent mechanic and a bearing supplier, and they also had a word with a local policeman who just happened to have an old BMW engine lying around in his lock-up. The engine was taken to the guesthouse to be used for spares. Vincent got his bike fixed and rode it all the way down to Pakistan, where he managed to break his collarbone and had to ship the bike home to France. AND the point of all this to *our* story is … that the old BMW engine was still lying around in the guesthouse garage when we arrived in UB.

Something that had also worried me about my engine was one of the adjusters on the valve gear, which seemed to have a dodgy thread (something to do with a ham-fisted home mechanic again). So I was delighted when we arrived in UB and there seemed to be a scrap engine begging to be cannibalised. I asked the guesthouse owners if I could take the part I needed. 'No, it's not ours to give' came the reasonable answer. Whereupon I turned from ham-fisted into light-fingered and stole the part I needed. But it would have been a pain to get the adjuster out of the rocker gear and then replace the rocker, so I undid the two large stud-nuts and stole the whole rocker arm, adjuster, shaft, supports and nuts. The assembly was a bit heavy but got secreted in with my tools and spare parts and promptly forgotten.

We rattled and smoked into Japan where the terribly nice, not-at-all-ham-fisted men at BMW took the bike apart to replace the worn-out noisy cam chain and the leaky piston rings. Wonderful, all fixed; or so we thought.

Then an easy month around Thailand followed by some serious riding in Cambodia hit the bike hard. All of a sudden we heard a terrible rattle from the top of the right-hand cylinder and the engine balance went to hell. Inspection showed that the valve clearances had increased, and repeated adjustment didn't stop the problem. A further check of the cylinder stud torques showed the problem was the stud I'd strained back in the UK. The Japanese mechanic had re-torqued the dodgy stud back up to the correct (very high) torque, and then a bit of hard riding in Cambodia had pulled the stud out. My chickens had come home to roost. Now the right hand cylinder was only held on by three studs rather than four, and the exhaust valve rocker shaft was only attached at one end rather than at both. As I revved the engine, the forces on the rocker shaft increased and bent the shaft rather than

As I revved the engine, the rocker shaft bent rather than opening the valve; I'd stumbled upon a bizarre form of variable valve timing.

opening the valve; I'd stumbled upon a bizarre form of variable valve timing. The standard fix for the problem is to do what I should have done before setting off from the UK; take the cylinder off and repair the stud hole in the crankcase using a clever little screwthread called a helicoil. But where to buy one in Southeast Asia? We knew of suppliers in Bangkok, but that would have added a five-day detour to our trip.

We crawled out of Cambodia on the damaged bike and into Thailand where we spent a week on the beach (it's not all motorcycle mayhem!). As the bike seemed to be doing sort of OK we decided to ignore the obvious need to repair it and head up to the Laos border.

On the way we spent a couple of nights in Ubon and I took the opportunity to see if the local bike shops could supply helicoils. The first one I came to said, 'Yes, what size do you need?' Whoo, excellent! So I took the rocker cover off and pulled out the stud (a loose fit by now) and showed the shop proprietor. No problem, he could helicoil the crankcase for me. An hour later the engine was opened up 'there you go mate, helicoil that'. But rather than getting out a box of delicate, precision-made helicoils and cutters, he got out a power drill, a box of huge great brass inserts and tatty cutters. He thought that I was going to let him play 'Driller Killer' with my bike, but he was wrong and 'politely' I told him so. Then I reminded him what helicoils are by showing him pictures of helicoils that I had downloaded from the web, and politely told him to call his tool suppliers.

An hour of calling and he said that he had found a supplier and he sent his son off on a bike to get the parts we needed. The promised hour's delay turned into three, and his son returned with another machined insert, made from steel and hot from the lathe. I lost my temper. To hell with the ethic of 'to lose one's temper is to lose face in Southeast Asia'; the guy got the rough edge of my tongue, but he kept coming towards the bike with that bloody power drill. Eventually I got loud enough to make him realise that I was dissatisfied with his service, about the time that I changed my approach to 'Why did you

lie to me?' I think the 'embarrassment' approach worked better than the decibels; I'll remember that next time. The bike went back together and we were back to Plan A; ride through Laos and fix the bike when we got back to Bangkok in a few thousand kilometres.

The next day we rattled off to Laos. To limit the stresses on the engine and the noise it made we decided to ride at 70kph (about 45mph), which is horribly slow by European standards but is not usually a problem in undeveloped countries where the roads are often so poor that higher speeds are dangerous. And all went well through Laos until we got to the hilly jungle tracks in the far north. There we were confronted by dozens of small streams to cross, each one requiring a muddy descent down one bank and then a steep ascent up the other side. During one such ascent, using a fist-full of revs, the engine started to rattle really loudly and the balance went to hell again. I'd taken the rocker cover off dozens of times before, but this time it was scary, in the jungle, miles from anywhere with a seriously sick engine. Somehow the valve clearance had opened up to a massive 6mm, and would not adjust down. The rocker shaft had bent a lot and wasn't keen to sit back where it should have been. What I didn't realise was that the rocker shaft had actually broken at the end where it was bolted down, and it was now only wedged in place.

Drastic circumstances need drastic measures, so I dived into my bag of spares and dug out a spare nut, added it to the end of the stripped stud and reattached the rocker cover. Now the thin aluminium rocker cover would press down on the sheared stud and its stack of nuts, holding the rocker gear in place. But we'd have to keep the speeds right down as thin alloy is not supposed to bear massive loads. And hey presto, the bodge worked, and after a night in a village brothel we limped out of the jungle and across the Mekong into Thailand.

Then we got really cocky and nearly blew things completely. The engine was running well (the valve timing seemed to be pretty near perfect), a clean Thai bed and a hot shower beckoned and I opened the bike up to a heady 90kph. Bad idea! A 'square law' governs the stresses on the valve gear; if you double the engine speed, the stresses on the gear quadruple. The increase in engine speed was enough to erupt the bodged stud right through the rocker case. It looked like I'd blown the engine big-time.

After a night in a village brothel we limped out of the jungle and across the Mekong into Thailand.

A detailed inspection (helped by the drunken village madman) was a real shock. I discovered the broken rocker shaft and it looked as if we'd be hiring a truck to move the bike. 'But wait a minute; what about the rocker I'd pinched in Ulaan Baator?' Would the shaft be the same size as in my engine? Of course it was the same size; BMW don't change anything unless there's a very good reason. A few minutes more bodging and we were back on the road again.

A couple of days later, in Chiang Mai, we found a shop that sold real helicoils and I did a few hours' work which I should have done a year before. Finally the bike was whole again, and it had survived through a combination of bullet-proof design, gentle treatment, severe thrashing, grand-theft-moto, pure luck, careful repairing and inspired bodging.

Up Top, Down Under

Sometimes you can have an adventure in your own country, especially if you decide to ride a GSXR up Australia's Cape York peninsula, as **David Brown** *recounts.*

The trip to the northernmost tip of Australia is a real outback adventure. North from Cairns it's 1000km of either corrugated dirt road or an overgrown twin-rut track winding through rainforest with several river crossings. Once you are on the Cape York track, you're part of a community that's either travelling 'up' or 'down'. People travelling to the tip have a concerned look on their faces; people returning have a satisfied look of accomplishment with an abundance of advice for those heading 'up'.

Our group of four consisted of Jeff and Rick on BMW 1100GSs, Brendan on a Dominator and me also on a sort of 1100GS – a Suzuki GSXR1100 to be precise. Rick and I had ridden up 3500km from Victoria, Jeff rode up from Sydney and Brendan freighted his Honda up and flew to Cairns.

The first day was taken up fitting knobblies and altering the GSXRs gearing. Off with the leathers and on with the body armour: much cooler and easier for fully-dressed swimming in the many river crossings along the track.

The bikes were loaded up with their fair share of equipment. Along with all the usual camping gear, we had enough video and photography equipment to reshoot *Star Wars*. As the trip progressed we realised the obvious: less weight meant more fun, and began posting stuff home. As the riding conditions deteriorated, we were having conversations like 'it takes 365 lentils to make a dish and we have 457, that means we can post back 92, although these tuna sachets contain more energy per gram'.

Not surprisingly my GSXR received a few modifications for the trip. Besides knobblies the standard suspension was raised 100mm using spacer tubes for the front and plates to reposition the top mount on the rear shocker. Motocross handlebars and a 57-tooth rear sprocket would make the bike more manageable in the sand, though the top speed was now down to 220kph.

The first leg of the journey was from Cairns to Cooktown, winding along the coast through rainforest with tropical mountains in the background. Not long after the road turned to dirt, with the steep hills and drizzle making the first day entertaining. We crossed several small streams and by the end of the day figured we'd cracked this river-crossing lark. Little did we know of what lay ahead.

Piloting the GSXR on the dirt for the first time was unnerving. It's not as if you can ask anybody what the limits are of a GSXR in the dirt. At first I would hit a patch of sand or gravel on a corner and be thinking to myself, 'This is it, I am off for sure at this speed', but every time it would make it easily. I could see it was going to take quite some time to retrain my reflexes that were built up over years of riding this bike on the bitumen. The suspension handled the dirt well, it didn't bottom out except for the severest of bumps and

absorbed most of the corrugations. The bike proved to be more capable in the dirt than I would have ever envisaged.

From Cooktown we headed up the Peninsula Developmental Track towards Coen. The first few hundred kilometres of the track are relatively easy; mostly open gravel road with the occasional patch of sand to keep you on your toes. The scenery changes from mountains and rainforest to flat sparsely-vegetated bush land.

Travelling in the outback is a serious adventure. After several days in rough terrain I really began to appreciate the remoteness of our journey. Calmness under pressure is compulsory – danger is just around the corner but can be easily avoided with the right attitude. The heat and humidity when paddling in the sand with the heat of the motor wafting up can be oppressive and a few hours without water all soon cause problems.

Ever tried skiing on a GSXR? Deep sand meant that the bike was quite often in a drift at both ends. My reflex vice-like grip on the handlebars caused my arms to pump up like Popeye's but without the tattoos; later I found that relaxing my arms caused the whole show to handle a lot better. Wherever I focused my eyes on the road was where the bike went. The concentration was so intense that looking momentarily at the speedo or a road sign resulted in fishtails in the sand. Relaxing my arms, focusing on the designated path and ignoring the brake levers delivered the goods. This is beginning to be fun!

After Coen the infamous Telegraph Track begins. This section is where the track is reduced to two parallel ruts in the soft sand with overhanging dense bush. There were several patches of sand where the speedo would be indicating 60 in second with the bike moving only at walking pace: one day we covered only 50km. This was where the real adventure began with river crossings and plenty of them.

River crossings are seriously entertaining. Approaching the first few caused me to outsweat the ambient humidity. Walking the river with a tank bag full of video equipment allowed further study of the optimal route. Jeff's BMW was already on the opposite bank, purging water from his cylinders. I sat with the bike idling close to the edge of the water and wondered what my chances were but once in motion, concentration soon overrides concern. Rocks the size of coconuts caused the bike to buck violently, definitely not what a road bike normally feels like. It's very tempting to stop and reassess halfway across, but this gets the frontal bow wave washing back into your engine. Gingerly I stumbled through to the far bank and gave the throttle a victorious blat. The deep roar of the 1100 was a new sound in the bush.

The GSXR surprised all of us with its ability to pull up riverbanks and steep hills. The rear knobbly and the broad but smooth power band created ideal traction, delivering that wonderful burble that only comes from a wide-open throttle under heavy load. Power was never an issue, rooster tails could be issued on command at any speed, which was always comforting.

Keeping a journal whilst travelling forms a record of events; once home I often refer to the journal and remember moments of the trip that would otherwise be lost forever. 'It is very peaceful by the fire tonight, everybody has gone to bed, and I am writing using the light of a candle. The wood burning in the fire smells very sweet, I can hear the sounds of wildlife and the nearby waterfall. I am sipping my coffee, ouch, I just got bitten on the lip by an ant, must remember not to put sweet things on the ground'.

After a few days and 370km since our last fuel, we arrived at Seisia, only 40km from the 'Tip'. Seisia has a fuel station, store and a caravan park so we relaxed for a day and caught up on the washing and bike maintenance before heading off for the final leg.

The last forty clicks was an easy track meandering through rainforest, paradise compared to the previous 1000km. The track stops about a kilometre short of the Tip, walking from here is the only option. We gathered around Australia's northernmost point for some photos, toasted each other with our remaining water and reflected on our achievement. The tradition amongst our group upon achieving our trip goal is to set the destination for the next adventure. Africa and South America were mentioned, perhaps with a west to east crossing of Russia in between.

Cape York is certainly a place that is all about the journey not the destination. After we all battled the extreme conditions to reach the Cape, the remoteness and ruggedness of this part of Australia hit home; we all hoped they'll never improve the track.

After reaching the top it was time to focus on the return journey. Brendan had booked his bike on the ship to be sent back and would fly to Cairns. Jeff would leave early by himself on his bike, Rick and I would travel together on our bikes. At first it was a bit daunting as it dawned on us we were really only halfway through our trip with another 1000km of sandy tracks ahead. But once underway we realised how much our skills had improved on the journey. Obstacles on the way up, went past almost unnoticed on the return. Those massive sandy patches we dreaded were attacked two gears faster and with one hand on our hip: all the hard-won landmarks seemed closer together. This was our return journey, it was our turn to exude achievement and dispense guidance to those on the way 'up'.

Desert Riders

Since his first XT500 trip back in '82, none of **Chris Scott**'s *Saharan rides have gone to plan so why should the Desert Riders Project be any different?*

The three of us reigned in our motorcycles, cut the engines and stared ahead. Around us the horizon was a flat 360° sweep – sky above and the sands of Niger's Ténéré Desert below. But those three silhouettes on the horizon – were they a trio of army or smuggler Land Cruisers, neither of which we particularly wanted to meet, or the desolate sandy mounds of the Lost Tree which we'd set course for yesterday? I zoomed in the camcorder but was none the wiser. Whatever, they'd have spotted us by now.

A couple of weeks earlier we'd taken a ferry to Tunis and crossed into Algeria a day or two later. We rode south through the oilfields and through the dunes of the Grand Erg Oriental sand sea, where we fitted fresh knobbly tyres and buried our road tyres for the ride back. The adventure was upon us.

Our plan was to explore challenging new routes in the central Sahara, a place I'd ridden for over 20 years. To help extend our range, three months earlier I'd driven out in my Toyota to bury fuel, water and food at three key locations in southern Algeria. The main cache at Erg Killian in the far south would enable us to make the 2000km round-trip to the Lost Tree in Niger. With no tracks, let alone wells, this sort of riding was extreme, even by Saharan standards.

With our Michelin knobblies primed and just enough fuel to get us to the first dump, we hit the sands on what we'd come to dub 'the Red Sheds'. It soon transpired that our out-of-the-crate Honda XRLs imported from Australia were a long way short of the more purposeful KTM Adventures we'd also considered, but after six months' tinkering they were as good as they could be.

The first part of the route led us into a sea of dunes, a route I'd blundered through before, but never the same way twice. With tyres sagging, our throttles were pinned as we ploughed our way into the Erg. Soon Andy's oil temperature gauge was reading 145°C, but on the dunes we had to keep moving or sink into the sands. After a few dead-ends and a well-timed 'emergency eject' right on the crest of a big drop-off, I located the old French colonial straw-bale 'road' which led out of the dunes into the valley and to a well for the night. The worst of the dunes were behind us and though on the limit, the 650s had pulled us through. But we knew there were more challenges ahead.

Next morning we passed the ruins of the old Legionnaires' fort at Ain El Hadadj, crossed another small dune barrier with some difficulty and with the GPS, located a pair of jerricans and some baked beans I'd left in a tree. From here we would leave the regular route and head south into the unknown. Our plan was to locate and follow the Oued Samene canyon 100km to its watershed on a huge escarpment, and hopefully ride down the far side to pick up the trans-plateau highway. It was ambitious in the extreme and though I'd studied maps and sat images for months, I still had no idea what to expect; no one I knew had ever travelled here.

We rode in a corridor between a ridge of huge dunes and the cliffs of the Tassili plateau with no tracks but our own. Most routes in the Sahara follow pistes (French for 'tracks'), which are generally easy, safe and sometimes even marked with posts. Cross-country or off-piste riding is another thing altogether. Here you ride not with maps or GPS, but where the terrain allows, and you're entirely on your own.

Being off-piste gave an edge to the experience that was exhilarating and liberating – picking our way over small scarps and huge dunes, vegetated creeks and rocky hills. The riding was perfect and by the evening we estimated we were within a few kilometres of the canyon rim.

Next morning that all changed; after an a hour of pushing, pulling and paddling we'd covered just one kilometre. A rock-strewn hillside lay between us and the GPS point we were aiming for on the canyon rim. We decided to ditch the bikes and recce on foot.

By late morning the cliff-rimmed canyon spread out 100m below us, clearly unrideable – but downstream a vast sandbank spilled down from the rim right to the canyon floor, providing a one-way slide into the canyon. It took the rest of the morning to push and ride the bikes to the top of the unrideably steep slope, and as long again to walk them down to the canyon floor. Here we called in a SatChat for the website and then wearily struggled up the riverbed, dodging boulders and trees, and spinning in the powdery creek sand. When we came across an abandoned encampment of grass huts we threw off our sweaty riding gear and exhausted, turned our backs on the cumbersome Sheds.

We'd bitten off more than we could chew with Oued Samene: our top-heavy, over-wide machines were a liability long before a rider got too tired to ride. Next morning we dropped our gearing and turned back along the riverbed out to the mouth and back north for 300km to Illizi town.

Showered and fed, bowed but not beaten, we had another new route lined up to cross the plateau close to the Libyan border. Sure enough it proved to be a classic mountain route – clear tracks most of the way following the base of the same 500-km long escarpment we'd planned to breach from Oued Samene. Towards evening Andy's pannier clipped a rock and sent him flying to land with a crunch, so we camped early in a shallow creek bed. By next morning he'd bounced back and we pursued the fabulous ride across the plateau.

You'd think we'd know better, being Desert Riders, but we'd run out of water. A hoped-for well did not materialise so we pressed on south on the promise of a waterhole 80km away. It took three hours of the roughest riding yet, a tyre-shredding, spoke-bending track with hairy 'one chance' launches out of rocky creek beds. We reached the waterhole at sundown, beaten to a pulp, and crashed out pretty much where we dropped.

By next afternoon we were sipping milky coffees in the lovely oasis of Djanet in Algeria's southeast corner, with steak-frites piled up in front of us. Our plan had been to get Niger visas in Tamanrasset or 'Tam' but that now involved a 1500km roundtrip that we just could not face. I was also in two minds about our planned route southeast into Niger: the last time I'd been here two Austrian parties heading for Cape Town had taken that route and been brutally robbed a day or two later.

Still, we had 120 litres of fuel, water and a Christmas hamper of food waiting for us way off the main piste at Erg Killian where there was little chance of meeting so much as a fly. Plan B was conceived: head cross-country for the stash, slip into Niger for a quick visit to the Lost Tree and nip back into Algeria before we got nailed.

We filled every last fuel container and headed with trepidation out of town and into the Erg Admer sand sea. I knew the way through but also knew that the final barrier dune would be a struggle for the tanked-up Hondas. But when the time came we hit the slope hard, sailed to the top, down the other side and on to the gravel plain below. Hereabouts longitude E8° 45' looked like a promising corridor on the map so we set our GPSs for the fuel dump, turned south and hoped for the best.

Initially the going was rough and slow but once we crossed the ancient floodplain of the Oued Tafassasset the desert finally opened out. Compared to the rock-bashing on the plateau the previous week, the riding here was serene: the typical Saharan pattern of dazzling sand plains and a distant rocky ridge which you eventually reach and cross to gaze across another shimmering sand plain.

No one was more surprised than me when we reached the fuel dump by 4pm – and we weren't even knackered! Sandstorms had blown through in the intervening months of course, but I recognised the rock-marker in the dunes where the handle of a jerrican poked out. A bit of digging revealed the water and, Hey Presto: a drum of food! We dragged it all back to the camp and by dusk lay bloated in the sands, blissed-out on an overdose of our favourite foods.

Today was the Big Day, hopefully a 300km run over the border to the Tree. The bikes were stripped of non-essential baggage and by mid-morning we were probably on the Algeria–Niger border. Our now empty fuel drums were fashioned into the historic 'DRP 2003' monument. We sang the hearty 'Desert Riders Song' and then keyed our Garmins to the Tree: bearing 134°, distance 242km. The legendary sands of the Ténéré were upon us.

You can't beat the thrill of riding on untouched terrain. The nearest piste was miles away and even then, was rarely used. But smugglers and bandits were travelling on our wavelength, as were the Algerian gunships which hunted them. We sincerely hoped to avoid both, which explains why we 'miraged' the unwanted Cruisers when, after a freezing overnight bivouac, we finally approached the Lost Tree.

We rode on warily but relaxed as the withered remains of the centuries-old tamarisk tree came into view, a lone living landmark in 100,000 square miles of barren desert – just a fraction of the Sahara's extent of course. In the bitter cold we hurriedly paid our respects to Thierry Sabine, the Paris–Dakar Rally founder whose ashes were scattered here in 1985 after his chopper crashed in a sandstorm near Timbuktu. That done, we belted back to Algeria before we got in trouble.

What a ride that was! In the Oued Samene we DNF'd after 4km; today we covered 400 and nothing could stop the 650s skimming over the sands back to the stash at Erg Killian.

What a ride that was! In the Oued Samene we DNF'd after just 4km; today we covered 400 and by the end nothing could stop the fuel-lightened 650s skimming over the sands back to the stash at Erg Killian. We ended the day buzzing after our adventure; job done!

But our good fortune was about to change. Heading back north I got a puncture and Andy ended the day with a series of flats that finished off his rear tyre. We repaired it as best we could on a sandy plain dotted with Neolithic tools dating back to a time when the Sahara was a grassy savannah. To the west lay the peaks of the Hoggar: no place for a split tyre and a patched-up tube. The plateau highway was only 100km away so Andy decided to call it a day; there was no chance of getting spares in Algeria so he'd struggle home as best he could (and a struggle it indeed turned out to be!).

Jon and I rode west along the tourist route I knew well, over dreary corrugations and bulldust. Out of water and food again, we hit Tam for some rest and repairs. It was the festival of Tabaski, the end of the Ramadan fast, and the campsite owner slaughtered a goat as four other bikers rocked up on a KTM, Paralever and an Africa Twin, including Dutchman Arjen who I'd met the year before. They were planning to take the Erg Killian route too, but with a guide in a pick-up to carry the extra fuel.

Jon and I said goodbye to the three guys next morning and headed up to the fabulous Assekrem Pass, one of the Sahara's highlights, especially at dawn, when the sun rises over the primeval panorama of volcanic cones. Riding down the rarely used far side of the Hoggar was rough; the pannier-bashing track really took it out of us and by nightfall we were back to that staggering, backachey worn-out feeling we knew so well.

Joining the sealed Trans Sahara highway for a bit, we filled the water bags and headed north to Garet El Djenoun or 'Mountain of Spirits', a striking granite peak which I'd passed many times and thought might be climbable. By the end of the next day Garet was in our sights, as were another 110 litres of fuel stashed among some rocks to the north, below the Tassili plateau …

> **The next thing I know, I'm lying on the ground with my helmet under my head ... Ouch! it hurts to breathe.**

The next thing I know, I'm lying on the ground with my helmet under my head. How did I get here? Ouch! it hurts to breathe. Over there Jon is kicking my bike straight. He comes over and points my Sony in my face…

After all the near-misses crossing sandy creeks, rocky plateaux and dunes, I'd flipped out on a virtual runway, landed badly and bust some ribs. Jon dragged me off the piste and a day later the sat phone got through to a German guy in a Unimog who took me back to Tam, gritting my teeth over every jarring bump. A couple of days after that, hobbling and breathing were less painful and we set about flying the bikes back to the UK.

Garet, the fuel stash and even Oued Samene would have to wait, for the party was about to end in Algeria.

A week after I got back Arjen and his mates were among 32 tourists abducted by terrorists near Oued Samene. Had I not crashed out it's likely Jon and I would have ridden straight into the multiple ambushes. Arjen's group were held captive in desert hideaways for six months, during which time one woman died of heatstroke; the rest of the hostages were finally released for a officially-denied €5 million ransom.

It's no longer possible to roam the wild Algerian borderlands. Now you need an expensive escort and can only drive on the highway. Our Project had unravelled, but what's new! We'd seen the promised land and tasted the thrill of unsupported cross-country riding. Regular tracks would never be the same again.

No Turning Back

For **Arno Backes**, *the daunting ride from Munich to Sydney had been a long-held dream. In 2003 he finally set off. Here's his story.*

After four months travel between Nepal and Sri Lanka, I knew it was time to leave India when a man died in front of my hotel. Another dead body, like those that floated down the Ganges and it didn't bother me. Definitely time to move on.

Half a year earlier a ferry had delivered me to Istanbul where my adventure was really to begin. After a few days exploring the city I travelled fast across Turkey and in Ankara met five other bikers heading the same way. We teamed up for the ride east, enjoying the welcoming Turkish people but constantly aware of the army around us. The Kurdish problem was very much in our thoughts and we could feel the tension in the air. On top of that Iran lay ahead – we seemed to get more and more nervous.

What did we know about Iran? From the TV it was just war, fanaticism and terror. As we reached the border, the girls among us put on their scarves with a moan, but it's only for a few weeks. Now the whole thing gets serious and it feels as if there's no turning back. The border, however, was easily crossed and we were soon on our way to a friendly welcome in Esfahan. We were marvelling at the beautiful blue-tiled mosque when we met a soldier who'd fought against the Iraqis. He could get arrested for just talking to us he said, but many people were increasingly less frightened of the 'Watchmen of the Revolution'. Iran was a wonderful experience and it was a shame we couldn't stay longer but we didn't want to be caught in snow on the Karakoram Highway (KKH).

At the Pakistani border, a friendly officer offered us mugs of tea and advised us that we should spend the night in the secure zone at the border post. We were told there were plenty of Afghani bandits wandering around Baluchistan waiting to rob us if we even so much as slowed down. We now had the sense of being deep in Asia: wild and wonderful at the same time. Weapons being carried as casually as umbrellas made me a bit nervous; one of the biggest Afghani refugee camps was just outside Quetta and gunfire could be heard there day and night. And not only light weapons, but artillery and anti-tank rockets too. As soon as it got dark we were warned to be off the street.

We shared a delicious, cheap, final meal together in an Afghani restaurant: some of my riding companions were going straight over to India while Mie, Hartmut and I planned to ride up the KKH to the Chinese border.

A few days later a time-consuming series of flat tyres had us stranded in the dark, something we'd been warned to avoid at any price. At one point someone jumped out of the dark and tried to grab one of us but missed. Luckily a Pakistani put Hartmut's bike in his pick-up and we reached the safety of the next town and stayed a few days.

More problems, this time for me, lay down the road. As in many places around the world, when a truck breaks down in Pakistan the drivers put big rocks around their vehicle instead of the red triangle. The trouble is, when they move on some of these untidy truckies leave the rocks on the road. One of these rocks was wailing 'Arno, Arnooo, come hither' like a siren and bedazzled by its alluring lament, I hit it head on.

One of these rocks was wailing 'Arnooo, come hither' like a siren and, bedazzled by its alluring lament, I hit it head on.

The result was a rim that now looked like a roller-coaster track. Time to wave down another pick-up.

In Islamabad we found a mechanic who restored old Triumphs which he sold to the elite. After introductions and a cup of tea he took the wheel, removed a couple of spokes and started to bash it about. I hoped he knew what he was doing – everything was done on the floor but by midnight he'd welded the crack, straightened the whole thing and replaced the spokes. We were finally ready for the KKH.

Not surprisingly it was the most wonderful stretch of the whole trip. Not only the breathtaking scenery but the tribesmen with their long beards, deep dark eyes, traditional dress and, of course, AKs swinging from their shoulders.

Climbing past Gilgit towards the Chinese border the air got thinner and soon I was wearing all my clothes and was still cold. We rode carefully to avoid the shady patches of black ice. At last we were on the Pakistan–China border and plenty of pictures were taken under the careful eyes of Big Chinese Brother under the red flag. Riding back down the Hunza valley, Pakistan continued to show me some of the most beautiful views I'd ever seen.

Meanwhile Hartmut came back from a short ride – but in a jeep and with a mashed leg. The guy who'd run him down felt very bad and helped us as much as he could as we sorted it all out. In the Gilgit clinic most of the other patients had gunshot wounds, but after the operation when Hartmut saw his X-rays he realised he had to get home fast. A month later I got a message his leg was infected; had he stayed he'd have lost it for sure.

Mie and I continued together towards India. At the border, the Pakistanis were as friendly as ever but the Indians were tiresome, wanted bribes, keeping us waiting taking the bikes apart. Even the tyre pressure was measured, just in case we were smuggling drugs in there. Even if we did have something in there it wouldn't make a difference to the pressure! But what the hell, I wasn't going to argue.

I don't know how to describe the traffic in New Delhi. Everything seems to happen on the road, people giving birth or taking a dump, buses blaring their horns, cows mooing, push bikes pottering and whole families on scooters bouncing from car to car like pinballs. When we stop people zoom in, their

faces right in ours asking endless questions: how many children, are the bikes petrol or diesel, why did I carry a spare cylinder. But no answer satisfies them, they have to touch everything until things break. In this mayhem Mie decided to head south for Christmas, I wanted to go to Nepal, and so for the first time in months I was riding alone.

It was good being independent again. In Nepal, the behaviour of the people changed immediately to calmness and friendliness. What a relief! The roads, however, were no better. In one day I had to cross nine rivers because the bridges were washed away. Nepal was the right place to spend Christmas and New Year, not too busy and I even managed to gain back the weight I'd lost in Pakistan. At the Indian Embassy I was told my three-month visa was extendable everywhere in India, 'No problem, new one not necessary…'

Back in India I went to Varanasi, the Hindus' holy place. Many come here to die, get cremated and then cast into the River Ganges. Bodies that are not burnt get wrapped in a white cloth, weighted with a heavy rock and thrown into the river. Some float back up until they disintegrate, while the living come to bath and launder by the shore. The river is holy so there is no fear of disease but every traveller experiences illness in Varanasi and I was no exception.

On the way to Rajasthan, I hit the tourist trail, Tantra temples in Katcharho and the Taj Mahal near Agra. In Rajasthan, the people were proud and much calmer. They wore huge colourful turbans and had a superb grasp of the concept of 'personal space'. Each city has a big fort with a long history and I spent more than a month in this part of India. Time which later I found out I could ill afford, my visa was expiring and the Indian High Commission had told me that they couldn't extend it, no matter how much money I offered. I had to reach Bombay before it ran out.

As my BMW was stamped into my passport I was not allowed to leave without it and there was no time to drive out of India. The only possibility was to leave it in Customs, while I left the country and pay a hell of a lot bribing money.

It was my only chance, so I decided to pay up and fly to Sri Lanka; a holiday compared to India. The people were more civilised and educated and to get a new Indian visa took only four hours. Back in Bombay I got my bike back with no problems and took the road down to Goa, one of the most dangerous in the world. On a stretch of 300km, I saw a dozen accidents and got pushed off the road more than five times. A hell of a ride!

Goa was backpacker party central, a different world. All this attracted crime and one night someone cut open my tent, gassed me and cleaned me out. That was the worst moment on the whole journey. Two days later I was so glad to run into Mie and Hartmut. The locals suggested I search in the bushes. Hartmut and Mie helped me and we found my passport, diary and papers, everything of little immediate value. Still, the shock was immense. I'd had enough of India and paid over the odds to ship out to Singapore.

One night someone cut open my tent, gassed me and cleaned me out. That was the worst moment on the whole journey.

Singapore: what a culture shock, no one looks at you strangely or tries to cheat you. To get the bike through Customs was not too bad, but I faced a new situation. In India I knew the tricks, here in Southeast Asia I had to learn them all anew. I headed up to Malaysia, Thailand and Laos, I learned how to convince people to help me even if it was only to give me directions and after I got the hang of it, it was a cruise.

It was time for Australia, my final destination. Back at Singapore, shipping was a doddle and after fourteen months on the road I reached Darwin and spent another three months riding the Outback desert tracks. Then one sunny morning I rode into Sydney. What a feeling, after all these years dreaming about it! I got terribly lost of course, but eventually found the Botanical Gardens and sat on the wall overlooking one of the most famous views in the world, reflecting on the events that had brought me to the other side of the planet.

Ladakh and the Valley of the Gods

*For **Sameer Shisodia** and his wife **Shubha**, the biggest unknown on the trip through the Indian Himalayas looked like being the landslide at Maling, where 1500m of missing road had been replaced by a makeshift wire cable that would hopefully transport the bike...*

For several years I'd dreamt of doing a long motorbike ride deep in the Himalayas so finally I bought a Bajaj Pulsar 180 and shipped it to Shimla at the base of the mountains. The first day was mostly about getting comfortable with the bike, especially for Shubha, whose first time it was on the Pulsar, which is not too friendly for long-distance pillions. We passed Narkanda, Theog, Matiana – villages that had just been names on a map not long before – and soon saw the magnificent Sutlej river, whose roar became evident as we descended to the bottom of the gorge and then rode along it. A few hours of easy roads brought us to Rampur Bushahr, at just over 1300m, but the news here was bad: the national highway beyond had been blocked for weeks and it was unclear if another route high up through the mountains was possible.

We decided to try the mountain route anyway. On reaching a stream where a section of the road had been washed away we were relieved to see a huge truck crossing without difficulty and quickly followed suit. Soon we were crossing stream after stream, the Pulsar pulling us through reliably, the knobbly tyres I'd picked up for the job handling the glacial slush and rocks beautifully. We were now probably at 2500 metres, in beautiful apple country, sampling the juiciest fruit offered by the friendly locals.

Pulling up at the end of a huge traffic jam, behind some truckers who'd been stranded there overnight, we saw more stationary vehicles a little further down the road, waiting for a bulldozer to clear another landslide. The adventure we'd come seeking was starting to happen. We moved on into lovely Kinnaur – starker, prettier and yet still only in the 'lower' Himalayas. The road was cut out of or into the steep hillsides, through tunnels and overhangs, but the little Pulsar did not miss a beat. We were soon to miss a few heartbeats though. By late afternoon the cloud broke into a drizzle and our surroundings became dark and menacing.

The next day was glorious. We crossed the Sutlej river for the first time at Wangtu, which used to be a village before it was inundated by the Sutlej in 1997, but now comprised nothing more than a bridge. A sign declaring the bridge to be unsuitable for heavy traffic convinced Shubha that we'd end up at the bottom of the gorge, but I persuaded her that a puny bike carrying two riders and some luggage was some way off being a 'heavy vehicle', and we made it to the other side.

From here we rode into the starkest, most unstable mountains we'd ever seen. The steep hillsides were a mass of fractured, cracking boulders and there were rockfalls in several places. All along the edges of the river you could see the scars that previous floods had left. A little before Morang the front wheel got stuck in a pile of rubble and before we knew it rock was falling all around us. I put the bike into first and scrammed out of there. That was scary and got our adrenalin pumping. Traversing the track along unstable hillsides was like playing chicken with the rock avalanches – even our rest stops were taken only along visible slopes for fear of getting swept into the valley without warning.

Following lunch and a warm welcome in the village of Puh (3300m), we bid farewell to the Sutlej river at Khab, where the calmer Spiti joined it, and crawled up the Ka-Zigs – a magnificent series of switchbacks that took us to the top of the ridge and rapidly towards Nako. The Pulsar – bad hooligan in the city – proved to be a sober, hardworking lad here; it kept breathing in the rarer air and didn't let us down. I loved the ease with which it handled curves without getting unsettled, and even Shubha was starting to enjoy them.

Arriving in Nako, a very picturesque village set at 3900m around a holy lake, we settled for a basic guesthouse and met travellers from all over the world, including a Dutch cyclist called Henk, and Nachiket Joshi, the first Indian I've ever met to give up a job and go backpacking for a few months. They were all surprised to meet an Indian couple doing the route on a little Bajaj.

We caught up with Henk next day at the dreaded Maling Nalah and saw with our own eyes the size of the landslide. The span was essentially a cable ropeway for ferrying goods over the slide – after about a third of the distance you'd need eagle eyes to keep track of whatever was being hauled across. With help from Henk and some locals, I lifted the bike onto some hooks and prayed hard as it started its uncertain flight. Then we started our own nerve-wracking trek across the shifting slope. The last part felt most dangerous, clambering fearfully over the boulders which had only partially completed their random slide down to the bottom and so blocked our way. It took us nearly three hours but at last Maling was behind us and we were re-united with the Pulsar.

> **I lifted the bike onto some hooks and prayed hard as it started its uncertain flight.**

The road flattened out before Tabo (3260m), where the monastic hostel had strict rules (including no sex!), but still seemed like a good place to stay. Surprisingly, the whole region – including the Buddhist monastic restaurant – serves and consumes meat. Quite a break for a strictly non-violent tradition – though I guess the lack of other sources of food accounts for this. We had been wearing our thermals for a couple of days but the next morning was so cold even they seemed insufficient. We rode along the river for a few kilometres and took a detour up to the cliffhanger village of Dhankar for spectacular views of the Spiti river far below. An hour or so later we reached Kibber, which, at 4000m, was until recently the highest village connected to a motorable road.

The road immediately after this was in amazing shape and we made good progress for an hour, but the nightmare started when we hit the beginning of 120kms of the worst road imaginable, a stretch that falls outside the remit of the Border Roads Organization (BRO) because it's of no strategic importance.

It was nothing more than a spillway of rocks and rubble brought down by melting ice. We slithered across extremely slowly, but thanks to the tyres managed to stay upright. Fresh mountain air, the poetic beauty and extreme desolation of the mind-boggling landscape, and the thrill of being there kept us going.

After lunch we started on our first Big One: the ascent of the 4551-metre Kunzom La. A series of rubble-strewn hairpins which had the 180 gasping for breath and the knobblies fighting for traction led all the way up to the top of the pass. I was glad Shubha was here to help push the bike over the nastier stretches as I got better at the art of using my feet along with the first cog and Shubha's shove to get past steep hairpins with loose mud and rock under the wheels. After a couple of hours the road suddenly flattened out and there in the distance marking the top was a huge *chorten* (stupa) with a zillion fluttering prayer flags. The ride down the other side was even worse and on reaching Batal we offered a thankful prayer to the relevant deities. An Australian riding a Bullet up to the pass eyed my tyres with anguish and envy – he had started from Manali that morning and had suffered three punctures already.

Soon after, we camped at a one-hut village called Chotta Darra. Our dinner companions were two guys from the Isle of Man who'd been climbing in the area for over two weeks, living in caves. This was our only camping experience of the whole trip and, at 3517m, we got chilled to the bone with rain, strong winds and fresh snow overnight on the surrounding mountaintops. As we packed up next morning a few hundred sheep passed by, looked after by a single shepherd and his dog. This guy had trekked for days with his sheep from the other side of Himachal to preserve their wool from the rain.

The road improved a little after a few kilometres and as we neared the Manali–Leh highway we crossed some breathtaking cliffs speckled with patches of green. Soon we joined the Manali–Leh road – a tarmac highway – which felt a little disappointing, especially when we overtook a couple of 'luxury' buses on their way to Leh. We filled up at Tandi – the last petrol before Leh, 365km away – and pushed on, passing hundreds of people returning from greeting an important lama who was visiting the region. At Jispa's Mountaineering Institute that night we dined with a trekking group and listened to the organiser, Manish Thakur, who spoke of the hills with a deep reverence and a little bit of fear. I could empathise after the experiences we had been through over the last few days. You don't conquer the Himalayas – they let you pass.

The next morning we passed the quaintly named Zing Zing army post before starting the 35km ascent. A couple of Bullets and quite a few trucks kept us company as we climbed up what were essentially layers and layers of broken mountainsides; the desolation all around was astounding. The little Pulsar did this climb with aplomb – managing to keep ahead of all the other traffic including the solo Bullet riders and causing no worried moments.

Near Sarchu the land flattened out and we saw swarms of tents pitched for renting out to travellers. We gladly took the warm beds and hot water offered, though the prices were steep. The guy who ran this place told us of the wildlife one could see around here – mainly ibex and mountain lions – but all we saw were large mole-like marmots.

The next day's climb up the 21 loops to Nakee La and Lachlung La was on great roads but Shubha was beginning to suffer from iron-butt – the well-known affliction of pillioning Pulsaristes. At Pang we found some more tents serving terrible food and caught Delhi Belly (it doesn't happen just to foreign tourists!). We crossed a deep river and came upon the remarkably flat More Plains, where Shubha rode the Pulsar for the first time.

It was around 5pm by the time we got to the base of Taglang La – the pass at the top of the second highest motorable road in the world. Since the pass was about 20km away we decided to chance it before nightfall and by coaxing the speedo above 40, we reached the summit in half an hour to enjoy a breathtaking 5328 metres (17,800 feet) above sea level. It was absolutely freezing up there! The BRO folks had a metal structure for shelter with a kerosene stove providing heat around the clock. They offered us butter tea, which we sipped politely (it's an acquired taste). In fact it was so cold it's permitted to enter the temple without taking off your shoes – probably the only such temple in India to allow this.

Dark, threatening clouds loomed above us so we decided to make a run for Rumtse, but even as we started hailstones waylaid us. I rushed down the slope like a maniac, skidding from bend to bend, feeling really fearful about the prospect of having to ride in the dark. We got to the BRO base at Rumtse just before nightfall and, inquiring at a restaurant, we were offered two beds in the restaurant itself. It claimed to be the highest idli-dosa (South Indian snacks) sales point in the world and was run by a Nepali who would have never heard of these snacks but for a southern idli-dosa-loving regiment that was posted there. He shut up the shop early to let us sleep well. The BRO brought us breakfast from their canteen next morning and a Sikh amongst them showed us the 'World's Highest Gurudwara' (Sikh Temple) next door. I'm sure we'd seen the highest number of 'World's Highest' whatevers on this trip already.

From here it was downhill all the way back to Leh. We caught our first glimpse of the legendary Indus river as the roads unrolled before us. The landscape was brutal by now, dotted with Buddhist chortens on both sides of the road. We crossed a bunch of villages with monasteries, a few army camps and the ancient palace at Shey before reaching crowded Leh.

Another trip took us up the Khardung La – at 5602 metres the highest motorable pass in the world.

Another trip took us up the Khardung La – at 5602 metres the highest motorable pass in the world – and beyond, into the Nubra Valley, which is culturally and geologically very different from the rest of Ladakh. We carried very little luggage on this trip but managed to get a broken carrier, which took the better part of a morning to repair once we found a welder in the middle of nowhere. On the way back we got drenched at Khardung La – our highest ride in the rain in the world!

The only puncture the rear Duro endured was on a short trip to a monastery a few kilometres out of Leh – and the only time I forgot to pack in the toolkit! Some army folks lent us a wrench to get the wheel off – I took a bus-ride to and from a nearby puncture-repair shop and fixed it back on screwing the axle nut with my fingers. Never left the toolkit behind after that!

Eventually the trip ended and we shipped the 180 back to Bangalore. We took home beautiful memories and experiences, inspiration, respect for the power that nature yields over us and a dream to do it again.

Let's Go, Mondo Enduro

In this excerpt from The Mondo Diaries, **Austin Vince** *and successive members of Mondo Enduro describe their agonisingly slow progress through the Zilov Gap in Far Eastern Russia. In the mid-1990s the Zilov was in a far worse state than the now notorious Road of Bones.*

The 'rump' of Mondo Enduro was chastised this morning by the urgent tones of Clive, lighting the fire, serving coffee and enthusing about the new day. A bright sun was quickly melting a blanket of white mist which signalled the start of a Siberian heatwave in miniature.

DAY 85
Tuesday 4 July
Mondo miles today: 18
Mondo mileage: 10,326

In the bright sunshine, our assault on Zilov did not at first seem daunting, especially when fortified by mushroom soup with stale bread croutons also prepared by our aforementioned and soon-to-be-deified chef. But any false bravado was quickly stifled by our realisation that our route, so easily negotiated by Clive/Austin on a clear evening two days ago has become a loamy morass of mud and water in the heavy rains. Coupled with the poor 'road' conditions was the perilous state of Gerald's health. His mild chill of yesterday, which had made him so strangely reluctant to complete the mechanical tasks which normally bring him so much joy, appeared to have developed into a full-on viral infection, leaving him useless and utterly exhausted. He needs rest so we are going to move ourselves and the bikes forward in short legs of 500m at a time. Gerald is too weakened to ride across the field and so he will walk whilst the rest of the team take turns shuttling his bike forward.

Austin, Clive and Chas were soon hard at work, ferrying luggage items to our first staging post by a bubbling stream some three-quarters-of-a-mile distant. It was with some, but not much regret, that we left the bridge and platelayer's hut combo which had served as a refuge in the storm. Our departure was watched by a group of recently dropped-off railway workers, clearly amused by our daft endeavour. The sun shone brightly.

The next section up a muddy and rutted track was if anything even more treacherous. Clive's bike was soon followed by Chas's in being nearly up to the rear wheel, each in a muddy puddle. Only massive muscular effort and much 'portage' – the posh word for the human hauling heavy luggage items across muddy fields – enabled us to complete this gruelling stage of Mondo Enduro.

The subsequent part of what by now was no longer the Krypton Factor but had turned into our own personal variation on the Ho Chi Minh Trail, was an assault on the sodden causeway which we had been led to believe was the route to the village. Clive drove Gerald's bike down a dirt track to a well-disguised swamp which soon claimed it in its muddy embrace. Chas's attempts to negotiate a similar trail was only successful thanks to a shove from Austin and a heave-ho from two jovial bulldozer drivers enjoying the perpetual lunch-break which renders real labour impossible in this erstwhile workers' paradise.

The incessant stress of the Road to Never (Never is a small town just east of Skovorodino; hopefully we will get there) now wreaked its revenge on Clive's bike which developed an electrical fault. As he

Staring down the barrel of yet another vodka binge, Chas faint-heartedly accepted the first deadly slug.

and Austin pummelled leads and massaged termini, Gerald and Chas negotiated an unforeseen obstacle in our path – a shack containing two vodka-wielding Siberians.

As deftly as The Man with No Name, Anatoly drew the bottle from a holster of flab beneath his shirt. Staring down the barrel of yet another vodka binge, Chas faint-heartedly accepted the first deadly slug.

Fortunately our Siberian friend and his hopelessly inebriated nephew proved amenable to our request for chai. Gerald staunchly defended Chas from further vodka volleys with the well-justified plea that he was officially off-games. To keep our hosts happy we stuffed ourselves with bread and chopped chives from their poorly-stocked table.

The final section to Zilov was tackled more or less without difficulty. As we rolled along the sandy road to the village store we counted the cost of the day's endeavours: Austin's badly gashed knuckle, Chas's and Clive's smashed wing mirrors and all of our creaking clutch cables. The shop itself contained the usual miscellaneous stock of cheap Chinese tracksuits, antique tools and inedible foodstuffs. We settled for three bags of 'recession', pasta, jars of Moldavian tomatoes, tinned Moloko and Hi-NRG peanuts and raisins. For Mondo readers we bought some more South Occotion Vino.

As we emerged onto the veranda of the humble wooden store we froze. Directly ahead of us was the ubiquitous Trans-Siberian Railway, another train creaking past at about 15mph. Nothing strange there, but suddenly the Australian white Land Rover appeared. We couldn't see the actual wagons it was resting on so it looked as if it was serenely floating through the town. Next to it were the Swiss bikes, gliding along too. How could it have taken them so long to get this far? We shouted and waved but they were about a hundred yards away so would never have heard us above the din of their railway heaven. It was all over in about seven seconds, they slid out of view behind some silver birch and their train was gone. Austin got a bit sad and with us barely a quarter of our way around the world the railway travellers seemed to have the right idea. We all tried not to dwell upon thoughts of anything along the lines of giving up.

A callow youth astride a grumbling Minsk 350cc motorcycle was happy to answer our plea to show us the road out of town. He proceeded to lead us through a labyrinth of railway track and sandy trails to a handsome trail leading eastwards. One particularly loathsome pool, which we had tried vainly to avoid, left us all spattered with an oily film of black brine.

After about ten miles of relatively problem-free motoring, past lonesome pines and bustling locomotives, the little Minsk tootles to a halt. Here, our

Life, we reflected, is not all bad unless you happen to live in Zilov all the time.

guide informed us, the good road ran out to be replaced with sixty miles of dirt track. At the time of writing Mondo Enduro is at a loss as to what to do. So many variables come into play: Gerald's health, Austin's rear sprocket and all our aforementioned clutches. Above all, we fear the weather which can change so whimsically in these parts from fly-blown heat to freezing downpours which dissolve riding surfaces like so much concentrated hydrochloric acid.

Our campsite was a rubble-strewn and midge-populated glade next to the Trans-Siberian railway. The day of many trials and much tribulation ended on a note of mild discord with Austin and Clive disagreeing over what attracted ants the most – snot or spittle?

As if seeking a metaphor for our mood, Clive torched an anthill with petrol. But we retired to our tent and poncho, filled up with 'Great Wall' Chinese tinned beef and a tot of Georgian brandy. Life, we reflected, is not all bad unless you happen to live in Zilov all the time.

DAY 86
Wednesday 5 July
Mondo miles today: 45
Mondo mileage: 10,371

So we awoke early (7am) and as usual on Mondo Enduro, we allowed ourselves a couple of hours to pack and have several brews before we hit the road.

Chas and Clive set off first to scout ahead, whilst Austin waited for Gerald to get dressed. We allowed him to have a lie-in in order to bring himself back to health: he had literally sweated the virus out – a quick sleeping bag change (his is now saturated with sweat so he got Austin's) in the morning and he was as right as rain. A barometer of his being back in good health came when he emerged from his second sweat-drenched sleeping bag and produced from his luggage his spare pair of underpants. They were clean white y-fronts and had been stored 'rolled up' like a cigar. Gerald deftly held one edge and flicked them open so they unrolled with an almost jubilant spring. At this very instant he made a 'boing' sound affect that perfectly accompanied this moment of rebirth. Whatever had smothered his normal good spirits these last 36 hours, it was certainly gone now. We had our leader back.

Chas and Clive had reached the point of no return after six miles when the pleasant sandy road turned into huge 6x6 mud tracks baked hard in the sun, with the occasional soft spot to keep you on your guard.

One eye on the road and the other on the weather as we knew we had roughly sixty miles of this and if it started raining we could well be stranded in the middle of nowhere with our limited supply of food, waiting for the inevitable perpetual rain to cease … moreover, after being held up under that bridge for two days, we knew very well that the Siberian weather had a mind of its own.

So the duo riding at point carefully made their way over this treacherous terrain for several miles when they came across one of the 6x6 Kamaz trucks by the Trans-Siberian. Surprisingly enough the railway workmen were having a break at the time. This is rapidly becoming a common feature in this land renowned for its hard workers. Clive and Chas got chatting to confirm their worried thoughts on how long this death road could possibly go on for. As per usual, the reply was a few k's down the line and it is 'Horosho' (good) all the way to Mogocha. Magocha is the next substantial town; it represents the halfway point from Chernyshevsk to Skovorodino.

As we trundle and struggle along this railside trail, it is becoming clear that in no way is it meant to be the 400-mile lifeline that spans what Austin has started calling 'The Zilov Gap'. These tracks are completely ad hoc and our desperate wish that suddenly it will all sort itself out and become rideable is clearly unrealistic. There is no traffic on the trail, even a 4x4 would struggle. All the little villages and towns we have encountered are on the railway. If you want to move around out here, you do it on the local one-carriage 'sprinter' service that we have observed, not by car. The one exception to this rule are these ginormous Russian Kamaz lorries that seem to be used to insert railway workers into position. Unfortunately for us, their 'off-road' capability is so superb that they do not need anything like the mollycoddling that we do. However, we keep encountering stretches of track that are about five miles long where the going is super easy and our spirits soar. The depressing thing is realising that this will never be the norm. We just don't know what's in store around the next corner. Nevertheless, we keep asking everyone we meet what's coming up next.

The Vince brothers turned up soon after Chas and Clive and we told them our news. However, their news that Austin's front sprocket was shagged set panic in the hearts of the Mondo Enduro team. Fortunately, Austin had kept Gerald's old front sprocket which was only semi-shagged.

As Austin changed sprockets there was a 'ping' and the circlip holding the front sprocket onto the driveshaft sprang away into the grass. Austin assembled the team and we crept forward on hands and knees combing the undergrowth for this vital retaining doo-dah. Their tea break over and vaguely curious, the rail workers drifted over and looked as well. Austin drew them the piece on a scrap of paper

> ... there was a 'ping' and the circlip holding the front sprocket onto the driveshaft sprang away into the grass

but they shrugged their shoulders. Gerald then had a brainwave and grabbed something from the floor, it was a piece of the thick copper wire used in the railway's overhead electrics. He carefully wound it around the shaft and tightened it into place with his leatherman pliers. Amazing, it looked delicate but better than nothing. Heaven knows if this sprocket will last though, the teeth are massively hooked and deformed and two of the fourteen have snapped off completely

A quick chai stop in the back of the 6x6 and we were back on the twisted track. The road improved slowly and before long we were on the sandy road again. Hurrah!! We were on a high note now, this had to be the road that went all the way, surely?

Gerald discovered for us, after a front wheel skid, that the road suddenly disappeared under water.

This was only a temporary set back, as we scrambled up the edge of a bank supporting a railway bridge. We proceeded a further thirty yards to find another river flowing straight across our path. A quick recce and we were over in no time – a film opportunity was taken … Great shot! Onwards once again making great progress until we encountered a village with no name – well, not listed on the map nor any welcoming signs. We were befriended by a local who guided us out of town and on the road to Never.

The sandy track was there again and it was not long out of this Town with No Name that the road split in two – we followed the better track for a few miles but it was unused and went in the wrong direction. About turn and back to the fork. Well, Plan B was afoot, the 'Bogus Route' in the right direction and through the first of what was to be huge puddle-ridden tracks... most of these were filmed with both Gerald and Chas caught with their engines stalled in the middle of the two-foot-deep, water-filled trenches, frantically and hopelessly trying to kick start them there. How we craved electric start.

The bikes were finally giving way – the weight was proving too much for their meagre 350 working bodies.

This wicked terrain went on endlessly until something had to give way and this time it was Chas's sprocket finally failing after going through the mother-of-all puddles. Close inspection revealed rounded-off sprocket teeth – the chain had started to jump! Hereafter Chas rode bravely and most carefully knowing the team was miles from any help and were more likely many miles from somewhere that could fabricate a sprocket. The bikes were finally giving way – the weight was proving too much for their meagre 350 working bodies.

Meanwhile, Clive had stripped his bike down (ditched the luggage) and cut ahead to see what he could find. It was truly a superb Enduro circuit and, unladen, a total joy to the DR – 3.7 miles later and the track once again disappeared into a river – this one 50m wide but fortunately no more than two feet deep – nothing our trail bikes couldn't handle.

Meanwhile, Austin had ditched half of his luggage and he followed in Clive's tyre marks in an attempt to make a little progress. Whilst negotiating a small lake he lost control and the whole bike was submerged in the silty soup. He was beside himself with fear and remorse, since we do not have any experience in the re-starting of water-logged bikes. Incredibly, it fired up second kick and he was able to catch up with Clive. They hooked up as Clive was on his return journey and Clive mooted the idea that they all get to the bridge he'd found, hole up there tonight and ride back tomorrow to collect the remainder of the luggage.

Back to the lads and they had made little progress, with Gerald's Givi hard luggage bracket bending in a crash and now catching in the back wheel. The sun is roasting us to a crisp and the biting flies love our pale flesh. Ironically, the byword for our overloadedness, the 4lb club hammer, proved most useful to Gerald, hunched at the rear of N1, straightening the Givi bracket!! Chas's Sprocket ailment is getting worse and now any attempt to even accelerate out of trouble sees his chain being dragged over the stumps of his back sprocket. The resulting harsh clattering and grinding sound is unbearable and cuts through us like a banshee wail of mechanical despair.

Wearily, the Mondo men soldiered on saturated with wet mud, slipping and sliding their way through this tricky Enduro circuit with obstacle after obstacle looming around each bend. Even more of the kit was left behind to preserve Chas's sprocket and make the journey to the bridge a little bit more bearable.

The resulting harsh clattering and grinding sound is unbearable and cuts through us like a banshee wail of mechanical despair.

The light was finally fading via a stunning Siberian sunset (at 10pm) when the huge girder bridge finally came into sight on the last stretch of track down to the water's edge. A sight to raise the sodden spirits of the physically and mentally shattered Mondo Enduro team. The campsite was on the sandy beach of the river's edge – a comfortable and convenient spot but there were only two lots of bedding between four men. We had left the rest back on the trail.

An emergency meal was the order of the day – after this marathon riding effort! A fire was soon started and bedding was improvised to cater for four. The team was too tired to have even their favourite drink of coffee, everyone sleeping in their leathers, soon fast asleep. We are about 100 miles in, 300 to go and only managed eighteen today. Can we keep this up?

The Mondo Diaries was published by Ripping Yarns in February 2006.

Jupiter in Acapulco

In this extract from his forthcoming book, Dreaming of Jupiter,
Ted Simon *describes his first visit to Acapulco.*

Acapulco is a place I had never been to although I'd heard about it all my life. John Wayne used to hang out there. So did Johnny 'Tarzan' Wiessmuller, and countless other stars of stage, screen and radio. It used to be on newsreels when I was a kid. I bet Carmen Miranda was there a lot. Everybody, I thought, should have their day in Acapulco, so I dragged myself off the beach at Puerto Angel and headed in that direction.

But a funny thing happened on my way to Acapulco.

With less than a hundred miles to go I was riding quite happily along a perfectly good straight road at about 55 mph. The air was coursing through my hyperventilated jacket and I was thinking about good times ahead, when suddenly I was sitting seven or eight inches lower than I had been an instant before.

> **Suddenly I was sitting seven or eight inches lower than I had been an instant before.**

Quick to realise that something was wrong, I stopped. The shoulder was an uncertain mixture of brush and loose earth so I had to stop on the tarmac.

Then I met my first predicament.

The side stand was useless because the engine was almost on the ground. Likewise it was impossible to lift the bike on to the centre stand. Evidently I was condemned to stand there holding the bike up for ever, or letting it drop. I still couldn't see what was wrong though I had a pretty good idea.

Still balancing the bike, I began to unstrap the soft luggage. Then I found I could put my main black bag under one of the panniers and lean the bike on it comfortably, allowing me to let go and view the damage.

My BMW had one shock absorber, a handsome and rather expensive thing called an Ohlins, with a big, beautiful yellow spring. It was still there, but at a jaunty angle, not at all where it was supposed to be. I took off the pannier that was obstructing my view and, applying my enviable intellect to the problem, I discovered what had happened.

A bolt that was supposed to hold the shock in place had sheared off, and the bottom end of the shock had jumped off its seat. This, I thought, was not supposed to happen to BMWs, but that was not a new thought. I'd had it before – in Bolivia.

Another thought was that the *topes* had finally got me. Ever since Africa speed bumps have been infuriating me, but they've never been as bad as they are here, where they are called *topes*. In Colombia they call them *policias* which at least gives them the minor satisfaction of driving over policemen.

Here in Mexico you run into them all the time, sometimes three or four in a row, even on major highways. Sometimes there's a sign to tell you they're coming, sometimes not. They can be ruinous to cars, which have to crawl over them. Usually I would slow down for them, too, but the bike can actually take them in its stride and I had another problem right now which inclined me to keep going and absorb the bump. My tyres were wearing out fast, especially the front one.

It was my own fault. Avon would have given me all the tyres I asked for. I just didn't want to bother them. Now the set I had would have to get me to the US, with another 1,700 miles to go, but they were looking awfully thin and nothing wears out tyres so much as banging on the brakes.

So I was trying to ride through Mexico without using my front brake. If somebody were to suggest that you do something impossible, like jump out of

It is a well-known fact that help will come.

a plane with an umbrella, you could say, 'Why? That would be like riding in Mexico with no brakes!'

Nevertheless, it's what I'm trying to do. And braking for every *tope* would skin the rubber off my front wheel before you could say Mazatlan.

Sometimes I changed down fast enough to avoid the jolt but mostly I just rode over them. The bike could do it. My Ohlins could take it. But maybe that bolt couldn't. Or maybe it fractured ages ago in Africa, and now was when it decided to pop.

Whatever. There I was on the edge of a not too wide road, with maniacs whizzing back and forth at the end of their Easter holiday. I stayed calm. It is a well-known fact that help will come. I busied myself taking everything I could off the bike to make it lighter. I knew it would have to be lifted into something.

A truck-load of police dressed in guns and dark blue cloth drove past waving and smiling.

'Well, Gee, thanks guys! What do you think I'm doing here?'

Then a *pesero*, which is a pick-up with seats in the back for passengers, came along and I stopped him.

'Hola hombre. Qué pasó?'

He said there was a mechanic just down the road. He would come back soon with three men to lift the bike into his pick-up. He drove off.

A white delivery van stopped behind me to let a bus pass in the opposite direction. A taxi driver travelling very fast behind the van was thinking of other things and woke up almost too late, stopping inches from the white van in a cloud of burnt rubber.

This made the van driver angry with me, and we had a futile conversation during which he told me to do all the things I couldn't do, like taking the bike off the road. I switched on the left indicator to please him, and he drove off.

Then I switched it off again. Anyone who couldn't see the bike wouldn't see the indicator. Then the police came past again, still waving and smiling.

I spread out my arms as if to say 'What the . . .!'

Having registered that I wasn't just stopping for a sandwich, they turned around and came back. There were six of them, and immediately two of them started directing traffic around me with red flags. Actually it was a good idea but it didn't look like an idea at all. I think they would have done it in the middle of a field.

But the others came to talk to me. They were sympathetic and nice, and wanted to help. They thought they would put the bike in their truck. I told them about the *pesero* but their boss, who was in plain clothes, said the *pesero* would not come back.

He turned out to be right, but I don't know how he knew. He didn't seem to know anything else. They tried to let down the tail gate of their truck, but it wouldn't open. Two of them struggled away at it for a long time. Then finally it popped down.

When it did I saw that there was a wooden structure right down the middle of the truck bed for cops to sit on. There was no room in there for a bike. As delicately as I could I pointed this out, and while they were absorbing this information, a highway patrol car stopped, and the officer stepped out.

He was in a different class, spick and span and spunky, with a polished badge and visible gleams of intelligence in his eyes. I was able to explain to him that if we could just lift the back of the bike high enough to get it on to the centre stand I might be able to perform some magic and get it running again.

So that's what we did, and I popped the end of the Ohlins back over its stub, good enough to get me to the next village, but obviously not much farther. Meanwhile two things happened.

First of all Officer Nambo (that was his name) told me he also rode motorcycles, and he knew a shop in Acapulco where they could fix me up.

Then another pick-up stopped, this time with a car mechanic in it, a dark bristly man with a cheerful smile, whose name was Angel – and he wanted to be my angel too.

We now had the elements of a plan. We had enough muscle to load the bike into Angel's pick-up, and he was willing to take me and the bike to Acapulco, for gas money and a little on top. Officer Nambo said he would phone the fellow he knew there and tell him to wait for us.

To do that, though, we had first to drive fifteen miles to Nambo's station house. There seemed to be communications equipment in his car, but for some reason he couldn't use it. So I rode with him that far and learned what it's like to be a highway patrol officer in Mexico.

He had a seventy-kilometre stretch to patrol. He worked twelve hours every day and had three days off a month all year long. There were no holidays. He had to deal with all and every kind of crime, whether highway related or not and, just a few weeks ago, one of his colleagues was shot dead when some robbers assaulted a bus.

**'If they paid us better, there would be less corruption.'
It wouldn't be long before I learned to truth of that.**

I said I thought that police in Mexico were better than they used to be. He agreed. I said of course there was also corruption, and he said it was mainly at the borders.

'If they paid us better, there would be less.'

It wouldn't be long before I learned to truth of that.

At the station house, Nambo gave Angel a piece of paper with the name and phone number of the fellow in Acapulco he knew, and also put some kind of rubber stamp on the paper. I moved in with Angel and his young assistant, and we set off on the seventy five-mile drive to Acapulco.

As it gradually sank in how far I'd come he whistled in amazement.

Angel had been in Salt Lake City for about seven years (illegally, I'm sure), sending money back to his family, until he had saved enough to buy a 1986 Nissan pick-up, the one we were in, and drive it back to Mexico. He was very interested in my journey. As it gradually sank in how far I'd come he whistled in amazement.

'I thought I'd come a long way from Utah.'

We stopped to buy petrol but not at a petrol station. It was a place where they were bagging limes. We ate some delicious mangoes, and I threw the peels to the pig that was wandering around the back of truck. A man brought out a big plastic jerry can of petrol and poured it into Angel's tank through a cloth. I gave Angel 200 pesos for petrol and a bit extra, meaning to give him more later.

'Why are you buying petrol at a fruit stand?' I asked him.

'It's cheaper here. Six pesos for a litre. The price went up today but here they will still sell at the old price.' Since I had bought petrol for six pesos a litre that morning at a regular petrol station this didn't make much sense. Probably I shouldn't have asked.

We chased the pig out from under the pick-up and set off again. I said how impressed I was with the police, how pleasant and co-operative they'd been.

'Didn't they ask you for anything back there?' he said. On the contrary, I replied. Nambo had even gone out of his way to get me some bottled water.

Angel said, Yes, things were better with the police these days, which it turned out later was a rather premature judgement.

I told him how I hated the *topes*. He said crazy drivers went so fast through his village that many people had been killed by them, so they had to have *topes*. We had lots of time for conversation. The drive took for ever, and it was getting dark when we got to Acapulco. The traffic was terrible, and we almost came to a halt squeezing through a long tunnel.

When we came out the other side a police car stopped us, shouting instructions through a loudspeaker. I could see that Angel was not amused.

We stopped. A perky, little cop came over. He looked suspicious from the start. He had lots of metal in his teeth, and wore a redesigned baseball cap, a white shirt, and pale pants with a stripe. He had a gun, a tin whistle, and a clip board. He thrust his chest out as he talked and tried to look pretty damned important.

There was a lot of to and fro between them, and you could tell from the cop's body language that he was inventing the whole incident. Angel showed the cop the piece of paper we had with Nambo's stamp on it, but it didn't shake the cop's confidence one bit. According to Angel, the cop was insisting that a fellow with a pick-up in Acapulco can't carry somebody else's motorcycle without a permit. It sounded like nonsense but Angel explained that

Nambo's stamp left something to be desired. What was desired was a 'mordi-ta', a bite, a pay-off. Otherwise the fine would be a thousand pesos.

Sad to say the only money I had on me was from the ATM machine, and it was all in 200 peso notes. It was a big 'bite' but I didn't even bother to ask for change.

In tortured English, with great ceremony the cop thanked me.

'Thank you for the tip,' he said and immediately became my best friend, explaining where the motorcycle shop was and escorting us to it. Actually it turned out to be the wrong shop, but it also happened by chance to be one where Angel's cousin worked, so we stopped there instead. It was a Yamaha shop but they said they could do the job and they'd start first thing in the morning.

It was time for Angel to go. I gave him another $20 and thanked him. I was giving away so much money that I wished I'd given some to Nambo as well. What can you do?

It was late. There was a $35 hotel nearby, an ugly place built round an asphalt parking lot. It was very hot, and I was definitely up the backside of Acapulco so I joined in with the mood of the place, bought some cheap take-away, drank beer and watched stupid television.

I was back at the shop early, drinking coffee from a paper cup until the work force arrived. The guy who did the work did it well. The bolt had sheared off inside the alloy casing and getting the broken-off stub out was difficult. He did it by welding a rod onto the broken end. I was afraid he might damage the casing but after several failed attempts he got a fix and was able to screw the thing out. Then we drilled right through the original BMW part and just put a plain bolt through the middle of it.

The people in the shop were terrific. Their accountant, however, was unsentimental. All in all it was a hundred-and-fifty-dollar breakdown. Coming from where I'd been that was a lot. It was a sign that I was coming back to what we like to call civilisation.

While they were working on the job, I went out to find a bank and an internet shop but the banks were either shut or uncooperative and Acapulco was having an internet blackout. I could see, walking down the main street, by the beach, how a person with a lot of money could have fun in Acapulco. The big Las Vegas names were there; Sands, Bali'hai, Flamingo. Personally I couldn't wait to get away from it. And at 2.30 pm I did.

Reflecting on my good fortune I have to admit that life's a beach.

About ten miles along the coast I found a much cooler place called Pie de la Cuesta, and found a great place on the coast, with beers for ten pesos, and a nice room for not too much money. The hotel was called Roxana and so was the black lady who owned it, and they were both lovely.

Reflecting on my good fortune, I have to admit that life's a beach.

Dreaming of Jupiter will be published by Little Brown in spring 2007. Ted Simon's website is www.jupitalia.com.

PART 4: APPENDIX

DVDS AND VIDEOS

Iceland
(Globeriders, 2002, dvd NTSC, 60 mins)
Photographer and tour organiser Helge Pedersen and his mate ride a couple of F650GSs over 4000km of dirt tracks in Iceland, exploring the black volcanic sands and huge waterfalls of the interior, while getting the BMWs a good rinsing in some metre-deep river crossings.

What sets this film apart are the high production values; a third rider Sterling Noren is behind the camera most of the time, delivering some great landscapes and action shots, and the whole effort is professionally packaged as you'd expect from Helge. This one's as good as it gets as a record of what riding in Iceland can really be like.

There's an instructional dvd for R1100/1150GSs (120 mins), showing you how his bike's set up, although most of the dvd is taken up with a very useful though rather drawn out (and seemingly duplicated) section on tyre changing and puncture repair. Nevertheless, a very handy step-by-step guide similar to that on p.66-67. There's a similar dvd for the 650 single too.

Up Top Down Under
(Gnarly Penguin, 2003, dvd PAL, 83 mins)
The film of the story on p.242: four Aussie blokes ride the classic tropical dirt trails to Cape York; the northeast spike of Australia. Again great filming when you consider the arduous nature of the ride and with a great soundtrack too. The star of course is the knobbly-tyred GSX11 whose high-rpm wail disrupted the cloth-eared bandicoot's mating activities for the rest of the season. My only complaint is the film should have ended right there on Cape York. There follows a rather dull and irrelevant excursion to Thursday Island which spoils the climax of a great adventure.

Terra Circa
(AIM Image, 2003, dvd PAL, about 150 mins)
Terra Circa include the guys who brought you the 'guerrilla'-filmed RTW classic, *Mondo Enduro*. The quintet took seven months to cross Russia and the US, roughing it all the way. Despite that, production values are higher than Mondo, and the innovative camcordery is still here. Originally broadcast on cable TV, if watched continuously the first three episodes

across Europe to Kazakhstan drag on like the ride itself. As you'd expect, the genuine rather than contrived action picks up when the going gets tough across the now plugged 'Zilov Gap' in Far Eastern Russia, followed by an upbeat jaunt through Japan. Trans America is knocked out in a couple of minutes.

A comparison with the *Long Way* dvd is irresistible, even if (or especially as) the productions could not be further apart in terms of budget or support. The same encounters with grinding Russian bureaucracy and heart-warming Russians are there but while *Terra Circa* may lack the raw appeal and global range of *Mondo Enduro*, these guys were still out there doing it hardcore. Traversing north Asia and America may not be everyone's definition of an RTW trip, but they might have subtitled it 'The Real Way Round'.

Miles Ahead – Endurance and Adventure Against the Clock
(Kevin & Julia Sanders, 2004, dvd PAL, 75mins)
Having rounded the world in record time, the Sanders knock out the Americas, from Alaska to the southern tip of Argentina, in less than five weeks, beating the previous record by twelve days. And they manage to do a pretty decent job of filming it too. There's no time for larking around or meeting the people, covering up to a thousand miles a day on their 1150 Adventure. Inevitably they come up against delays in Central America but press on through to claim their record. A testament to the Sanders' endurance and the bike; the amazing thing is, both make it look so easy.

Long Way Round
(Virgin, 2004 dvd PAL, 2 discs)
This event seemed to polarise opinions: either you're a Ewan fan or you ride bikes and it's just show business. For a trip that claimed it would be 'just us on our own, meeting the locals like any other travellers and dealing with problems ourselves', this must have been the most expensive, lavishly-equipped and fixer-supported 'RTW' ride since Jim Rogers rode his BSA Gold Card in Investment Biker. How could the 'Long Machine' fail to deliver TV, print, interviews and disc in time for Christmas? Need some credibility? Parachute Ted Simon in to Ulaanbator for a minute.

At one point early in the book Boorman bleats: '…nothing was going right. We had no bikes or offices, no money, no staff, no camping equipment, no bike gear'. But what would you really expect? One may not admire the manner in which they did it or believe McGregor's claim of wanting a career break. But because of who he is as much as what they did, the film is fun to watch, skimming over the detail featured in the less larky book.

Jupiter's Travels
(VHS PAL, 89mins, 2001)
Twenty-five years after his RTW epic, aged 70 but looking pretty good for it, Ted Simon sets off to see what's changed as well as to try and locate some faces from the past. *'My purpose really is to show how it is possible, perhaps, to live a heroic life without being a hero'* he says with typical humility. You do feel for the bloke, he's never mastered the knack of self-promotion ('having

to sell myself was a miserable prospect' he admits on his website). One suspects he takes on the daunting trip, part-funded by fans, because old age finds him skint.

Manfred Waffender's film follows his departure and catches up in Tunis, Sudan, in Kenya nursing a broken shin, and finally in Cape Town acting out a seemingly tokenistic charity gig. It's good to put a face to the book and occasionally some erudition comes forth; the pace of the production befits its subject. But other ramblings may indeed show his age and the futility of trying to relive times past. One can't help feeling that he was a reluctant performer in the whole enterprise and there's a certain melancholy that was perhaps always part of his persona; a thoughtfulness that, through no fault of Waffender, reflects best in the written word rather than on film.

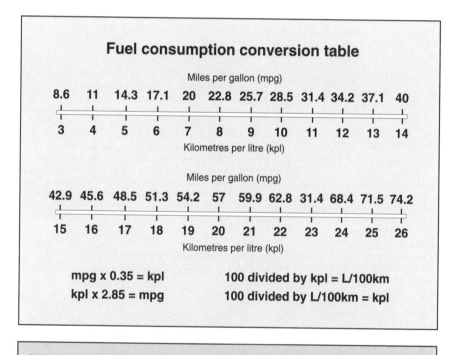

Fuel consumption conversion table

Miles per gallon (mpg)

8.6	11	14.3	17.1	20	22.8	25.7	28.5	31.4	34.2	37.1	40
3	4	5	6	7	8	9	10	11	12	13	14

Kilometres per litre (kpl)

Miles per gallon (mpg)

42.9	45.6	48.5	51.3	54.2	57	59.9	62.8	31.4	68.4	71.5	74.2
15	16	17	18	19	20	21	22	23	24	25	26

Kilometres per litre (kpl)

mpg x 0.35 = kpl
kpl x 2.85 = mpg

100 divided by kpl = L/100km
100 divided by L/100km = kpl

Other conversion figures

1 kilogram (kg) = 2.2lb
1 pound = 454 grams (0.45kg)

1 metre = 3 feet 3.4 inches
1 kilometre (km) = 0.62 miles
1 mile = 1.6 km

1 litre = 0.22 Imperial gallons
1 litre = 0.26 US gallons
1 US gallon = 3.78 litres
1 US gallon = 0.8 Imperial gallons
1 Imperial gallon = 4.55 litres

CONTRIBUTORS

German pastry-chef **Arno Backes** fulfilled a long-held dream by riding from Munich to Sydney, meeting his partner along the way. In 2002 they left again for an 18-month trip to Latin America, published the book *Motoqueros* on their return and now live in Melbourne: www.bikeactive.de.

Andy Bell (andy@desertbiking.com) is 31 and lives in South Africa. He has travelled off-road by motorcycle in much of North Africa, as well as in Europe and Iceland and was one of the Desert Riders. He currently has plans to explore Angola and Namibia by 4x4 with a view to running supported motorcycle expeditions there in the future.

Chris Bright, a Brit who for years thought he needed a career etc. Realised that biking around interesting parts of the world was more fun. Always dreaming of the next jolly. The story so far: www.TheBright Stuff.com.

Jeremy Bullard spent 10 weeks on his first trip and 8 months on the next. He came back for a rest after 15 months on his third and is about to start again for another year. 'It's just too much fun, totally addictive and beats the shit out of working: www.fowb.co.uk.

Professional motorcycle adventurer Dr **Gregory W Frazier** is the only motorcyclist to have circumnavigated the globe four times. No stranger to danger, his adventures include being shot at by rebels, jailed by unfriendly authorities, bitten by snakes and smitten by a product of Adam's rib.

Robert Goggs (aka: Bob). Yorkshire born, Yorkshire bred, strong in arm and thick in head. Started riding at six years old and hasn't improved much since. Aircraft engineer in his spare time; lived, worked and travelled extensively throughout the world. Currently riding RTW with his wife, Danielle.

Tom Grenon Born in Vancouver and started riding at 15. Worked on logging camps in BC, and from 1981 lived in Paris, Milan, Barcelona, NYC and Seattle before returning to BC to focus on motorcycle-adventure touring, photography, and computer graphics.

Former motorcycle mechanic, dealer and racer, from 1987 **Grant Johnson** spent eleven years riding the world with his wife Susan. On their return, he embarked on www.HorizonsUnlimited.com. It was supposed to be the diary of their trip, but has since grown to become the foremost online resource for motorcycle travellers.

Simon McCarthy rode the wrong bike on the right terrain for 25 years. Burnt three tonnes of petrol riding from the UK to Japan and back. Co-author of *Sorebums – Rattling Around Asia* available from sorebums@ yahoo.co.uk. Partner of Georgie Simmonds – 'I liked the pillion so much, I married her'.

Cynthia Milton had travelled in North Africa and the Middle East on her 1985 R80G/S. But after being made redundant in June 2004, shortly before her 50th birthday, she decided that enough was enough and embarked on an RTW ride on the same bike.

In the Zilov Gap **Mondo Enduro** added up to Chas Penty, Clive Greenhough, Gerald and Austin Vince. A tight-knit team hopelessly out of its depth. Not a single moment of 'off-road' experience between them, no Russian, no GPS, no idea what would happen next.

A native New Zealander, **Shaun Munro** has spent the last 15 years travelling the various areas of the world in a variety of ways. Recently completing a circumference on a BMW Dakar 650, Shaun is actively planning his next big journey by air or sea. His website is www.blue-dunes.com.

Weary of the daily grind in jargon-infested London media-land, **Lois Pryce** left her job at the BBC to ride from Alaska to Tierra del Fuego astride her XT225. Her motorcycling fun had previously revolved around a couple of ropey old BSAs, so this adventure seemed alarmingly hi-tech and comforting. Read about the book at www.loisonthe loose.com

Dr Paul Rowe is a UK-based anaesthetist who spent his first pay cheque on a bike and never looked back. He is most grateful to his physiotherapist wife Jenni for inventing motorcycle pilates, recently while crossing Australia and promises just one more trip before settling down to make babies.

CONTRIBUTORS (cont'd)

Georgie Simmonds learnt to ride in the Pennines on a Yamaha Serow. She was persuaded to go two-up on an 18-month Asian tour with now-husband Simon McCarthy. In Kathmandu, 28,000 miles later, she bought her own Enfield to ride home on. Her body is still recovering two years later!

Ted Simon has had many different interests in his 75 years but the one constant has been a passion for travel. He took up motorcycling at the age of 42 as a way of travelling around the world, and wrote *Jupiter's Travels*, still a steady favourite after 25 years. Recently he repeated the journey 'to see how things have changed'.

Alec Simpson grew up in PNG, rode around Australia in 1986. In 2003-4 he rode through 19 countries in an attempt to reach Lake Baikal, Siberia, on a 1984 BMW G/S.

Previous travels include Europe, Asia, South America, Middle East and North Africa. Active in Ralphino Verde's BMW owners psychological support group.

Maciek Swinarski: 26-year-old computer programmer living in Gdansk, Poland. Motorcycle trips: Poland–Dakar, Poland–Mongolia, Europe. Other travels: Siberia, Africa. Hobbies motorcycling, white-water kayaking, paragliding, snowboarding, watching and making movies.

Richard Virr was born in England in 1968. Lived for a few years in the USA and Turks and Caicos Islands. Has been travelling since 1986 and in 2000 decided to combine this with his other passion of motorcycling and head east. Now lives and works in London as a Project Manager.

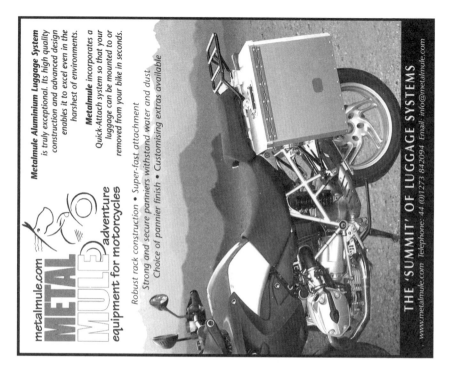

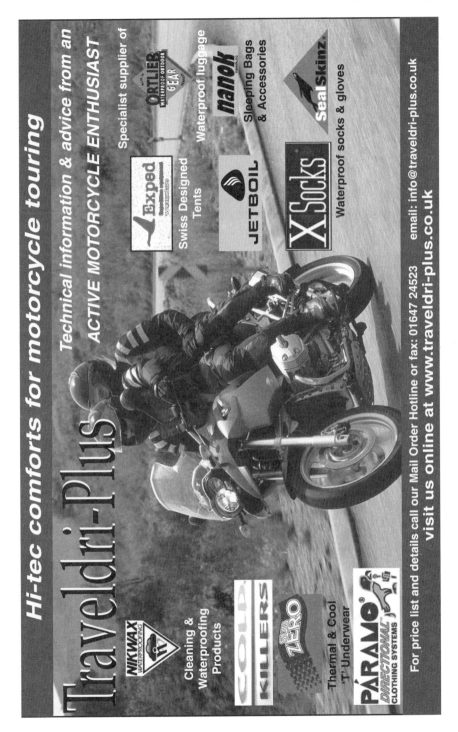

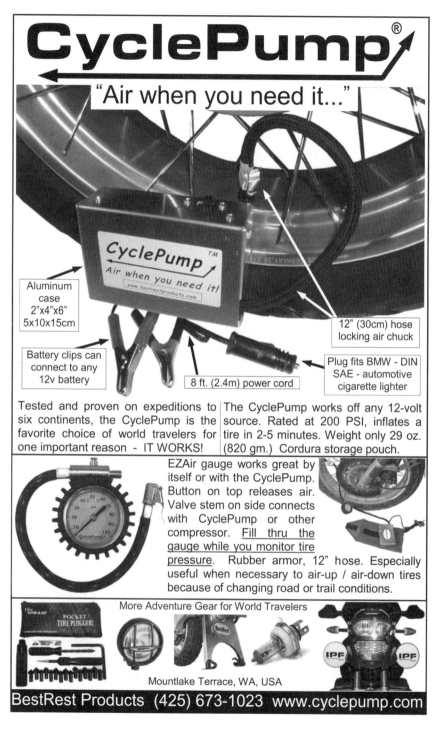

INDEX

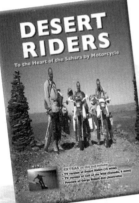
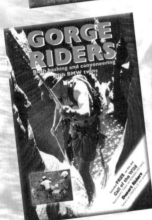